# FROMMER'S
## *EasyGuide*

### TO

P9-CNI-867

# ALASKAN CRUISES AND PORTS OF CALL

*By*
Fran Wenograd Golden
and Gene Sloan

NO LONGER PROPERTY OF
SEATTLE PUBLIC LIBRARY

*EasyGuides are* ✦ Quick To Read ✦ Light To Carry
✦ For Expert Advice ✦ In All Price Ranges

RECEIVED
JAN. 1 4 REC'D
By

## FrommerMedia LLC

Published by

**FROMMER MEDIA LLC**

Copyright © 2014 by Frommer Media LLC, New York City, New York. All rights reserved. No part of this publication may be reproduced, stored in a retrieval system, or transmitted in any form or by any means, electronic, mechanical, photocopying, recording, scanning or otherwise, except as permitted under Sections 107 or 108 of the 1976 United States Copyright Act, without the prior written permission of the Publisher. Requests to the Publisher for permission should be addressed to the Permissions Department, Frommer Media LLC at partnerships@frommermedia.com.

Frommer's is a registered trademark of Arthur Frommer. Used under license. All other trademarks are the property of their respective owners. Frommer Media LLC is not associated with any product or vendor mentioned in this book.

ISBN 978-1-62887-014-5 (paper), 978-1-62887-044-2 (ebk)

Editorial Director: Pauline Frommer
Editor: Alexis Lipsitz
Production Editor: Jana M. Stefanciosa
Cartographer: Roberta Stockwell
Cover Design: Howard Grossman

For information on our other products or services, see www.frommers.com.

Frommer Media LLC also publishes its books in a variety of electronic formats. Some content that appears in print may not be available in electronic formats.

Manufactured in the United States of America

5   4   3   2   1

# CONTENTS

## ABOUT THE AUTHORS

**Fran Wenograd Golden** is a well-known travel writer and the cruise expert blogger for *USA TODAY*'s Experience Cruise website. She is also a contributing editor and chief blogger for *Porthole* cruise magazine. Former travel editor of the *Boston Herald*, she writers for numerous newspapers and magazines including the *New York Daily News*, *Miami Herald* and *Virtuoso Life*. When not at sea, she and her partner, David Molyneaux, make their home in Oberlin, Ohio.

**Gene Sloan** writes about cruising for *USA TODAY* and oversees *USA TODAY*'s online cruise site, The Cruise Log (cruises.usatoday.com), as well as *USA TODAY*-owned VacationCruises Info.com. Sloan's stories are also distributed by the Gannett News Service to more than 80 other U.S. newspapers. A travel writer for nearly 20 years, Sloan has sailed on almost 100 cruise ships. He lives near Philadelphia with his wife and three daughters.

## ABOUT THE FROMMER TRAVEL GUIDES

For most of the past 50 years, Frommer's has been the leading series of travel guides in North America, accounting for as many as 24% of all guidebooks sold. I think I know why.

Though we hope our books are entertaining, we nevertheless deal with travel in a serious fashion. Our guidebooks have never looked on such journeys as a mere recreation, but as a far more important human function, a time of learning and introspection, an essential part of a civilized life. We stress the culture, lifestyle, history and beliefs of the destinations we cover, and urge our readers to seek out people and new ideas as the chief rewards of travel.

We have never shied from controversy. We have, from the beginning, encouraged our authors to be intensely judgmental, critical—both pro and con—in their comments, and wholly independent. Our only clients are our readers, and we have triggered the ire of countless prominent sorts, from a tourist newspaper we called "practically worthless" (it unsuccessfully sued us) to the many rip-offs we've condemned.

And because we believe that travel should be available to everyone regardless of their incomes, we have always been cost-conscious at every level of expenditure. Though we have broadened our recommendations beyond the budget category, we insist that every lodging we include be sensibly priced. We use every form of media to assist our readers, and are particularly proud of our feisty daily website, the award-winning Frommers.com.

I have high hopes for the future of Frommer's. May these guidebooks, in all the years ahead, continue to reflect the joy of travel and the freedom that travel represents. May they always pursue a cost-conscious path, so that people of all incomes can enjoy the rewards of travel. And may they create, for both the traveler and the persons among whom we travel, a community of friends, where all human beings live in harmony and peace.

Arthur Frommer

# THE BEST OF ALASKA CRUISING

A laska is one of the top cruise destinations in the world, and when you're sailing through the calm waters of the Inside Passage or across the Gulf of Alaska, it's easy to see why: The jaw-dropping scenery is simply breathtaking.

Much of the coastline is wilderness, with snowcapped mountain peaks, immense glaciers that create a thunderous noise as chunks break off into the sea (a process known as calving), emerald rainforests, fjords, icebergs, soaring eagles, lumbering bears, and majestic whales—all easily visible from the comfort of your ship.

Visit the towns and you'll find people who retain the spirit of frontier independence that brought them here in the first place. Add Alaska's colorful history and heritage, with its European influences, its spirit of discovery, and its rich Native cultures, and you have a destination that is utterly, endlessly fascinating. Even thinking about it, we get chills of the good kind.

The state celebrated its 50th anniversary of statehood in 2009. It was in January 1959 that the Union accepted what had once been a territory as a full-fledged state—the 49th. Every city, town, and hamlet seemed to hold celebrations in honor of the event, showing their Alaskan spirit.

The number of cruise passengers visiting the state was expected to top 1 million in 2013. In summer, some towns still turn into tourist malls. We're talking seasonal vendors, including jewelry stores geared towards the cruise crowd and shelves filled with imported souvenirs. However, the port towns you'll visit—from Juneau, the most remote state capital in the country, to Sitka, with its proud reminders of Native and Russian cultures—manage to retain much of their rustic charm and historical allure. Sure, you may have to jostle for a seat in Juneau's popular Red Dog Saloon (a must-do beer stop, and the oldest tourist attraction in the state) or ask other visitors to step out of the way as you try to snap a picture of Skagway's historic gold-rush buildings or Ketchikan's picturesque Creek Street, but these are minor hassles for cruise-ship passengers. If you want to get away from the crowds by taking an organized shore excursion, touring on your own, or booking a small-ship cruise that goes to more remote parts, there's opportunity for that, too. In addition, by signing up for the cruise lines' pre- or post-cruise land-tour packages (known as "cruisetours" or land + sea adventures), you can also visit less-populated inland destinations such as Denali National Park, Fairbanks, the Kenai Peninsula, the Yukon Territory, or the Canadian Rockies.

Even before you cruise, we can predict you'll want to visit again. This is a place that puts a spell on you. Fran first visited some 15 years ago and found her view of the world was forever changed. She quickly put the state at the top of her list of cruise destinations; numerous visits since have just confirmed her initial impression. She even traveled here in winter for the first time a few years ago, attending the Fur Rendezvous (Fur Rondy) in Anchorage, and discovered a whole new side to Alaska (where they know how to have fun even in the cold). Gene has also become a big fan of the cruising scene—he found himself doing three cruises in 3 months at one point. Alaska is like that. It grabs you by the scruff of the neck and won't let you go.

Whether you're looking for pampering and resort amenities or a "you and the sea" adventure experience, you'll find it all on cruise ships in Alaska. Here are some of our favorites, along with our picks of the best ports, shore excursions, and sights.

The relationship between cruise lines, state politicians, and the populace can be a hot potato—so much so Alaska Governor Sean Parnell took to annually attending Cruise Shipping Miami, the cruise industry's largest gathering, to show his support. Obviously, Alaska coffers want cruisers—when numbers decline, they take a hit (a loss of $150 million alone when several lines pulled ships in 2010 after a dispute over a passenger head tax, since settled in favor of the cruise lines). There was some fear in Alaska, as expressed in a lawsuit filed by the state, that new federal North American Emissions Control Area (ECA) regulations requiring all large ships to use low-sulfur fuel within 200 miles of U.S. and Canadian shores could discourage cruise-ship traffic—by increasing operating costs for the cruise lines. The cleaner fuel standards didn't appear to have had much impact on the market as of press time, but the standards are set to become more stringent in 2015 (barring a court ruling to the contrary). Cruise lines were talking about using "scrubbers" to modify engines.

Alaska environmentalists have had a mixed record of victories and losses when it comes to wastewater treatment on cruise ships, emissions, and more. Consumer-protection officials in the state have had better luck, coming down hard, for example, on three companies that run port shopping programs onboard cruise ships (in a settlement, the companies agreed to pay $200,000 and to promise that their port lecturers would disclose the sessions are about advertising certain stores). In some ports, there have been complaints that cruise ships and their passengers tie up cellular phone service, impact electrical grids and water service, and otherwise impact the lives of Alaskans. We tell you this only because you may hear such from the locals.

# THE best OF ALASKA'S SHIPS

o **The Best Ships for Luxury:** Luxury in Alaska is defined in 2014 by **Regent Seven Seas** and **Silversea.** If you want a more casual kind of luxury (a really nice ship with a no-tie-required policy), Regent Seven Seas' *Navigator* offers just that on an all-suite vessel (most cabins have private balconies) with excellent cuisine. **Silversea,** with its *Silver Shadow,* represents a slick, Italian-influenced, slightly more formal luxury experience with all the perks—big suite cabins and excellent food, linens, service, and companions. Both Regent and Silversea include fine wine and booze in their cruise fares, and Regent also includes airfare and shore excursions. For a luxury Alaska experience in a small-ship setting, check out the three "Luxury Adventures" vessels of **Un-Cruise Adventures,** where soft adventure comes with upscale acoutrements, and **American Cruise Lines'** *American Sprit,* which boasts the most well-appointed cabins of any small ship in the region (they even have balconies!).

o **The Best of the Mainstream Ships: Celebrity**'s *Solstice* is a contemporary stunner, with a half-acre of real grass on its top deck, a beautifully dramatic main dining room, an extensive modern-art collection, cushy public rooms, and an expanded spa area. Celebrity has a formidable presence in Alaska—the older Celebrity *Millennium* is none too shabby either. You can't go wrong with the modern ships of Princess Cruises as well, including the *Crown Princess*.

o **The Best of the Small Ships:** The "Luxury Adventures" vessels of **Un-Cruise Adventures** are the most intimate and upscale of the small-ship players. You can't get much more personal or pampering than the line's 22-person *Safari Quest*. That said, if it's new and shiny you want, American Cruise Lines' upscale *American Spirit* is by far the youngest vessel in Alaska's small-ship fleet. **Lindblad Expeditions,** on the other hand, shines with its on-board naturalists, *National Geographic* tie-in, and overall soft-adventure expertise.

o **The Best Ships for Kids/Families:** All the major lines have well-established kids' programs, with **Carnival, Royal Caribbean,** and **Norwegian Cruise Line** leading the pack in terms of facilities and activities. **Princess** gets a nod for its National Park Service Junior Ranger program, designed to teach kids about glaciers and Alaska wildlife—the kids can even earn a Junior Ranger badge—and for recently increasing its shore excursions geared toward families. **Holland America**'s Culinary Arts program includes cooking classes that are a favorite of teens. But no one can beat **Disney,** returning for its 4th year in Alaska in 2014 and cruising from Seattle with the *Disney Wonder*—and with its presence really responsible for putting Alaska cruising on the family travel map.

o **The Best Ships for Pampering: Celebrity**'s *Solstice* and *Millennium* have wonderful AquaSpas, complete with thalassotherapy pools and a wealth of soothing and beautifying treatments, and the solariums on **Royal Caribbean**'s *Rhapsody of the Seas* and *Radiance of the Seas* have relaxing indoor pool retreats. We are also big fans of the thermal suite (complete with a hydrotherapy pool) in the Greenhouse Spas on **Holland America**'s *Zuiderdam* and *Westerdam*. Luxury line **Regent Seven Seas,** of course, pampers all around. Ditto for the very posh **Silversea Cruises.**

o **The Best Shipboard Cuisine: Oceania Cruises,** with its *Oceania Regatta,* is tops in this category—even the hamburger grills impress with such options as the Kobe Burger (made with Wagyu beef and topped with truffle sauce). **Regent Seven Seas** appeals to foodies, especially in the creative department. **Silversea** impresses with its emphasis on preparation—if you want your filet rare, you'll get it rare. If you try the Le Cirque dinner experience on Holland America's ships you will certainly be pleased, and we have to give high marks to the overall cuisine on **Celebrity** ships—but especially the food-as-theater experience at Qsine on Celebrity's *Millennium*.

o **The Best Ships for Onboard Activities:** The ships operated by **Carnival** and **Royal Caribbean** have rosters teeming with onboard activities that range from the sublime (such as lectures) to the ridiculous (such as contests designed to get passengers to do or say outrageous things). **Princess**'s ScholarShip@Sea program is a real winner, with exciting packaged classes in such diverse subjects as photography, computers, cooking, and even ceramics, so you can make your own take-home souvenirs. **Holland American Line** has particularly impressive culinary classes.

o **The Best Ships for Entertainment:** Look to the big ships here. **Carnival** and **Royal Caribbean** are tops when it comes to an overall package of shows, nightclub acts, lounge performances, and audience-participation entertainment. **Princess** also presents particularly well-done—if somewhat less lavishly staged—shows. **Holland**

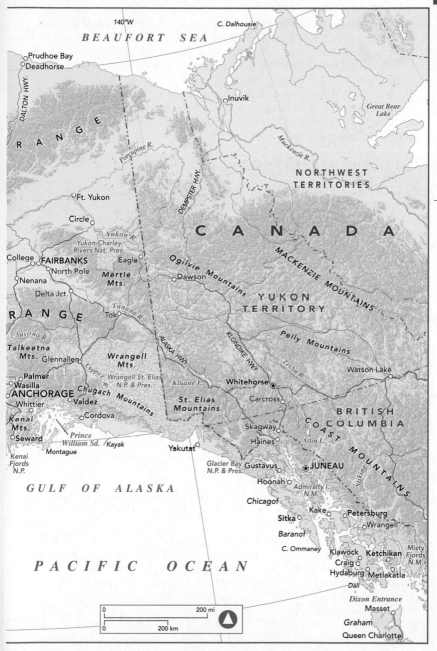

BEAUFORT SEA

140°W

C. Dalhousie

Prudhoe Bay
Deadhorse

DALTON HWY.

Inuvik

Great Bear
Lake

R  A  N  G  E

Porcupine R.

Mackenzie R.

NORTHWEST
TERRITORIES

Ft. Yukon

Circle

Yukon R.
Yukon-Charley
Rivers Nat. Pres.

DEMPSTER HWY.

C  A  N  A  D  A

College  FAIRBANKS
North Pole

Nenana

Delta Jct.

Eagle

Dawson

Ogilvie Mountains

MACKENZIE MOUNTAINS

Mertle
Mts.

Tanana R.

R  A  N  G  E

Tok

YUKON
TERRITORY

Pelly Mountains

Susitna R.

ALASKA HWY.

Talkeetna
Mts.  Glennallen

Copper R.

KLONDIKE HWY.

Teslin R.

Watson Lake

Palmer
Wasilla

ANCHORAGE
Whittier

Wrangell
Mts.

Wrangell St. Elias
N.P. & Pres.

Kluane L.

Whitehorse

Chugach Mountains

Valdez

Cordova

St. Elias
Mountains

Carcross

BRITISH
COLUMBIA

Kenai
Mts.

Seward

Prince
William Sd.  Kayak

Montague

Yakutat

Skagway

Haines

Atlin L.

COAST MOUNTAINS

Kenai
Fjords
N.P.

GULF  OF  ALASKA

Glacier Bay
N.P. & Pres.  Gustavus

Hoonah

JUNEAU

Stikine

Chicagof

Admiralty I.
N.M.

PACIFIC  OCEAN

Sitka

Baranof

C. Ommaney

Kake

Klawock

Craig

Hydaburg

Dall

Petersburg

Wrangell

Misty
Fjords
N.M.

Ketchikan

Metlakatla

Dixon Entrance

Masset

Graham

Queen Charlotte

0          200 mi
0          200 km

**America** has made recent improvements in this area, including adding very funny comedians and magicians to its roster. Of course, **Disney** is also tops in this area with its family-oriented fare.

o **The Best Ships for Whale-Watching:** If the whales come close enough, you can see them from any ship in Alaska—Fran spotted a couple of orcas from her balcony cabin on a Holland America ship. But smaller ships—such as those operated by **Lindblad, Un-Cruise Adventures,** and **Alaskan Dream Cruises**—might actually change course to follow a whale. Get your cameras and binoculars ready!

o **The Best Ships for Cruisetours:** With their own fleets of deluxe motorcoaches and railcars, **Princess, Holland America,** and **Royal Caribbean Cruises** (which owns Royal Caribbean and Celebrity) are the market leaders in getting you into the Interior of Alaska, either before or after your cruise.

# THE best PORTS

Juneau and Sitka are our favorite ports. **Juneau** is one of the most visually pleasing small cities anywhere and certainly the prettiest capital city in America (once you get beyond all the tourist shops near the pier). It's fronted by the Gastineau Channel and backed by Mount Juneau and Mount Roberts, lies near the very accessible Mendenhall Glacier, and is otherwise surrounded by wilderness—and it's a really fun city to visit, too.

**Sitka**'s Russian architecture, the totem-pole park, and the Raptor Rehabilitation Center are all top-flight attractions. And what we like most about Sitka is that it hasn't been overrun with stuff for tourists—it still feels like a small-town place. Sitka is the kind of place real travelers (as opposed to tourists) will adore.

No town in Alaska is more historically significant than **Skagway,** and the old buildings are so perfect you might think you stepped into a Disney version of what a gold-rush town should look like. But you must first get over the presence of a Starbucks, more than a dozen upscale jewelry shops that have followed cruise passengers from the Caribbean, and all the other tourist shops and attractions. In short, Skagway has become hokey and touristy. For a more low-key Alaska experience, take the ferry from Skagway to **Haines,** which reminds us of the folksy, frontier Alaska depicted on the old TV show *Northern Exposure* and is a great place to spot eagles and other wildlife. Some ships also stop at Haines as a port of call, usually for a few hours after Skagway, and we're pleased to report this is one town that has not been changed by the advent of cruise-ship visitors.

# THE best SHORE EXCURSIONS

Flightseeing by **floatplane** or **helicopter** in Alaska is an unforgettable way to check out the scenery—if you can afford it. Airborne tours tend to be pretty pricey, from $215 to more than $600 per head. However, a helicopter trip to a dog-sled camp at the top of a glacier (usually among the priciest of the offerings) affords both incredibly pretty views and a chance to try your hand at the truly Alaskan sport of dog sledding, and it's a great way to earn bragging rights with the folks back home.

For a less extravagant excursion, nothing beats a ride on a clear day on the **White Pass & Yukon Route Railway** out of Skagway to the Canadian border or beyond. The steep train route is the same one followed by the gold stampeders of 1898. While you're riding the rails, try to imagine what it was like for those gold seekers crossing the same path on foot!

We also like to get active with **kayak** and **mountain-biking** excursions offered by most cruise lines at most ports. In addition to affording a chance to work off those shipboard calories, these excursions typically provide optimum opportunities for spotting eagles, bears, seals, and other wildlife. **Ziplining** is just plain fun for those who want to try soaring on a wire above the treetops—the adrenaline rush can be addictive. Recently, Fran has also gotten into snorkeling in Alaska (less cold than you think!).

Another popular (and less hectic) excursion is **whale-watching.** On one evening excursion out of Juneau in May, passengers on a small whale-watching boat got the thrill of seeing an entire pod of orcas, more than a dozen of the giant creatures, frolicking before their eyes.

# CHOOSING YOUR IDEAL CRUISE

**2**

Just like clothes, cars, and gourmet coffee, Alaska cruises come in all different styles to suit all different tastes. The first step in ensuring that you have the best possible vacation is to match your expectations to the appropriate itinerary and ship.

In this chapter, we explore the advantages of the two main Alaska itineraries; examine the differences between big-ship cruising and small-ship cruising; pose some questions you should ask yourself to determine which cruise is right for you; and give you the skinny on cruisetours, which combine a cruise with a land tour that gets you into the Alaska Interior.

## THE ALASKA CRUISE SEASON

Alaska is very much a seasonal, as opposed to year-round, cruise destination; the season generally runs from May through September, although a few ships get an early jump, starting up in late April. May and September are considered the shoulder seasons, and lower brochure rates and more aggressive discounts are offered during these months. We particularly like cruising in May, before the crowds arrive, when we've generally found locals to be friendlier than they are later in the season, at which point they're pretty much ready to see the tourists go home for the winter.

Also, at the Inside Passage ports, May is one of the driest months in the season. Though we have done late-May cruises where temperatures were in the 70s, perfect weather for hiking and biking, Alaska weather is unpredictable. Last year, in Southeast Alaska, it snowed in early June. September also offers the advantage of fewer fellow cruise passengers clogging the ports. The warmest temperatures are in late June, July, and August, which generally see temperatures of around 50°F to 80°F during the day and cooler nights. Some years the temperature has soared higher—Juneau has been known to hit the 90s. When this happens, you'll hear much local speculation about global warming. As for clothing, the trick in coping with Alaska weather is to dress in layers, with a lightweight waterproof jacket on top and a sweater and T-shirt underneath. You may not need a parka, but you will need to bring along outerwear and rain gear. Pack T-shirts, too.

## SHORE excursions: THE WHAT, WHEN & WHY

Shore excursions offered by the cruise lines provide a chance for you to get off the ship and explore the sights up close. You'll take in the history, nature, and culture of the region, from strolling gold-rush-era streets to experiencing Native Alaskan traditions such as totem carving.

Some excursions are of the walking-tour or bus-tour variety, but many others are activity-oriented: Cruise passengers have the opportunity to go sea kayaking, mountain-biking, horseback riding, salmon fishing, ziplining, and even rock climbing. There are tours by motorcycle and ATV. You can see the sights by seaplane or helicopter—and maybe even land on a glacier and go for a walk or a dog-sled ride. Occasionally, with some of the smaller cruise lines, you'll find quirky excursions, such as visits with local artists in their studios. Some lines even offer scuba diving and snorkeling (highly recommended!).

With some lines, including Regent Seven Seas and the small ships of Un-Cruise Adventures, Alaskan Dream Cruises, American Cruise Lines, and Lindblad Expeditions, shore excursions are included in your cruise fare, but with most lines they are an added (though sometimes very worthwhile) expense. See chapters 7 and 8 for details on the excursions available at the various ports. For more information, see "Cruisetours: The Best of Land & Sea," later in this chapter, and chapter 9.

June tends to be drier than July and August. (We have experienced trips in July during which it rained nearly every day.) If you are considering traveling in a shoulder month, keep in mind that some shops and a few attractions don't open until Memorial Day, and the visitor season is generally considered over on Labor Day (although cruise lines operate well into Sept).

# THE INSIDE PASSAGE OR THE GULF OF ALASKA?

For the purposes of cruising, Alaska can be divided into two separate and distinct areas, known generically as "the Inside Passage" and "the Gulf."

## The Inside Passage

The Inside Passage runs through the area of Alaska known as Southeast (which the locals also call "the Panhandle"). It's the narrow strip of the state—islands, mainland coastal communities, and mountains—that runs from the Canadian border in the south to the start of the Gulf in the north, just above the Juneau/Haines/Skagway area. The islands on the western edge of the area afford cruise ships a welcome degree of protection from the sea and its attendant rough waters (hence the name "Inside Passage"). Because of that shelter, such ports as Ketchikan, Wrangell, Petersburg, and others are reached with less rocking and rolling and thus less risk of seasickness. Sitka is not on the Inside Passage (it's on the Pacific Ocean side of Baranof Island), but is included in a fair number of Inside Passage cruise itineraries because it is a beautiful little port, with architecture and historical sites strongly reflective of Alaska's Russian past.

Southeast encompasses the capital city, **Juneau,** and townships influenced by the former Russian presence in the state (**Sitka,** for instance), the Tlingit and Haida Native cultures (**Ketchikan**), and the great gold rush of 1898 (**Skagway**). It is a land of rain-forests, mountains, inlets, and glaciers (including Margerie, Johns Hopkins, Muir, and the others contained within the boundaries of **Glacier Bay National Park**). The region is rich in wildlife, especially of the marine variety. It is a scenic delight. But then, what part of Alaska isn't?

## The Gulf of Alaska

The other major cruising area is the **Southcentral** region's Gulf of Alaska, usually referred to by the cruise lines as the "Glacier Discovery Route" or the "Voyage of the Glaciers," or some such catchy title. "Gulf of Alaska," after all, sounds pretty bland.

The coastline of the Gulf is that arc of land from just north of Glacier Bay to the Kenai Peninsula. Southcentral also takes in **Prince William Sound;** the **Cook Inlet,** on the northern side of the peninsula; **Anchorage,** Alaska's biggest city; the year-round **Alyeska Resort** at Girdwood, 40 miles from Anchorage; the **Matanuska** and **Susitna** valleys (the "Mat-Su"), a fertile agricultural region renowned for the record size of some of its garden produce; and part of the Alaska Mountain Range.

The principal Southcentral terminus ports are **Seward** or **Whittier** for Anchorage. Rarely do ships actually head for Anchorage proper, because that adds another full day to the route; instead, they carry passengers from Seward or Whittier to Anchorage by bus or train. (In 2010, Holland America made news by becoming the first big ship to visit Anchorage in 25 years, and in 2014 the cruise line will make a full-day call at Anchorage on its 14-night itinerary on the *Amsterdam* out of Seattle.)

Let us stress that going on a Gulf cruise does not mean that you don't visit any of the Inside Passage. The big difference is that, whereas the more popular Inside Passage cruise itineraries run 7 nights round-trip to and from Seattle or Vancouver, BC, the Gulf routing is one-way—either northbound or southbound—between Vancouver and Seward or Vancouver and Whittier. A typical Gulf itinerary still visits such Inside Passage ports as **Ketchikan, Juneau,** and **Skagway.**

The Gulf's glaciers are quite dazzling and every bit as spectacular as their counter-parts to the south. **College Fjord,** for instance, is lined with glaciers—16 of them, each one grander than the last. On one cruise, Fran saw incredible calving at **Harvard Glacier,** with chunks of 400- and 500-year-old ice falling off and crashing into the water to thunderous sounds every few minutes. (Concerns about global warming aside, it was spectacular.) Another favorite part of a Gulf cruise is the visit to the gigantic **Hubbard Glacier**—at 6 miles, Alaska's longest—at the head of Yakutat Bay, where the chunks in the water may remind you of ice in a giant punch bowl. Nothing beats a sunny day watching the glacier—hyperactive, popping and cracking, and shedding tons of ice into the bay. We should mention that on one visit to Hubbard Glacier we couldn't even get into the bay because another ship was blocking our path (and hog-ging the optimum views). Our fear is that, with so many new ships in Alaska, glacier viewing could become a blood sport.

2

CHOOSING YOUR IDEAL CRUISE | The Inside Passage or the Gulf of Alaska?

And then there's the fact that, sadly, what you're really seeing is Alaska's glaciers in retreat, some receding quite rapidly.

## Which Itinerary Is Better?

It's really a matter of personal taste. Some people don't like open-jaw flights (flying into one city and out of another)—which can add to the air ticket price—and prefer the round-trip Inside Passage route. Some have Glacier Bay on the mind, a visit to the national park high on their "Bucket List." Others don't mind splitting up the air travel because they want to enjoy the additional glacier visits on the Gulf itineraries.

It wasn't so long ago that you wouldn't have had a choice. A few years back, there were practically no Gulf crossings. Then Princess and its tour-operating affiliate decided to accelerate the development of its land components (lodges, railcars, motor coaches, and so on), particularly in the Kenai Peninsula and Denali National Park areas, for which Anchorage is a logical springboard. To feed these land services with cruisetour passengers, Princess beefed up its number of Gulf sailings, and the line will still have three ships in the Gulf this year—as well as a formidable Inside Passage capacity. The other Alaska cruise giant, Holland America Line (HAL), will have five of its seven vessels in the Inside Passage (three out of Vancouver, two out of Seattle), and two vessels cruising across the Gulf (out of Vancouver and Seward). HAL tends to go more heavily into the Inside Passage than Princess because it is arguably stronger in Yukon Territory land services, which are more accessible from Juneau or Skagway.

# BIG SHIP OR SMALL SHIP?

Picking the right ship is the most important factor in ensuring that you get the vacation you're looking for. Cruise ships in Alaska range from **small, adventure-type vessels** to **really big, resortlike megaships,** with the cruise experience varying widely depending on the type of ship you select. There are casual cruises and luxury cruises; there are educational cruises, where you attend lectures, and entertainment-focused cruises, where you attend musical revues; there are adventure-oriented cruises, where hiking, kayaking, and exploring remote areas are the main activities, and resortlike cruises, where aquatherapy and mud baths are the order of the day.

Besides the availability (or nonavailability) of the programs, the spas, the activities, and the like, there is another question you have to answer before deciding on a ship. Do you want, or do you need, to be with people and, if so, in an intimate daily setting or only on an occasional basis? On a small ship, there's no escape. The people you meet on a 12-passenger or even a 138-passenger vessel are the ones you're going to be seeing every day of the cruise. And woe betide you if they turn out to be boring, or bombastic, or slow-witted, or in some other way not to your taste. Some people may think that the megaships are too big, but they do have at least one saving grace: On a 2,670-passenger ship, there's plenty of room to steer clear of people who turn you off. And because all these big, newer ships have lots of alternative restaurants, it's even easier to avoid those types at mealtimes, something that's not so easy on a smaller ship.

Personal chemistry plays a big part in the success or failure of any cruise experience—especially a small-ship cruise experience.

You'll need to decide what overall cruise experience you want. Itinerary and type of cruise are even more important than price. After all, what kind of bargain is a party cruise if you're looking for a quiet time? Or an adventure-oriented cruise if you're not physically in the best of shape? Your fantasy vacation may be someone else's nightmare, and vice versa.

Unlike the Caribbean, which generally attracts people looking to relax in the sun or possibly party 'til the cows come home, Alaska attracts visitors with a different goal: They want to experience Alaska's glaciers, forests, wildlife, and other natural wonders. All the cruise lines recognize this, so almost any cruise you choose will give you opportunities to see what you've come for. The main question, then, is how you want to see those sights. Do you want to be down at the waterline, viewing them from the deck of an adventure vessel, or do you want to spot them from a warm lounge or your own private veranda?

The hotel director on a Holland America ship once noted, "If you want to stay out until 4am, gamble wildly, and pass out in a lounge, you don't come on Holland America." And he's right. Picking the ship that's right for you is the key to a successful Alaska cruise experience.

In this section, we'll run through the pros and cons of the big ships and the small and alternative ships. (See chapters 5 and 6 for detailed descriptions of the ships cruising in Alaska.)

## The Big Ships

Big ships operating in Alaska vary in size, amenities, and activities, and include really big and really new megaships (the *Celebrity Solstice* and *Crown Princess* are the biggest; the *Norwegian Pearl* and *Celebrity Solstice* the newest). All the big ships provide a comfortable experience, with virtual armies of service employees overseeing your well-being and ship stabilizers ensuring smooth sailing.

The size of the current crop of ships may keep Alaska's wildlife at a distance (you may need binoculars to see the whales), but they have plenty of deck space and comfy lounge chairs for relaxing as you take in the gorgeous mountain and glacier views, and sip a cup of coffee or cocoa (and, on Holland America, the famous Dutch pea soup). Due to their deeper drafts (the amount of ship below the waterline), the big ships can't get as close to the sights as the smaller ships, and they can't visit the more pristine fjords, inlets, and narrows. However, the more powerful engines on these ships do allow them to visit more ports during each trip—generally, popular ports where your ship may be one of several and where shopping for souvenirs is a main attraction. Some of the less massive ships in this category also visit alternative ports, away from the cruise crowds.

It should be noted, too, that the bigger ships being built nowadays are equipped with some pretty powerful stabilizers—something to think about if you have the occasional bout with seasickness.

The big-ship cruise lines put a lot of emphasis on **shore excursions,** which often take you beyond the port city to explore different aspects of Alaska—nature, Native culture, and so on. (See the shore excursion listings in chapters 7 and 8 for more information.) Dispersing passengers to different locales on these shore trips is a must. When 8,000 passengers from several visiting ships converge on a small Alaska town, much of the ambience goes out the window. On particularly busy days, there are more cruise passengers in some ports than locals. Take Skagway, for instance: In midsummer, even counting the influx of seasonal tourist-services-related employees, its population is far short of 1,000. One large cruise ship will deposit at least twice that many people onto the streets—and on busy days, there may be as many as *four* ships in port!

The larger ships in the Alaska market fall into two categories: midsize and megaships. **Midsize ships** in Alaska for 2014 are the luxurious Silversea's *Silver Shadow* and Regent Seven Seas' *Navigator,* Oceania Cruises' upscale *Regatta,* the modern midsize *Volendam, Amsterdam, Zaandam,* and *Statendam* of Holland America Line and Princess' *Pacific Princess.* In general, the size of these ships is less significant than the general onboard atmosphere. Holland America's midsize ships, for example, all have a similar calm, adult-oriented feel, as does the *Pacific Princess;* Oceania's *Regatta* has an ambience akin to a floating country hotel; the *Navigator* offers a casual luxury (think country-club set); and the *Silver Shadow* oozes ultraluxury with sleek, Italian flair.

Carrying as many as 2,670 passengers, the **megaships** look and feel like floating resorts. Big on glitz, they offer loads of activities, attract many families and seniors, have many public rooms (including fancy casinos and fully equipped gyms and spas), and provide a wide variety of meal and entertainment options. Although they may feature 1 or 2 formal nights per trip, the ambience is generally casual. The Alaska vessels of the Carnival, Celebrity, Princess, and Royal Caribbean fleets all fit in this category, as do Norwegian Cruise Line's *Sun, Star,* and newer *Pearl,* Holland America's

---

### Weighing the Dining Options on Various Cruises

Smaller ships usually serve dinner at a certain time and with open seating, allowing you to sit at any table you want but at a set time. Large ships may offer only two fairly rigid, set seating times, especially for dinner; this means that your table will be preassigned and remain the same for the duration of the cruise. Increasingly, however, there are exceptions to the rule in the large-ship category. The ships of Norwegian Cruise Line, Oceania, Regent Seven Seas, and Silversea serve all meals with open seating—dine when you want and sit with whom you want (within the restaurants' open hours and sometimes requiring reservations to be made in the morning for dinner). Princess, Holland America,

Carnival, Royal Caribbean, and Celebrity have their own systems, allowing guests to choose before the cruise between traditional early or late seating, or open restaurant-style seating. Most large ships today also offer multiple alternative-dining options, featuring casual buffets and specialty restaurants, some with an additional charge (as a gratuity) of up to $35, or more if you choose a fancy Chef's Table where dishes are paired with wines (costing $89 on Norwegian Cruise Line, for example). See "Choosing Your Dining Options," in chapter 3, for more information on dining choices, and see the individual ship reviews in chapters 5 and 6 for ship-specific dining information.

*Oosterdam, Zuiderdam,* and *Westerdam,* and Disney's *Wonder. **Word of caution:*** Due to the number of people onboard, debarkation from the biggest ships can be a lengthy process.

Both the midsize ships and the megaships have a great range of **facilities** for passengers. There are swimming pools, health clubs, spas (of various sizes), nightclubs, movie theaters, shops, casinos, bars, and kids' playrooms. In some cases, especially on the megaships, you'll also find sports decks, virtual golf, computer rooms, and cigar clubs, as well as quiet spaces where you can get away from it all. There are so many public rooms that you more than likely won't feel claustrophobic. **Cabins** range from cubbyholes to large suites, depending on the ship and the type of accommodations you book. Cabins provide TVs and telephones, and some have minibars, picture windows, and private verandas.

These ships have big dining rooms and buffet areas and serve a tremendous variety of **cuisine** throughout the day, often with 24-hour food service. There may also be additional dining venues, such as pizzerias, hamburger grills, ice cream parlors, alternative restaurants (typically for an extra service charge), wine bars, cigar bars, champagne bars, caviar bars, and patisseries. Note that because these ships carry a lot of people, there may be lines at the buffets and in other public areas.

In most cases, there are lots of **onboard activities** to keep you occupied when you're not whale- or glacier-watching, including games, contests, and classes and lectures (sometimes by naturalists, park rangers, or wildlife experts; sometimes on topics such as line dancing and napkin folding). These ships also have a variety of entertainment options that may even include celebrity headline acts and often stage-show productions, some pretty extravagant (those of Carnival come to mind).

## The Small & Alternative Ships

While big cruise ships are mostly for people who want every resort amenity, small or alternative ships are best suited for people who prefer a casual, crowd-free cruise experience that gives passengers a chance to get up close and personal with Alaska's **natural surroundings** and **wildlife.**

Thanks to their smaller size, these ships, carrying only 22 to 100 passengers, can go places where larger ships can't, such as narrow fjords, uninhabited islands, and smaller ports that cater mostly to small fishing vessels. Due to their shallow draft, they can nose right up to sheer cliff faces, bird rookeries, bobbing icebergs, and cascading waterfalls that you can literally reach out and touch. Also, sea animals are not as intimidated by these ships, so you might find yourself having a rather close encounter with a humpback whale or watching other sea mammals bobbing in the ship's wake. You may catch excellent glimpses of land animals, too—while on a small ship in the Misty Fjords (a place big ships can't even go), Fran and her fellow passengers watched through binoculars as a brown bear shoreside stood to its full height, the captain positioned the ship a safe distance from the creature for a good half-hour so everyone could take in the sight. The decks on these ships are closer to the waterline, too, giving passengers a more intimate view than they would get from the high decks of the large cruise ships. Some of these ships stop at ports on a daily basis, like the larger ships, while some avoid ports almost entirely, exploring natural areas instead. Small ships also have the flexibility to change direction as opportunities arise—say, to go where whales have been sighted and to linger awhile once a sighting has been made.

The alternative-ship experience is all about a sense of **adventure** (usually of a soft rather than rugged sort), and it's a generally casual cruise experience: There are no dress-up nights, and food may be rather simple (although there are notable exceptions—on the luxury ships of Un-Cruise Adventures the chefs show a deft hand with fresh Alaskan seafood, and on Alaskan Dream ships the Asian dishes are particularly tasty). These ships have so few public areas to choose from—usually only one or two small lounges—that camaraderie tends to develop more quickly between passengers than aboard larger vessels, which can be as anonymous as a big city. **Cabins** on these ships don't usually offer TVs or telephones and tend to be very small and in some cases downright spartan (though the luxury ships of Un-Cruise Adventures include some cabins and suites with Jacuzzis and French balconies). Meals are served at a set time, with open seating (seats are not assigned), and dress codes are usually nonexistent.

None of these ships has the kind of significant exercise or spa facilities that you'll find on the big ships—your best exercise bet is usually a brisk walk around the deck after dinner—but many compensate by providing more **active off-ship opportunities,** such as hiking or kayaking. The alternative ships are also more likely to feature in-depth **lectures** on Alaska-specific topics, such as marine biology, history, and Native culture.

There are few if any stabilizers on most of these smaller ships, and the ride can be bumpy in open water—which isn't much of a problem on Inside Passage itineraries, when most of the cruising area is protected from sea waves. With no elevators, these ships can also be difficult for travelers with disabilities. And the alternative-ship lines do not offer specific activities or facilities for children, although you will find a few families on some of these vessels.

# CRUISETOURS: THE BEST OF LAND & SEA

Most folks who go to the trouble of getting to a place as far off the beaten path as Alaska try to stick around for awhile once they're there, rather than jetting home as soon as they hop off the boat. Knowing this, the cruise lines have set themselves up in the land-tour business as well, offering a number of great land-based excursions that can be tacked onto your cruise experience.

We're not just talking about an overnight stay in Anchorage or Juneau before or after your cruise; almost any cruise line will arrange an extra night of hotel accommodations for you. Enjoyable as that may be, it doesn't begin to hint at the real opportunities available in Alaska. No, the subject here is **cruisetours,** or Land + Sea Journeys, as Holland America now calls them, a total package with a cruise and a structured, prearranged, multiday land itinerary already programmed in—for instance, a 7-day cruise with a 5-day land package. There are any number of combinations between 10 and 20 days in length.

In this section, we'll discuss the various cruisetour itineraries that are available through the lines. See chapter 10 for details on the various cruisetour destinations.

## Cruisetour Itineraries

Many parts of inland Alaska can be visited on cruisetour programs, including Denali National Park, Fairbanks, Wrangell–St. Elias, Nome, and Kotzebue. If you're so inclined, you can even go all the way to the oil fields of the North Slope of Prudhoe Bay, hundreds of miles north of the Arctic Circle.

Three principal tour destination areas can be combined with your Inside Passage or Gulf of Alaska cruise—two major ones, which we'll call the **Anchorage/Denali/Fairbanks** corridor and the **Yukon Territory,** and one less-traveled route that we'll call the **Canadian Rockies Route,** which is an option because of Vancouver's position as an Alaska cruise hub.

## ANCHORAGE/DENALI/FAIRBANKS CRUISETOUR

A typical Anchorage/Denali/Fairbanks cruisetour package (we'll use Princess as an example because it is heavily involved in the Denali sector) might include a 7-day Vancouver-Anchorage cruise, followed by 2 nights in Anchorage and a scenic ride in a private railcar to **Denali National Park** for 2 more nights at Princess' Denali Lodge or Mount McKinley Lodge (or 1 night at each) before heading on to Fairbanks. On a clear day, the McKinley property affords a panoramic view of the Alaska Mountain Range and its centerpiece, **Mount McKinley,** which, at 20,320 feet, is North America's highest peak. A full day in the park allows guests to explore the staggeringly beautiful wilderness expanse and its wildlife before reboarding the train and heading into the Interior of Alaska, to **Fairbanks,** for 2 more nights. Fairbanks itself isn't much to look at, but the activities available in outlying areas are fantastic—the *Riverboat Discovery* paddlewheel day cruises on the Chena and Tanana rivers and an excursion to a gold mine are two excellent activity options in the area. Passengers on that particular cruisetour fly home from Fairbanks.

A shorter variation of that itinerary might be a cruise combined with an overnight (or 2-night) stay in Anchorage along with the Denali portion, perhaps with rail transportation into the park and a motorcoach back to Anchorage, skipping Fairbanks. Princess has cruisetours that include visits to a hitherto largely inaccessible area, **Wrangell–St. Elias National Park,** where it has built the Copper River Princess Wilderness Lodge, the fifth hotel in the company's lodging network.

## YUKON TERRITORY CRUISETOUR

Another popular land itinerary offered along with Alaska cruises typically involves a 3- or 4-day cruise between Vancouver and Juneau/Skagway (you either join a 7-day sailing late or get off early), combined with a land program into the **Klondike,** in Canada's Yukon Territory, then through the Interior of Alaska to Anchorage. En route, passengers experience a variety of transportation modes, which may include rail, riverboat, motorcoach, and/or air—Holland America now flies passengers between Fairbanks and Dawson City. The flight takes an hour and saves 2 days of motorcoach travel and a hotel overnight.

Although located in Canada, the Yukon is nevertheless an integral part of the overall Alaska cruisetour picture because of its intimate ties to Alaska's gold-rush history. The overnight stops are **Whitehorse,** the territorial capital, and **Dawson City,** a remote, picture-perfect gold-rush town near the site where gold was found in 1896. Holland America offers a drive through Canada's **Kluane National Park,** a Yukon Territory wilderness area designated a UNESCO World Heritage Site, and also through Tombstone Territorial Park, about a 90-minute drive from Dawson City and an area of stunning scenery, Native architecture, and abundant wildlife. Kluane Park contains 5 of

## SHOULD YOU TAKE YOUR cruisetour BEFORE OR AFTER YOUR CRUISE?

Though the land portion of both the Denali and the Yukon itineraries can be taken either before or after the cruise, we feel it's better to take the land portion pre-cruise rather than post-cruise. Why? After several days of exploring the wilderness, it's nice to be able to get aboard a ship to relax and be pampered for a while.

Because of the distances that must be covered on some wilderness cruisetour itineraries, passengers often have to be roused out of bed and ready to board the motorcoach by, say, 7:30am. And the day may seem to go on forever, with a stop to view this waterfall, or that river, or that mountain. Then, upon arrival at the next stop—in the early evening usually—the request is, "Hurry and get cleaned up for dinner." By the time

you've crawled into your new bed, often quite late at night, you're beat. It's a nice kind of tired, as the saying goes, but it's tired nevertheless. After a few days of that, it's great to get on a luxurious cruise ship, unpack just once, and rise when you feel like it, comfortable in the knowledge that you haven't missed your transportation and that you'll still make it in time to have a leisurely breakfast.

That, at any rate, is the conventional wisdom, and there's more of a demand for pre-cruise land packages than for post-cruise. As the lines obviously can't always accommodate everybody on a land itinerary before the cruise (they're hoping to even out the traffic flow by having a like number of requests to go touring after the voyage), it's smart to get your bid in early.

North America's 10 tallest peaks. If it's wilderness scenery you want, you'll be hard-pressed to find anything more awesome.

### CANADIAN ROCKIES CRUISETOUR

A Canadian Rockies tour is easily combined with a Vancouver-originating (or -terminating) Inside Passage or Gulf cruise. In 5-, 6-, or 7-day chunks, you can visit such scenic wonders as **Banff, Lake Louise,** and **Jasper National Park** in conjunction with an Alaska sailing.

The Canadian Rockies have some of the finest **mountain scenery** on Earth. It's not just that the glacier-carved mountains are astonishingly dramatic and beautiful; it's also that there are hundreds and hundreds of miles of this wonderful wilderness high country. Between them, Banff National Park and Jasper National Park preserve much of this mountain beauty. Other national and provincial parks make accessible more vast and equally spectacular regions of the Rockies, as well as portions of the nearby Columbia and Selkirk mountain ranges. Beautiful Lake Louise, colored deep green from its mineral content, is located 35 miles north of Banff.

## Battle of the Top Players

If we talk in this section more about **Princess** and **Holland America (HAL)** than we do about other lines, it's because their significant financial investments in land components of Alaskan tourism have allowed them to become the 800-pound gorillas duking it out for regional dominance. Other lines offer some of the same cruisetours as these two, but many buy at least some of their cruisetour components from Princess and/or Holland America's land operations. It may seem odd to have companies buying from (or selling to) competitors, but with tourism in Alaska, there's practically no other way. As recently as the early 1980s, when Holland America–Westours owned the bulk of the land-tour components, Princess, its number-one rival, was also its number-one customer! Hey, a 4-month season makes for strange bedfellows.

It was partly to carve out a niche for itself and, at the same time, to lessen its reliance on the services of a competitor that Princess plunged heavily into the lodging and transportation sectors. Princess is arguably stronger in the Denali corridor than any other line, while Holland America could be said to have the upper hand in the Yukon/ Klondike market. But each line offers tours to both of these areas, among other options.

Princess owns railcars (the *Midnight Sun Express*) in the Denali corridor. Holland America also owns railcars there (the *McKinley Explorer*). Both, incidentally, rely on the Alaska Railroad to pull them. Princess owns five wilderness lodges; Holland America owns primarily city hotels (the Westmark Fairbanks and Anchorage recently renovated; the Skagway property updated including with an expansion). Princess and Holland America have a fleet of motorcoaches (some of Holland America's very recently updated).

But HAL and Princess have not gone unchallenged. With its Royal Caribbean International and Celebrity Cruises brands, Royal Caribbean has become the third well-established player in the game. The company will have two Royal Caribbean ships and three Celebrity ships in the 49th state in 2014. A few years ago, it formed Royal Celebrity Tours to operate its own land packages. Its motorcoaches are luxurious, and its railcars are truly state of the art, with business-class-style leather seas, a fine kitchen on the lower level (meals are extra, with a variety of menus), and a friendly, knowledgeable staff.

# QUIZ TIME: QUESTIONS TO ASK WHEN CHOOSING YOUR CRUISE

After you've decided which itinerary and what kind of ship appeals to you, we suggest you ask yourself some questions about the kind of experience you want, and then read through the cruise-line and ship reviews in chapters 5 and 6 to see which ones match your vision of the perfect Alaska cruise vessel.

When looking at the attributes of the various ships to make your choice, some determining factors will be no-brainers. For instance, if you're traveling with kids, you'll want a ship with a good kids' program. If you're a foodie, you'll want a ship with gourmet cuisine. If you're used to staying at a Ritz-Carlton hotel when you travel, you'll probably want to cruise on a luxury ship. If you usually stay at B&Bs, you'll probably prefer one of the small ships.

Also ask yourself whether you require resortlike amenities, such as a heated swimming pool, spa, casino, aerobics classes, and state-of-the-art gym. Or do you care more about having an adventure or an educational experience? If you want the former, choose a large cruise ship; if you prefer the latter, a small ship may be more your speed.

Here are some more pertinent questions to help you narrow the field:

**HOW DO YOU GET A DEAL, AND WHAT'S NOT INCLUDED?**   The best way to get a deal on a cruise in Alaska is usually to book early, but this is hardly a hard and fast rule. Virtually all the lines (with the exception of some of the small-ship lines) offer early-booking discounts. The numbers and dates may vary a bit, but the formula has been fairly standard: When you **book in advance,** in a typical year, you can expect to save 25 percent to 50 percent off the brochure rate if you book your Alaska cruise by mid- to late February of the year of the cruise. If the cabins do not fill up by the cutoff date, the early-bird rate may be extended. We were seeing starting early-bird brochure prices for 2014 as low as $499 for an inside cabin on an early-season 7-night cruise.

If the cabins are still not full as the cruise season begins, cruise lines typically start marketing special deals, usually through their top-producing travel agents and with savings that can run as high as 50 percent to 75 percent. Last year, which proved a tough one for the cruise lines, you could nab a last-minute fare of under $300 if you waited to book in early July. Such bargain-basement fares generally apply to the lowest category of inside cabins, and the number of cabins offered at said prices is very limited. To get the best deal in 2014, we suggest you book your Alaska cruise, and particularly your Alaska cruisetour (because these are increasingly popular), as early as possible.

Cruise fares cover accommodations, meals, shipboard entertainment, and most shipboard activities. There are, however, a number of expenses not covered in the typical cruise package, and you should factor these in when planning your vacation budget. Airfare to and from your port of embarkation and debarkation is usually extra (though cruise lines sometimes offer reduced rates). Necessary hotel stays before or after the cruise are also usually not included. Gratuities, taxes, and trip insurance are typically extra as well. Shore excursions are rarely included in the cruise fare (Regent Seven Seas is the only big ship line that includes a free option at each port), and if you opt for pricey excursions, such as flightseeing, you can easily add $600 to $1,000 per person to your total. Alcohol is typically extra (though Regent and Silversea include all drinks in the cruise fare), as are sodas and such incidentals as laundry, Internet access (which can run as much as 75¢ per minute!), telephone calls from the ship, and babysitting. And then there are such optional splurges as beauty and spa services, wine tastings, dining in alternative restaurants, select fitness classes, fancy ice cream sundaes, and photos taken by ship photographers.

Because travel agents constantly keep abreast of the latest bargains, we believe they are best equipped to advise you on the best Alaska cruise deals.

See chapter 3 for details on when to book for the best prices.

**HOW MUCH TIME IS SPENT IN PORT & HOW MUCH AT SEA?**   Generally, ships on 7-night itineraries spend 3 or 4 days in port and cruise in natural areas such as Glacier Bay, College Fjord, or Tracy Arm during the other days.

Coming into port, ships generally dock right after breakfast, allowing you the morning and afternoon to take a shore excursion or explore on your own. Ships usually depart in the early evening, giving you an hour or two to rest up before dinner (although some ships do stay in Juneau as late as 10pm, giving passengers a chance to sample a dinner of halibut burger, salmon steak, or similar local fare off the ship, if you so choose). On rare occasions, a ship might cruise through a glacier area in the morning and dock at the next port in the early afternoon, not leaving until 10 or 11pm.

On days at sea, the emphasis will be on exploring natural areas, viewing glaciers, and scanning for wildlife. Big ships stick to prearranged schedules on these days, but on small-ship, soft-adventure-type cruises, days at sea can be unstructured, with the captain choosing a destination based on reports of whale sightings, for example. Some small-ship itineraries include almost no ports, sticking instead to isolated natural areas that passengers explore by kayak or Zodiac boat or on foot.

**IS THE CRUISE FORMAL OR CASUAL?**   If you don't care to get dressed up, select a less formal cruise, such as those offered by many of the small ships, such as Regent's luxurious, but casual *Seven Seas Navigator,* or the Norwegian Cruise Line ships, which do not have official formal nights (but usually set aside 1 night for those who want to dress up). If, on the other hand, having the chance to put on your finery appeals to you, select Princess, Celebrity, or Holland America (and, to a lesser extent, mass-market lines such as Royal Caribbean and Carnival) or the posh *Silversea.* These ships will have casual and formal nights, meaning women can show off everything from a sundress to an evening gown (though on formal nights, most show up in cocktail dresses) over the course of a week, and men will go from shirtsleeves 1 night to jacket and tie the next (you can wear a tuxedo if you like, but many men are now opting for dark suits). All the lines also now have an option for those who do not want to dress up on formal nights—you can skip the dining room and eat casually at the buffet.

**WHAT ARE THE OTHER PASSENGERS USUALLY LIKE?**   Each ship attracts a fairly predictable type of passenger. On small ships, you'll find a more physically active bunch that's highly interested in nature, but you'll find fewer families and single travelers. Larger ships cater to a more diverse group—singles, newlyweds, families, and couples over 55. Alaska sailings out of Seattle attract a younger, more family-oriented crowd. If you're looking for nightlife, you may want to look at Carnival, Norwegian Cruise Line, and Royal Caribbean cruises from this port. Disney of course attracts a family crowd, but also a number of adult couples. We've included information on typical passengers in all the cruise-line reviews in chapters 5 and 6.

**I'LL BE TRAVELING ALONE. WILL I HAVE FUN? AND DOES IT COST MORE?**   A nice thing about cruises is that you're seated with other guests, so you never have to dine alone. (If you don't want to be seated with other guests, seek a ship with alternative-dining options—although a steady diet of "Table for one, please" is likely to raise a few eyebrows among your shipmates.) You also needn't worry much about finding people to talk to because the general atmosphere on nearly all ships is very congenial and allows you to find conversation easily, especially during group activities. Some ships host a party to give singles a chance to get to know one another, and some ships provide social hosts as dance partners.

The downside is that you may have to pay for the privilege of traveling solo. Because rates are based on two people per cabin, some lines charge a "single supplement" fee (aka, an extra charge) that ranges from 10 percent to 100 percent of the double-occupancy fare. As a single person, you have two choices: Find a line with a reasonable single supplement rate (Regent Seven Seas, Holland America, and Silversea have all lowered their supplements to 25 percent or less), or ask if the line has a cabin-share program, under which the line will pair you with another single so you can get a lower fare. Some lines also have a single-guarantee program, which means if they can't find you a roommate (of the same sex), they'll book you in a cabin alone but still honor the shared rate. Single cabins designed for one person are available on some ships; these tend to be small, however, and sell out fast.

**IS SHIPBOARD LIFE HEAVILY SCHEDULED?**   That depends to a certain extent on you and the ship you choose. Meals are generally served during set hours, though on larger ships, you'll have plenty of alternative options if those hours don't suit you. On smaller ships, you may be out of luck if you miss a meal, unless you can charm the cook. On both large and small ships, times for disembarking and reboarding at the ports are strict: If you miss the boat, you miss the boat. (See chapter 4 for tips on what to do in this situation.) Other than these two considerations, the only schedule you'll have to follow on board is your own. It all depends on how busy you want to be.

**WHAT ARE THE CABINS LIKE?**   Cabins come in all sizes and configurations. See "Choosing Your Cabin," in chapter 3, for a detailed discussion.

**WHAT ARE MEALS LIKE?**   Meals are a big part of the cruise experience. The larger the ship, the more dining options you'll find. When booking on large ships that feature two dining-room seatings each evening, you'll be asked ahead of time to decide on your preferred dinner hour, with tables assigned. On Princess, Royal Caribbean, Carnival, Holland America, and Celebrity ships, you choose in advance whether to dine traditional- or restaurant-style. Norwegian, Silversea, Oceania, and Regent ships have open, restaurant-style seating, meaning that you can dine when you want with whomever you choose, but you are encouraged to make reservations each morning for tables at dinner. On smaller ships, you can sit where you want, but dinner will be called for a set time. In the reviews in chapters 5 and 6, we discuss dining options for each line.

If you have any special dietary requirements (vegan, kosher, gluten-free), be sure the line is informed well in advance, preferably when you book your cruise. Almost all ships have vegetarian and low-fat options available at every meal (sugar-free desserts, too), and those that don't can usually meet your needs with some advance warning.

**WHAT ACTIVITIES & ENTERTAINMENT DOES THE SHIP OFFER?**   On small ships, activities are limited by the available public space and are usually up to the passengers to organize—maybe a game of Scrabble or Trivia Pursuit. There may be a showing of a video or two, and there will typically also be a lecture series dealing with the flora, fauna, and geography of Alaska, usually conducted by a naturalist. These lectures are also becoming more popular on the larger ships.

The big ships have activities such as fitness, personal finance, photography, and art classes; Ping-Pong and bingo tournaments; audience-participation games; art auctions; and parties. Show productions at night are almost de rigueur. Cooking classes and demonstrations are the *in* thing. (See the general big-ship and small-ship descriptions earlier in this chapter for more information on activities and entertainment.)

**DOES THE SHIP HAVE A CHILDREN'S PROGRAM?**   Many parents are taking their kids with them on cruise vacations. The big ship lines have responded by adding youth counselors and supervised programs, fancy playrooms, teen centers, and even video-game rooms to keep kids entertained while their parents relax. Some lines offer special shore excursions for children and teens, and most ships provide babysitting (for an extra charge). You may even find reduced cruise fares for kids.

It's important to ask whether a supervised program will be available on your specific cruise, because sometimes the programs operate only if a certain number of children are on board. If your kids are TV addicts, you may want to make sure that your cabin has a TV. Even if it does, though, channel selection will be limited, so consider bringing along a portable DVD player (or a laptop with DVD capabilities) and a selection of movies in the event that your ship is not equipped with in-cabin DVD players.

## I HAVE A DISABILITY. WILL I HAVE ANY TROUBLE TAKING A CRUISE?

It's important to let the cruise line know about any special needs when you make your booking. If you use a wheelchair, you'll need to know if wheelchair-accessible cabins are available (and how they're equipped), as well as whether public rooms are accessible and can be reached by elevator, and whether the cruise line has any special policy regarding travelers with disabilities—for instance, whether it's required that a fully mobile companion accompany you. Based on various court cases, it's clear that when operating in U.S. waters, ships are expected to comply with the Americans with Disabilities Act (ADA). Newer ships tend to be better equipped, however, offering a larger number of cabins at various price points for passengers in wheelchairs as well as those who are sight- or hearing-impaired. But even older ships undergoing renovations are being retrofitted to provide more access.

Travelers with disabilities should inquire when booking whether the ship docks at ports or uses "tenders" (small boats) to go ashore. Tenders cannot always accommodate passengers with wheelchairs; in most cases, wheelchair-bound passengers require crew assistance to board tenders—though Holland America, for one, uses a special lift system to get passengers into the tenders without requiring them to leave their wheelchairs. Once aboard the ship, travelers with disabilities will want to seek the advice of tour staff before choosing shore excursions that are wheelchair-friendly.

If you have a chronic health problem, we advise you to check with your doctor before booking a cruise and, if you have any specific needs, to notify the cruise line in advance. This will ensure that the medical team on the ship is properly prepared to offer assistance. There is another, somewhat sensitive, consideration for some would-be small-ship passengers: obesity. We mention this only because we once met, on a small ship, a charming young lady who stood a little over 5 feet tall and weighed about 250 pounds. She told us that she had been advised by the cruise line not to book passage on the ship she first chose because she wouldn't fit in the shower. Instead, the company put her on a ship for which her girth would not be a problem. Understand, please, that the cruise operator is not being judgmental. But if you don't mention such things and end up on an inappropriate ship, you're in for a miserable time. So assess the situation realistically.

## WHAT IF I WANT TO TAKE A CRUISE FOR MY HONEYMOON?

One-week Alaska cruises start not only on Saturdays and Sundays, but also on Mondays, Wednesdays, Thursdays, and Fridays, which should help you find an departure date that doesn't have you running out of your wedding reception to catch a plane. You will want to make sure that the ship you choose has double, queen-, or king-size beds; you may also want to request a cabin with a Jacuzzi. Rooms with private verandas are particularly romantic; you can take in the sights in privacy and even enjoy a quiet meal, assuming the veranda is big enough for a table and chairs (some are not) and the weather doesn't turn chilly. If you want to dine alone, make sure the dining room has tables for two or the ship provides room service. Your travel agent can fill you in on these matters. You may also want to ask whether other honeymooners your age will be on the ship. Some ships—among them those of Princess, Royal Caribbean, Carnival, Celebrity, and Holland America—offer special honeymoon packages and sometimes honeymoon suites. Most lines provide special perks such as champagne and chocolates if you let them know in advance that you'll be celebrating your honeymoon on the ship.

**CAN I GET MARRIED ON BOARD?** Yes. You can get married at sea in the chapel on any of the Princess ships, with the nuptials conducted by the ship's captain. You can also get married at sea on the *Carnival Miracle*, which has a nice wedding chapel. Other big ships permit you to get married on board, but only if you're willing to bring your own clergyman along with you at full price. Of course, you can also get married while the ship is in port, but you will have to provide your own officiate (sea captains are able to legally marry couples only in international waters). Ships without wedding chapels will usually agree to clear a public room for your nuptials and may even provide flowers and light refreshments.

**WILL I GET SEASICK?** On Inside Passage itineraries, most of your time will be spent in protected waters with islands between you and the open sea, making for generally smooth sailing. At certain points, however, such as around Sitka and at the entrance to Queen Charlotte Strait, there is nothing between you and Japan but a lot of wind, water, and choppy seas. Ships with sailing itineraries on the Gulf of Alaska and those sailing from San Francisco, out of necessity, will spend more time in rough, open waters. Although ships that ply these routes tend to be very stable, you'll probably notice some rocking and rolling. Keep in mind that big ships tend to be more stable than smaller ships.

Unless you're particularly prone to seasickness, you probably don't need to worry much. But if you are, there are medications that can help, including Dramamine, Bonine, and Marezine, which are available over the counter and also stocked by most ships—the purser's office may even give them out for free. Another option is the Transderm patch, available by prescription only, which is applied behind your ear and has time-released medication. The patch can be worn for up to 3 days, but you should be aware that it comes with a slew of warnings about side effects. Some people have also had success in curbing seasickness by using ginger capsules, which are available at health food stores, or acupressure wristbands, which are available at most pharmacies. Our best advice is to ask for recommendations from your doctor before your cruise. If you do get sick onboard, the ship's doctor may have additional recommendations.

**IS THERE SMOKING ON SHIPS?** The short answer is yes. Recently, however, cruise lines have been reevaluating their smoking policies. Some, including Celebrity, Princess, Oceania, Silversea, and Regent Seven Seas, now ban smoking in cabins and on cabin balconies. Carnival, Royal Caribbean, Holland America, Norwegian, and Disney Cruise Line do not allow smoking in cabins, but do allow it on cabin balconies.

Smoking is generally not allowed in shipboard theaters, show lounges, or dining rooms and may be restricted to certain bars (many ships now have cigar lounges) or even certain sides of the ship (open decks on starboard side only on Royal Caribbean vessels, for instance). Smoking is generally allowed in ship casinos. Celebrity, for one, prohibits smoking even on cruisetours. Small ships typically allow smoking only in certain outdoor areas. If you are a smoker, check with your line in advance—several lines were considering stricter policies at press time. If you are not a smoker, you will no doubt be relieved by the new policies being adopted.

# BOOKING YOUR CRUISE

O kay, you've thought about what type of cruise vacation experience you have in mind. You've decided when and for how long you'd like to travel. Read through our ship reviews in chapters 5 and 6, narrow down your focus to the lines that appeal to you, and then you'll be ready to get down to brass tacks and make your booking.

**3**

## BOOKING A CRUISE: THE SHORT EXPLANATION

Cruise lines have detailed websites and brochures, or sometimes many different brochures—including e-brochures—full of beautiful glossy photos of beautiful glossy people enjoying fabulous vacations. They're colorful! They're gorgeous! They're enticing! They're confusing!

You'll see low starting rates on the charts, but look further and you'll realize those are for tiny inside cubicles; most of the cabins sell for much more. Sometimes the brochures have published rates that are nothing more than the pie-in-the-sky wish of cruise lines for the rate at which they'd like to sell the cruise (most customers will pay less). We strongly suggest you look at the early-bird savings column and book your cruise early (by mid-Feb at the latest for an average savings of 25–30 percent, and sometimes as much as 50 percent). You can pretty much count on last-minute offers of cheaper fares, too. Widespread discount pricing was a factor in 2013. In early July of last year, you could snag a last-minute, weeklong Alaska cruise for under $400, and in some cases under $300. But then again it was a tough year for cruise sellers in general, especially after huge media coverage of a fire that knocked out generators on the Carnival *Triumph* in the Caribbean (well, who can resist a story about cruise passengers stranded at sea for days without basic services including toilets?).

Whether or not bargain-basement discounting will continue in Alaska in 2014 remains to be seen. At press time, everyone was predicting that Alaska would be popular—especially since an improving U.S. economy translates to more people with money to spend on vacations. How will that reflect in prices? Our take: You may be able to save by taking your chances, but if you don't reserve space early, you may be left out in the cold (cold in Alaska, get it?). Keep in mind that the most expensive and cheapest cabins tend to sell out first. As they say in the cruise business, ships sell out from the top and bottom first. For the 2014 season, we were seeing some exceptionally low early-bird prices at press time. For example, Princess launched its 2014 brochure with a price tag of $899 for 1 weeklong early-season cruise, but promptly put the cruise on sale for $598.

So how do you book your cruise? Traditionally (meaning over the past 30 years or so), people have booked their cruises through **travel agents.** But you may be wondering: Hasn't the traditional travel agent gone the way of typewriters and eight-track tapes and been replaced by the **Internet?** Not exactly. Travel agents are alive and kicking, though the Internet has indeed staked its claim alongside them and knocked some out of business. In an effort to keep pace, nearly every traditional travel agency (and many individual agents too) have their own websites.

### Past-Passenger Deals

Many of the most intense deals are marketed first to past passengers. So if you've cruised at all before—Caribbean, Europe, Bermuda—check with the cruise line to see if you qualify for a past-passenger deal.

So what's the best way to book a cruise these days, online or with an agent? Good question. The answer depends. If you're computer-savvy, have a good handle on all the elements that go into a cruise, and have narrowed down the choices to a few cruise lines that appeal to you, websites are a great way to trawl the seas at your own pace and check out deals, which can be dramatic. On the other hand, you won't get the same personalized service searching for and booking a cruise online. If you need help getting a refund, arranging special meals or other matters, or deciding which cabin to choose, you're on your own. In addition, agents usually know about cruise and airfare discounts that the lines won't necessarily publicize on their websites.

However you arrange to buy your cruise, what you basically have in hand at the end is a contract for transportation, lodging, dining, entertainment, housekeeping, and assorted other miscellaneous services that will be provided to you over the course of your vacation. That's a lot of services involving a lot of people. It's complex, and like any complex thing, it pays (and saves) to study up. That's why it's important that you read the rest of this chapter.

# BOOKING THROUGH A TRAVEL AGENT

The majority of cruise passengers still book through agents. The cruise lines are happy with this system and have only small reservations staffs themselves (unlike airlines). In some cases, if you try to call a cruise line directly to book your own passage, the line will advise you to contact an agent in your area. The cruise line may even offer a choice of names from its list of preferred agencies, and you'll often find links to preferred agencies on cruise-line websites.

A good travel agent can save you both time and money. If you're reluctant to use an agent, consider this: Would you represent yourself in court? Perform surgery on your own abdomen? Tackle complicated IRS forms without seeking help? You may be the rare type that doesn't need a travel agent, but most of us are better off working with one.

Good agents can give you expert advice, save you time, and (best of all) will usually work for you for free or a nominal fee—the bulk of their fees are paid by the cruise lines. (Many agents charge a consultation fee—say, $25 or $50—which is refunded if you eventually give them the booking.) In addition to advising you about the different ships, an agent can help you make decisions about the type of cabin you need, your dining-room seating choices, any special airfare offerings from the cruise lines, pre- and post-cruise land offerings, and travel insurance—all of which can have a big impact on your cruise experience. We have seen complaints by people who booked a really cheap inside cabin and were angry that it was "a noisy cabin." Had they asked an experienced cruise agent, they might have been advised that the cabin was cheap because it was practically in the engine room—and that paying only a few bucks more would have resulted in a nice, quiet cabin.

It's important to realize that not all agents represent all cruise lines. To be experts on what they sell, and to maximize the commissions the lines pay them (they're often paid more based on volume of sales), some agents may limit their offerings to, say, one luxury line, one midprice line, one mass-market line, and so on. If you have your sights set on a particular line or have narrowed down your preferences to a couple of lines, you should find an agent who handles those choices. As we mentioned above, the lines themselves can often recommend the name of an agent near you. It's also a good idea to ask the agent you are working with if he or she has actually been to Alaska. *Note:* Be wary of an agent promising to give you a cash rebate. It's against the rules of most cruise lines, and the lines have been clamping down on violators—most legit agents follow the rules. The cruise lines themselves post Internet specials on their websites, and the same deals are usually also available through travel agents. The lines don't want to upset their travel-agent partners and generally try not to compete against them.

Travel agents are frequently in contact with the cruise lines and are continually alerted by the lines about the latest and best deals and special offers. The cruise lines tend to communicate such deals and offers to their top agents first before they offer them to the general public—in fact, some of these deals will never appear in your local newspaper, on bargain travel websites, or even on the websites of the cruise lines themselves.

Experienced agents know how to play the cruise lines' game and get you the best deals. For example, the lines run promotions that allow you to book a category of cabin rather than a specific cabin, and guarantees that you'll be placed in that category or better. An informed agent will know about these offers but may also be able to direct you to a category on a specific ship in which your chances of an upgrade are better. The cruise lines sometimes even upgrade passengers as a favor to their top-producing agents or agencies.

To keep their clients alert to specials, agencies may offer newsletters or communicate through other means, such as e-mail or postcards, or post specials on their websites. Depending on the agency you choose, you may run across other incentives for booking through an agent. Some agencies buy big blocks of space on a ship in advance and offer it to their clients at a group price available only through that agency. These are called group rates, although "group" in this instance means savings, not that you have to hang out with the other people booking through the agency. In addition, some agencies are willing to negotiate, especially if you've found a better deal somewhere else. It never hurts to ask. Finally, some agencies are willing to give back to the client a portion of their commissions from the cruise line to close a sale—in the form of a perk such as a free bottle of champagne, onboard spending credit (that you can use

# WATCH OUT FOR scams

It can be difficult to know whether the travel agency you're dealing with to book your Alaska cruise is or isn't reliable, legitimate, or, for that matter, stable. The travel business tends to attract more than its share of scam operators trying to lure consumers with incredible come-ons. If you get a solicitation by phone, fax, mail, or e-mail that just doesn't sound right, or if you are uneasy about an agent you are dealing with, call your state consumer-protection agency or the local office of the Better Business Bureau. Or you can check with the cruise line to see whether they have heard of the agency in question. Be wary of working with any company, be it on the phone or Internet, that won't give you its street address.

- **Get a referral.** A recommendation from a trusted friend or colleague is one of the best ways to hook up with a reputable agent.
- **Use the cruise lines' agent lists.** Many cruise-line websites include agency locator lists, naming agencies around the country with which they do business. These are by no means comprehensive lists of all good or bad agencies, but an agent's presence on these lists is usually a good sign of experience.
- **Beware of snap recommendations.** If an agent suggests a cruise line without first asking you a single question about your tastes, beware. Because agents work on commissions from the lines, some may try to shanghai you into cruising with a company that pays them the highest rates, even though that line may not be right for you.

- **Always use a credit card to pay for your cruise.** A credit card gives you more protection in the event the agency or cruise line fails. (Trust us! It happens occasionally.) When your credit card statement arrives, make sure the payment was made to the cruise line, not the travel agency. If you find that payment was actually made to the agency, it's a big red flag that something's wrong. If you insist on paying by check, you'll be making it out to the agency, so it may be wise to ask if the agency has default protection. Many do.
- **Always follow the cruise line's payment schedule.** Never agree to a different schedule the travel agency comes up with. The lines' terms are always clearly printed in their brochures and usually require an initial deposit, with the balance due no later than 45 to 75 days before departure, depending on the cruise line. If you're booking 2 months or less before departure, the full payment is often required at the time of booking (but cruise lines have been making changes in this regard, so read the fine print carefully).
- **Keep on top of your booking.** If you ever fail to receive a document or ticket on the date it's been promised, inquire about it immediately. If you're told that your cruise reservation was canceled because of overbooking and that you must pay extra for a confirmed and rescheduled sailing, demand a full refund and/or contact your credit card company to stop payment.

toward your bar bill or other shipboard treats), or a limo ride to the ship. These hardly reasons to book in and of themselves but make nice little perks.

## Finding a Great Agent

As we said, if you don't know a good travel agent, ask your friends for recommendations, preferably those who have cruised before. For the most personal service, look for an agent in your area, and for the most knowledgeable service, look for an agent who has cruising experience. It's perfectly okay to ask an agent questions about his or her personal knowledge of the product, such as whether he or she has ever cruised in Alaska or with one of the lines you're considering. But the easiest way to be sure that the agent is experienced in booking cruises is to work with an agent at a **cruise-only agency** (that's all they book) or to find an agent who is a **cruise specialist** within a full-service agency. If you are calling a full-service travel agency, ask for the **cruise desk.** A good and easy rule of thumb to maximize your chances of finding an agent who has cruise experience and won't rip you off is to book with an agency that's a member of the **Cruise Lines International Association** (CLIA; ℂ **754/224-2200;** www.cruising.org), the main industry association. Members are cruise specialists; agents accredited as Certified Cruise Counselors by CLIA have particularly extensive training. Membership in the **American Society of Travel Agents** (ASTA; ℂ **800/275-2782;** www. asta.org) ensures that the agency is monitored for ethical practices, although it does not designate cruise experience. Tap into the websites of these organizations to find reliable agents in your area.

## Booking with Discounters

Keep in mind that discounters, who specialize in great-sounding, last-minute offers (usually without airfare) and whose ads you can find in the Sunday papers and all over the Internet, don't necessarily offer service that matches their prices. Their staffs are more likely to be order-takers than advice-givers. Go to these companies to compare prices only when you know exactly what you want.

## Booking a Small-Ship Cruise

The small-ship companies in Alaska—Un-Cruise Adventures, Alaskan Dream Cruises, American Cruise Lines, and Lindblad Expeditions—all provide niche-oriented cruise experiences, attracting passengers who have a very good idea of the kind of experience they want (usually educational or adventurous, and always casual and small-scale). In many cases, a large percentage of passengers on any given cruise will have sailed with the line before. Because of all this, and because the passenger capacity of these ships is so low (22–100 passengers), in general you don't find the kinds of deep discounts often offered by the large ships. For the most part, these lines rely on agents to handle their bookings, taking very few reservations directly. All the lines have a list of agents with whom they do considerable business; just call or e-mail the cruise line and ask for an agent near you.

# CRUISING ON THE INTERNET

For those who know exactly what they want (we don't recommend online shopping for first-time cruisers) and don't need the personalized care a smaller travel agency re are deals to be had on the Internet. Those sites that sell cruises include travel agencies (**Expedia.com** and **Orbitz.com**) and big agencies that ruises (**icruise.com, Cruise.com, Cruise411.com,** and **7blueseas.com**). numbers you can call or chat forums where you can ask questions (it's to get the name of anyone you deal with so you can follow up, if necessary). Also selling cruises on the Web are travel discounters (**Bestfares.com, Onetravel.com,** and **Lowestfare.com**), search engines (**Kayak.com**), and auction sites (**Allcruiseauction.com** and **Priceline.com**).

The Internet also has some good sites that specialize in providing cruise information rather than selling cruises. A popular cruise fan site is **Cruisecritic.com** (now owned by TripAdvisor). This website features reviews by professional writers, ratings and reviews by cruise passengers, plus useful tips, frequent chat opportunities, and message boards. See, too, *USA Today*'s "Experience Cruise," with a lot of content written by Fran (www.usatoday.com/experience/cruise). For updated cruise news, no one does it better than Gene, at his **USA Today Cruise Log Blog** (www.cruises.usatoday.com), where you'll also find a very active discussion forum. **AlaskaCruisingReport.com** tracks what's happening specifically in Alaska. In addition, nearly all the cruise lines have their own sites, which are chock-full of information—some even give virtual tours of specific ships. You'll find the websites for the various cruise companies in our cruise-line reviews in chapters 5 and 6.

# CRUISE COSTS

In chapters 5 and 6, we've included the brochure rates for every ship reviewed, but as noted above, these prices may actually be higher than any passenger will pay. Prices constantly fluctuate based on special deals the cruise lines may be running. Rates are heavily influenced by the volume of travelers interested in cruising Alaska. If the sales season (Sept–Jan are the key months) fails to achieve certain predetermined passenger volume goals, the lines are very quick to start slashing rates to goose the market. The prices we've noted are for the following three basic types of accommodations: inside cabins (without windows), outside cabins (with windows), and suites. Remember that cruise ships generally have several different categories of cabins within each of these three basic divisions, all priced differently. That's why we give a range. See "Choosing Your Cabin," below, for details on cabin types.

The price you pay for your cabin represents the bulk of your cruise vacation cost, but there are other costs to consider. Whether you're working with an agent or booking online, be sure that you really understand what's included in the fare you're being quoted. Are you getting a price that includes the cruise fare, port charges, taxes, fees, and insurance, or are you getting a cruise-only fare? Are airfare and airport transfers included, or do you have to book them separately (either as an add-on to the cruise fare or on your own)? One agent might break down the charges in a price quote, while another might bundle them all together. Make sure you're comparing apples with apples when making price comparisons. Read the fine print!

It's important when figuring out what your cruise will cost to remember what extras are **not included** in your cruise fare. The items discussed in the section below are not included in most cruise prices and will add to the cost of your trip.

## Shore Excursions

The priciest additions to your cruise fare, particularly in Alaska, will likely be shore excursions. Rates on cruise-line-planned tours range from about $39 to $99 for a sightseeing tour by bus (the higher-priced tours usually include visits to museums or other local attractions) to $500 and up (sometimes as high as $600) for a lengthy helicopter or seaplane flightseeing excursion. Although these sightseeing tours are designed to help cruise passengers make the most of their time at the ports the ship visits, they can add a hefty sum to your vacation costs, so be sure to factor these expenses into your budget. Of course, whether you take any excursions at all is a personal choice, but we suggest setting aside at least $600 per person for trips in port, which might just about cover a short flightseeing trip, a kayak or jeep safari, and a bus tour. You may be able to save by booking your tours through a private company such as **Viator** (www.viator. com) or **ShoreTrips** (www.shoretrips.com), which may offer the same excursions as the cruise lines at reduced prices.

## Tips

Be sure to add tips for the ship's crew to your budget calculations. Crewmembers are usually paid low base wages with the expectation that they'll make up the difference in gratuities. Exceptions in Alaska this year, as far as the big ships are concerned, are Regent Seven Seas and Silversea Cruises, which include tips in the cruise fare (but you can still leave a few bucks for your favorite crew members if you want to).

Because some people find the whole tipping process confusing, the big ship lines automatically add tips to guests' shipboard accounts. Carnival, Holland America, Royal Caribbean, Norwegian Cruise Line, and Princess, for instance, all add a standard tip of $11 to $12.50 per passenger per day. You are free to adjust the amount up or down as you see fit, based on the service you received. The tips cover the room steward, waiter, and busperson. In practice, we find many people tend to give a little more—maybe leaving some extra cash in the cabin for the cabin steward. Additional tips to other personnel, such as the headwaiter or maitre d', are at your discretion. If you have a room with a butler, slip him or her $5 a day. Most lines automatically add 15 percent to bar bills, so you don't have to tip your bartender. There may be an automatic tip of 15 percent for spa services as well. If not, you can add a tip to the bill.

On small ships, tips are typically pooled among the crew: You hand over a lump sum in cash, and they divvy it up. Because tipping etiquette on small ships varies, we include information on tipping specifics for each small-ship line on p. 129 in chapter 6, and general guidelines in "Tips on Tipping," in chapter 4.

## Booze & Soda

Most ships charge extra for alcoholic beverages (including wine at dinner) and soda. Nonbubbly soft drinks, such as lemonade and iced tea, and hot drinks such as coffee and tea are included in your cruise fare. On Disney ships, soda from fountains and at meals is free, but if you want a can, you pay extra. A can of soda will cost about $2.50, beer $3.50 and up, a glass of wine or mixed drinks $6 and up. Bottled water is extra too, from $2 per bottle. A bottle of wine with dinner will run anywhere from $15 to upwards of $300. If you're a big soda drinker, you'll want to consider buying a soda package that offers unlimited refills. Prices vary by cruise line but start at around $42

**Fancy Dining Choices for a Fee**

As if multicourse dining-room meals and endless buffets were not enough, cruise lines have added premium restaurant venues where, in most cases, a fee is charged to cover especially attentive service and a menu featuring extra-special cuisine. These alternative restaurants tend to be small venues done up in fancy furnishings—just the kind of place you'd want for a date night or special celebration. In most cases, the spaces are reserved for adults only.

Prices vary from line to line and restaurant to restaurant. For example, you can dine for $20 per person at Disney Cruise Line's impressive Northern Italian Palo. Carnival's steakhouses serve extravagant prime aged cuts for $35. Norwegian Cruise Line charges $75 and Royal Caribbean $95 for a Chef's Table experience where multiple courses are presented by the ship's executive chef and accompanied by specially paired wines.

for adults ($28 for kids) for a weeklong cruise. You may be required to book the package in advance of your cruise, so check the information sent from the cruise line. Some cruise lines also offer bottled water packages or wine packages (you buy, say, five bottles for a discounted price). Celebrity Cruises, Carnival, Norwegian Cruise Line, and Royal Caribbean also offer all-you-can-drink alcohol and wine packages. You'll have to do the math to figure out if you can drink enough to make it worth it.

## Port Charges, Local Taxes & Fees

Every ship has to pay docking fees at each port. It also has to pay some local taxes per passenger in some places. Port charges, taxes, and other fees are sometimes included in your cruise fare, but not always, and these charges can add on average between $200 and $250 to the price of a 7-day Alaska cruise. A $34.50 per passenger head and berth tax imposed by the State of Alaska and $7 and $8 taxes in Juneau and Ketchikan, respectively, are usually melded into this figure and not paid by passengers separately. Make sure you know whether these fees are included in the cruise fare when comparing rates.

## Fuel Surcharges

Cruise lines have instituted fuel surcharges in the past, and you'll see a note that they have a right to impose such fees in their customer contracts. Last time we saw them was in 2008, when fees ranged from $8 to $11 per passenger per day, less for a third or fourth person in the cabin. If reinstated, these surcharges are a significant addition to the cruise fare.

# MONEY-SAVING STRATEGIES
## Early-Bird & Last-Minute Discounts

As we said earlier, in our opinion the best way to save on an Alaska cruise is to **book in advance.** In a typical year, lines offer early-bird rates, usually 25 percent to 50 percent off the brochure rate, to those who book their Alaska cruise by mid-February of the year of the cruise. If the cabins do not fill up by the cutoff date, the early-bird rate may be extended, but it may also be lowered—say, a 15 percent or 20 percent savings. Offers made to past cruisers may present even bigger discounts. For the 2014 season, we were seeing early-bird fares 10 months in advance starting at $619 on Carnival, $544 on Royal Caribbean, $598 on Princess, $499 on Norwegian, and $899 on Holland America. Early-bird rates offer consumers the best selection of cabins. If the cabins are still not full as the cruise season begins, cruise lines typically start marketing special deals, usually through their top-producing travel agents and sometimes, but rarely, with crazy savings of up to 75 percent. Last year's limited last-minute deals for an Alaska cruise included: $279 per person on Norwegian (practically cheaper than staying home!), $399 on Royal Caribbean, and $499 on Princess. Still, in terms of cabin selection and value, we say planning your Alaska cruise vacation in advance and taking advantage of early-booking discounts is the best way to go.

## Shoulder-Season Discounts

You can also save by booking a cruise in the shoulder months of **May** or **September,** when cruise pricing is usually lower than during the high-season summer months (though in 2013 there were deals even in July and Aug). Typically, Alaska cruises are divided into budget, low, economy, value, standard, and peak seasons, but since these overlap quite a bit from cruise line to cruise line, we can lump them into three basic periods:

1. **Budget/Low/Economy Season:** May and September
2. **Value/Standard Season:** Early June and late August
3. **Peak Season:** Late June, July, and early to mid-August

## Third- & Fourth-Passenger Discounts

Most ships offer highly discounted rates for third and fourth passengers sharing a cabin with two full-fare passengers, even if those two have booked at a discounted rate. You can add the four rates together and then divide by four to get your per-person rate. This is a good option for families (or very good friends) on a budget, but remember that it will be a tight fit, since most cabins aren't all that big to begin with.

## Group Discounts

One of the best ways to get a cruise deal is to book as a group, so you may want to gather family together for a reunion or convince your friends or colleagues they need a vacation, too. A "group," as defined by the cruise lines, is generally **at least 16 people** in at least eight cabins. Not only do the savings include a discounted rate, but at least the cruise portion of the 16th ticket will be free. On some upscale ships, you can negotiate a free ticket for groups of 10 or more. The gang can split the proceeds from the free berth or hold a drawing for the ticket, maybe at a cocktail party on the first night. If your group is large enough, you may even be able to get that cocktail party for free, and perhaps some other onboard perks as well.

Some travel agencies buy big blocks of space on a ship in advance and offer it to their clients at a group price available only through that agency. These are called group rates, although, as we mention earlier in the chapter, "group" in this case means savings, not that you have to hang out with (or even know) the other people booking through the agency.

## Senior Citizen & Military Discounts

Senior citizens might be able to get extra savings on their cruise. Some lines will take 5 percent off the top for those 55 and older on select sailings, and the senior rate applies even if the second person in the cabin is younger. Membership in groups such as AARP is not required, but such membership may bring additional savings. Discounts may also be available for active or retired military personnel, so let your travel agent know if you fit into this category.

## Other Deals

If you like your Alaska cruise so much that you decide to take a vacation with the cruise line again, consider booking your next cruise on the spot. Cruise lines cannily recognize the value in having a captive audience to whom to pitch future vacation plans. Before you sign on the dotted line, though, make sure the on-the-spot discount can be combined with other offers you might uncover later. Keep in mind that if you do choose to book on board, you can still do the reconfirmation and ticketing through your travel agent by giving the cruise line his or her name.

In addition, lines tend to offer cut rates when they are introducing a new ship or moving into a new market. So it pays to keep track of what's happening in the cruise industry—or have your agent do so—when looking for a deal.

Finally, check each cruise line's website for the latest savings plans.

# AIRFARES & PRE-/POST-CRUISE HOTEL DEALS

Also see the information on cruisetours in chapter 9.

## Air Add-Ons

Unless you live within driving distance of your port of embarkation, you'll probably be flying to Vancouver, Anchorage, Seattle, or one of the other ports to join your ship. Your cruise package is not likely to include air (unless you are on Oceania or Regent Seven Seas, which do include air, or snag a special air-inclusive promotion), so you will have to make air arrangements. You are free to book your air separately, but keep in mind the lowest discount fares may not apply—especially if your cruise departs on the peak travel days of Friday or Saturday. A better option may be to take advantage of the cruise lines' air add-ons. Why? First of all, as frequent customers of the airlines, cruise lines tend to get decent (if not the best) discounts on airfare, which they pass on to their customers. They also tend to book up the prime flights. Booking air with the cruise line also allows the line to keep track of you. If your plane is late, for instance, they may actually hold the ship, though not always. When you book air travel with your cruise line, most lines will include **transfers** from the airport to the ship, saving you the hassle of getting a cab. (If you do book your air travel on your own, you may still be able to get the transfers separately—ask your agent about this.) *Tip:* Be aware that once the air ticket is issued by the cruise line, you usually aren't allowed to make changes.

The only time it really pays to book your own air transportation is if you are using frequent-flier miles and can get your air travel for free, or if you are particular about which carrier you fly or which route you take. You are more or less at the mercy of the cruise line in terms of carrier and route if you take its air deals. Princess, for one, has a program that does let you choose the airline you want to fly, but most other lines may charge a "deviation" fee if you want to fly a specific airline or route. The deadline for these requests is usually 60 days before the sailing date or, if you book later, the day your cruise reservations are made. *Tip:* If you're determined to book your own air and your travel schedule is flexible, it's often easier to get the carrier and the flight time you prefer if you choose a cruise that leaves on a Wednesday or Thursday—or other times considered nonpeak by the airlines.

On the plus side, if airfare is part of the cruise package but you choose to book your air transportation, you will be refunded the air portion of the fare.

## Pre- & Post-Cruise Hotel Deals

Even if you don't take a cruisetour (a land trip combined with your cruise), you may want to consider spending a day or two in your port of embarkation or debarkation either before or after your cruise. (See details on exploring the port cities in chapters 7 and 8.) An advantage to coming in a day or two early is that you don't have to worry if your flight is running late. (Gene has a personal policy of always flying into his embarkation port at least a day early, to be safe; he's never missed a ship!) Plus, Vancouver, Anchorage, and Seattle—the cities into which most passengers fly—happen to be great cities to explore.

Just as with airfare, you need to decide whether you want to buy your hotel stay from the cruise line or make arrangements on your own. The cruise lines negotiate **special deals with hotels** at port cities, so you will often get a bargain by booking through the cruise line.

When evaluating a cruise line's hotel package, make sure you review it carefully to see what's included. See whether the line provides a **transfer** from the airport to the hotel and from the hotel to the cruise ship (or vice versa); make sure that the line offers a hotel that you will be happy with in terms of **type of property and location;** and inquire if any **escorted tours, car rental deals, or meals** are included. You'll also want to compare the price against booking on your own. (See chapters 7 and 8 for information on hotels in the various ports.) *Note:* Keep in mind that cruise lines usually list rates for hotels on a per-person basis, whereas hotels post their rates on a per-room basis.

# CHOOSING YOUR CABIN

Once you've looked at the ship descriptions in chapters 5 and 6, talked over the options with your travel agent, and selected an itinerary and ship, you'll have to choose a cabin. The cruise lines have improved things a bit since Charles Dickens declared that his stateroom reminded him of a coffin, but cramped, windowless spaces can still be found. On the other hand, so can penthouse-size suites with expansive verandas, Jacuzzis, and butler service. Most cabins on cruise ships today have twin beds that are convertible to queen-size (you can request which configuration you want), plus a private bathroom with a shower. Some cabins have bunk beds, which are obviously not convertible. Most ships also have cabins designed for three or four people, which will include two twin beds plus one or two bunks that fold down from the wall in some way.

In some cases, it is possible to add a fifth bed to the room. Some lines have special cabins designed for families, with "regular" twin beds that can be pushed together to create a double bed, plus fold-down bunks. Families may also be able to book connecting cabins (although they'll have to pay for two cabins to do so). Cabins for travelers with disabilities are ideally located near elevators and close to the ship's entrances.

### Bed Lingo

On cruise ships, "lower beds" refer to standard twin beds, while "bunks" (or, less commonly, "upper beds") refer to beds that passengers pull out from the wall to sleep in.

Most cabins, but not all, have TVs (often flatscreen). Some have extra amenities, such as safes, minifridges, DVD players, bathrobes, and hair dryers. A bathtub is considered a luxury on ships and is usually found only in more expensive cabins.

## Cabin Types

What kind of cabin is right for you? Price will likely be a big factor here, but so should the vacation style you prefer. The typical ship has several types of cabins, which are illustrated by floor plans in the cruise line's brochure. The cabins are usually described by **price** (highest to lowest), **category** (suite, deluxe, superior, standard, economy, and other types), and **furniture configuration** ("sitting area with two lower beds"). The cabins will also be described as being **inside** or **outside.** Simply put, inside cabins do not have windows (or even portholes), and outside cabins do. However, views from some outside cabins may be obstructed—usually by a lifeboat—or look out onto a public area; an experienced travel agent should be able to advise you on which cabin to choose if full views and privacy are important.

On the big ships, deluxe outside cabins may also come with **verandas** (also known as **balconies**), giving you a private outdoor space to enjoy the sea breezes—a great thing to have in Alaska. You can throw on your bathrobe and view the glaciers and wildlife. But remember that the verandas vary in size, so if you're looking to do more than stand on your balcony, make sure the space is big enough to accommodate deck chairs, a table, or whatever else you require. Also keep in mind that these verandas are not completely isolated—your neighbors may be able to see you and vice versa. With few exceptions, veranda cabins will not have obstructed views.

**Noise** can be a factor that may influence your cabin choice. If you take a cabin on a lower deck, you may hear engine noises; in the front of the ship, anchor noises; and in the back of the ship, thruster noises. A cabin near an elevator may bring door opening and closing sounds (though proximity makes it easier to get around the ship), and a cabin above or below the disco may pulse until all hours of the night. Cabins near children's facilities may not be the quietest places, at least during the day. The loudest areas of a ship vary depending on how well insulated the different areas are, so if noise will be a problem for you, ask what the quietest part of the ship is when you are booking your cabin. We would say that, generally, midship on a higher deck will be the quietest part of the ship (unless, of course, it's near a disco).

Cabins on upper decks can be affected by the motion of the sea. If you're abnormally susceptible to **seasickness,** keep this in mind. Ditto for cabins in the bow. Cabins in the stern can be affected by the motion of the sea and tend to be subject to engine vibration. Cabins midship are the least affected by the motion of the sea, especially if they're on a lower deck.

If you plan to spend a lot of quiet time in your cabin, you should probably consider booking the biggest room you can afford, and you should also consider taking a cabin with a picture window or, better still, a private veranda. If, conversely, you plan to be off on shore excursions or on deck checking out the glaciers and wildlife, and using your cabin only to change clothes and collapse in at the end of the day, you might be happy with a smaller (and cheaper) cabin. Usually, cabins on the higher decks are more expensive and much nicer, with plusher amenities and superior decor, even if they are the same size as cabins on lower decks. **Luxury suites** are usually on upper decks. The top suites on some ships are actually apartment size, and you'll get lots of space to stretch out. A quirky thing about cabin pricing is that the most stable cabins during rough seas are those in the middle and lower parts of the ship.

> ### Cabin Size by Square Foot
>
> The size of a cabin is described in terms of square feet. This number may not mean a lot unless you want to mark it out on your floor at home. But to give you an idea: 120 square feet and under is low end and cramped, 180 square feet is midrange (and the minimum for people with claustrophobia), and 250 square feet and up is suite size.

On the small ships, cabins can be truly tiny and spartan, though some give the big-ship cabins a run for their money. Generally, the difference lies in the orientation of the cruise line: Those promising a real adventure experience tend to feature somewhat utilitarian cabins.

Aboard both large and small ships, keep in mind that the most expensive and least expensive cabins tend to sell out fast. Inside cabins (without windows), for example, can be real money-savers. Also keep in mind that, just as with real estate, it's sometimes better to take a smaller cabin in a nicer ship than a bigger cabin in a less pleasant ship.

# CHOOSING YOUR DINING OPTIONS

**Smaller ships** usually serve dinner at a certain time, with unassigned seating, allowing you to sit at any table you want. So if you plan to sail on one of the smaller lines, you don't have to read this section at all. Because most dining rooms on **larger ships** are not large enough to accommodate all passengers at once, large ships typically offer the option of traditional seating, which means two different seating times, especially for dinner. In this case, your table will be preassigned and remain the same for the duration of the cruise. You will generally make your choice of seating time and table size when you book your cruise. You will also have the option of open seating, as noted in the "Open Seating" portion of this section.

## Mealtimes

If you choose traditional seating, there are set dinner times, with early or main seating typically at 6pm and late seating at 8:30pm. There are advantages and disadvantages to both times, and it basically comes down to personal choice. **Early seating** is usually less crowded and the preferred time for families and seniors. The dining experience can be a bit more rushed (the staff needs to make way for the next wave of guests), but the food may be fresher. You can see a show right after dinner and have first dibs on other nighttime venues as well. And you just may be hungry again in time for the midnight buffet.

**Late seating,** on the other hand, allows you time for a good long nap or late spa appointment before dining. Dinner is not rushed at all. You are free to linger—unless, that is, you choose to go catch a show, which usually starts at 10:15 or 10:30pm.

You can also choose to eat **breakfast** and **lunch** in the dining room as opposed to more casual venues on the ship. The times will be set and the seating is on a de facto "open seating" basis for both of these meals (typically you are escorted to an open table by dining room staff).

Most large ships today also have **alternative dining options.** Most have a casual, buffet-style restaurant, usually located on the lido deck, with indoor and outdoor pool-side seating and an extensive spread of both hot and cold food items at breakfast, lunch, and dinner (as a casual alternative to the dining room). Some ships also have **reservations-only restaurants,** seating fewer than 100, where—except on some luxury ships—a small fee is charged, mainly to cover gratuities.

## Table Size

Do you mind sitting with strangers? Are you looking to make new friends? Your dinner companions can make or break your cruise experience. Most ships have tables configured for two to eight people. For singles or couples who want to socialize, a table of eight seats generally provides enough variety that you don't get bored and also allows you to steer clear of any individual you don't particularly care for (tables are assigned, not seats). Couples may choose to sit on their own, but singles may find it hard to secure a table for one. A family of four may want a table for four, or request to sit with another family at a table for eight.

You need to state your table-size preference in advance, unless you are on a ship with an open-seating policy. If you change your mind once you're on board, don't worry; you'll probably have no trouble moving around. Just tell the dining-room maitre d', and he or she will review the seating charts for an opening.

## Open Seating

Put off by all this formality? Want guaranteed casual all the way? Norwegian Cruise Line's ships, Regent's *Seven Seas Navigator,* Oceania's *Regatta*, and Silversea's *Silver Shadow* serve all meals with open seating—dine when you want (within the restaurants' open hours, of course) and with whom you want. The catch is, particularly with Norwegian, you are best off deciding in the morning where you want to have dinner and reserving a table; otherwise, the restaurant of your choice may be full when you decide to eat. Princess, Carnival, Royal Caribbean, Holland America, and Celebrity all have a version of this system, allowing guests to choose traditional early or late seating or open restaurant-style seating (you make your choice before the cruise but may be able to change your mind once you're on board).

## Special Menu Requests

The cruise line should be informed at the time you make reservations about any special dietary requirements you have. Some lines provide kosher menus, and all have vegetarian, vegan, low-fat, low-salt, gluten-free, and sugar-free options.

# DEPOSITS & CANCELLATION POLICIES

You'll be asked by your travel agent to make a **deposit,** either a fixed amount or some percentage of your total cruise cost. You'll then receive a receipt in the mail from the cruise line. You'll typically be asked to pay the remaining fare usually no later than 60 to 90 days before your departure date.

Cruise lines have varying policies regarding **cancellations,** and it's important to look at the fine print in the line's brochure to make sure you understand the policy. Most lines allow you to cancel for a full refund on your deposit and payment anytime up to 75 days before the sailing, after which you have to pay a penalty.

# TRAVEL INSURANCE

Hey, stuff happens. Given today's unpredictable geopolitical situation, economic woes, and extreme weather conditions, you just never know what might occur. A cruise could be canceled, for example, because of mechanical breakdowns (such as nonfunctioning air-conditioning or an engine fire), the cruise line going out of business, or an act of war. For all these reasons—worries about travel, worries about cruise lines canceling, sudden illness or other emergencies, missed flights that cause you to miss the ship, or even if you just change your mind—you may want to think about purchasing **travel insurance.**

Now, if you're just worried about missing the ship, go a day early and spend your money on a hotel and a nice dinner instead. If you're worried about medical problems occurring during your trip, on the other hand, travel insurance may be more vital. Except for small coastal cruisers, most cruise ships have an infirmary staffed by a doctor and a nurse or two, but in the event of a dire illness, the ship's medical staff can only do so much. Therefore, you may want a policy that covers **emergency medical evacuation** (having a helicopter pick up a sick person on board a ship will cost a bundle without insurance) and, if your regular insurance doesn't cover it, the potential cost of major medical treatment while away from home (especially vital if you're covered primarily by Medicare, which won't cover you in international destinations—and most ships are flagged internationally, so they don't qualify for coverage). There are policies sold through the cruise lines and others sold independently through third-party insurers, and both have pros and cons.

A good travel agent can help you parse policies sold through the cruise lines and ones sold independently of the lines. No matter what you choose, it's absolutely crucial to read the fine print, because terms vary from policy to policy and even line to line.

Both kinds typically reimburse you in some way when your trip is affected by unexpected events (such as flights canceled due to bad weather, plane crashes, dockworkers' strikes, or the illness or death of a loved one, as late as the day before or day of departure) but not by "acts of God," such as hurricanes and earthquakes (the exception being if your home is made uninhabitable, putting you in no mood to continue with your cruise plans). Both also typically (but not always—check!) cover **cancellation of the cruise** for medical reasons (yours or a family member's, whether he or she was a part of your traveling party or not); **medical emergencies** during the cruise, including evacuation from the ship; lost or damaged luggage; and a cruise missed due to weather-related airline delays (though some only cover if the delay is more than 3 hr.). Neither kind of policy will reimburse you if your travel agent didn't send in your payment and ships usually have a fully equipped medical facility and staff (a doctor and a nurse or two) on board to handle any emergency. They work in a medical center that typically offers set office hours but is also open on an emergency basis 24 hours a day. A fee (sometimes a steep one) is charged. The staff is equipped to do some surgery, but in cases of major medical emergencies, passengers may be airlifted off the ship by helicopter to the nearest hospital.

goes bankrupt, so using a travel agent you're very familiar with or one who's recommended is the safest precaution you can take. (And, of course, *always use a credit card,* never a check. If a corrupt travel agent cashes it or a decent one just goes out of business, you could get screwed.)

Reputable insurers include **Allianz** (© 800/284-8300; www.accessamerica.com), **Travel Guard International** (© 800/826-4919; www.travelgaurd.com), and **Travel Insured International** (© 800/243-3174; www.travelinsured.com). A useful website, **Squaremouth** (© 800/240-0369; www.squaremouth.com), lets you easily compare various third-party insurance options. For evacuation coverage in the event of a major medical emergency, **MedJet Assist** (© 800/527-7478; www.medjetassist.com) has both short-term and annual policies. Be aware that travel insurance does not cover changes in your itinerary, which are at the discretion of the cruise line.

# [FastFACTS] ALASKA

**Area Code** Almost all of Alaska is in area code **907.** The tiny community of Hyder, about 90 miles northeast of Ketchikan, lies on the Alaska/British Columbia border. For practical and technical reasons, Hyder uses the same area code as nearby Stewart, BC: **250.**

**Banks & ATMs** There are banks and automated teller machines (ATMs) in all but the tiniest towns. They may charge a nominal fee.

**Business Hours** In the larger cities, major **grocery stores** are open 24 hours a day and carry a wide range of products (even fishing gear) in addition to food. At a minimum, stores are open Monday through Friday from 10am to 6pm and Saturday afternoons, but closed on Sunday. However, many are open for longer hours, especially in summer. **Banks** may close an hour earlier and, if open on Saturday, only in the morning. Under state law, **bars** don't have to close until 5am, but many communities have earlier closing times (around 2am).

**Cellphone Coverage** Most of the populated portion of the state has cellular coverage. The largest provider is an Alaskan company, Alaska Communications, which posts maps of its coverage area at **www.alaskacommunications.com**. AT&T and Verizon have coverage in Alaska— though we've found that usable coverage is often less than what the companies claim.

**Emergencies** Generally, you can call © **911** for medical, police, or fire emergencies. On remote highways, there sometimes are 911 coverage gaps, but dialing 0 will generally get an operator, who can connect you to emergency services. Citizens-band channels 9 and 11 are monitored for emergencies on most highways, as are channels 14 and 19 in some areas.

**Holidays**  Besides the normal national holidays, banks and state and local government offices close on two state holidays: Seward's Day (the last Mon in Mar) and Alaska Day (Oct 18, or the nearest Fri or Mon if it falls on a weekend).

**Liquor Laws**  The minimum drinking age in Alaska is 21. Most restaurants sell beer and wine, and a minority have full bars that serve hard liquor as well. Packaged alcohol, beer, and wine are sold only in licensed stores, but these are common and are open long hours every day. Some rural communities have laws prohibiting the importation and possession of alcohol (known as being "dry") or only the sale but not possession of alcohol (known as being "damp"). Before bringing alcohol into a Native village, ask about the law—bootlegging is a serious crime (and serious bad manners).

**Newspapers**  The state's dominant newspaper is the **Anchorage Daily News** (www.adn.com); it's available everywhere, but it's harder to find in Southeast Alaska. Seattle newspapers and **USA Today** are often available, and in Anchorage you can get virtually any newspaper.

**Taxes**  There is no state sales tax, but most local governments have a sales tax and a bed tax on accommodations.

**Telephone**  We have been assured that all major calling cards will work in Alaska, but this hasn't been the case in the past. To make sure, contact your long-distance company or buy a by-the-minute card.

**Time Zone**  Although the state naturally spans five time zones, in the 1980s Alaska's middle time zone was stretched so almost the entire state would lie all in one zone, known as Alaska Time. It's 1 hour earlier than the U.S. West Coast's Pacific Standard Time and 4 hours earlier than Eastern Standard Time. Crossing over the border from Alaska to Canada adds an hour and puts you at the same time as the West Coast. As with almost everywhere else in the United States, daylight saving time is in effect from 2am on the second Sunday in March (turn your clocks ahead 1 hr.) until 2am on the first Sunday in November (turn clocks back again).

**Water**  Unpurified river or lake water may not be safe to drink. Handheld filters available from sporting goods stores for around $75 are the most practical way of dealing with the problem. Iodine kits and boiling also work.

# THE CRUISE EXPERIENCE

N ow that you've made most of the hard decisions—choosing and booking your cruise—the rest of your vacation planning should be relatively easy. From this point on, the cruise lines take over much of the work, particularly if you've booked a package that includes air travel. Carefully read the pretrip information sent to you by your chosen cruise line, because most lines' pretrip packets include sections that address commonly asked questions.

Most of this information can also be found on each line's website. In this chapter, we'll add our own two cents' worth on these matters and provide some practical hints that'll help you be prepared for all you'll find in the 49th state, both aboard your ship and in the ports of call.

## PACKING FOR YOUR CRUISE

### Preparing for the Weather

The sometimes extreme and always unpredictable Alaska weather will be a big factor in the success of your vacation. During your summertime cruise, you may experience temperature variations from the 40s to the 80s or even low 90s (single digits to low-30s Celsius). The days will be long, with the sun all but refusing to set, especially in the more northern ports, and people will be energized by the extra daylight hours. You'll likely encounter some rain, but there could also be weeks of sunny skies with no rain at all. You're less likely to encounter snow, but it is a remote possibility, especially in the spring (in fact, last year cruisers encountered snow in early June).

Weather plays a factor in what you need to pack, with the must-haves on an Alaska cruise including a raincoat, an umbrella, and comfortable walking shoes that you don't mind getting wet or muddy. A swimsuit is also a must if your ship has a pool (sometimes covered, sometimes heated) or hot tubs.

Even in the summer, temperatures in Alaska may not go much higher than the 50s or 60s (low or high teens Celsius), although they also may go into the 70s or 80s (low to high 20s Celsius). Having **layers of clothing** that you can peel off if the weather is hot and add if the weather is cold is the most convenient approach.

# Essentials

What you choose to pack is obviously a personal choice, but here's a [list?] that everyone should bring along:

o A waterproof parka or jacket or lightweight raincoat (big enou[gh to wear?] underneath)
o Two sweaters or fleece pullovers, or substitute a warm vest or sw[eater]
o A warm hat and gloves
o Two to four pairs of pants or jeans
o Two pairs of walking shoes (preferably waterproof)
o Sunscreen (SPF 15 or higher)
o Bug spray (Alaska has 55 different kinds of mosquitoes, although the Inside Passage ports in the south are not as affected as the areas farther north)
o Sunglasses
o Binoculars (Some small ships stock them for free guest use, but on the bigger ships, it will cost you—if they even have pairs for rent.)
o A camera, preferably with a telephoto or zoom lens, and a drypack to protect the camera (you may also want to bring a crappy second camera that you don't mind getting wet)
o Extra flash cards and batteries for your camera
o Formal wear (with accessories) if your ship has formal nights (not all do)
o Semiformal wear if your ship has informal nights (not all do)
o Long underwear if you're on a shoulder-season cruise (especially if a shore excursion will get you on a glacier)

## Alaska's Climate, by Months & Regions

### ANCHORAGE: SOUTHCENTRAL ALASKA

|  | MAY | JUNE | JULY | AUG | SEPT |
|---|---|---|---|---|---|
| Avg. high/low (°F) | 54/39 | 62/47 | 65/52 | 63/50 | 55/42 |
| Avg. high/low (°C) | 12/4 | 17/8 | 18/11 | 17/10 | 13/6 |
| Avg. hours of light | 17:45 | 19.30 | 18:15 | 15:30 | 12 |
| Avg. sunny days | 11 | 10 | 9 | 9 | 9 |
| Avg. rainy days | 7 | 8 | 11 | 13 | 14 |
| Avg. precipitation (in.) | .7 | 1.1 | 1./ | 2.4 | 2.7 |

### JUNEAU: SOUTHEAST ALASKA

|  | MAY | JUNE | JULY | AUG | SEPT |
|---|---|---|---|---|---|
| Average high/low (°F) | 55/39 | 61/45 | 64/48 | 63/47 | 56/43 |
| Average high/low (°C) | 13/4 | 16/7 | 18/9 | 17/8 | 13/6 |
| Avg. hours of light | 17 | 18:15 | 17:30 | 15:30 | 12:30 |
| Avg. sunny days | 8 | 8 | 8 | 9 | 6 |
| Avg. rainy days | 17 | 15 | 17 | 17 | 20 |
| Avg. precipitation (in.) | 3.4 | 3.1 | 4.2 | 5.3 | 6.7 |

# Packing for Formal, Informal & Casual Events

Some people agonize over what to pack for a cruise, but there's no reason to fret. Except for the addition of a formal night or two, a cruise vacation is really no different from any resort vacation. And in some cases, it's much more casual.

Many ships offer dry-cleaning and laundry services (for a fee, of course; look for deals where they will wash whatever you can squeeze into a laundry bag for a set price, usually around $25), and some offer either free or coin-operated laundry facilities (the latter requiring quarters or tokens that you can get at the reception desk). Using these services can save you a lot of packing. Check the line's brochures for details.

Don't feel you have to go out and buy "cruise wear." Sweatshirts, jeans, and jogging outfits are the norm during the day. Dinner is dress-up time on most ships, although several have begun to offer more casual alternatives. And the small adventure-type ships are all casual, all the time.

Generally, ships describe proper dinner attire as formal, informal, or semiformal (the two terms mean the same thing in this case), smart casual or country club, or casual. There are usually either 2 formal nights and 2 informal (or semiformal) nights during a weeklong cruise or 2 formal nights and the rest "smart casual" or all smart casual/country club casual; check with your line for specifics. Although the term has gotten somewhat more relaxed in recent years, **formal** generally means a dark suit with tie for men (some still wear a tuxedo) and a nice cocktail dress, long dress, or dressy pantsuit for women. **Informal** (or **semiformal**) is a jacket, tie, and dress slacks, or a light suit, for men, and a dress, skirt and blouse, or pants outfit for women (the ubiquitous little black dress is appropriate here). **Smart casual** or **country club** casual is pretty much the same as informal without the tie. **Casual** at dinner means a sports shirt or open-collar dress shirt with slacks for men (some will also wear a jacket), and a casual dress, pants outfit, or skirt and blouse for women. In other words, for casual nights, dress as you would to go out to dinner at a midrange restaurant. Men who want to wear a **tuxedo** and women who want to wear a **gown** and don't own one may be able to rent one in advance through the ship. In all cases, don't be surprised if some people ignore the dress code altogether.

*Tip:* If you are bringing a bunch of electronic gadgets—cellphones, cameras that need recharging, an iPad, a laptop—you might want to bring a power strip. Don't expect to find more than two electrical outlets in your cabin.

# MONEY MATTERS

There are few forms of travel that are as easy as a cruise, at least as far as money is concerned. That's because you've already paid the lion's share of your all-inclusive vacation by the time you board the ship.

When you check in for a large-ship cruise, either at the terminal or online, the cruise line will ask for a major credit card to charge your onboard expenses (although most lines now allow you to also process this information in advance online). They will typically preauthorize your account (with your credit card company) for $50 to $70 per person per day, an amount refunded if you don't spend it. On some ships, you must report to the purser's office once on board to establish your onboard credit account. On all cruises, you also have the option of paying your account with cash, traveler's checks, or, in some cases, a personal check. Check the cruise line's brochure for specific rules on this. You may be asked to leave a deposit if you are paying with cash, usually $250 to $350 per person for a 1-week sailing. You should let the cruise line know as early as possible if you wish to pay with cash or checks (some lines like to know at the time you make your cruise reservations). One thing to keep in mind is that if you plan to put down a deposit in cash and you're departing out of Vancouver in Canada, you need to have enough U.S. dollars—the accepted currency of the ships in Alaska—with you before leaving home. The ATMs in Vancouver, as you might expect, dispense Canadian dollars, not U.S. dollars.

Whether you check in online (which the lines are encouraging to speed up the process) or at the terminal, the staff at the check-in counter will give you a special **ship charge card** (sometimes called a "signature card") that you use for the length of your cruise. From this point on, on most ships, your time aboard is virtually cashless, except for any gambling you do in the casino. On many ships, you can even put your crew tips on your credit card, though on some you're expected to use cash (more on tipping later in this chapter). The same electronic card, by the way, also will likely serve as your cabin key.

On most small ships, things aren't so formal. Because there are so few passengers, and because the only places to spend money aboard are at the bar and the small gift counters, the staff will just mark down your purchases and you'll settle your account at the end of the week.

In all cases, you will need some cash on hand for port stops: to pay for cabs, make small purchases, buy sodas and snacks, tip your tour guides, and so on. Having bills smaller than $20 is useful for these purposes (especially some $1 bills). At all the ports described in this book (even the Canadian ones), U.S. dollars are accepted, as are major credit cards. If you prefer to deal in Canadian currency in Canada, most ports will have exchange counters, banks, and ATMs. Ships in Alaska do not usually offer currency-conversion services.

Some ships have their own ATMs aboard, most often located, not surprisingly, in the casino. These give out U.S. dollars. A fee may be involved.

It's recommended that you not leave large amounts of cash in your room. All ships have some sort of safes available, either in-room or at the purser's desk, and passengers are wise to use them. You should also store your plane ticket and passport or ID papers there.

## Budgeting

Before your trip, you may want to make a tentative budget. It's a good idea to set aside money for **shore excursions** ($600 per person or more if you plan to do several) and **tips** ($11–$12.50 per passenger per day). You might also want to budget in such extras as **bar drinks, dry cleaning, phone calls, massage and other spa services, salon services, babysitting, photos taken by the ship's photographer, wine at dinner, souvenirs,** and costs for any other special splurges your particular ship might offer (items at the caviar bars or cigar bars, time on the golf simulator, and so on). Above are some rough prices for the more common incidentals.

We suggest you keep careful track of your onboard expenses to avoid an unpleasant surprise at the end of your cruise.

On big ships, a final bill will be slipped under your door on the last night of your cruise. If everything is okay and you're paying by credit card, you don't have to do anything but keep the copy. If there's a problem on the bill, or if you are paying by

| THE COST OF COMMON CRUISE INCIDENTALS | US$ |
|---|---|
| Alternative dining (service charge) | 10.00–75.00 |
| Babysitting (per hour) | |
| Group | 6.00–8.00 |
| Private | 15–19 |
| Beverages | |
| Beer (domestic/imported) | 3.50–6.00 |
| Latte | 3.25–4.25 |
| Mineral water | 2.00–3.95 |
| Mixed drink (more for fine liquors) | 5.95–7.95 |
| Soft drink | 2.50–2.75 |
| Wine with dinner (per bottle) | 15.00–300.00 |
| Cruise-line-logo souvenirs | 3.00–60.00 |
| E-mail (per minute) | 0.40–0.75 |
| Haircuts | |
| Men's | 29.00–35.00 |
| Women's | 52.00–77.00 |
| Laundry/Dry-cleaning | 1.25–7.00 per item |
| Massage (50 minutes) | 119.00–169.00 |
| Phone calls (per minute) | 4.95–12.00 |
| Photos | 9.95–17.95 |
| Fitness classes | 10 |

cash, traveler's check, or personal check, you will have to go down to the purser's or guest-relations desk and wait in what will likely be a very long line. On small ships, you usually settle up directly with the purser on the last full day of the cruise.

# YOUR VERY IMPORTANT PAPERS

About 1 month (and no later than 1 week) before your cruise, you should receive in the mail your **cruise documents,** including airline tickets (if you purchased them from the cruise line), a boarding document with your cabin and dining choices on it, boarding forms to fill out, luggage tags, and your prearranged bus-transfer vouchers from the airport to the port (if applicable). Also included will likely be a description of shore excursions available for purchase either on board or, in some cases, in advance, as well as additional material detailing things you need to know before you sail. Most lines also now allow you to download this information online.

All this information is important. Read it carefully. Make sure that your cabin category and dining preference are as you requested, and also check your airline tickets to make sure everything checks out in terms of flights and arrival times. Make sure that there is enough time to arrive at the port no later than a half-hour before departure time, and preferably a lot earlier. Be sure to carry these documents in your carry-on rather than in your luggage, since you can't board without them.

## Important Rule Change

A Department of Homeland Security regulation requires cruise ships to deliver a final passenger manifest at least an hour before sailing, and most lines are now requiring passengers to check in at least 1½ hours before sailing and to complete a check-in form online (with your name, address, and passport or other ID information) at least 3 days prior to sailing. If you do not complete the form, you may be required to show up at least 3 hours before your sailing so that the cruise line has time to prepare and transmit your information. If you don't comply, you may be denied boarding (with no refund).

## Passports & Necessary Identification

These days you are required to have a valid passport (whereas a photo ID and birth certificate used to suffice) for all Alaska cruises that begin or end in Canada. On cruises that begin and end in the same port in the U.S. (from Seattle or Juneau, for instance), a government-issued birth certificate and government-issued photo ID (such as a driver's license) will suffice—though cruise lines highly recommend a passport, because if for some reason you need to leave the cruise early at a Canadian port you may be in for a big hassle. If you are not a U.S. citizen but live in the United States, you will have to carry your alien registration card and passport. Foreign-born travelers who do not reside in the U.S. will be required to show a valid visa to enter the U.S. through Canada. For more information about passports and to find your regional passport office, consult the Department of State website (http://travel.state.gov) or call the **National Passport Information Center**'s automated service at ☎ **877/487-2778.**

Even if your cruise doesn't visit Canada, you'll still be required to show photo ID when boarding the ship; in this case, however, a driver's license is sufficient.

# GETTING TO THE SHIP & CHECKING IN

Before you leave for the airport, attach to each of your bags one of the luggage tags sent by the cruise line. Make sure that you correctly fill in the tags with your departure date, port, cabin number, and so forth. You can find all this information in your cruise documents. Put a luggage tag on your carry-on as well.

## Airport Arrival

If you booked your air travel and/or transfers with the cruise line, you should see a **cruise-line representative** holding a card with the name of the line either when you get off the plane or at the baggage area. (If you're arriving on a flight from the United States to Vancouver, you will need to clear Customs and Immigration. Follow the appropriate signs. The cruise-line rep will be waiting to greet you after you've cleared.) Check in with this person. If you are on a precruise package, the details of what to do at the airport will be described in the cruise line's brochure.

When you arrive at your gateway airport, you will be asked by a cruise-line representative to identify your luggage, which will then go straight to the ship for delivery to your cabin. It won't necessarily go in the same bus as you, and it may not (almost certainly will not) be waiting for you when you board, but it'll arrive eventually, have no fear. Make certain that your bags have the cruise line's tags on them, properly filled out, before you leave the airport for the ship.

You'll have to turn over to the bus driver the **transportation voucher** received with your cruise documents, so do have it handy.

If you're flying independent of the cruise line, claim your luggage at the baggage area and proceed to the pier by cab, rental car, or whatever other transportation you have arranged. And again, remember to put the luggage tags provided by the cruise line on your bags at this point if you haven't already, because when you get to the pier, your bags will be taken from you by a porter for loading onto the ship. The porter who takes your bags may expect a tip of $1 per bag (some will be more aggressive than others in asking for it).

> ### Where's My Luggage?!
>
> Don't panic if your bags aren't in your cabin when you arrive: Getting all the bags on board is a rather slow process—on big ships, as many as 6,000 bags need to be loaded and distributed. If it's close to sailing time and you're concerned, call guest relations or the purser's office. If your luggage really is lost rather than just late, the cruise line's customer-relations folks will track it down and arrange for it to be delivered to the ship's first port of call.

On the question of identifying your luggage, don't rely simply on appearances; one Samsonite looks just like another, even though yours may have a distinctive yellow ribbon on its handle. Check the ID tags as well! There's nothing worse than boarding a cruise that starts with 2 days at sea with somebody else's luggage and only the clothes on your back.

## WHAT TO DO IF YOUR FLIGHT IS DELAYED

First of all, tell the airline personnel at the airport that you are a cruise passenger and that you're sailing that day. They may be able to put you on a different flight. Second, have the airline folks call the cruise line to advise them of your delay—your cruise documents should include an emergency number. Keep in mind that you may not be the only person delayed, and the line just may hold the ship until your arrival.

## WHAT TO DO IF YOU MISS THE BOAT

Don't panic. Go directly to the cruise line's port agent at the pier (the name, phone number, and address of the port agent should be listed in your cruise documents). You may be able to get to your ship via a chartered boat or tug, assuming that the vessel isn't too far out at sea by that time. (Be aware that if you do follow in a small boat, you'll have to transfer from it to a moving ship at sea—not an exercise to be taken lightly!) Or you may be put up in a hotel for the night and flown or provided with other transportation to the next port the next day. If you booked your flight on your own, you will likely be charged for this service.

## At the Pier

Most ships start embarkation in the early afternoon and depart between 4 and 6pm. You will not be able to board the ship before the scheduled embarkation time, usually about 3 or 4 hours before sailing, and even then it's likely that you'll have to wait in line unless you're sailing on a small ship carrying very few passengers. If you've booked a suite, you may get priority boarding at a special desk. Special-needs passengers may also be processed separately. Ship personnel will check your boarding tickets and ID and collect any documents you've been sent to fill out in advance. You will then be given a boarding card and your cabin key. (On some lines, your key may be waiting in your cabin.)

You have up to 90 minutes before departure to board (see "Important Rule Change," above), but there are some advantages to boarding earlier, like getting first dibs on spa-treatment times. Plus, if you're early enough, you can eat lunch on the ship.

Protocol for establishing your **dining-room table assignment,** if one is required (you may instead have open seating), varies by ship. You may be given your assignment in advance of your sailing (shown on your tickets), you may be advised of your table number as you check in, or a card with your table number may be waiting for you in your cabin. If you do not receive an assignment by the time you get to your cabin, you will be directed to a maitre d's desk, set up at a convenient spot on board. This is also the place to make any changes if your table assignment does not meet with your approval.

# KEEPING IN TOUCH WITH THE OUTSIDE WORLD

## Getting the News & Keeping in Touch

Newshounds don't have to feel out of touch on a cruise ship. Most big ships offer CNN or Fox News on in-room TVs, and nearly every ship—even small ships without TVs—will post the latest news from the wire services outside the purser's office. Some lines excerpt information from leading newspapers each day and deliver the news to your room (if you are British, you may even be able to get British news).

Most ships will provide the opportunity to make satellite phone calls, but these can be exorbitantly expensive—usually anywhere from $4.95 to $12 per minute. You should be able to use your cellular phone in some of the more populated areas of Alaska (see "Fast Facts: Alaska," in chapter 3). Check with your cellular provider for details. Many ships have added service that allows you to use your cellphone at sea, although you will have to pay what can be expensive roaming rates—again, check with your provider for details (and smartphone users should be aware that even if you have calling capability, your e-mail service and Internet access may not work). If you don't have a cellphone, consider buying a prepaid phone card to use at a public phone on shore.

Another alternative is shipboard e-mail, which all the big ships now have. Rates range from 40¢ to 75¢ per minute. It is generally cheaper if you buy a set plan—for instance, paying in advance for 4 hours of usage throughout your cruise (plans vary by line, so check with your ship's Internet cafe to see what plans are available; special discounts may be offered if you sign up the first day of your cruise). In recent years, some lines, including Holland America, have been offering discount packages toward the end of the cruise as well (on a recent Norwegian Cruise Line cruise, there was an offer of free bingo cards if you booked certain Internet packages). Some of the small ships also provide e-mail access. The port cities you'll be visiting are also likely to have Internet cafes—charging cheaper rates than ships.

## Sending Mail

If you want to send mail from the ship, the purser's office should have postage stamps and a mailbox.

# VISITING THE PORTS OF CALL

Here's where the kind of ship you chose for your cruise, and the itinerary, comes into play. On a big ship, you will likely visit the popular ports of Skagway, Juneau, and Ketchikan (and possibly Sitka or Victoria, depending on your itinerary) and will have several days at sea to enjoy the glorious glaciers, fjords, and wildlife, as well as participate in shipboard activities and relax. On a smaller ship, you may also visit several smaller ports of call and head into wilderness areas that cannot accommodate larger vessels.

On **days in port,** you need a plan for what you want to see on land (more on that in this section). On **days at sea,** you will probably want to be out on deck much of the time looking for whales and listening to the commentary of glacier and wildlife experts. There will be plenty of activities offered, but these may be reduced at certain times—for instance, when the ship is scheduled to pass one of the famous glaciers.

Nearly every ship in Alaska has naturalists and other Alaska experts on board to share their expertise on glaciers, geography, plant life, and wildlife. Sometimes these experts are on for the entire cruise and give lectures complete with slides or films; other times they are National Park Service rangers who come on board at glacier sites (particularly in Glacier Bay) to provide commentary, usually over the ship's PA system. Depending on the ship, local fishermen, Native Alaskans, teachers, photographers, librarians, historians, and anthropologists may come on board to teach about local history and culture.

Cruise lines carefully arrange their itineraries to visit places that have a little something for everyone, whether your interest is nature, museum hopping, barhopping, or no hopping at all. You can take in the location's ambience and natural beauty, learn about the local culture and history, eat local foods, and enjoy sports activities. And you'll have the opportunity to shop to your heart's content.

## Shore Excursions

When the ship gets into port, you'll have the choice of going on a shore excursion organized by the cruise line or going off on your own. The shore excursions are designed to help you make the most of your limited time at each port of call, to get you to the top natural or historical attractions, and to make sure you get back to the ship on

---

### Religion on the High Seas

Religious services depend, of course, on the ship and the clergy on board. Most ships have a nondenominational service on Sunday and a Friday-night Jewish Sabbath service, usually run by a passenger. On Jewish and Christian holidays, clergy are typically on board large ships to lead services, which are usually held in the library or conference room. If you are looking for a daily Catholic Mass, you may have to visit churches at the ports.

time. But shore excursions are also a moneymaking area for the cruise line, and they can add a hefty sum to your vacation costs. Whether you choose to take one of these prearranged sightseeing trips is a matter of both personal preference and budgetary concerns; you should in no way feel that you must do an excursion in every port. Our picks of some of the best shore excursions in Southeast and Southcentral Alaska, as well as in Vancouver and Victoria, are included with all the port listings in chapters 7 and 8, along with advice on exploring on your own.

At most ports, the cruise lines have **guided tours** to the top sights, usually by bus. The most worthwhile tours take you outside the downtown area or include a meal, a dance or music performance, or a crafts demonstration (or sometimes all the above). There's a guide on each bus, and the excursion price includes all incidental admission costs. The commentary is sometimes hokey, other times educational.

In most Alaska ports, it's easy to explore the downtown area on your own. There are advantages to independent exploration: Walking around is often the best way to see the sights, and you can plan your itinerary to steer clear of the crowds. In some ports, however, there's not much within walking distance of the docks, and it's difficult to find a cab or other transportation. In these cases, the cruise line's excursion program may be your best and most cost-effective option. For instance, a typical **historical tour** in Sitka will take in the Russian St. Michael's Cathedral in the downtown area plus two great sights a little way out of downtown: Sitka National Historic Park, with its totem poles and forest trails; and the Alaska Raptor Rehabilitation Center, where injured bald eagles and other birds of prey are nursed back to health. The tour may also include a Russian dance performance by the all-female New Archangel Dancers. Although you could visit the church on your own, it's a long walk to the park, and the bus is the best way to get to see the eagles (otherwise you're talking $20-plus cab fare each way).

There are plenty of shore excursions in Alaska for those who want to get active, such as **mountain-bike trips, fishing, snorkeling,** and **kayak voyages,** all of which get you close to nature and afford stunning views. These trips are generally worth taking. They usually involve small groups of passengers, and by booking your activity through the cruise line, you have the advantage of knowing that the vendors have been pre-screened: Their prices may be slightly higher than those offered by the outfitters that you'll find once you disembark at the port, but you can be assured that the outfitters the cruise lines work with are reputable.

For those who enjoy trips in small planes or helicopters and are willing to pay for the experience (they are on the pricey side), **flightseeing trips,** offered as shore excursions at many of the ports of call, are a fascinating way to see the Alaska landscape. Again, the ship's tours may be priced slightly higher than those offered at the port, but by booking the ship's package, you should be able to avoid touring with Reckless Mike and His Barely Flying Machine. The extra few bucks you pay will be worth it.

That said, in some cases you can lock in the exact same tour your cruise line is selling you (with the exact same outfitter) at a lower price by cutting out the middleman (the line) and going straight to the source (the outfitter). The trick is finding the same operator, which takes a fair amount of legwork. But it's doable, and it can result in significant savings. One summer, for instance, during an Alaskan cruise with his family, Gene decided to splurge on one of the flightseeing trips offered on Alaska cruises (something he feels every Alaska visitor should do at least once). But the particular outing he was eyeing cost nearly $400 a person through the cruise line! By tracking down the outfitter that arranges the tour for the line and talking with them directly, he was able to get the price knocked down about 20 percent, or $80 per person—a significant savings (and he never once mentioned his affiliation with Frommer's or *USA Today;* as far as they were concerned, he was just another cruiser looking for a deal).

If you try the direct route, keep in mind that a fair number of the outfitters in Alaskan towns won't budge from quoting you the same price whether you book on the ship or off it. It's no secret that the cruise lines discourage their preferred outfitters from undercutting them by taking bookings directly from cruisers at lower prices, and the last thing an outfitter in Alaska wants is to be put on the naughty list of a cruise line that's one of its biggest customers. The outfitters that do offer you a discount often will ask you not to mention it to anyone back at the cruise line—lest they find themselves in the hot seat.

As for tracking down the operators that cruise lines use, the secret is to examine in great detail the tour you're interested in on your cruise line's website, noting the wording of the description and even the photos you find there, and then comparing that to the descriptions and photos of tour options you'll find on the websites of Alaska's main port towns such as Juneau and Skagway (in many cases, you'll find an exact match). In some of the towns that are small, such as Skagway, it's fairly obvious once you do a little digging which particular outfitter does what for the cruise lines. Keep in mind that some of the port towns, such as Skagway, are so small that they might only have one operator offering such activities as hiking, biking, climbing tours, and the like, so no matter where you book, you're probably going to end up with the same folks.

There are also private companies that specialize in selling shore excursions at a discount (See Chapter 3 for details.)

A fairly new trend is private shore excursions—the cruise line arranges a guide just for you and others you want to invite along. For instance, in Sitka, Holland America Line will arrange for a party of up to six people to head off for 3½ hours in a 38-foot expedition-style catamaran, and you help determine the course; price tag: $1,994. It's the best of both worlds—you get to see what you want to see with an experienced guide—but naturally, these tours are pricey.

Regular shore excursions usually range in price from about $35 to $99 for a bus tour to $229 and up for elaborate trips such as flightseeing by floatplane or helicopter (sometimes $600 and up if you add in thrills such as dogsledding on a glacier). You may be in port long enough to book more than one option or take an excursion and still have several hours to explore the port on your own. You may well find that you want to do a prearranged shore excursion at one port and be on your own at the next.

The best way to decide which shore excursions you want to take is to do some research in advance of your trip. In addition to our descriptions in chapters 7 and 8, which detail the most common and popular excursions offered in the various ports, your cruise line will probably send you a booklet listing its shore excursions with your cruise tickets. You can compare and contrast. You are best off booking shore excursions online before your trip, as the most popular ones tend to sell out fast. But if you wait until you are on board, you'll find a shore-excursion order form in your cabin, at the purser's desk or shore-excursion desk, or at the shore-excursion lecture offered the first day of your cruise. To make your reservations, check off the appropriate places on the shore-excursion order form, sign the form (include your cabin number), and drop it off as directed, probably at the ship's shore-excursion desk or at the purser's office. Your account will be automatically charged, and tickets will be sent to your cabin before your first scheduled tour. Tickets will include such information as where and when to meet for the tour. Carefully note the time: If you are not at the right place at the right time, the tour will likely leave without you.

*Remember:* The most popular excursions (such as flightseeing trips) sell out fast. For that reason, you're best off booking your shore excursions online before your cruise or at least by the first or second day of your cruise.

## Arriving in Port

When the ship arrives in port, it will either dock at the pier or anchor slightly offshore. You may think that when the ship docks right at the pier, you can walk right off, but you can't. Before the gangway is open to disembarking passengers, lots of papers must be signed, and local authorities must give their clearance, a process that can take as long as 2 hours. Don't even bother going down to the gangplank until you hear an announcement saying the ship has been cleared.

If your ship anchors rather than docks (as in Sitka, for instance), you will go ashore in a small boat called a launch or tender, which ties up next to your ship and shuttles passengers back and forth all day. Getting on the tender may require a helping hand from crew members, and the waves may keep the tender swaying, sometimes requiring passengers to literally jump to board. (The tenders, by the way, are part of the ship's ample complement of lifeboats, lowered into the water, usually four at a time, for the day in port.)

Whether the ship is docked or anchored, you are in no way required to get off at every port of call. The ship's restaurants will remain open, and there will still be activities, though usually on a limited basis.

If you do disembark, before you reboard, you may want to use the pay phones at the docks to call home. This is *much* cheaper than making calls from the ship. But be prepared to wait for a phone. No matter how many telephones there are on the pier, you will invariably find that off-duty members of the crew, who generally get off the ship earlier than passengers, have beaten you to them. It's an interesting exercise to stand near a dozen public telephones and listen to the Filipino, cockney, French, Norwegian, and other languages and dialects being spoken by the users. The same goes for Internet cafes near the pier—crew members may flock there—though without the audio aspect.

## Tips for Your Port Visits

### THE ESSENTIALS: DON'T LEAVE THE SHIP WITHOUT 'EM

You must bring your **ship boarding pass** (or shipboard ID) with you when you disembark or you will have trouble getting back on board. (You probably have to show it as you leave the ship anyway, so forgetting it will be hard.) You may also be required to show a photo ID (such as your passport or driver's license). The ship will let you know if you have to carry this as well. And don't forget to bring a little cash—although your ship operates on a cashless system, the ports do not. Many passengers get so used to carrying no cash or credit cards while aboard the ship that they forget them when going ashore. (Gene admits to doing just this when popping off a ship in Ketchikan; luckily, all he had planned was a long hike, so there was little need for paper money, though he says it was a bit disconcerting when he realized halfway out of town that he was wandering off sans wallet.)

## WATCH THE CLOCK

If you're going off on your own, whether on foot or on one of the alternate tours or transportation options that we've listed, remember to be very careful about timing. You're generally required to be back at the dock at least a half-hour before the ship's scheduled departure. Passengers running late on one of the line's shore excursions needn't worry: If an excursion runs late, the ship accepts responsibility and won't leave without the late passengers.

If you're on your own, however, and miss the boat, immediately contact the cruise-line representative at the port. (Most lines list phone numbers and addresses for their port agent at each stop in the newsletter delivered to your cabin daily; be sure to take it ashore if you are going any distance from the ship!) You'll probably be able to catch your ship at the next port of call, but you'll have to pay your own way to get there.

# TIPPING, PACKING & OTHER END-OF-CRUISE CONCERNS

A few hints that should save you time and aggravation at the end of your cruise:

## Tips on Tipping

Tipping is a subject that some people find confusing. First, let's establish that you are expected on most ships to tip the crew at the end of the cruise—in particular, your cabin steward, server, and busperson—and *not* to tip is bad form. Recently, lines including Carnival, Holland America, Princess, and Norwegian Cruise Line have made the process easier, adopting a system whereby they automatically add tips of $11 to $12.50 per passenger per day to your shipboard account. You can visit the purser's office and ask to increase or decrease the amount, depending on your opinion of the service you received. Other lines may suggest that you tip in cash, but some also allow you to tip via your shipboard account. Bar bills usually automatically include the tip (usually 15 percent), but if the dining room wine steward, for instance, has served you exceptionally well, you can slip him or her a few bucks, too.

If there is no automatic tip, the cruise line will give suggested tip amounts in the daily bulletin and in the cruise director's debarkation briefing, but these are just suggestions—you can tip more or less, at your own discretion. Keep in mind, though, that stewards, servers, and buspersons are often extremely underpaid and that their salaries are largely dependent on tips. Many of these crew members support families back home on their earnings.

We think the **minimum tip** you should consider is $4 per passenger per day for your room steward and your waiter, and $3 per passenger per day for your busperson. That's a total of up to $77 per passenger for a 7-night cruise (you don't have to include debarkation day). We also recommend leaving about half of these amounts on behalf of child passengers 12 and under. Some lines recommend more, some a little less. Of course, you can always tip more for good service. You'll also be encouraged to tip the dining room maitre d', the headwaiter, and other better salaried employees. Whether to tip these folks is your decision. If you have a cabin with butler service, tip the butler about $5 per person per day, provided he has been visible throughout your cruise (if he hasn't, reduce that amount). The captain and his officers should not be tipped—it'd be like tipping your doctor.

Regent Seven Seas Cruises and Silversea Cruises include tips in the cruise fare, although some people choose to tip key personnel anyway—it's really up to you. Small-ship lines have their own suggested tipping guidelines. (See chapter 6.)

If you have spa or beauty treatments, you can tip at the time of service (just add it to your ship account; be aware some ships add 15 percent automatically). Most ships now automatically add a gratuity to bar tabs, but if not, you can hand a bartender a buck if you like. Otherwise, tips are usually given on the last night of your cruise. On some ships (especially small ships), you may be asked to submit your tips in a single sum that the crew will divide among itself after the cruise, but generally, you reward people individually, usually in little preprinted envelopes that the ship distributes.

If a staff member is particularly great, a written letter to a superior is always good form and may earn that person an employee-of-the-month honor, and maybe even a bonus.

## Settling Your Shipboard Account

On big ships, your shipboard account will close just before the end of your cruise, but before that time, you will receive a preliminary bill in your cabin. If you are using a credit card, just make sure the charges are correct. If there is a problem, you will have to go to the purser's office, where you will likely encounter long lines. If you're paying by cash or traveler's check, you'll be asked to settle your account during the day or night before you leave the ship. This will also require that you go to the purser's office. A final invoice will be delivered to your room before departure.

On small ships, the procedure will be simpler. Often you can just mosey over to the purser's desk on the last evening, check to see that the bill they give you looks right, and sign your name.

## Luggage Procedures

With thousands of suitcases to deal with, big ships have established the routine of requiring guests to pack the night before they disembark if they don't want to carry their bags off the ship themselves. You will be asked to leave your bags (except for your carry-ons) in the hallway before you retire for the night—usually by midnight. The bags will be picked up overnight and placed in the cruise terminal before passengers are allowed to disembark. It's important to make sure that your bags are tagged with the luggage tags given you by the cruise line toward the end of your cruise. These are not the same tags you arrived with; rather, they're color-coded to indicate deck number and debarkation order—the order in which they'll likely be arranged on the dock. If you need more tags, alert your cabin steward or the purser's staff. You may also have the option of carrying your own bags off if they aren't too heavy for you to do so.

If you booked your air travel through the cruise line, you may be able to check your luggage for your flight at the cruise terminal (or even on board the ship for a small fee). Make sure you receive your luggage claim checks. You may even be able to get your flight boarding passes at the cruise terminal, saving you a wait in line at the airport. A bus will then take you to the airport.

If you're signed up for a **post-cruise tour,** special instructions will be given to you by the cruise line.

# Debarkation

You won't be able to get off the ship until it is cleared by Customs and other authorities, a process that usually takes 90 minutes or more. In most cases, you'll be asked to vacate your cabin by 8am and wait in one of the ship's lounges. If you have a flight home on the same day, you will disembark based on your flight departure time. Passengers with mobility problems, those who booked suites, and travelers who will be staying on at the port will often disembark early. If you have booked a land package through the cruise line, transportation will be waiting to take you from the ship to your hotel.

# Customs & Immigration

If your cruise begins or ends in Canada, you'll have to clear Canadian Customs and Immigration, which usually means that your name goes on a list that is reviewed by authorities. You must fill out a Customs declaration form, and you may be required to show your passport.

When disembarking in U.S. ports after starting out from Vancouver, non–U.S. citizens (including green-card holders) will be required to meet with U.S. Immigration authorities, usually in a lounge or theater, when the ship arrives at the port. Bring your passport receipt; all family members must attend.

The U.S. Customs & Border Protection Service has a preclearance program in Vancouver that allows cruise passengers to go through Customs before boarding their flights home.

Tipping, Packing & Other End-of-Cruise Concerns

THE CRUISE EXPERIENCE

# THE CRUISE LINES: THE BIG SHIPS

H ere's where the rudder hits the road: It's time to choose the ship that will be your home away from home for the duration of your Alaska cruise.

As we said earlier, your biggest decision is whether you want to sail on a big ship or a small ship. So that you can more easily compare like with like, in this chapter, we'll deal with the big and midsize ships; in chapter 6, we discuss the small ships.

For some years, the ships in Alaska have been getting bigger and bigger. In terms of total tonnage, **Princess** ships still lead. Indeed, four of the seven vessels the company is sending to Alaska in 2014 are more than 100,000 tons, putting them among the bigger cruise ships in the world. The largest, the 113,000-ton *Crown Princess,* is capable of carrying 3,080 passengers, and at 107,500 to 109,000 tons, the *Grand Princess, Golden Princess,* and *Star Princess* are not far behind. Two of Princess's three other ships in the region also are relatively large at 92,000 tons.

There are other megaships that don't sport the Princess colors. **Celebrity Cruises'** *Solstice* and *Millennium* measure 122,000 tons and 91,000 tons, respectively, and carry 2,850 and 1,950 passengers. **Royal Caribbean's** 90,000-ton, 2,112-berth *Radiance of the Seas* will be spending its 11th summer in Alaska, joined by the slightly smaller *Rhapsody of the Seas.* **Norwegian Cruise Line** is sending three large ships to Alaska in 2014, led by the 93,000-ton *Norwegian Pearl* and the 93,502-ton *Norwegian Jewel.* And as in past years, even Caribbean-focused **Carnival Cruise Lines** is positioning one ship in Alaska, the 88,500-ton, 2,124-passenger *Carnival Miracle.*

For those looking for a slightly more intimate experience, midsize-ship-focused **Holland America Line** has seven vessels in Alaska this year. The largest of the lot—the *Ooosterdam, Zuiderdam,* and *Westerdam*—are "only" a little in excess of 80,000 tons and carry fewer than 2,000 passengers apiece, while several other Holland America ships, such as the *Statendam,* are under 60,000 tons. (By today's standards, such ships are definitely midsize!)

Perhaps the biggest news in Alaska cruising in recent years was the arrival of the **Disney Cruise Line** in 2011, and it must have been a success for the company, as Disney has returned every year since. The family-friendly operator's 83,000-ton, 1,754-passenger *Disney Wonder* once again will sail 7-night voyages to Alaska, this time out of Vancouver, BC (the line has switched back and forth between the city and Seattle as its Alaska base).

Another recent newcomer to Alaska that is returning for 2014 is **Oceania Cruises,** which offers a more upscale (and pricey) experience than the likes of Princess and Holland America. Consider it a step up from the mass-market lines. Lovers of ultra-luxury, meanwhile, can choose between **Regent Seven Seas'** *Seven Seas Navigator* and **Silversea's** *Silver Shadow*, the only true luxury ships in the market. Both are tiny compared to most of the vessels we mention here; however, they're a good bit bigger than the ships in the next chapter, and they have a full range of big-ship amenities, so we've kept them in with the big guys.

The beauty of some of the latter-day megaships is that they're designed so that you won't feel as if you're sharing your vacation with thousands of others. There have lots of nooks and crannies in which to relax and hide far from the maddening crowd, so to speak.

The evolution of cruise ships is almost worth a chapter all by itself, but we'll address it here in shorter order. A few decades ago, major cruise lines operated ships that ranged from about 20,000 to 40,000 gross registered tons (GRT). These were considered "big" ships. The cabins had portholes or, at best, picture windows that didn't open. The ships had one dining room, with two seatings for lunch and dinner, and a snack bar/buffet as pretty much the only alternative. Many of them had large numbers of inside cabins, and all the cabins, inside and outside, tended to be rather basic (in some cases, downright spartan). Only the very best half-dozen or so suites on some of them had private balconies.

Things began changing in the 1980s, when ships began getting bigger—and debuting with not just a few but rows of balcony cabins. As the demand for cruises grew—stoked by the popular TV show *The Love Boat*—the lines also began looking for ways to make life at sea more enjoyable for their passengers, adding everything from larger showrooms with more sophisticated acts to more deck-top amenities. Advances in shipbuilding technology allowed them to move up from 45,000 tons to 70,000 tons and, by the middle of the 1990s, more than 100,000 tons, adding ever more onboard attractions (from miniature golf courses to climbing walls) along the way. But the growth of cruise ships wasn't over. Early last decade, lines such as Cunard and Royal Caribbean rolled out ships as big as 160,000 tons, and in 2009 Royal Caribbean upped the ante again with the unveiling of the 225,282-ton *Oasis of the Seas*—by far the biggest ship ever built. (***Note:*** None of these biggest-of-the-big vessels—aimed primarily at the Caribbean market—sail in Alaska.)

All the new ships, but especially those built this century, have more technologically advanced showrooms, million-dollar collections of original art, better trained and higher-paid entertainment directors, flashy and extensive children's and teens' centers—and alternative dining facilities. Lots and lots of alternative dining facilities! Nowadays the roster of available food choices on cruise ships would do credit to the Manhattan telephone directory. Depending on your ship, you can have Italian, Tex-Mex, Cajun, Asian fusion, top-flight steakhouse, French, even good old British fish and chips. More and more cruise ships are also going to an open seating policy (come when you like, eat with whom you like). On some ships, it is possible nowadays to eat dinner in a different restaurant every night of your cruise.

The ships featured in this chapter vary in size, age, and amenities, but they share the common thread of having scads of activities and entertainment. You will not be roughing it: On these ships, you'll find swimming pools, health clubs, spas, nightclubs, movie theaters, shops, casinos, multiple restaurants and bars, special kids' playrooms (in most cases, special club spaces for teens as well), sports decks, virtual golf, computer rooms, martini and cigar bars, as well as the aforementioned quiet spaces where you can get away from it all. Onboard activities generally include games, contests, classes, and lectures, plus a variety of entertainment options and show productions, some very sophisticated. There's usually a vast array of shore excursions for which you will have to pay extra. Cabins vary in size and amenities but are usually roomy enough for the time you'll be spending aboard. And with all the public rooms, you won't be spending much time in your cabin anyway.

# SOME COMPONENTS OF OUR CRUISE-LINE REVIEWS

Each cruise line's review begins with a quick word about the line in general and a short summation of the kind of cruise experience you can expect to have aboard that line. The text that follows fleshes out the review, providing all the details you need to get a feel for what kind of vacation the cruise line will provide.

The individual ship reviews following the general cruise-line description then get into the nitty-gritty, giving you all the details on the ships' accommodations, facilities, amenities, comfort levels, and upkeep.

People feel very strongly about ships. For centuries mariners have imbued their vessels with human personalities, usually referring to an individual ship as "her." In fact, an old (really old) seafaring superstition holds that women should never be allowed aboard a ship because the ship, being a woman herself, will get jealous. It's a fact that people bond with the ships aboard which they sail. They find themselves in the gift shop loading up on T-shirts with the ship's name emblazoned on the front. They get to

## A Note for New Cruisers

There is a saying in the industry that nobody should cruise just once. On any voyage, a ship could encounter bad weather. On any given day at sea, the only seat left in the show lounge might be behind an unforgiving pillar. Or a technical problem might affect the enjoyment of the onboard experience. Gene remembers vividly one occasion when the air-conditioning on a ship on which he was traveling—which shall remain nameless—went out for a half-day. It was an uncomfortable time and could have turned a neophyte off cruising forever. That would have been a mistake. In travel there is liable to be an occasional snafu. Your hotel room may not be available, even though you have a valid confirmation number. Your flight might be canceled. The luxury car you thought you rented might not be on the lot, and all that's available is a miniature subcompact. But you don't stop flying, you don't refuse to stay in a hotel ever again, and you don't stop renting cars. Nor should one unforeseen problem on a cruise ship cause you to swear off the product forever. Give it another go, on a different cruise line if you prefer. If you still haven't had the enjoyable experience that millions of others have discovered, then, and only then, is it perhaps time to abandon hope of becoming a cruise aficionado.

port and the first question they ask other cruisers they meet is "Which ship are you sailing on?" They engage in a (usually) friendly comparison, and both parties walk away knowing in their hearts that their ship is the best. We know people who have sailed the same ship a dozen times or more and feel as warmly about it as their summer cottage. That's why, when looking at the reviews, you want to look for a ship that says "you."

We've listed some of the ships' vital statistics—ship size, years built and most recently refurbished, number of cabins, number of crew—to help you compare. Size is listed in tons. Note that these are not actual measures of weight but gross register tons (GRTs), a measure of the interior space used to produce revenue on a ship. One GRT equals 100 cubic feet of enclosed, revenue-generating space. Among the crew/officers statistics, an important one is the **passenger/crew ratio,** which tells you, in theory, how many passengers each crew member is expected to serve and, thus, how much personal service you can expect.

*Note:* When several vessels are members of a class—built on the same design, with usually only minor variations in decor and attractions—we've grouped the ships together into one class review.

## Stars
### THE RATINGS

To make things easier on everyone, we've developed a simple ratings system that covers those things that vary from vessel to vessel—quality and size of the cabins and public spaces, comfort, cleanliness and maintenance, decor, number and quality of dining options, gyms/spas (and for the small-adventure lines that don't have gyms and spas, a slightly different system; see p. 130), and children's facilities—plus a rating for the overall enjoyment of the onboard experience. We've given each ship an overall **star rating** (for example, ★★★) based on the combined total of our poor-to-outstanding ratings, translated into a 1-to-5 scale:

| | | | | | |
|---|---|---|---|---|---|
| 1 | = | **Poor** | 4 | = | **Excellent** |
| 2 | = | **Fair** | 5 | = | **Outstanding** |
| 3 | = | **Good** | | | |

In instances when the category doesn't apply to a particular ship (for example, none of the adventure ships have children's facilities), we've simply noted "not applicable" (N/A) and absented the category from the total combined score, as these unavailable amenities will be considered a deficiency only in certain circumstances (for instance, if you plan to travel with kids).

Now for a bit of philosophy: The cruise biz today offers a profusion of experiences so different that comparing all ships by the same set of criteria would be like comparing a Park Avenue apartment to an A-frame in Aspen. That's why, to rate the ships, we've used a sliding scale, rating ships on a curve that compares them only with others in their category. Once you've determined what kind of experience is right for you, you can look for the best ships in that category based on your particular needs.

## Itineraries

Each cruise-line review includes a chart showing itineraries for each ship the line has assigned to Alaska for 2014. Often a ship sails on alternating itineraries—for instance, sailing southbound from Seward or Whittier to Vancouver, BC, 1 week and doing the same route in reverse the next. When this is the case, we've listed both and noted that they alternate. These one-way cruises are known as Gulf of Alaska cruises, as opposed to Inside Passage cruises, which generally are round-trip out of either Seattle or Vancouver, BC. (Some longer round-trip cruises depart from San Francisco.) All itineraries are subject to change. Consult the cruise-line websites or your travel agent for exact sailing dates.

The variety of cruise itineraries and of ports of embarkation (and debarkation, for that matter) also demonstrates the maturation of the cruise industry and growth in demand for the product. Not so long ago, just about the only thing you could do in Alaska cruising was a Vancouver-to-Vancouver Inside Passage loop; very few lines had one-way Gulf itineraries. It was simply easier for the ship operators to stick with the tried and true. People wanted it. Ships' crews got into a rhythm—arrive in Vancouver, BC, at 8am, discharge passengers, take on new ones, and start all over again. But demand began to outstrip the available berths. San Francisco became an attractive alternative, then Seattle. People who had done the Inside Passage round-trip began to demand a new experience—a cruise across the Gulf. Princess and Holland America, sister companies in the Carnival Corp. family who had invested heavily in a physical presence in Alaska (hotels/lodges, motorcoaches, railcars for land tour add-ons in the Denali Park corridor btw. Anchorage and Fairbanks), began to see that route as the way to go. Princess tweaked the itinerary further, using Whittier rather than Seward as the northern terminal of its Gulf cruises because it was closer to Anchorage. (Not much, but when you're on vacation, every minute counts!) Royal Caribbean Cruises also has invested heavily in Denali railcars and motorcoaches for its Royal Caribbean International and Celebrity brands. Those lines that do not have a strong investment in Alaska land components still tend to stick with the Vancouver, BC—or Seattle-originating round-trip.

For your convenience, we've listed the **cruisetours and add-ons** you can book with your cruise, and we've provided brochure prices for these as well where possible—though some lines make their plans (and set their prices) early, others do not. Therefore, at press time, some of the numbers were not available.

## Prices: Don't Get Sticker Shock

We've listed the prices for cabins and suites. We stress that all the prices listed reflect the line's **brochure rates,** so depending on how early you book and any special deals the lines are offering, you may get a rate substantially below what we've listed. (Discounts can run as high as 60 percent or thereabouts.) Rates are per night for a 7-night cruise, per person, and are based on double occupancy. If the ship does not sail 7-night itineraries, we've noted that and given per diem rates for whatever itineraries it does sail. (The *Star Princess,* for instance, operates a 10- and 11-night round-trip Inside Passage pattern out of San Francisco.)

Our rates are based on the basic types of accommodations:

o Inside cabin (without windows)
o Outside cabin (with windows)
o Suite

Remember that cruise ships generally have several different categories of cabins within each of these three basic divisions, all priced differently, which is why, on some ships, you'll see a rather broad range in each category.

# weddings AT SEA

Lovers long have known that there is nothing as romantic as cruising. Luxury cruise ships have been vastly popular honeymoon vehicles for decades. And recently, with the growing popularity of cruises, they have assumed new significance in the marriage business. Ship operators now make it easier to tie the knot either in a port of call during the voyage or on board the vessel. Most lines will help you set it all up—for a fee, of course (and assuming you give them enough advance notice). They will provide the music, photographer, bouquets, champagne, hors d'oeuvres, cake, and other frills and fripperies. All you have to do is bring somebody to share your "I do" moment. The wedding package might cost you $1,000 or so in addition to the price of your cabin.

In Alaska this year, Carnival, Celebrity, Norwegian Cruise Line, Royal Caribbean, and Holland America Line allow you to hold your marriage ceremony in a specially decorated lounge on board while in port, officiated by a local clergyman or justice of the peace. Princess goes one better: Whereas before you could be married only on a handful of ships equipped with wedding chapels in which the captain himself would conduct the ceremony, now you can be wed on any ship in the Princess fleet, including those in Alaska in 2014. It's all perfectly legal. The ships now sail under a Bermuda registry, the authority under which your nuptials will be certified.

If you want guests to attend your special onboard moment while in port, the ship line must be notified well in advance, and your guests will be required to produce valid ID and to go through the same kind of screening process that passengers go through. Princess makes it easy for friends and family on shore to share the event by filming the entire process and then posting it on a special webcam found on its website (www.princess.com). Click on "Ships" and then "Bridge Cams." And, no, it's not really live. The images are there for all to see long after the rites are concluded.

No matter where you wed, you have to have a valid U.S. marriage license (or a Canadian license if you want to bid farewell to the single life in one of the British Columbia ports). The cruise line's wedding planner will help you set that up. Just remember to plan in advance—these things take time.

Please keep something else in mind. As they say in the business, "Buy as much cruise as you can afford." If you go in with the attitude that you refuse to buy anything but the least-expensive inside cabin, you may be doing yourself a disservice. The idea that "Oh, I'm not going to spend any time in my cabin anyway, so what does it matter if it's inside or outside, big or small?" isn't really valid. You *will* spend time in your cabin, and sometimes having no exposure to the outside world can be awfully claustrophobic. You may find that for a few hundred dollars more, you can upgrade to an outside room. Or if you're planning to pay for an outside cabin, you may find that you could reserve a room with a balcony if you dug just a little deeper into the purse. This is not to say you have to go deeply into debt to buy the best—just that you should investigate the possibility of buying something a little better.

# CARNIVAL CRUISE LINES

Carnival Place, 3655 NW 87th Ave., Miami, FL 33178-2428. ℰ **888/CARNIVAL** (227-6482). Fax 866/857-7090. www.carnival.com.

## Pros

- **Entertainment.** Carnival's entertainment is among the industry's best, with each ship boasting a large cast of dancers and singers who perform lively production numbers in a big theater, along with comedians, jugglers, and numerous live bands, as well as a big casino. Most recently, the line added the new Punchliner Comedy Club presented by George Lopez as well as Superstar Live—a karaoke-like experience where passengers can belt out tunes backed up by a live band and even backup singers.
- **Children's program.** Carnival long has had one of the best children's programs in the industry, and it keeps getting better. The line now has separate facilities, counselors, and nearly around-the-clock activities for each of three different age groups. Carnival's Alaska cruises, moreover, include Alaska-specific activities thrown into the mix, including a special series of shore excursions designed for teens.

## Cons

- **Service.** The international crew doesn't provide the type of service typically found on higher-end brands, but that's not the point here, is it?
- **Crowds.** This is a big ship with lots of people on board, and you are occasionally aware of that fact, like when you want to get off at a port and have to wait in line.

**THE LINE IN A NUTSHELL** Almost the definition of mass market, Carnival is the Big Kahuna of the industry, boasting a modern fleet of flashy megaships that cater to a fun-loving crowd. Nonstop entertainment (if you have the energy after a busy day of Alaska cruising) is the name of the game on board.

**THE EXPERIENCE** Carnival ships are known for spectacularly glitzy decor that some people love and others find overwhelming (and that's putting it nicely). Translating the line's warm-weather, fun-in-the-sun experience to Alaska has meant combining the "24 hours of good times" philosophy with opportunities to experience the natural wonders of the state, so you may find yourself bellying up to the rail with a multicolored umbrella drink to gawk at a glacier. The casino is nearly always hopping, although the festive atmosphere is a little more subdued in Alaska than on the line's Caribbean sailings. This, of course, is either a plus or a minus, depending on your taste. Carnival does not pretend to be a luxury experience. It doesn't claim to have gourmet food (although it's routinely praised for serving some of the best meals of any massmarket ship), and it doesn't promise around-the-clock pampering. The motto is "fun," and with a big focus on entertainment, friendly service, and creative cruise directors (they can be corny sometimes, but at least they're lively), that's what Carnival delivers.

**THE FLEET** Carnival has the biggest cruise fleet in the world with 24 ships, but only one, the 2,124-passenger *Carnival Miracle,* sails in Alaska. It has plenty of activities, great pool and hot-tub spaces (some covered for use in chillier weather), a big oceanview gym and spa, and more dining options than your doctor would say are advisable.

**PASSENGER PROFILE**   Overall, Carnival has some of the youngest demographics in the industry. But it's far more than age that defines the line's customers. Carnival executives are fond of using the word "spirited" to describe the typical Carnival passenger, and indeed, it's right on target. The line's many fans increasingly come from a wide range of ages as well as occupations, backgrounds, and income levels, but what they share is an unpretentious, fun-loving, and outgoing demeanor. This is a line for people who don't mind at all that their dinner will be interrupted by the loud music and flashing lights of a dance show starring their waiters. If anything, the typical Carnival passenger will want to jump right into the fray. On Carnival, you'll find couples, a few singles, and a good share of families (in fact, the line carries more than 725,000 kids a year—the most in the cruise industry). But the bottom line is this is not your average sedentary, bird-watching crowd. Passengers want to see whales, but they will also dance the Macarena.

**DINING OPTIONS**   Food is bountiful, and the cuisine is traditional American: Red meat is popular on these ships. In addition, delicious preparations of more "nouvelle" dishes include broiled Chilean sea bass with truffle butter or smoked turkey tenderloin with asparagus tips. The line features fresh salmon on Alaska sailings. Gourmet Spa Carnival Fare is on menus for those seeking healthier options. Pasta and vegetarian choices also are served nightly. Until recently, meals were always served at assigned tables, with two seatings per meal. But the line has also rolled out an alternative, eat-when-you-want dining option for passengers called Your Time dining. Passengers must sign up for Your Time dining in advance, in lieu of fixed seatings. The casual lunch buffets include international (Italian, Indian, and so on, with a different cuisine featured daily), deli, rotisserie, and pizza stations; the breakfast buffet has everything from made-to-order egg dishes to cold cereals and pastries. Many passengers prefer to eat their meals in the buffet rather than in the main dining room. As on many Carnival ships, the *Carnival Miracle* also adds the special treat of a truly superb reservations-only steakhouse, where, for a fee of $35 per person, you can dine on a great steak and other upscale culinary choices.

**ACTIVITIES**   If Atlantic City and Las Vegas appeal to you, Carnival will, too. What you'll get is fun—lots of it, professionally and consistently delivered and spangled with glitter. Cocktails inevitably begin to flow before lunch. You can learn to country line dance or play bridge, take cooking lessons, and watch first-run movies. Among the newer offerings on Alaska sailings is a photo safari in Juneau led by a professional photographer. Plus, there are always the onboard staple activities of eating, drinking, and shopping, and the Alaska-specific naturalist lectures that are delivered daily. Once in port, Carnival lives up to its "more is more" ethos by providing more than 120 shore excursions in Alaska. These are divided into categories of easy, moderate, and adventure. Internet cafes allow Internet access for 75¢ a minute, with a 10-minute minimum (discounted bulk-use packages also are available). The *Miracle* has also been outfitted with Wi-Fi for those who bring their own laptops (for the same fee as above).

**CHILDREN'S PROGRAMS**   Camp Carnival is an expertly run program for children ages 2 to 11, and it's loaded with kid-pleasing activities, allowing Mom and Dad some downtime. In Alaska these activities include everything from Native American arts-and-crafts sessions to lectures conducted by wildlife experts. On the *Carnival Miracle,* parents of little kids even can request beepers so that they can keep in touch. In recent years, Carnival also has added separate programs called Circle "C" for 12- to

| SHIP | ITINERARIES |
| --- | --- |
| *Carnival Miracle* | 7-night Inside Passage: Round-trip from Seattle, visiting Skagway, Juneau, Ketchikan, and Victoria, and cruising Tracy Arm Fjord (May–Aug) |

14-year-olds and Club O2 for children ages 15 to 17, each with dedicated facilities and separate staffs.

**ENTERTAINMENT** Carnival consistently has the most lavish entertainment extravaganzas afloat, spending millions on stage sets, choreography, and acoustical equipment that leave many other floating theaters in their wake. Each Carnival megaship carries flamboyantly costumed dancers and singers (the *Carnival Miracle* has a cast of about 20) and a 10-piece orchestra, plus comedians, magicians, jugglers, acrobats, and live bands playing everything from rock 'n' roll and country to big-band music. Carnival also is rolling out what it's calling Playlist Productions—featuring interactive high-tech LED screens and shorter, more frequent performances—to several ships as part of a multi-year, $500-million fleetwide upgrade.

**SERVICE** As we said before, Carnival service isn't exactly "refined" in the way you'd find on a luxury line, but it is certainly friendly and professional. A Carnival ship is a well-oiled machine, and you'll certainly get what you need—but not much more. When you board the ship, for instance, you're welcomed by polite staff at the gangway, given a diagram of the ship's layout, and then pointed in the right direction to find your cabin on your own, carry-on luggage in tow. On Carnival, gratuities of $11.50 per passenger per day are automatically charged to your shipboard account, but you can increase or decrease the amount by visiting the guest services desk on board.

A laundry service on board (for washing and pressing only) charges by the piece; it also has a handful of self-service laundry rooms with irons and coin-operated washing machines and dryers. Dry cleaning is not available.

**CRUISETOURS & ADD-ON PROGRAMS** None.

# Carnival Miracle

## The Verdict

The *Carnival Miracle* is glitzy Vegas, with more bars and lounges than you'll be able to visit. The dining room is two decks high, and it offers such cool extras as a reservations-only steakhouse and a wedding chapel.

## Specifications

| | | | |
| --- | --- | --- | --- |
| Size (in Tons) | 88,500 | Crew | 930 |
| Passengers (Double Occ.) | 2,124 | Passenger/Crew Ratio | 2.3 to 1 |
| Space/Passenger Ratio | 41.7 | Year Launched | 2004 |
| Total Cabins/Veranda Cabins | 1,062/682 | Last Major Refurbishment | N/A |

## Frommer's Ratings (Scale of 1–5)                              ★★★★

| | | | |
| --- | --- | --- | --- |
| Cabin Comfort & Amenities | 4 | Dining Options | 4 |
| Ship Cleanliness & Maintenance | 4 | Gym, Spa & Sports Facilities | 4.5 |
| Public Comfort/Space | 4 | Children's Facilities | 5 |
| Decor | 4 | Enjoyment Factor | 4 |

**THE SHIP IN GENERAL** The *Carnival Miracle* is big and impressive, even if some may find the interior a bit over-the-top (but after a few days on board, it may grow on you). Rooms are themed around "fabulous fictional icons" from Batman and Superman to characters from a Dashiell Hammett novel, with all sorts of (sometimes clashing) materials, from ebony paneling to faux stone walls, and lots of flash. In other words, legendary Carnival designer Joe Farcus has shown little restraint. Love it or not, you'll certainly be wowed.

**CABINS** Some 80 percent of the cabins on this ship boast ocean views; of those, 80 percent have private balconies, a big plus in a market like Alaska where views are the main draw. Cabins are larger than those you'll find on other lines in the same price category and are mostly furnished with twin beds that can be converted to king size. (A few have upper and lower berths that cannot be converted.) All cabins come with a TV, a wall safe, and a telephone; oceanview cabins also come with bathrobes and coral-colored leather couches with nifty storage drawers underneath. Connecting cabins are available for families or groups traveling together. Suites are offered at several different levels, each with separate sleeping, sitting, and dressing areas, plus double sinks, a bathtub, and a large balcony. Sixteen cabins are wheelchair-accessible. Carnival features the Carnival Comfort Bed sleep system with plush mattresses and fluffy duvets (no more scratchy wool blankets for this line). And not to miss a marketing opportunity, if you fall in love with the new linens and more, you can buy them online at **www.carnivalcomfortcollection.com**.

## CABINS & RATES

| CABINS | PER DIEM RATES | SQ. FT. | FRIDGE | HAIR DRYER | SITTING AREA | TV |
|---|---|---|---|---|---|---|
| **Inside Passage** | | | | | | |
| Inside | $125 | 185 | yes | yes | no | yes |
| Outside | $161 | 220–260* | yes | yes | yes | yes |
| Suites | $261 | 340–430* | yes | yes | yes | yes |
| **Gulf of Alaska** | | | | | | |
| Inside | $128 | 185 | yes | yes | no | yes |
| Outside | $164 | 220–260* | yes | yes | yes | yes |
| Suites | $264 | 340–430* | yes | yes | yes | yes |

*Includes veranda*

**PUBLIC AREAS** The ship's soaring atrium spans 11 decks. There are dozens of bars and lounges, including a piano bar, a sports bar, and a jazz club. A lobby bar provides live music and a chance to take in the vast dimensions of the ship. A particularly fun room is the two-level disco; depending on your particular Alaska sailing, it may be hopping until dawn or may just host a few stragglers late at night. A better hangout spot, we think, is the nearby Deco bar, where a combo plays nightly (we've even seen the captain hanging out here).

The ship, which is part of the line's Spirit class, consciously offers the best features of the line's earlier Fantasy class ships, including an expansive outdoor area with four swimming pools (a retractable dome over the main pool lets you can take a dip no matter what the weather), four whirlpools, and a waterslide; a high-tech children's play center with computers and a wall of video monitors; a multilevel oceanview fitness facility; numerous clubs and lounges; and a variety of eating and entertainment options. Among the interesting features is a wedding chapel, as well as a mostly outdoor promenade (if you are doing a full tour around the ship, you have to take a few steps inside). The ship also has ultramodern engines and waste treatment and disposal systems to make it more environmentally friendly. And the *Carnival Miracle* offers more space per passenger than most ships in the Alaska market.

The hundreds of onboard activities for which Carnival is famous, including Vegas-style shows and casino action (the ship's Mr. Lucky's casino, themed after a 1943 Cary Grant movie, is one of the largest at sea), keep passengers on the *Carnival Miracle* on the fast track to that famous and oft-mentioned fun. It's up to you to find time to stop and catch the scenery, which you can do both from the generous open-deck spaces and from some (but not many) indoor spaces. For kids, there's a children's playroom, children's pool, and video arcade. The *Carnival Miracle*'s library doubles as an Internet cafe, though the clicking of computers may be annoying to those who want to read a book. Shoppers will find plenty of enticements at the ship's shopping arcade, including Fendi and Tommy Hilfiger products.

Carnival passengers also have the capability of using their personal cellphones anywhere at sea.

**DINING OPTIONS** The ship's handsome atrium is topped with a red stained-glass dome that is part of Nick & Nora's steakhouse, a reservations-only ($35 per person supplement) restaurant. Some people might consider the nightspot a little pricey, but this is not your run-of-the mill restaurant operating by filling tables with two or three changes of customers in the evening. Rather, it's an intimate room in which passengers are encouraged to linger and savor a truly elegant and enjoyable experience. The two-level main dining room is done up in Napoleonic splendor. A 24-hour poolside pizzeria and 24-hour room service keep you from getting hungry.

**POOL, FITNESS, SPA & SPORTS FACILITIES** The ship has three pools, including one with a retractable dome, as well as a children's splash pool. A freestanding waterslide is on the top deck. The gym has an interesting tiered design and more than 50 exercise machines, as well as a spacious aerobics studio. There are windows, so you won't miss the scenery. The spa has a dozen treatment rooms and an indoor sunning area with a whirlpool. The ship also has three additional whirlpools and a jogging/walking track (10 laps=1 mile).

# CELEBRITY CRUISES

1050 Caribbean Way, Miami, FL 33132. ℂ **800/647-2251** or 305/262-8322. Fax 800/437-5111. www.celebritycruises.com.

## Pros

○ **Spectacular spas and gyms.** Beautiful to look at and well stocked, the spas and gyms on *Celebrity Solstice, Celebrity Century,* and *Celebrity Millennium* (and Celebrity's other non-Alaska megaships) are among the best at sea today and set the standard followed by other lines.

○ **Fabulous food.** Celebrity cuisine is rated high among mainstream cruise lines.

○ **Innovative everything.** Celebrity's entertainment, art, service, spas, and cuisine are some of the most groundbreaking in the industry. Its ships were among the first in the industry to display major art collections on board, and its menus have long recognized the need for vegetarian, low-sodium, heart-conscious, and other healthy dishes.

## Cons

○ **Occasional crowding.** Pack a couple thousand people onto a ship (pretty much any ship), and you'll get crowds at times, such as during buffets and when disembarking.

○ **So-so kids programs.** While Celebrity ships offer a full day of activities for children, kids' facilities and programs are less elaborate and enticing than those found on more family-focused mainstream lines such as Carnival, Princess, and Disney.

**THE LINE IN A NUTSHELL**   With a premium fleet that's among the best designed in the cruise industry, Celebrity Cruises offers a great experience: classy, tasteful, and luxurious. You'll be pampered at a relatively reasonable price.

**THE EXPERIENCE**   Each of the Celebrity ships is spacious and comfortable, mixing modern and Art Deco styles and boasting an astoundingly cutting-edge art collection. The line's genteel service is noticeable: Staff members in our experience are polite and professional and contribute greatly to the cruise experience. Dining-wise, Celebrity shines, offering innovative cuisine that's a cut above the fare served by some of the other mainstream lines.

Celebrity gets the "best of" nod in a lot of categories: The AquaSpa by Elemis on the line's megaships are tops for mainstream lines, the art collections fleetwide are the most compelling, and the onboard activities are among the most varied. Like all the big-ship lines, Celebrity has lots for its guests to do, but it focuses on mellower pursuits and innovative programming.

It's interesting to note that Celebrity (and its sister company, Royal Caribbean International) has been an early champion of the new Alaska port of Icy Strait Point. The port is growing—it was created from a cannery dock—and lies between Juneau and Glacier Bay, with a prime vantage point for whale- and wildlife-watching and easier access to the Alaskan wilderness.

**THE FLEET**   Celebrity's current Alaska fleet comprises one of the line's newest, most celebrated ships, the *Celebrity Solstice* (122,000 tons, 2,850 passengers) and the somewhat older *Celebrity Millennium* (91,000 tons, 2,158 passengers) and *Celebrity Century* (71,545 tons, 1,814 passengers). All three ships have a high degree of decorative panache and just the right combination of elegance, artfulness, excitement, and fun.

**PASSENGER PROFILE**   The typical Celebrity guest is one who prefers to pursue his or her R&R at a relatively relaxed pace, with a minimum of aggressively promoted group activities. The overall atmosphere leans more toward sophistication and less to the kind of orgiastic Technicolor whoopee that you'll find aboard, say, a Carnival ship. Celebrity passengers are the type who prefer wine with dinner and maybe a tad more decorum than on some other ships, but they can kick up their heels with the beer-and-pretzels crowd just fine if the occasion warrants. Most give the impression of being prosperous but not obscenely rich, congenial but not obsessively proper, animated and fun but not the type to wear a lampshade for a hat. You'll find everyone from kids to retirees, with a good number of couples in their 40s.

**DINING**   Celebrity's cuisine, plentiful and served with style, is extra special and leans toward American/European. This means that dishes are generally not low-fat, although the line has eliminated trans fats and in 2013 brought in healthy-eating organization SPE Certified to consult on and certify dozens of dishes in Celebrity's main restaurants. The company's dining program is under the leadership of John Suley, a highly talented and experienced chef who was once nominated as a "rising star" by the prestigious James Beard Foundation.

Celebrity's Alaska cruises serve an array of Pacific Northwest regional specialties, and vegetarian dishes are featured at both lunch and dinner. If three meals a day in both informal and formal settings are not enough for you, Celebrity has one of the most extensive 24-hour room-service menus in the industry, plus themed lunch buffets and one to two (depending on the itinerary length) special brunches. Meals in the alternative dining rooms on *Century, Millennium,* and *Solstice,* served on a reservations-only basis, generally are worth the extra charges of up to $45 per person; in some cases, they are among the best romantic restaurants at sea.

You can dine formally in the dining room or informally at buffets for breakfast and lunch, with a sushi bar and made-to-order pastas and pizzas served nightly in the Oceanview Cafe. Dinner is served at two seatings in the main dining room. Four years ago, the line also introduced the option of open seating in the dining room; you choose either traditional or open seating Celebrity Select Dining before your cruise. The AquaSpa Cafe, in a corner of the Solarium pool area, serves low-cal treats, including raw veggie platters, poached salmon with asparagus tips, vegetarian sushi, and pretty salads with tuna or chicken (this is a hidden secret worth finding).

**ACTIVITIES**    The line offers a laundry list of activities through its all-encompassing enrichment program. A typical day might involve a Rosetta Stone language course, bridge, a culinary demonstration, a chef's cook-off, distinct wine tastings in partnership with the renowned Riedel Crystal, an art auction, and a volleyball tournament. Lectures on the various ports of call, some by Smithsonian speakers, the Alaska environment, glaciers, and Alaska culture are given by resident naturalists, who also provide commentary from the bridge as the ships arrive in port and at other times are available for one-on-one discussions with passengers. Celebrity iLounge, the brand's chic version of the Internet cafe, allows e-mail access for 75¢ a minute, with discount packages also available. The line was among the first to offer an Acupuncture at Sea program.

**CHILDREN'S PROGRAMS**    For children, Celebrity ships employ a group of counselors who direct and supervise a camp-style children's program with activities geared toward different age groups. Though not as elaborate as the kids' facilities on the ships of some other mainstream lines, Celebrity's ships offer kids' play areas and a separate lounge area for teens that, among other things, now feature Xbox-themed spaces for organized Xbox-related activities and games (new as of mid-2013). Private and group babysitting are both available.

**ENTERTAINMENT**    Although entertainment is not generally cited as a reason to sail with Celebrity, the line's stage shows are none too shabby. You won't find any big-name entertainers, but you also won't find any obvious has-beens either—there's just a whole lot of singin' and dancin'. If you tire of the glitter, you can always find a cozy lounge or piano bar to curl up in, and if you tire of that, the disco and casino stay open late.

**SERVICE**    In the cabins, service is efficient and so unobtrusive that you might never see your steward except at the beginning and end of your cruise. In the dining rooms, service is polite, professional, and cheerful. Five-star service can be had at the onboard beauty salon or barbershop, and massages can be scheduled at any hour of the day in the AquaSpa. Laundry, dry cleaning, and valet services are also available. If you stay in a suite, you really will be treated like royalty, with a tuxedo-clad butler at your beck

## Celebrity Fleet Itineraries

| SHIP | ITINERARIES |
|---|---|
| *Celebrity Solstice* | 7-night Tracy Arm Fjord: Round-trip cruises from Seattle visiting Ketchikan, Juneau, Victoria, BC, and Skagway, in addition to cruising the Inside Passage and beside Sawyer Glacier (May–Sept) |
| *Celebrity Century* | 7-night Hubbard Glacier: Round-trip cruises from Vancouver, BC, visiting Ketchikan, Hubbard Glacier, Icy Strait Point, Juneau, and Inside Passage (May–Sept) |
| | 11-night "Golden Light" itinerary: One-way from Vancouver, BC to San Francisco, visiting Ketchikan, Icy Strait Point, Juneau, Skagway, Tracy Arm, and Victoria, BC (Aug. 24) |
| | 12-night "Golden Gate" itinerary: Round-trip from San Francisco, visiting Ketchikan, Icy Strait Point, Juneau, Skagway, Tracy Arm, Victoria, BC, and Astoria, Ore. (Sept. 4) |
| *Celebrity Millennium* | 7-night North- and Southbound Gulf of Alaska: Sails from Vancouver, BC, to Seward and reverse, visiting Juneau, Skagway, Icy Strait Point, Ketchikan, and Hubbard Glacier (May–Sept) |

and call. The butler will serve you afternoon tea (or free cappuccino or espresso) and bring predinner hors d'oeuvres. And yes, the butler will gladly shine your shoes, too, at your request. Also available for those who can't quite afford a suite are Concierge Class rooms that come with such perks as fresh flowers and fruit, a choice of pillow types, and oversize towels. On Celebrity ships, gratuities of $12 per passenger per day are automatically charged to your shipboard account ($12.50 per person per day for those staying in Concierge Class and AquaClass cabins), but you can increase or decrease the amount by visiting the guest relations desk on board.

**CRUISETOURS & ADD-ON PROGRAMS** Celebrity is offering 9 cruisetours in 2014 in conjunction with its sailings on *Celebrity Millennium,* ranging in length from 10 to 13 nights. All of Celebrity's cruisetours include a combination of travel through the interior of Alaska in deluxe motorcoaches and the company's Wilderness Express glass domed railcars, at least 1 night visiting Denali National Park, and the expert advice of a tour director who travels with customers for the entire journey. For vacationers seeking the ultimate cruisetour experience, there also is a 19-night package available that includes a 6-night pre- or post-cruise Canadian Rockies land tour, a 7-night Alaska cruise, and a 6-night pre- or post-cruise Alaska land tour.

## Celebrity Solstice

### The Verdict

This ship is a true winner, combining the kind of luxury you'd expect at a great contemporary hotel with all the leisure, sports, and entertainment options of megaships. If this ship was a high school senior, it'd be heading to Harvard. It is best in its class.

### Specifications

| | | | |
|---|---|---|---|
| Size (in Tons) | 122,000 | Crew | 1,250 |
| Passengers (Double Occ.) | 2,850 | Passenger/Crew Ratio | 2 to 1 |
| Space/Passenger Ratio | 43 | Year Launched | 2008 |
| Total Cabins/Veranda Cabins | 1,426/1,216 | Last Major Refurbishment | 2010 |

## Frommer's Rating (Scale 1–5)                          ★★★★★

| | | | |
|---|---|---|---|
| Cabin Comfort & Amenities | 5 | Dining Options | 5 |
| Ship Cleanliness & Maintenance | 5 | Gym, Spa & Sports Facilities | 5 |
| Public Comfort/Space | 4.5 | Children's Facilities | 4 |
| Decor | 5 | Enjoyment Factor | 5 |

**THE SHIP IN GENERAL**  Heralded as groundbreaking when it debuted in 2008, *Celebrity Solstice* remains one of Celebrity's most stunning ships. Stylish and contemporary, the line's first Solstice class vessel (there are now five) features interiors created by noted designer Adam Tihany, including a dramatic, two-level dining room that features a soaring glass wine tower; a pool deck with a sleek, South Beach vibe; a sumptuous spa; and some of the most enticing specialty restaurants at sea. It also boasts the industry's first deck-top "lawn club" with a half-acre of live grass—a place for outdoor games such as bocce that has proven a hit with customers (there is now one on each of Solstice's four sisters).

**CABINS**  Celebrity took its cabins up a notch with the debut of the Solstice class. *Celebrity Solstice*'s cabins are about 15 percent larger, on average, than those on earlier classes of Celebrity ships. Even the smallest inside cabins are a respectable 183 square feet and boast relatively large bathrooms (with new touches such as footrests in showers), sitting areas with sofas, and entertainment units. Slightly smaller are the ship's 70 ocean-view cabins without balconies, which measure 176 square feet, while the majority of ocean-view cabins with balconies measure 192 square feet, not including 53 square feet of outdoor space on their balconies (floor-to-ceiling sliding glass doors lead to the outside). Suites come in several sizes and offer such accoutrements as whirlpool tubs, DVD players, and walk-in closets. The fanciest suites also have whirlpools on the veranda. The two apartment-size Penthouse Suites (1,291 sq. ft. each, not including their balconies) feature bedrooms with walk-in-closets, marble-lined master baths with whirlpool tubs and separate showers; living rooms with dining areas, a baby grand piano, and a full bar with lounge seating. Thirty cabins are wheelchair-accessible, including several suites.

### CABINS & RATES

| CABINS | PER DIEM RATES | SQ. FT. | FRIDGE | HAIR DRYER | SITTING AREA | TV |
|---|---|---|---|---|---|---|
| **Celebrity Solstice** | | | | | | |
| Inside | $135–$225 | 183 | yes | yes | no | yes |
| Outside | $163–$314 | 176–192 | yes | yes | yes | yes |
| Suites | $342–$1,085 | 251–1,291 | yes | yes | yes | yes |

**PUBLIC AREAS**  A highlight of *Celebrity Solstice* is the Lawn Club, a half-acre hideaway at the top of the ship that features a broad expanse of live grass and such outdoor games as lawn bowling. It's a cruise ship rarity, for sure, and a hit with passengers (enough so that Celebrity installed similar Lawn Clubs on the ship's four sisters). The Lawn Club is home to a small putting green and, perhaps most notably, an outdoor glass-blowing studio where passengers can watch periodic glass-blowing demonstrations. Snacks are available at the adjacent Patio on the Lawn, and the adjacent Sunset Bar is a haven. Down below, on the ship's interior decks, there's also a grand shopping boulevard, casino, champagne bar, theater, beauty salon, library, Celebrity iLounge, children's center, teen room, arcade, and more.

**DINING OPTIONS** Noted designer Adam Tihany designed the ship's dramatic, two-story main dining room, the 1,429-seat Grand Epernay, which features a two-story glass wine tower. It serves elaborate, multicourse dinners nightly in two seatings and is also open for breakfast and lunch. The ship also has a wide array of alternative dining venues that, alas, come with fairly steep extra charges, including the Tihany-designed, 132-seat Italian steakhouse Tuscan Grille ($35 per person); the 88-seat Asian fusion eatery Silk Harvest ($30 per person); and 76-seat Murano ($45 per person), which serves classic and modern international cuisine. Located near the top of the vessel is the Oceanview Cafe, the ship's casual buffet eatery. With 632 seats, it's not only spacious, but one of the most diverse buffets at sea, with a wide range of choices. The ship also has a creperie called Bistro on Five ($5 per person) and the upscale Cafe al Bacio and Gelateria, which serves gourmet coffees, pastries and ice cream at an extra charge.

After dinner, Michael's Club, decorated with leather chairs and men's club coziness, offers piano entertainment. More than half a dozen other bars are spread around the ship, including a Martini Bar and a separate wine bar called CellarMasters that boasts a state-of-the-art "Enomatic" wine serving system.

**POOL, FITNESS, SPA & SPORTS FACILITIES** Celebrity Solstice is home to one of the most lovely spas at sea, the AquaSpa, which is run by spa company Elemis, Ltd., a division of spa giant Steiner. It features the Persian Garden, a tranquil area that includes a coed sauna and steam room, tropical rain shower, and heated relaxation chairs that face the sea (passengers can pay a daily or weekly fee for access). Nearby is the adults-only Solarium, a soaring, glass-enclosed space with plush chairs, a lap pool and two whirlpools. The ship also has a striking main pool area with a pool and four hot tubs and a South Beach vibe. For exercise fans, a very large, well-equipped fitness center is located near the spa, with dozens of cardio and weight machines, and a jogging track is up on one of the ship's top decks (8 laps equals 1 mile). The top decks also have facilities for basketball, volleyball, and paddle tennis.

## Celebrity Millennium

### The Verdict

A recent overhaul has breathed new life into this 14-year-old vessel, which remains a solid option for cruisers looking for a stylish, contemporary experience.

### Specifications

| Size (in Tons) | 91,000 | Crew | 999 |
|---|---|---|---|
| Passengers (Double Occ.) | 2,158 | Passenger/Crew Ratio | 2 to 1 |
| Space/Passenger Ratio | 46 | Year Launched | 2000 |
| Total Cabins/Veranda Cabins | 975/590 | Last Major Refurbishment | April 2012 |

### Frommer's Rating (Scale 1–5)                    ★★★★ ½

| Cabin Comfort & Amenities | 4 | Dining Options | 4.5 |
|---|---|---|---|
| Ship Cleanliness & Maintenance | 5 | Gym, Spa & Sports Facilities | 4 |
| Public Comfort/Space | 4 | Children's Facilities | 3.5 |
| Decor | 4 | Enjoyment Factor | 4 |

**THE SHIP IN GENERAL**   When *Celebrity Millennium* debuted in 2000, it was hailed as one of the most spectacular ships afloat. While no longer the belle of the ball at Celebrity (that distinction now goes to the line's new Solstice class ships), it's still an elegant vessel with a lot to offer—particularly after a massive overhaul in April 2012. The ship now boasts several new eateries and other features that first debuted on Solstice class ships as well as revamped cabins that reflect the latest in cruise ship style.

**CABINS**   During the April 2012 overhaul, which took place in an extended dry dock, the Celebrity Millennium's cabins received all new upholstery, bedding, and carpeting, as well as new flatscreen TVs. The smallest inside cabins are 170 square feet and boast minibars, sitting areas with sofas, and entertainment units. Premium oceanview cabins measure 191 square feet, and large oceanview cabins with verandas that are indeed large—271 square feet, with floor-to-ceiling sliding glass doors leading outside. Suites (also completely redone during the ship's overhaul) come in several sizes and offer such accoutrements as whirlpool tubs, DVD players, and walk-in closets. The fanciest suites also have whirlpools on the veranda. The two apartment-size Penthouse Suites (1,432 sq. ft. each), designed to evoke Park Avenue apartments, have all the above plus separate living and dining rooms, a foyer, a grand piano, a butler's pantry, a bedroom, exercise equipment, an outbound fax, and—sure to be a favorite accessory—motorized drapes. Twenty-six cabins are wheelchair-accessible.

### CABINS & RATES

| CABINS | PER DIEM RATES | SQ. FT. | FRIDGE | HAIR DRYER | SITTING AREA | TV |
|--------|----------------|---------|--------|------------|--------------|-----|
| Inside | $100–$149 | 170 | yes | yes | yes | yes |
| Outside | $128–$328 | 170–191 | yes | yes | yes | yes |
| Suites | $357–$999 | 251–1,432 | yes | yes | yes | yes |

**PUBLIC AREAS**   Like all Celebrity ships, the Millennium features a stylish, contemporary decor, with a splash of old-world charm. The dramatic, three-deck high Grand Foyer, with its sweeping staircase, is the heart of the vessel's interior. It's home to the ship's guest relations and shore excursion desks, a concierge, and the Captain's Club for frequent Celebrity cruisers. From the Grand Foyer, passengers can stroll up to Deck 4, the hub of the ship's evening entertainment, with bars, eateries, and other venues including the photo gallery. The Emporium, an area for shopping, is one more deck up on Deck 5, and Deck 6 is home to a Celebrity iLounge, an iMac-lined Internet cafe developed in partnership with Apple and also used for (extra-charge) technology classes that focus on Apple products. The Millennium also has a two-story library, Words, on Decks 8 and 9, with the floors connected by a spiral staircase. A top spot for looking out over the ocean is Cosmos, a lounge at the front top of the ship with floor-to-ceiling windows. There's also a casino on board (isn't there always?).

**DINING OPTIONS**   The ship has a two-tier dining room that features live music by a pianist or a quartet. It also provides a gourmet dining experience in a wonderfully intimate and romantic alternative restaurant called the Olympic (reservations required; it costs an extra $35 per person for dinner). Dinner is served in the main dining room in two seatings, as well as in the Oceanview Cafe and the AquaSpa Cafe. New since the ship's 2012 overhaul is Qsine, the playful, food-as-art eatery first unveiled in 2010 on the line's *Celebrity Eclipse,* and Blu, the Mediterranean-themed specialty restaurant for AquaClass passengers that debuted on *Celebrity Solstice* in 2008. Qsine costs $45 per person; Blu comes with no extra charge for passengers in AquaClass spa cabins and a small charge (currently $5) for passengers in suites. The ship also got a creperie called Bistro on Five ($5 per person) and a Cafe al Bacio and Gelateria (both venues that first appeared on *Celebrity Solstice*).

After dinner, Michael's Club, decorated like the parlor of a London men's club and devoted to the pleasures of live jazz and piano entertainment and fine cognac, comes into its own. Several other bars are tucked into the nooks and crannies of the ships, including a new ice-topped Martini Bar and a separate wine bar called CellarMasters that boasts a state-of-the-art "Enomatic" wine serving system.

**POOL, FITNESS, SPA & SPORTS FACILITIES**   Spa aficionados, listen up: The *Millennium* will not disappoint. The ship's 25,000-square-foot AquaSpa complex provides a range of esoteric hydrotherapy treatments; a suite of beautiful New Age steam rooms and saunas; and a huge free-of-charge thalassotherapy whirlpool. In addition, there is the usual array of massage and beauty procedures, plus some unusual ones, such as an Egyptian ginger-and-milk treatment. Next door to the spa is a very large, well-equipped cardio room and a large aerobics floor. On the top decks are facilities for basketball, volleyball, quoits (a game akin to horseshoes), and paddle tennis; a jogging track; a golf simulator; two pools; four whirlpools; and a multitiered sunning area. The swimming pool features a waterfall.

# Celebrity Century

### The Verdict

Nearly 2 decades old, but still a charmer.

### Specifications

| Size (in Tons) | 71,545 | Crew | 860 |
|---|---|---|---|
| Passengers (Double Occ.) | 1,814 | Passenger/Crew Ratio | 2.1 to 1 |
| Space/Passenger Ratio | 41 | Year Launched | 1995 |
| Total Cabins/Veranda Cabins | 639/220 | Last Major Refurbishment | 2006 |

### Frommer's Rating (Scale 1–5)                                    ★★★★

| Cabin Comfort & Amenities | 4.5 | Dining Options | 4 |
|---|---|---|---|
| Ship Cleanliness & Maintenance | 4 | Gym, Spa & Sports Facilities | 4 |
| Public Comfort/Space | 4 | Children's Facilities | 4 |
| Decor | 4 | Enjoyment Factor | 4.5 |

**THE SHIP IN GENERAL**   It's hard to say what's most striking about *Celebrity Century.* The elegant spa and its 15,000-gallon thalassotherapy pool? The twin three-and four-story atria with serpentine staircases that seem to float without supports and domed ceilings of painted glass? The two-story, classically designed dining room set back in the stern, with grand floor-to-ceiling windows, allowing diners to spot the glow of the wake under moonlight? The industry's first "ice" martini bar? The Murano specialty restaurant? An intriguing modern-art collection? Take your pick: Any one points to a winner. We really like this ship!

**CABINS**   Inside cabins are about par for the industry standard, but outside cabins are larger than usual, and suites, which come in five different categories, are particularly spacious. Some, such as the Penthouse Suites, have more living space than you find in many private homes, and the Sky Suites have verandas that, at 179 square feet, are among the biggest aboard any ship. During the ship's 2006 dry-dock, 314 new verandas were added.

All cabins are accented with wood trim and outfitted with built-in vanities. Closets and drawer space are roomy, and all standard cabins have twin beds that, when pushed together, convert into one full-size bed. Bathrooms are sizable and stylish. Celebrity is fond of high-tech gizmos, and you can actually order food, gamble, or check your bill from the comfort of your cabin via your interactive TV.

Butler service is provided to suite guests. Ten cabins are wheelchair-accessible.

## CABINS & RATES

| CABINS | PER DIEM RATES | SQ. FT. | FRIDGE | HAIR DRYER | SITTING AREA | TV |
|--------|----------------|---------|--------|------------|--------------|-----|
| Inside | $99–$221 | 175 | yes | yes | no | yes |
| Outside | $157–$304 | 210 | yes | yes | yes | yes |
| Suites | $271–$785 | 1,433 | yes | yes | yes | yes |

**PUBLIC AREAS**   The interior of this ship is the product of a collaboration between a dozen design firms that have created a diverse yet harmonious whole providing just the right atmosphere without resorting to glitz. Our favorite is the champagne bar with champagne bubbles etched into the wall.

Throughout the ship, artwork from a multimillion-dollar art collection sometimes greets you at unexpected moments. Read the tags and you'll be impressed to find names such as Sol LeWitt, who designed a mural specifically for the vessel. There is a coffee bar for those craving caffeine, and various other bars pepper the ship and are great venues for spending time with friends.

The ship has a two-deck theater with an unobstructed view from every seat if you want to take in a stage show, and a cinema if you're in the mood for film. If you're looking for more active pleasures, there's always the disco and casino. For kids there's a children's playroom, a children's pool, a teen center, and a video arcade. When the ship was refurbished in 2006, besides tacking on 314 new verandas, Celebrity added a specialty restaurant called Murano, a new Spa Cafe, and a new martini "ice" bar, as well as a new reception area in the AquaSpa and 10 new sea-view treatment rooms.

**DINING OPTIONS**   In addition to a main dining room, the ship has the Oceanview Cafe, which serves up breakfast, lunch, and a more casual dinner (the latter with menu as well as buffet service). The Lido Buffet also is home to a made-to-order pasta and pizza bar. But the most upscale venue on the ship is Murano, a $45-per-person specialty restaurant. There's also a AquaSpa Cafe.

**POOL, FITNESS, SPA & SPORTS FACILITIES**   Mercury's AquaSpa features a Moorish theme, with ornate tile work and latticed wood. It has a large thalassotherapy pool, plus steam rooms and saunas. The spa also features sometimes pricey Elemis of London health and beauty services, including hairdressing, pedicures, manicures, massages, and various herbal treatments. The attached fitness area has exceptionally large cardiovascular floors and a full complement of exercise machines. Prearranged spa packages that you book before your cruise are also available.

The ship features a pair of good-size swimming areas rimmed with teak benches for sunning and relaxation. Even when the ship is full, these areas don't seem particularly crowded. A basketball court, jogging/walking track, fitness center, golf simulator, and volleyball court also are available.

# DISNEY CRUISE LINE

P.O. Box 10238, Lake Buena Vista, FL 32830. ℂ **888/325-2500.** Fax 407/566-3541. www.disney cruise.com.

## Pros

- **Great children's program.** Would you expect anything less from Disney? In both the size of facilities and the range of activities, this is a line that's hard to beat.
- **Disney-quality entertainment.** The line shows family-oriented musicals that are some of the best onboard entertainment today.
- **Family-style cabins.** It's rare in the cruise business to find so many large, family-friendly cabins that can sleep three, four, or even five people.

## Cons

- **Limited adult entertainment.** Forget about a night out gambling—this is one of just a few ships at sea without a casino. There's an adult-only night entertainment area on board, but it's often quiet.
- **Crowded pools.** Disney ships are kid magnets, and that can have a downside on sunny days when children come out of the woodwork to hit the pools.
- **The cost.** Compared to other big ship lines such as Carnival and Norwegian, Disney is pricey, running at least a few hundred dollars more per person for a week. In short, you pay a premium for The Mouse.

**THE LINE IN A NUTSHELL**  Disney's cruising arm isn't large (just four ships), but the company is the Big Kahuna when it comes to family-geared cruising. Though a number of big lines including Royal Caribbean, Carnival, and Norwegian Cruise Line have long offered wonderful programs for children, it was Disney that first set out to create a family vacation that would be as relaxing for parents as for their offspring. If you love Disney's resorts on land, you'll love the company's ships.

**THE EXPERIENCE**  Both classic and ultra-modern, the line's ships (only one of which will be in Alaska in 2014) are like no others in the industry, designed to evoke the grand transatlantic liners of old but also boasting some truly innovative features, such as extra-large cabins for families and a trio of restaurants through which passengers rotate on every cruise. Disney is known for entertainment, of course, and its ships don't disappoint, with Disney-inspired shows. The vessels also boast separate adult pools and lounges and the biggest kids' facilities at sea. In many ways, the experience is more Disney than it is cruise (for instance, there's no casino); on the other hand, the ships are surprisingly elegant and well laid out, with little Disney touches sprinkled all around.

**THE FLEET**  The 1,754-passenger *Disney Wonder* is the line's only ship in Alaska, a relatively new destination for Disney (the company didn't offer cruises in the region until 2011). The streamlined vessel is chock-full of activities for kids, with great pools (including one shaped like Mickey's head) and adult-only areas, too.

**PASSENGER PROFILE** Disney's ships attract a wide mix of passengers, from honeymooners to seniors, but as one might expect, a big percentage is made up of young American families with children. (This isn't a big line for foreign passengers, though you'll see a few.) Because of the allure to families with younger children, the average age of passengers tends to be lower than aboard most other cruise ships. Many adult passengers are in their 30s and early to mid-40s. The bulk of the line's passengers are first-time cruisers, and because the line attracts so many families (sometimes large ones), many of its bookings are for multiple cabins.

**DINING** Disney offers a traditional fixed-seating type plan for dinners, but with a twist. Each of its ships has three main restaurants—each with a different theme—among which passengers (and their servers) rotate over the course of a cruise. On one night, passengers dine on dishes such as roasted duck or garlic-roasted beef tenderloin in a green peppercorn sauce in the nautical-themed Triton's restaurant. On another night, they enjoy the likes of potato-crusted grouper, baby-back pork ribs, or mixed grill in the tropical Parrot Cay restaurant. And then it's on to Animator's Palate, a bustling eatery with a gimmick: It's a sort of living animation cell, with walls decorated with black-and-white sketches of Disney characters that over the course of the meal gradually become filled in with color. Video screens add to the illusion, and even the waiters' outfits change as the evening wears on. Disney also offers a romantic, adults-only Italian specialty restaurant on board its ships called Palo that comes with an extra charge ($20 per person). Breakfast and lunch are served in several restaurants, both sit-down and buffet. Pluto's Dog House, on the main pool deck, serves up kid-friendly basics such as chicken fingers, fries, burgers, and nachos; nearby Goofy's Galley offers wraps, fresh fruit, and other more healthful fare. One notable feature of Disney ships that sets them apart from other big, mass-market vessels is that soft drinks are included in the fare, and you can find self-serve soda machines around the pool deck and in the buffet area.

**ACTIVITIES** Disney offers an array of activities similar to other big-ship lines, with one big exception: There's no casino. (Disney executives apparently decided a casino just didn't fit with the line's family-friendly image.) Besides lounging at the pool or (for kids) heading to the kids' program, the array of options on board includes basketball, Ping-Pong, and shuffleboard tournaments; sports trivia contests; weight-loss, health, and beauty seminars; bingo, Pictionary, and other games; wine tastings; and singles mixers (though these family-focused cruises aren't the best choice for singles). Each ship also has a spa and gym, and enrichment activities include galley tours; backstage theater tours; informal lectures on nautical themes and Disney history as well as current Disney productions; animation and drawing classes; and home entertainment and cooking demonstrations. All these activities come with no extra charge except for wine tastings, which cost a hefty $15 per person. There also are dance classes and movies, and all voyages include a captain's cocktail party with complimentary drinks once per cruise, where the master of the ship and (this being Disney) a gaggle of characters make an appearance.

**CHILDREN'S PROGRAMS** Disney's kids' facilities are, famously, the most extensive at sea, spreading across a good part of an entire deck (what the ship lacks in

| SHIP | ITINERARIES |
| --- | --- |
| *Disney Wonder* | 7-night Inside Passage: Round-trip from Vancouver, BC, visiting Skagway, Juneau, and Ketchikan, and cruising Tracy Arm Fjord (May–Sept.) |

casino space it makes up for with extra kids' space). The ships carry dozens of children's counselors who look after groups split into five age groups. Broken up into several areas, the children's zone generally is open between 9am and midnight. The **Oceaneer Club,** for ages 3 to 10, is a kiddie-size playroom themed around Captain Hook. Kids can climb and crawl on the bridge, ropes, and rails of a giant pirate ship, as well as on jumbo-size animals, barrels, and a sliding board; play dress-up from trunks full of costumes; dance with Snow White and listen to stories by other Disney characters; or play in the kiddie computer room on PlayStations. The interactive **Oceaneer Lab** offers kids ages 3 to 10 a chance to work on computers, learn fun science with microscopes, do arts and crafts, hear how animation works, and direct their own TV commercial.

New to the *Disney Wonder* is Edge, an exclusive hangout for tweens (ages 11–13). The club is located on Deck 2, midship. For teens the Wonder has a hangout called Vibe that has two separate rooms, one with video screens for movies and the other a disco with a teens-only Internet center. Dance parties, karaoke, trivia games, improv comedy lessons, and workshops on photography are offered for teens on every voyage.

One thing Disney doesn't do is private babysitting. Instead, there's Flounder's Reef Nursery for kids ages 3 months to 3 years ($6 per hour for the first child, $5 per each additional child; hours vary depending on the day's port schedule, and space is limited, so book well in advance). No other lines offer such extensive care for babies.

**ENTERTAINMENT** Family-friendly entertainment is one of the highlights of being on a Disney ship, and as one might expect, Disney characters and movies often are front and center in the line's onboard productions. Performances by Broadway-caliber entertainers in the nostalgic Walt Disney Theatre include *Disney Dreams: An Enchanted Classic,* a musical medley of Disney classics from *Peter Pan* to *The Lion King,* and *Golden Mickeys,* a tribute to Disney films through the years that combines song and dance, animated films, and special effects. Family game shows (including a trivia contest called "Mickey Mania") and karaoke take place in the **Studio Sea family nightclub.** Adults 18 years and older, meanwhile, have their own play zone, an **adults-only entertainment area** in the forward part of Deck 3 with three themed nightclubs. Another nightspot is the **Promenade Lounge,** where live music is featured daily. The **Buena Vista Theatre** shows movies day and evening.

**SERVICE** Just as at its parks, Disney's cruise ships feature staff that come from around the globe. Service in the dining rooms is efficient and precise but leans toward friendly rather than formal. The crew keeps the ship exceptionally clean and well maintained. Overall, things run very smoothly.

Services include laundry and dry cleaning. (The ship also has self-service laundry rooms and 1-hr. photo processing.) Tips can be charged to your onboard account, for which most passengers opt, or you can give them out in the traditional method: cash.

Disney suggests a gratuity of $28 per person per week for the dining room server, $21 for the assistant server, and $28 for the cabin steward. Disney also recommends tipping the dining room head server $7.

**CRUISETOURS & ADD-ON PROGRAMS**   None.

# Disney Wonder

### The Verdict

Whether you're a Disney fanatic or just someone looking for a heavily family-focused experience while sailing in Alaska, this is your ship. Just keep in mind you'll be paying a bit of a "Disney premium" for the privilege.

### Specifications

| | | | |
|---|---|---|---|
| Size (in Tons) | 83,000 | Crew | 950 |
| Passengers (Double Occ.) | 1,754 | Passenger/Crew Ratio | 1.8 to 1 |
| Space/Passenger Ratio | 47.3 | Year Launched | 1999 |
| Total Cabins/Veranda Cabins | 877/378 | Last Major Refurbishment | 2009 |

### Frommer's Ratings (Scale of 1–5)                    ★★★★½

| | | | |
|---|---|---|---|
| Cabin Comfort & Amenities | 5 | Dining Options | 4.5 |
| Ship Cleanliness & Maintenance | 5 | Gym, Spa & Sports Facilities | 3 |
| Public Comfort/Space | 4 | Children's Facilities | 5 |
| Decor | 5 | Enjoyment Factor | 5 |

**THE SHIP IN GENERAL**   This sleek homage to ocean liners of old carries 1,754 passengers at "double occupancy"—the standard industry measuring stick for passenger capacity that assumes two people per cabin. But with all the kids packing into rooms with their parents, the double occupancy rating for this particular vessel is less indicative of the crowds that will be on many sailings. Built to be family-friendly, many cabins can hold four or even five people (some two-bedroom family cabins can hold up to seven!), and theoretically, the *Wonder* could carry 2,700 people if every possible berth was filled. Though service is a high point of a Disney cruise and the ships are well laid out, the large numbers of passengers means some areas of the ship can feel crowded at times, most notably the kids' pool area and the buffet eatery.

**CABINS**   As noted above, the *Disney Wonder* is all about family-friendly cabins, and the rooms on the ship have a number of features that make them unusually appealing to parents with kids. In addition to being able to hold up to five people in some cases (a rarity in the cruise world), cabins are about 25 percent larger on average than the industry standard. All 877 cabins have at least a sitting area with a sofa bed to sleep families of three. Some cabins also have one or two pull-down bunks to sleep families of four or five. Nearly half have private balconies. One-bedroom suites have balconies and sleep four or five comfortably; two-bedroom suites sleep up to seven. Outside cabins that don't have balconies have large-size porthole windows.

One big twist aimed at families: The majority of cabins have two bathrooms—a sink and toilet in one and a shower/tub combo and sink in the other.

As for decor, it's virtually identical from cabin to cabin, combining modern design with nostalgic ocean-liner elements such as a steamer-trunk armoire for kids, globe- and telescope-shaped lamps, map designs on the bedspreads, and a framed black-and-white shot of Mr. and Mrs. Walt Disney aboard the fabled ocean liner *Rex*. Warm wood tones predominate, with Art Deco touches in the metal and glass fittings and light fixtures.

## CABINS & RATES

| CABINS | PER DIEM RATES | SQ. FT. | FRIDGE | HAIR DRYER | SITTING AREA | TV |
|---|---|---|---|---|---|---|
| **Inside Passage** | | | | | | |
| Inside | $155–$266 | 184–214 | yes | yes | yes | yes |
| Outside | $228–$393 | 226–268 | yes | yes | yes | yes |
| Suites | $8,109–$1,050 | 259–1,029 | yes | yes | yes | yes |

**PUBLIC AREAS**   The *Wonder* has several theaters and lounges, including an adults-only area with three venues: a piano/jazz lounge, a disco, and a sports bar. A family-oriented entertainment lounge called Studio Sea offers game shows, karaoke, and dancing; the Promenade Lounge has classic pop music in the evenings; and a 24-hour Internet cafe has eight flatscreen stations. The Cove Cafe is a comfy place for gourmet coffees (for a price) or cocktails in a relaxed setting with books, magazines, Internet stations, Wi-Fi access, and TVs. A 270-seat cinema shows mostly recent-release Disney movies. The ship also has a jumbo 336-square-foot screen attached to the forward funnel outside on Deck 9 that shows classic Disney animated films. The children's facilities, as you'd expect, are the largest of any ship at sea. In preparation for its Alaska sailings, the *Wonder* received a new venue in dry dock called Outlook Cafe. Located high atop Deck 10, the 2,500-square-foot observation lounge is designed as a place for passengers in Alaska to relax with a drink as they peer out through floor-to-ceiling, curved-glass windows at the region's vistas. A spiral staircase connects Outlook Café with the existing Cove Cafe one deck below.

**DINING OPTIONS**   Disney's unique rotation dining system has passengers tasting three different eateries at dinner over the course of their cruise, with an adults-only specialty restaurant also available by reservation. Exclusive to Alaska sailings, Disney adds Alaska-themed items to menus and holds a weekly Taste of Alaska dinner featuring Alaska king crab legs, honey-mustard-marinated Alaskan salmon, and juniper-spiced elk tenderloin. At breakfast and lunch, the buffet-style spread in *Wonder*'s Beach Blanket restaurant offers deli meats, cheeses, and rice and vegetable dishes, as well as a carving station, a salad bar, and a dessert table with yummy chocolate chip cookies. Though the culinary offerings are par for the course in the cruise business, an oft-heard critique of the buffet area is that it's too small for the number of people who are on board and poorly designed for passenger flow, resulting in bottlenecks—particularly during the morning rush.

Options for grabbing a bite next to the pool include Pinocchio's Pizzeria, Pluto's Dog House (for hot dogs, hamburgers, chicken tenders, fries, and more), and an ice-cream bar (which also includes a generous selection of toppings). There's 24-hour room service from a limited menu but no midnight buffet.

**POOL, FITNESS, SPA & SPORTS FACILITIES**   The pool deck has three pools: Mickey's Kids' Pool, shaped like the mouse's big-eared head, with a great big white-gloved Mickey hand holding up a snaking yellow slide (expect a crowd at this pool!); Goofy's Family Pool, where adults and children can mingle; and the Quiet Cove Adult Pool, with whirlpools, gurgling waterfalls, a teak deck and lounge chairs with plush cushions, a poolside bar, and a coffee spot called Cove Cafe. For families with young children, adjacent is a splash pool with circulating water for diaper-wearing babies and toddlers. It's the only one at sea, as the lines' official party line is no diaper-wearing children allowed in any pool (and that includes Pull-Ups and swim diapers).

Just behind the pool at the stern is a spa and gym, which was refurbished a few years ago and expanded to twice its original size. The Steiner-managed Vista Spa & Salon is impressive, with attractive tile treatment rooms and a thermal suite with a sauna, a steam room, a misting shower, and heated contoured tile chaise lounges. Among the many treatments is a selection geared to teens.

The *Wonder* has an outdoor Sports Deck with basketball and paddle tennis. It also has shuffleboard and Ping-Pong, and joggers and walkers can circuit the Promenade Deck.

# HOLLAND AMERICA LINE

300 Elliott Ave. W., Seattle, WA 98119. © **877/932-4259** or 206/286-3900. Fax 206/286-7110. www. hollandamerica.com.

## Pros

- **Expertise that comes with experience.** Holland America's ships may be young, but not the company itself. Formed in 1873 as the Netherlands-America Steamship Company, it's been around more than 140 years, a lot of time to learn a little about operating oceangoing vessels.
- **Warm interiors.** Holland America ships, especially the more recent ones, tend to be understated, inviting, and easy on the eye; nothing garish here.
- **Signature of Excellence.** This multi-year, mega-upgrade program has enhanced a lot of shipboard features and activities to create a more premium experience.

## Cons

- **Sleepy nightlife.** If you're big on late-night dancing and barhopping, you may find yourself partying mostly with the entertainment staff, although the company has been offering more for night owls in recent years. If you're looking for a lot of late-night action, you're probably better off on one of the bigger, more bustling ships operated by rivals Norwegian, Carnival, or even Princess.

**THE LINE IN A NUTSHELL**  More than any other cruise company in Alaska, Holland America Line (HAL) has managed to hang onto some of its seafaring history and tradition, with its moderately priced, classic, casual yet refined, ocean-liner-like cruise experience. The line also has somewhat smaller, more intimate vessels than its main competitors, Princess and Celebrity.

**THE EXPERIENCE**  In Alaska terms, everybody else is an upstart when it comes to the cruise and even land tour business. The line calls itself Alaska's most experienced travel operator, and the key to that claim is HAL's 1971 acquisition of the tour company Westours, founded in 1947 by the late Charles B. "Chuck" West, often called

"Mr. Alaska" and widely recognized as the absolute pioneer of tourism to and within the state.

Cruising with HAL is less hectic than cruising on most other ships. The line strives for a less intrusive, sometimes almost sedate, presentation, although it has brightened up its entertainment package—with offerings including a "Dancing with the Stars"–inspired dance contest—and its menus in recent years. Overall, the ships tend to be more evocative of the days of grand liners, with elegant, European styling and displays of nautical artifacts.

About a decade ago, the company embarked on a Signature of Excellence product- and service-enhancements program aimed at elevating the quality of the dining experience, service, and enrichment programs on older ships. One problem that always faces cruise lines is ensuring that their newly built vessels—invariably outfitted with all the latest bells and whistles—don't overshadow their existing, older fleetmates. HAL's still-ongoing $525-million investment is one way to minimize the disparity between the old and the new.

Under the Signature of Excellence program, HAL has spent much of the upgrade dollars on such items as new amenities in cabins—massage showerheads, lighted magnifying makeup mirrors, hair dryers, extra-fluffy towels, terry-cloth robes, upgraded mattresses, and Egyptian-cotton bed linens. Passengers in all rooms are welcomed with a complimentary fruit basket. Suites have plush duvets on every bed, a VCR/DVD player, access to a well-stocked library of DVDs, and a fully stocked minibar.

Another focus has been on branded partnerships to offer passengers the chance to try new things. The Culinary Arts Center presented by *Food & Wine* magazine is a show kitchen with free cooking demonstrations several times during each cruise, where video cameras allow you to watch every move the chefs make. For those who prefer a more hands-on experience, cooking classes cost $29 per person. (The classes are limited to about 12 people and highly popular, so sign up early on your cruise.) Over 60 guest chefs and culinary experts sail on Holland America ships each year (the line's website lists specific sailings).

Another branded offering on Holland America vessels is the Digital Workshop, powered by Windows, which has free sessions on a variety of topics related to camera basics and photo editing, moviemaking, PC security, and more. "Techsperts" trained by Microsoft are on hand. In addition, the recently launched On Location activity program brings local experts on board ships to offer personal insights into each destination through lectures, demonstrations, and cultural entertainment performances.

**THE FLEET**   Over the years, Holland America Line has picked up a lot of "stuff"—Holland America Line Tours (formed by the merger of Westours and Gray Line of Alaska); Westmark Hotels; the *MV Ptarmigan* day boat that visits Portage Glacier outside Anchorage; a fleet of railcars (some built in the Old West style, but with better viewing opportunities, and some built in a more contemporary style); an almost completely new fleet of motorcoaches; and a lot more.

HAL's control of so many of the components of tour packages once gave the cruise company a position of preeminence in the Alaska market, though that's been well and truly challenged in the past decade by Princess, which now has a heavy presence in the accommodations and ground-transportation business as well. (Actually, the similarities don't end there: Both lines have large fleets of primarily late-model ships, both strive for and achieve consistency in the cruise product, and both are pursuing and acquiring younger passengers and families. And both are owned by Carnival Corp.) HAL's philosophy is to stick with ships of fewer than 2,500 passengers—many of them significantly smaller—eschewing the 3,000- to 5,000-passenger megaships being built by some other lines, including Princess.

The company's *Statendam*-class ships—the 1,260-passenger *Statendam* (1993), 1,258-passenger *Maasdam* (1993), 1,260-passenger *Ryndam* (1994), and 1,350-passenger *Veendam* (1996)—are virtual carbon copies of the same attractive, well-crafted design, with a dash of glitz here and there. The 1,432-passenger *Volendam* officially debuted in 1999, and the 1,432-passenger *Zaandam* debuted in 2000. Brighter and bolder than the earlier ships, the *Volendam* and *Zaandam* share many features of the *Statendam*-class ships, though they are slightly larger in size (nearly 62,000 tons, as opposed to approximately 56,000) and carry more passengers (1,432, against the *Statendam* class's 1,260). The 1,380-passenger *Amsterdam* is 62,735 tons and is one of two flagships in the fleet. (The other is the *Amsterdam*'s sister ship, the *Rotterdam*.) The *Westerdam* (2004), *Oosterdam* (2003), and *Zuiderdam* (2000) represent the Vista class in Alaska, each at 82,350 tons and carrying 1,916 passengers—sister ship *Noordam* (2006) is cruising elsewhere. The company's smallest ship is the luxurious *Prinsendam,* just 38,000 tons and with a passenger capacity of 835. The Signature-class ships include the 2,104-passenger *Eurodam* (2008) and the 2,106-passenger *Nieuw Amsterdam.*

Holland America has never shown any inclination to plunge into the 100,000-plus-ton megaship market (even the new, larger Pinnacle Class ship it has on order for 2016 will top out at just 99,000 tons). Keeping the size down allows HAL to maintain its high service standards and a degree of intimacy while offering all the amenities of its larger brethren.

In 2014, the line will offer eight different itineraries in Alaska, operated by seven different ships (for a total of 135 sailings in all). The line is bringing back its unusually long Gulf of Alaska itinerary that lasts 14 days (twice as long as the typical 7-night offering in the region) and includes a regular stop in Anchorage—a first for a major line in Alaska when HAL introduced the itinerary in 2010. Offered on just one of Holland America's seven ships in Alaska, the *Amsterdam,* the round-trip voyages out of Seattle also include one other relatively rare port of call in Alaska—Homer—as well as Sitka.

**PASSENGER PROFILE**  Holland America's passenger profile used to reflect a somewhat older crowd than on other ships. Now the average age is dropping, thanks to both an increased emphasis on the line's Club HAL program for children and some updating of the onboard entertainment offerings. HAL's passenger records in Alaska show a high volume of middle-age and older vacationers (the same demographic as aboard many of its competitors' ships), but on any given cruise, records are also likely to list a hundred or more passengers between the ages of, say, 5 and 16. This trend gathered its initial momentum a few years ago in Europe, a destination that, parents seem to think, has more kid appeal. It's spilled over into Alaska more recently, mainly thanks to the cruise line's added emphasis on generational travel with programs such as Club HAL, the Culinary Arts Center, and family reunion travel, a growing segment of the market.

The more mature among Holland America's passengers are likely to be repeat HAL passengers, often retirees. They are usually not Fortune 500 rich—they are looking for solid value for their money, and they get it from this line.

**DINING OPTIONS**   Years ago, HAL's meals were as traditional as its architecture and its itineraries—almost stodgy. But today the variety of dishes on the menu matches those of other premium lines, and the quality of the food is generally good throughout the fleet. Vegetarian options are available at every meal, and the line has excellent veggie burgers at the on-deck grill. We've also found that Holland America does a particularly good job of catering to special diets, ranging from vegan to kosher to gluten-free. On menus in the main dining room, look for selections from top chefs like Marcus Samuelsson and David Burke, who advise the line as members of its Culinary Council.

The kids' menu usually includes spaghetti, pizza, hamburgers, fries, and hot dogs. In addition, a few variations on what's being offered to the adults at the table are often served.

Buffets are offered at the Lido Restaurant as an alternative to breakfast and lunch and dinner in the main dining room (a large percentage of passengers dine in the Lido for breakfast and lunch, occasionally leading to some serious waiting times for tables and on lines during those times). Canaletto is a waiter-service casual Italian restaurant open for dinner on the Lido Deck, for a $10 extra charge (reservations are recommended). For a fancier meal, the Pinnacle Grill is the line's excellent steak and seafood venue on all the ships, priced at $25 for dinner and $10 for lunch; reservations are required. It's money well spent. One night a cruise, the Pinnacle Grill hosts An Evening at Le Cirque dining experience ($39 per person, and totally worth it), featuring the cuisine of the famed Le Cirque restaurant in New York.

**ACTIVITIES**   Young hipsters need not apply. Holland America's ships are heavy on more mature, less frenetic activities and light on boogie-till-the-cows-come-home, party-hearty pursuits. You'll find good cooking classes at the Culinary Arts Center and music to dance to or listen to in the bars and lounges, plus health spas, and all the other standard activities found on most large ships—photography classes, golf-putting contests (on the carpet in the lobby), art auctions, and the like. Dance classes include the opportunity to be paired with a member of the production show team to compete in an onboard contest themed on the TV show "Dancing with the Stars." Sometimes stars from the show are also onboard to lend a hand. All ships provide Internet access for 75¢ a minute; less if you buy a multi-minute package. Piano bars are lively.

Local travel guides sail on all Alaska-bound ships as part of the new On Location program. The guides bring their knowledge of local culture, history, art, and flora and fauna, giving lectures and interacting one-on-one with guests. The program also includes food and beverage events, including an Alaskan Brewing Company beer tasting and Pacific Northwest wine-tasting. The travel guides also sell stuff including artwork by Alaska Natives. In addition, a Tlingit cultural interpreter from Hoonah boards each ship at Glacier Bay and Hubbard Glacier to give talks explaining the origins of the Huna people—a tribe that has called Glacier Bay home for centuries. At the glaciers, there is also commentary by National Park Service employees.

**CHILDREN'S PROGRAMS**   Club HAL is more than just one of those half-hearted give-'em-a-video-arcade-and-hot-dogs-at-dinner efforts. This children's program has

# Holland America Fleet Itineraries

| SHIP | ITINERARIES |
|---|---|
| **Amsterdam** | 7-night Alaskan Adventurer: Round-trip from Seattle, visiting Ketchikan, Juneau, Sitka, and Victoria, BC, and scenic cruising in Tracy Arm (May–Sept) |
| | 14-night Alaskan Adventurer: Round-trip from Seattle, visiting Ketchikan, Juneau, Icy Strait Point, Anchorage, Homer, Sitka, and Victoria, BC, and scenic cruising in Tracy Arm and at Hubbard Glacier (May–Sept) |
| **Westerdam** | 7-night Alaskan Explorer: Round-trip from Seattle, visiting Juneau, Glacier Bay, Sitka, Ketchikan, and Victoria, BC (May–Sept) |
| **Volendam/Zaandam/ Zuiderdam** | 7-night Inside Passage: Round-trip from Vancouver, BC, visiting Juneau, Skagway, Ketchikan, Glacier Bay orTracy Arm (May–Sept) |
| **Oosterdam/ Statendam** | 7 night Glacier Discovery: North and southbound between Vancouver, BC, and Seward/Anchorage, visiting Juneau, Ketchikan, Skagway or Haines, and Glacier Bay (May–Sept) |

expert supervisors, a fitness center, and dedicated kids' rooms and teen club rooms (adults, keep out!).

Kids' activities are arranged in three divisions, by age—3 to 7, 8 to 12, and teens. The youngest group might have, say, crafts and games; there's golf putting and disco parties for 'tweens, and, for the older kids, a chance to try their hand at karaoke and teen sports tournaments. When there are more than 100 kids on board, a Talent Show is presented. On the *Statendam, Volendam, Zaandam,* and *Amsterdam* in Alaska, teens also get their own outdoor sunning area called The Oasis.

**ENTERTAINMENT**  The line has been making great strides in entertainment over the past decade, bringing in Broadway veterans to play the main theaters of its ships as well as top-notch illusionists, comedians, and musicians. On one ship, the *Eurodam* (not in Alaska, alas), the line in 2013 opened a B.B. King's Blues Club, and other vessels in 2013 began seeing "Dancing with the Stars"–themed programming as well as such big-name guest performers as Las Vegas' Recycled Percussion. The change, to a large extent, reflects the tastes of the younger passengers who are starting to book in greater numbers with HAL. Overall, the quality of the professional entertainers on HAL ships has perceptibly improved over the past decade. And then there are the amateurs! Each week includes a crew talent show in which the international staff members perform their countries' songs and dances. Even if that sounds a bit corny, try it—many of the staff members are fabulous! Your fellow passengers might also be quite the surprise—HAL ships offer live karaoke and an "American Idol"–style competition that sometimes deliver professional-caliber performances.

**SERVICE**  The line employs primarily Filipino and Indonesian staff members who are generally gracious and friendly without being cloying.

On one occasion, one of our contributors somehow managed to get his baggage on board a Holland America ship in Vancouver, BC—while the keys to the bags were lying on the bedside table at home 1,000 miles away! The cabin steward refused to let him break the locks and ruin the rather expensive (and brand-new) luggage. Instead, he called an engineer, and together they toiled patiently with a variety of tools—and a huge ring of keys—until, about a half-hour after boarding, they managed to free the offending locks. Luggage saved—and score one for the HAL service spirit!

Onboard services on every ship in the fleet include laundry and dry cleaning. On Holland America ships, a gratuity of $11 per person per day is automatically charged to your shipboard account, but you can increase or decrease the amount by visiting the guest services desk on board.

**CRUISETOURS & ADD-ON PROGRAMS**   As might be expected of a cruise line that owns its own land-tour company in Alaska (Royal Caribbean and Princess also own tour companies in the market), HAL offers a variety of land arrangements in combination with its cruises, and they are extensive. Newly dubbed Land + Sea Journeys for 2014, HAL's cruisetours range from 10 to 20 days in length, including a 3- to 7-day cruise, a 1- to 3-day visit to Denali National Park, and, in some cases, a few days visiting the Yukon Territory. In a big change for 2014, the line's tours that visit the Yukon include a 1-hour flight to the region from Fairbanks that replaces up to 2 days of motorcoach travel and a hotel overnight (in our eyes, a great improvement!). It's just the latest innovation when it comes to tours to the Yukon for Holland America, which has been a tourism pioneer in the region. While other lines have focused their land-tour options on the Anchorage-Denali-Fairbanks corridor and the Kenai Peninsula, Holland America also has poured resources into the Yukon and is the clear leader there; if you want to see the Yukon as part of your Alaska trip, Holland America is your line. Other notable land-tour changes for 2014 at Holland America include a new schedule for the McKinley Explorer domed rail cars the line uses to bring customers from Anchorage to Denali and back, with departures from Anchorage now occurring later in the morning and return trips from Denali now coming back earlier, with arrival back in Anchorage before dinnertime. The Holland America–owned Westmark hotels used on the company's tours in Fairbanks, Anchorage, and Skagway also recently have gotten substantial upgrades. Prices for Land + Sea Journeys vary widely depending on the type of cabin chosen for the cruise portion of the trip, level of hotel for the land portion, and length of the trip. Starting fares for 2014 for an 11-day trip are $999 per person.

# Statendam

## The Verdict

The smallest of Holland America's ships in Alaska, this vessel is a good choice for cruisers looking for a more intimate, less crowded experience than found on many mass-market lines.

## Specifications

| Size (in Tons) | 55,819 | Crew | 580 |
| --- | --- | --- | --- |
| Passengers (Double Occ.) | 1,258 | Passenger/Crew Ratio | 2.2 to 1 |
| Space/Passenger Ratio | 43 | Year Launched | 1993 |
| Total Cabins/Veranda Cabins | 630/149 | Last Major Refurbishment | April 2010 |

## Frommer's Ratings (Scale of 1–5)                    ★★★★

| Cabin Comfort & Amenities | 4 | Dining Options | 3.5 |
| --- | --- | --- | --- |
| Ship Cleanliness & Maintenance | 4 | Gym, Spa & Sports Facilities | 4 |
| Public Comfort/Space | 4 | Children's Facilities | 4 |
| Decor | 4 | Enjoyment Factor | 4 |

**THE SHIP IN GENERAL**   This ship is part of Holland America's *Statendam* class of vessels built between 1993 and 1996. While among the oldest in the line's fleet, it remains a wonderful ship that, at under 60,000 tons, offers a decidedly more intimate experience than the 100,000-ton megaships of, say, Princess Cruises. Moreover, in 2009, Holland America began a massive overhaul of the entire *Statendam* class that included a complete renovation of rooms; the addition of new, more open and contemporary public lounges and bars; the addition of innovative "Lanai cabins" with sliding doors that open onto the Promenade Deck; and other big changes. The *Statendam* received its $40-million revamp in April 2010. The overhauls are bringing a decidedly more contemporary vibe to the vessels while maintaining many of the classic touches for which Holland America is known for. Public areas still feature a healthy sprinkling of the antique furniture, Delft pottery, seafaring-themed artwork, and historic textiles that are a hallmark of the line, but they now also boast a more stylish feel than in the past. In one of the biggest changes, several walls have been knocked out on Deck 7 to create a more contemporary lounge and bar area called Mix, which includes a martini bar, champagne bar, and spirits-and-ales bar.

**CABINS**   All cabins have at least a small sitting area, plus lots of closet and drawer space. The outside doubles have either picture windows, verandas, or a sliding door that opens onto the Promenade Deck (the so-called Lanai cabins that the line began adding to the ships in 2009). *Note:* Like most ships built more than a decade ago, Holland America's *Statendam*-class vessels have relatively few cabins with verandas—at least compared with the line's newer ships. If a balcony is something you won't sail without (and many travelers to scenic Alaska demand a balcony), be sure to book early. The least-expensive inside cabins run almost 190 square feet (quite large by industry standards) and have many of the amenities of their higher-deck counterparts—sofas, chairs, desks-cum-dressers, stools, hair dryers, safes, and coffee tables. The overhaul that we mentioned earlier in this section has made the rooms much more welcoming—and functional. All cabins have TVs and telephones, and some have bathtubs (including some whirlpool tubs), DVD players, and minibars. A single penthouse is huge—almost 1,200 square feet. Six cabins on the ship are wheelchair-accessible.

## CABINS & RATES

| CABIN | PER DIEM RATES | SQ. FT. | FRIDGE | HAIR DRYER | SITTING AREA | TV |
|---|---|---|---|---|---|---|
| Inside | $118–$140 | 182 | no | yes | yes | yes |
| Outside | $147–$194 | 197 | no | yes | yes | yes |
| Suites | $355–$754 | 282–1,149 | yes | yes | yes | yes |

**PUBLIC AREAS**   The striking dining room and two-tiered showroom are among the ship's best features; the latter is comfortable and has great views of the stage area from all seats. It helps, of course, that Holland America has made huge strides in upgrading its entertainment package.

The lobby area is not just the place to board the ship; it's a place to hang out in as well. The *Statendam*'s lobby houses a magnificent three-story fountain.

Other public rooms include a recently redesigned Explorations coffee bar/library/game area, a casino, a children's playroom, a cinema, and conference facilities. We especially like the forward-facing Crow's Nest bar and lounge up on the top deck of the ship, an inviting place from which to view the spectacular Alaska scenery for an hour or three.

**DINING OPTIONS**  The overhaul of the *Statendam* in 2010 brought a new alternative eatery, the Italian-themed Canaletto, available to passengers at a $10 extra charge (reservations recommended). In addition, as on other Holland America vessels, the ship has the line's signature, reservations-only Pinnacle Grill ($25-a-head charge for dinner, $10 for lunch) and the casual Lido buffet, which is open in the evenings as well as for breakfast and lunch.

**POOL, FITNESS, SPA & SPORTS FACILITIES**  The *Statendam* has a sprawling expanse of teak-covered aft deck surrounding a swimming pool. The ship also has a main swimming pool plus a wading pool, with a spacious deck area, a bar, and two hot tubs in the middle of the top deck (all of which can be sheltered from inclement weather with a sliding glass roof—a godsend in sometimes chilly Alaska). Both areas are well planned and wide open. There's a practice tennis court and an unobstructed track on the Lower Promenade Deck for walking or jogging. The ship's roomy, windowed gym has a couple dozen exercise machines, a large separate aerobics area, steam rooms, and saunas. The spa lacks pizzazz, but provides the typical treatments.

# Amsterdam • Volendam • Zaandam

## The Verdict

More than a decade after debuting, these three markedly similar vessels remain an attractive choice for cruisers looking for a midsize vessel in the Alaska market. At 62,000 tons, they are just a tad bigger than the *Statendam*, mentioned above.

## Specifications

| Size (in Tons) | 62,000 | Crew | 615 |
|---|---|---|---|
| Passengers (Double Occ.) | 1,380/1,432/1,432 | Passenger/Crew Ratio | 2.2/2.3/2.3 to 1 |
| Space/Passenger Ratio | 43 | Year Launched | 2000/1999/2000 |
| Total Cabins/Veranda Cabins | 716/197 | Last Major Refurbishment | 2010/2011/2010 |

## Frommer's Ratings (Scale of 1–5)                              ★★★★

| Cabin Comfort & Amenities | 4 | Dining Options | 3.5 |
|---|---|---|---|
| Ship Cleanliness & Maintenance | 4.5 | Gym, Spa & Sports Facilities | 4 |
| Public Comfort/Space | 4 | Children's Facilities | 4 |
| Decor | 4 | Enjoyment Factor | 4 |

**THE SHIPS IN GENERAL**  Holland America pulled out all the stops on these ships. The centerpiece of the striking, triple-decked, oval atrium on the *Volendam,* for instance, is a glass sculpture by Luciano Vistosi, one of Italy's leading practitioners of the art—and that's just part of the ship's $2-million art collection, which reflects a flower theme. On the *Zaandam,* the focal point of the atrium is a 22-foot-tall pipe organ that is representative of the ship's music theme, which is filled out by a collection of guitars signed by rock musicians, including the Rolling Stones, Iggy Pop, David Bowie, and Queen (an attempt to attract a younger clientele?). Apart from the artwork and overall decorating motifs, there aren't many differences among these magnificent vessels; they really are virtually indistinguishable from one another. The *Zaandam* may look just the teeniest bit brighter than the *Volendam* and the *Amsterdam,* but hardly enough to make a real difference.

**CABINS**   The 197 suites and deluxe staterooms on each ship have private verandas, and the smallest of the remaining 523 cabins is a comfortable 182 square feet. All cabins come complete with sofa seating areas, hair dryers, telephones, and TVs. The suites and deluxe rooms also have VCRs, whirlpool tubs, and minibars. The ships have more balcony cabins than other HAL vessels. Twenty-one cabins on the *Amsterdam* are equipped to accommodate wheelchairs; 22 cabins a piece on *Zaandam* and *Volendam* are so equipped.

## CABINS & RATES

| CABINS | PER DIEM RATES | SQ. FT. | FRIDGE | HAIR DRYER | SITTING AREA | TV |
|---|---|---|---|---|---|---|
| **Amsterdam** | | | | | | |
| Inside | $147–$176 | 182 | no | yes | yes | yes |
| Outside | $176–$220 | 197 | no | yes | yes | yes |
| Suites | $297–$768 | 292–1,159 | yes | yes | yes | yes |
| **Volendam** | | | | | | |
| Inside | $147–$183 | 182 | no | yes | yes | yes |
| Outside | $183–$231 | 187 | no | yes | yes | yes |
| Suites | $297–$933 | 292–1,159 | yes | yes | yes | yes |
| **Zaandam** | | | | | | |
| Inside | $133–$161 | 182 | no | yes | yes | yes |
| Outside | $161–$206 | 197 | no | yes | yes | yes |
| Suites | $276–$933 | 292–1,159 | yes | yes | yes | yes |

**PUBLIC AREAS**   Each ship has five entertainment lounges, including the main two-tiered showroom. The Crow's Nest, a combination nightclub and observation lounge, is a good place to watch the passing Alaska scenery during the day. Each ship also has a casino, a children's playroom, a cinema, a library, an arcade, and an Internet center where you can surf for 75¢ a minute, with a 5-minute minimum.

**DINING OPTIONS**   All three ships have an alternative restaurant, the Pinnacle Grill (a staple on all HAL ships), which features steak and seafood, available on a reservations-only basis ($25-per-person supplement for dinner; $10 per person for lunch). Designed to inspire an artsy bistro vibe, these restaurants also have a display of drawings and etchings on the walls. A second alternative option on the vessels is Italian eatery Canaletto, which comes with a $10 per-person charge.

**POOL, FITNESS, SPA & SPORTS FACILITIES**   The gym is downright palatial on these ships, with dozens of state-of-the-art machines surrounded by floor-to-ceiling windows. There is an adjacent aerobics room. The spa and hair salon are not quite as striking. Three pools are on the Lido Deck, with a main pool and a wading pool under a retractable glass roof that also encloses the cafelike Dolphin Bar. A smaller and quieter aft pool is on the other side of the Lido buffet restaurant. On the Sports Deck is a pair of paddle-tennis courts as well as a shuffleboard court. Joggers can use the uninterrupted Lower Promenade Deck for a good workout.

# Westerdam • Zuiderdam • Oosterdam

## The Verdict

The biggest of the HAL ships in Alaska, these three are nevertheless intimate and certainly well equipped to support HAL's position as a force in the Alaska market.

## Specifications

| Size (in Tons) | 82,300 | Crew | 817 |
|---|---|---|---|
| Passengers (Double Occ.) | 1,916 | Passenger/Crew Ratio | 2.3 to 1 |
| Space/Passenger Ratio | 44 | Year Launched | 2004/2002/2003 |
| Total Cabins/Veranda Cabins | 958/640 | Last Major Refurbishment | 2010/2010/2011 |

## Frommer's Ratings (Scale of 1–5)                      ★★★★

| Cabin Comfort & Amenities | 4 | Dining Options | 3.5 |
|---|---|---|---|
| Ship Cleanliness & Maintenance | 5 | Gym, Spa & Sports Facilities | 4 |
| Public Comfort/Space | 4 | Children's Facilities | 4 |
| Decor | 4 | Enjoyment Factor | 4 |

**THE SHIPS IN GENERAL**   The *Zuiderdam* comes back to Alaska this year after spending last summer in the Caribbean. The *Westerdam* is in its third season in the North Country, and the *Oosterdam* has been sailing in Alaska on and off for years. The ships' thoughtful layout prevents bottlenecks at key points—outside the dining room, for instance, and at the buffet and the pool area. Art worth about $2.5 million, according to HAL, is well displayed throughout each of the vessels, and the decor reflects Holland's (and Holland America's) contribution to the development of cruising and, indeed, of ships as a trade and transportation medium. The nautical pieces on display are plentiful but never overwhelming.

**CABINS**   Nearly 85 percent of the ships' cabins have ocean views, 67 percent of them with verandas. The smallest of the inside cabins is just 170 square feet, and the standard outside rooms start at 185 square feet. Suites here go up to 1,318 square feet, making them some of the biggest in the HAL fleet. All rooms have Internet/e-mail dataports. All the rooms—even the smallest—have ample drawer and closet space, are tastefully decorated in quiet colors, and have quality bathroom fittings. All have DVD players and minibars. On each ship, 28 cabins, in several categories, are wheelchair-accessible.

## CABINS & RATES

| CABINS | PER DIEM RATES | SQ. FT. | FRIDGE | HAIR DRYER | SITTING AREA | TV |
|---|---|---|---|---|---|---|
| **Westerdam** | | | | | | |
| Inside | $147–$183 | 154–185 | yes | yes | yes | yes |
| Outside | $176–$290 | 171–185 | yes | yes | yes | yes |
| Suites | $318–$490 | 389–1,318 | yes | yes | yes | yes |
| **Zuiderdam** | | | | | | |
| Inside | $161–$197 | 154–185 | yes | yes | yes | yes |
| Outside | $197–$311 | 171–185 | yes | yes | yes | yes |
| Suites | $347–$526 | 398–1,318 | yes | yes | yes | yes |
| **Oosterdam** | | | | | | |
| Inside | $161–$197 | 154–185 | yes | yes | yes | yes |
| Outside | $197–$311 | 171–185 | yes | yes | yes | yes |
| Suites | $347–$526 | 398–1,318 | yes | yes | yes | yes |

PUBLIC AREAS   The ships include a disco; a two-level main dining room; a library; an alternative, reservations-requested restaurant; and seven lounges/bars, including HAL's signature splendid Crow's Nest observation lounge/nightclub. And each ship has not one, but two showrooms—a three-level main showroom (sadly, with some rather obstructed sightlines) and a more intimate "cabaret-style" venue for smaller-scale performances.

The Club HAL children's facilities are extensive and have both indoor and outdoor components. The ships have two interior Promenade Decks, affording walkers protection against the elements—these decks can prove very useful in Alaska!

Wheelchair users are well catered to on these vessels. Besides the 28 cabins specially designed for them, they have wheelchair elevators dedicated for use in boarding the tenders in port, two tenders equipped with special wheelchair-accessible platforms, and accessible areas at virtually all public decks, bars, and lounges.

The ships have well-equipped casinos, offering passengers the chance to try their luck at stud poker, slots, craps, and roulette. Dozens of original works of art, with combined values ranking in the millions, dot the public areas. Each of the ships also features Explorations Cafe, a coffeehouse environment in which passengers can browse the Internet, check e-mail, or just read the *New York Times*—transmitted electronically to the ships daily.

DINING OPTIONS   All three of these ships have HAL's signature Pinnacle Grill (for a supplemental charge) and a more casual buffet. There is also 24-hour room service for those who prefer in-cabin dining.

POOL, FITNESS, SPA & SPORTS FACILITIES   The main pool on the Lido Deck has a retractable dome—a feature that has proven popular on other ships in Alaskan waters. A couple of hot tubs and a smaller pool complement the main pool. A huge spa, complete with the usual array of treatments and services, occupies part of the Lido Deck.

# NORWEGIAN CRUISE LINE

7665 Corporate Center Dr., Miami, FL 33126. ℂ **866/234-7350** or 305/436-4000. Fax 305/436-4120. www.ncl.com.

## Pros

o  **Flexible dining.** Norwegian's dining policy lets you sit where and with whom you want, dress as you want (within reason), and dine when you want (dinner is served 5:30–10pm; guests must be seated by 9:30pm) at a wide variety of restaurants, including one that's open 24 hours. Room service is also available.

o  **Smoke-free zones.** Norwegian promotes a smoke-free environment for those who want it, and all dining rooms are smoke-free.

## Cons

o  **It's not all Freestyle.** While Norwegian promotes its pioneering "Freestyle Cruising" (see below), shows and activities have specific start and end times; it's not up to the passenger.

o  **Few quiet spots.** Other than the library, there's not a quiet room to be found indoors, but Norwegian has added adult quiet zones at its pool decks.

o  **Crowded dining areas.** The most popular of the alternative restaurants can get booked up early; it's best to make reservations as quickly as one can.

**THE LINE IN A NUTSHELL**   The very contemporary Norwegian Cruise Line ("Norwegian," for short) offers an informal and upbeat Alaska program on three large ships: the 8-year-old *Norwegian Pearl,* 9-year-old *Norwegian Jewel,* and 13-year-old *Norwegian Sun.* The first two vessels will spend most of the summer sailing round-trip out of Seattle on 7-night Inside Passage itineraries that include a stop in Victoria, BC. The *Norwegian Sun* is sailing one-way Gulf of Alaska itineraries between Vancouver, BC, and Whittier.

**THE EXPERIENCE**   Norwegian excels in activities, a lack of regimentation, and alternative dining. Recreational and fitness programs are among the best in the industry. The line's youth programs for kids and teens are also top-notch. The company offers what it calls "Freestyle Cruising," which makes life a whole lot easier for passengers. Norwegian was, in fact, the pioneers of the concept in the North American cruise market. One of the main components of Freestyle Cruising is freedom in when, where, and with whom passengers dine. Guests can eat in their choice of a variety of restaurants pretty much any time between 5:30pm and 10pm (you must be seated by 9:30pm), with no prearranged table assignment or dining time. Other features of Freestyle Cruising are that daily service charges are automatically charged to room accounts, dress codes are more relaxed (resort casual) at all times, and at the end of the voyage, passengers can remain in their cabins until their time comes to disembark, rather than huddling in lounges or squatting on luggage in stairwells until their lucky color comes up. Freestyle Cruising has since been copied, to whatever extent possible, by other lines operating in the U.S.

Naturally, with each new ship in a line's fleet, there usually comes innovation. In this case, one special addition was added on the *Norwegian Pearl:* a four-lane bowling alley tied in with an ultrachic South Beach–like lounge.

Top suites in the line's exclusive complex called The Haven also get a dedicated restaurant for breakfast and lunch, key-card access courtyard, and butler service, among other perks.

**THE FLEET**   *Norwegian Jewel* joined the fleet in 2005 and is a tad smaller than the newer *Norwegian Pearl.* Both ships have lots of windows for great viewing. Though these ships are relatively large and have a lot of public areas, some of the cabins are on the small side, and some have insufficient closet space. The *Norwegian Sun* is somewhat smaller than the other two vessels but still features Norwegian's signature wide array of eateries.

**PASSENGER PROFILE**   In Alaska, the overall demographic tends to be more toward older, affluent retirees than on the line's warmer-climate sailings, but you'll find an increasing number of younger couples and families as well, attracted by the line's flexible dining policy and relaxed dress code. Generally, passengers are not seeking high-voltage activities or around-the-clock action. The disco is seldom the most frequented room on a Norwegian ship, the exception being the Bliss Lounge on *Norwegian Pearl.* There is a good mix of first-timers and veteran cruisers (many of whom have cruised with this line before).

**DINING OPTIONS**   The cruise line handles the business of dining in an innovative way, with an extensive number of alternative restaurants (albeit, many at an extra charge) in addition to two traditional (and subsequently smaller) main dining rooms. And you can dress pretty much however you like, too—guests are allowed to wear blue jeans, shorts, and T-shirts in the evenings at the buffets, outdoor barbecues, and 24-hour venues. There is one optional formal night for those who want to dress up. As on all ships, breakfast and lunch are available either in the dining room, on an open-seating basis, or in the buffet up top, where passengers can help themselves, dress pretty much as they please, and enjoy a more relaxed meal—chefs manning cooking stations at the buffet prepare food right in front of your eyes. In addition to the main dining rooms, both ships have a variety of other food options—more than a dozen a piece. Included in the mix, depending on the ship, are French; sushi, sashimi, and Teppanyaki; Brazilian-style churascaria; and a signature steakhouse for which reservations are strongly recommended. There are now delicious signature dishes in all specialty restaurants. Pricing for the specialty restaurants is known to bounce around a bit as the line manages crowds by adjusting prices, but it's typical to pay $15 to $30 per person for many of the eateries. A chocolate buffet, presented on select cruises, was an industry first, and it's probably still the best.

**ACTIVITIES**    In Alaska, the line has a destination lecturer or two on the history, landscape, and culture of the state; wine-tasting demonstrations; art auctions; dance classes and a fitness program; daily quizzes; crafts; board games; and bingo, among other activities. Passengers also tend to spend time at sports activities, which include basketball and mini-soccer. The ships all have Internet cafes that cost 75¢ a minute a la carte, with package rates available. In addition, Alaska sailings feature more than 130 options for shore excursions, including the Dogsledding & Glacier Flightseeing Helicopter, the Whale Watching and Wildlife Quest, and the Historic Gold Mine, Panning & Salmon Bake. Like other lines, Norwegian also offers one-of-a-kind, customized private shore tours on all cruises calling in Juneau and Ketchikan. Dubbed Freestyle Private Tours, the outings offer a personalized experience with a personal guide, giving passengers an exclusive insider's perspective. The cost of the Chauffeur-Driven Hummer Freestyle Private Tour begins at $599 per group of four for a 4-hour personalized tour, including special tour options and custom stops.

**CHILDREN'S PROGRAMS**    Norwegian ships tend to be very family-friendly: There's at least one full-time youth coordinator per age group, a kids' activity room, video games, an ice-cream stand, and group babysitting for ages 3 and up, plus a Nickelodeon Pajama Jam Breakfast (on Norwegian Jewel) and a visit from a park ranger for the ships that sail to Glacier Bay National Park. The line is constantly upgrading its kids' program. More family features aboard ships include exclusive Nickelodeon at Sea programming on *Norwegian Jewel,* with character meet-and-greets and special Nickelodeon game shows; a bowling alley and a jungle gym with a ball pit and tunnels on the *Pearl;* and arcades on all Norwegian ships.

**ENTERTAINMENT**    Entertainment is a Norwegian hallmark, with Vegas-style productions that are surprisingly lavish and artistically ambitious; the gymnasts are superb. On some nights, the showrooms also feature magic, comedians, and juggling acts. The three ships boast the Norwegian fleet's big, splashy casinos, and all have intimate lounges that present pianists and cabaret acts. Music for dancing—usually by a smallish band and invariably the kind of dancing that mature passengers can engage in (that is, not a lot of rock 'n' roll)—is popular and takes place before or after shows. Each ship also has a late-night disco for those who prefer a more frenetic beat. Norwegian's ultra-hip theme party—"White Hot Night"—really keeps the ship lively into the wee hours.

## Norwegian Fleet Itineraries

| SHIP | ITINERARIES |
|------|-------------|
| **Norwegian Pearl** | 7-night Inside Passage/Glacier Bay: Round-trip from Seattle, visiting Juneau, Skagway, Ketchikan, and Victoria, BC (May–Sept) |
| **Norwegian Jewel** | 7-night Inside Passage/Sawyer Glacier: Round-trip from Seattle, visiting Ketchikan, Juneau, Skagway, and Victoria, BC (May–Sept) |
| **Norwegian Sun** | 7-night Glacier Bay from Vancouver: Northbound from Vancouver, BC, to Whittier, visiting Ketchikan, Juneau, Skagway, Glacier Bay and Hubbard Glacier (May–Sept) |
| | 7-night Sawyer Glacier from Whittier: Southbound from Whittier to Vancouver, BC, visiting Ketchikan, Juneau, Skagway, Glacier Bay, Hubbard Glacier, Sawyer Glacier and Icy Strait Point (May–Sept) |

**SERVICE**   Generally, room service and bar service fleetwide are speedy and efficient, and the waitstaff is attentive and accommodating. In the alternative dining rooms, service can be somewhat slow if it's a large group at one table, but at least on the *Norwegian Pearl,* they have made great strides in improving this. With the introduction of the line's flexible dining program, additional crew members, mostly waiters and kitchen staff, have been added to each ship. To eliminate tipping confusion, the line automatically adds a charge of $12 per passenger per day to shipboard accounts, which also can be prepaid at the time of booking (you are free to adjust the amount up or down as you see fit based on the service you received). Full-service laundry and dry cleaning are available.

**CRUISETOURS & ADD-ON PROGRAMS**   Norwegian offers four cruisetours before the 7-day southbound cruise or after the 7-day northbound cruise: the Denali Express, Denali/Alyeska Explorer, the Denali/Fairbanks Explorer, and the Authentic Alaska. All Cruisetours are fully escorted by local Alaskan guides, feature 2 nights in Denali, include a stop at an Iditarod Sled Dog musher's house, and have an airport meet and greet by a representative.

# Norwegian Pearl

### The Verdict

Norwegian's newest ship in Alaska is an evolutionary step forward with such features as bowling. It's the perfect ship for those who like lots of things to do and places to eat without much regimentation.

### Specifications

| Size (in Tons) | 93,530 | Crew | 1,084 |
|----------------|--------|------|-------|
| Passengers (Double Occ.) | 2,394 | Passenger/Crew Ratio | 2.2 to 1 |
| Space/Passenger Ratio | 37 | Year Launched | 2006 |
| Total Cabins/Veranda Cabins | 1,197/360 | Last Major Refurbishment | N/A |

### Frommer's Ratings (Scale of 1–5)     ★★★★

| Cabin Comfort & Amenities | 4 | Dining Options | 5 |
|---------------------------|---|----------------|---|
| Ship Cleanliness & Maintenance | 4 | Gym, Spa & Sports Facilities | 4 |
| Public Comfort/Space | 4 | Children's Facilities | 4.5 |
| Decor | 4 | Enjoyment Factor | 4 |

**THE SHIP IN GENERAL**  Launched in December 2006, *Norwegian Pearl* was the line's first ship with a bowling alley, among other new features.

**CABINS**  *Norwegian Pearl* has 1,197 cabins, 360 of which have balconies. The smallest of the rooms is about 142 square feet, average for this new breed of ship—not big, but not cramped, either. The ship's biggest accommodations—the spectacular, three-bedroom Garden Villa—runs to a staggering 4,390 square feet. One oft-voiced complaint in some of the lower-end cabins is an age-old Norwegian bugbear: not enough closet and drawer space. (That doesn't apply, of course, to the suites, and most assuredly not to the Garden Villa.) This should not be an issue for a 1-week Alaska cruise when there are two to a cabin. Freestyle 2.0 improvements have been added as noted above.

## CABINS & RATES

| CABINS | PER DIEM RATES | SQ. FT. | FRIDGE | HAIR DRYER | SITTING AREA | TV |
|---|---|---|---|---|---|---|
| Inside | $112–$135 | 143 | no | yes | no | yes |
| Outside | $140–$209 | 161 | no | yes | yes | yes |
| Suites | $240–$1,429 | 285–4,390 | some | yes | yes | yes |

**PUBLIC AREAS**  Public areas are bright and airy, if just a tad too colorful and varied (the nightclub's lilac and blue chairs and carpeting are definitely a bit over-heated). The Library, on the other hand, is a tastefully decorated, relaxing room and the only quiet room on the ship. As part of the "Freestyle" concept, *Pearl* has a vast array of eating and drinking spots. Other spaces include a huge casino, offering black-jack, roulette, craps (with wonderfully fair, Las Vegas–type odds), Caribbean Stud Poker—plus more than 200 slot machines—and a Texas Hold 'em table. The main showroom, the two-story Stardust Theater, holds about 1,100 in comfy seating, with good sightlines from either floor (and an air-conditioning flow from the back of each chair, helping to keep the room nice and cool). With its massive stage and loads of technological bells and whistles, the Stardust pulls off some pretty ambitious Broad-way-style revues. The Internet cafe isn't a cafe at all (no coffee or pastries here), but it can keep you in e-touch with the outside world for 75¢ a minute; packages lowering the per-minute cost are available. Splash Academy and Entourage, for ages 3 through 17, have trained supervisors and are fully equipped with TVs, PS3, Wii, a disco floor, foosball tables, an air hockey tables, a nursery, and a sleep/rest area.

**DINING OPTIONS**  In addition to its two main dining rooms (Indigo and the Summer Palace), the ship houses several other eateries in keeping with Norwegian's prom-ise of providing maximum dining flexibility. Guests choose from two main dining rooms; a French bistro; an Italian trattoria; a Brazilian churascaria complete with passadors; a signature steakhouse; eateries for teppanyaki, sushi, tapas, and more; and the Blue Lagoon, open 24 hours a day. Supplemental fees ($15–$30 per person) are added for some of the restaurants. Colorful electronic signage around the ship lets guests know which restaurants are full and which ones have space. Even late in the afternoons, it's often possible to book a table in any restaurant for prime or near-prime dining times.

**POOL, FITNESS, SPA & SPORTS FACILITIES**  *Pearl* has an adult pool, six hot tubs, a kiddie pool, a spa with exceptional thermal offerings highlighted by the large thalassotherapy pool, and a salon. Active types should check out the Body Waves fit-ness center, the jogging/walking track, the rock-climbing wall, the bowling alley, and the court used for basketball, volleyball, mini-soccer, and tennis. Also nice in this day and age is the Deck 7 promenade, which goes around the entire ship (2⅔ laps to a mile).

# Norwegian Jewel

## The Verdict

The first of Norwegian's popular *Jewel*-class series of ships is lively and fun, with lots of restaurants and nightspots to keep cruisers busy in the evening.

## Specifications

| | | | |
|---|---|---|---|
| Size (in Tons) | 93,502 | Crew | 1,100 |
| Passengers (Double Occ.) | 2,376 | Passenger/Crew Ratio | 2.2 to 1 |
| Space/Passenger Ratio | 39 | Year Launched | 2005 |
| Total Cabins/Veranda Cabins | 1,163/510 | Last Major Refurbishment | N/A |

## Frommer's Ratings (Scale of 1–5)    ★★★★

| | | | |
|---|---|---|---|
| Cabin Comfort & Amenities | 4 | Dining Options | 5 |
| Ship Cleanliness & Maintenance | 4 | Gym, Spa & Sports Facilities | 4 |
| Public Comfort/Space | 4 | Children's Facilities | 3.5 |
| Decor | 4 | Enjoyment Factor | 4 |

**THE SHIP IN GENERAL**    From the outside, the *Norwegian Jewel* looks a lot like its slightly younger sister, the *Norwegian Pearl,* and it's similar on the inside, too, with a few key differences—the most notable being the lack of a bowling alley (a trademark feature that is found on every Norwegian ship built after the *Pearl*). Like many Norwegian ships, the *Jewel* has a flashy, Las Vegas casino–influenced decor that is heavy on the purples, golds, and blues. Subtle it is not, and Norwegian's customers seem to like it that way. One big difference from the *Pearl:* The *Jewel* is home to Nickelodeon programming that exists on four other Norwegian ships and brings Nickelodeon characters such as SpongeBob SquarePants and Dora the Explorer on board for character breakfasts, meet-and-greets, and more.

**CABINS**    Almost 540 cabins have a private balcony. The inside cabins are smallish, ranging from 142 to 150 square feet. Suites have floor-to-ceiling windows, refrigerators, and private balconies. All cabins are equipped with TVs, telephones, small dressing tables, soundproof doors, individual climate control, and sitting areas that are actually big enough to stretch out in. Closet and drawer space is quite limited, so pack lightly. There are 27 wheelchair-accessible cabins, including suites, and they all feature collapsible shower stools mounted on shower walls; all toilets feature collapsible arm guards and lowered washbasins.

## CABINS & RATES

| CABINS | PER DIEM RATES | SQ. FT. | FRIDGE | HAIR DRYER | SITTING AREA | TV |
|---|---|---|---|---|---|---|
| Inside | $107–$132 | 142–150 | yes | yes | no | yes |
| Outside | $128–$161 | 160–205 | yes | yes | some | yes |
| Suites | $214–$2,407 | 285–4,891 | yes | yes | yes | yes |

**PUBLIC AREAS** Norwegian boasts that the *Jewel* has 16 eateries and 13 bars and nightspots, an unusually large number for a ship its size—all part of the line's "freestyle" concept of offering passengers lots of choices. The *Jewel*'s two main dining rooms (Azura and Tsar's Palace) offer traditional (that is to say, multicourse) meals and a range of lighter fare, but dining doesn't involve the traditional assigned seating found on some other lines ("If it's 8pm, it must be dinnertime"). Instead, the ship follows a no-reservations, come-as-you-please format in a wide variety of restaurants. Public rooms include a casino, a conference center, a disco, a library, a karaoke bar, a martini bar, a champagne and wine bar, a beer and whiskey pub, and a three-level show lounge. For kids, in addition to the scheduled Nickelodeon activities, there's a children's playroom (Splashdown Academy Youth Center), teen center (Entourage), and a video arcade.

**DINING OPTIONS** Rest assured, you won't go hungry on the *Jewel*. Among the unusually wide (for a cruise ship) assortment of restaurants available at night are Le Bistro, a French restaurant; Chin Chin, serving Asian cuisine; a sushi bar; the line's signature Cagney's Steakhouse; Teppanyaki Room; and an Italian eatery. As if that weren't enough, the Blue Lagoon serves hamburgers, hot dogs, soups, salads, and pizza 24 hours a day. For the little ones, Garden Cafe also includes a buffet for kids with small seats and tables. *A caveat:* As on other Norwegian ships, while the *Jewel*'s main dining rooms come at no extra charge, most of the specialty restaurants on board have a per-person service charge ranging from $15 to $30.

**POOL, FITNESS, SPA & SPORTS FACILITIES** The *Jewel* is well equipped for the sports-minded and active vacationer. In addition to the fitness center, there are heated pools (two main pools with a waterslide and a children's pool), hot tubs, a jogging/walking track (3½ laps is 1 mile), and an array of sports facilities, including a basketball/volleyball/tennis court. Adults now can experience quiet zones poolside. The Body Waves Fitness Center and Mandara Spa, located on Deck 12, are well stocked with Jacuzzis, hydrotherapy baths, and saunas. The spa has facilities for couples to take their treatments together.

# Norwegian Sun

## The Verdict

One of Norwegian's smaller ships, which may appeal to passengers looking for a more intimate experience.

## Specifications

| Size (in Tons) | 78,309 | Crew | 953 |
|---|---|---|---|
| Passengers (Double Occ.) | 1,936 | Passenger/Crew Ratio | 2.1 to 1 |
| Space/Passenger Ratio | 40 | Year Launched | 2001 |
| Total Cabins/Veranda Cabins | 1,025/432 | Last Major Refurbishment | N/A |

## Frommer's Ratings (Scale of 1–5)                    ★★★★

| Cabin Comfort & Amenities | 4 | Dining Options | 4 |
|---|---|---|---|
| Ship Cleanliness & Maintenance | 4 | Gym, Spa & Sports Facilities | 4 |
| Public Comfort/Space | 4 | Children's Facilities | 4 |
| Decor | 4 | Enjoyment Factor | 4 |

**THE SHIP IN GENERAL**  Launched in 2001, the *Norwegian Sun* was the first Norwegian ship purposely built with the line's signature "freestyle" dining in mind, and its nine restaurants make it possible to eat in a different location every night of a Alaskan cruise. It's a peaceful ship, with plenty of room to get away from it all.

**CABINS**  The Norwegian Sun has a large number of windowless "inside" cabins (375), which can be a tough sell in a destination known for its beauty. Another 650 have ocean views, of which 432 also have balconies. The smallest of the rooms is about 145 square feet and come with a small desk area, but some categories of standard cabins are 170 up to 221 square feet. The ship also has several categories of suites, including 828-square-feet owner's suites that feature a living room, dining room, and separate bedroom as well as large balcony. Suites come with a butler and concierge service. The ship has 20 wheelchair-accessible cabins.

## CABINS & RATES

| CABINS | PER DIEM RATES | SQ. FT. | FRIDGE | HAIR DRYER | SITTING AREA | TV |
|--------|----------------|---------|--------|------------|--------------|-----|
| Inside | $112–$135 | 145-191 | no | yes | no | yes |
| Outside | $140–$209 | 145-221 | no | yes | yes | yes |
| Suites | $240–$1,429 | 332-828 | some | yes | yes | yes |

**PUBLIC AREAS**  Located midship, the glass-domed, eight-story atrium of the ship is a striking feature, built to offer at least the illusion of space. Bright and airy, it's home to Guest Services, the Shore Excursions desk, and a port and cruise consultant. Four glass elevators whisk passengers to the higher decks. A grand spiral staircase, located midship, links the Atlantic Deck with the International Deck, two flights up. Internet facilities (24 terminals) are available for 75¢ a minute (lower bulk rates available). Also entertaining is the Sun's large casino and a choice of nine lounges.

**DINING OPTIONS**  Besides Le Bistro, a standard on all Norwegian ships, the *Sun* offers Il Adagio, a rather informal Italian dining room; Ginza, for Japanese food; East Meets West steakhouse; a Spanish tapas bar called Las Ramblas; newly added Moderno Churascaria; the Garden Buffet/Great Outdoor Cafe, serving lunch and dinner; and two main dining rooms (some of the alternative restaurants come with a surcharge). Have a sweet tooth? Look no further than Sprinkles Ice Cream Bar near the pools. There also is a 24-hour room service menu.

**POOL, FITNESS, SPA & SPORTS FACILLITIES**  The ship has two pools and two hot tubs on Pool Deck 11 and a children's splash pool one deck up on the Sports Deck. The Sports Deck features a net for driving golf balls, a basketball/volleyball court, a batting cage, shuffleboard courts, and sunbathing areas. Mandara, one of the premier spa operators in the world, manages this spa, as well as the spas on all Norwegian ships. Simultaneous spa treatments for couples and in-cabin spa services, hydrotherapy baths incorporating milk and honey or mineral salts, exotic Asian treatments, de-stress treatments, and all of Mandara's signature "Best of the East and West" techniques are available here.

# OCEANIA CRUISES

8300 NW 33rd St., Suite 308, Miami, FL 33122. ℰ **800/531-5658.** www.oceaniacruises.com.com.

**THE LINE IN A NUTSHELL**  Oceania Cruises entered the cruise industry in 2003 when it launched *Regatta*, formerly the R Two from Renaissance (which went belly-up after 9/11). It was an interesting beginning for *Regatta,* along with its sister ship, *Insignia,* formerly the R One, as the ships were being positioned above the premium lines and below the luxury lines. It was essentially a new category they called "upper premium" and it's been very successful, with Oceania adding a third former Renaissance ship to the fleet in 2005 (*Nautica,* formerly the R Five) and two newbuilds, *Marina* and *Riviera,* in February 2011 and May 2012, respectively. Oceania and luxury line Regent Seven Seas Cruises make up Prestige Cruise Holdings, a cruise division of the Apollo Management investment firm, which also owns a big portion of Norwegian Cruise Line.

**THE EXPERIENCE**    Oceania truly offers a deluxe or, said another way, upscale, experience. There's little glitz or hoopla on board, and the hallmarks are dining, service, and itineraries. The no-charge alternative restaurants are way above the norm. But one of the line's biggest strengths is the size of its first three vessels (one of which, *Regatta,* is Oceania's only ship in Alaska). At 30,277 tons and carrying 684 guests, these ships are really small-to-midsize by today's standards. It's an informal setting (Oceania calls it country-club casual) without crowds and lines. Oceania is a relative newcomer to Alaska, having not entered the market until 2011. After a 1-year hiatus, the line returned in 2013, and in 2014 Regatta will offer 10 sailings in the region with four new itineraries.

### Pros

o **Excellent dining.** Whether you're dining in the main dining room or the two alternative restaurants, food is a focus at Oceania.

o **Small ship size.** The relative small size of the ships makes for an intimate, warm experience without masses of people.

o **Longer itineraries than the industry norm.** In the case of Alaska, the line offers 9- and 10-day trips, giving plenty of time to experience the destination.

o **Pretty public rooms.** Many public rooms, including the library, the Grand Bar, and the main atrium, are as pretty as any at sea.

### Cons

o **Cabin size.** Cabins are relatively small.

o **Low ceilings.** In some areas, the ship's low ceilings make for a somewhat cramped feeling; in the case of the main dining room, it gets quite noisy.

**THE FLEET**    This will be *Regatta's* 3rd year in Alaska, but the line's sister company Regent Seven Seas has more than a decade's experience for them to draw from. The ship's size is excellent for the destination, making it easier to navigate closer to the highlights. Carrying only 684 passengers, *Regatta* offers a midsize alternative compared to the much larger premium ships and provides plenty of really upscale features at way-lower cruise fares than the luxury lines. In 2010, *Regatta,* along with sister ships *Insignia* and *Nautica,* underwent a multimillion-dollar refurbishment, including enhanced cabins, expanded menus, new production shows, faster Internet, and more (all three ships are scheduled for even more updates in 2014).

**PASSENGER PROFILE**    The basic profile is one of couples in their 50s and 60s, but Oceania's ships are equally comfortable for both younger and older cruisers. The line is appropriate for those looking for a somewhat informal cruise, where dining and excellent service take a higher priority than glitz, glamour, and nonstop activity. Historically, itineraries have been very port-intensive, with few sea days, so a busy shipboard agenda has never been a priority to passengers.

THE CRUISE LINES: THE BIG SHIPS

Oceania Cruises

# Oceania Cruises Fleet Itineraries

| SHIP | ITINERARIES |
| --- | --- |
| *Regatta* | 10-day between San Francisco and Vancouver, BC: Astoria, Sitka, Juneau, Ketchikan and Victoria; scenic cruising of the Inside Passage, Hubbard Glacier and Outsided Passage (May and Aug) |
| | 10-days between Vancouver and Seattle: Sitka, Juneau, Skagway, Hoonah, Ketchikan and Victoria; scenic cruising: Inside Passage, Hubbard Glacier, Outside Passage (June and July) |
| | 10-day roundtrip Seattle: Ketchikan, Juneau, Hoonah, Sitka, Wrangell, Victoria; scenic cruising: Inside Passage, Hubbard Glacier, Outside Passage (June and July) |
| | 7-day roundtrip Seattle: Ketchikan, Wrangell and Prince Rupert; scenic cruising: Inside Passage, Outside Passage, Tracy Arm Fjord and Sawyer Glacier (July) |
| | 9-day roundtrip Vancouver: Sitka, Hoonah, Skagway, Juneau, Ketchikan; scenic cruising: Inside Passage and Hubbard Glacier (Aug) |

**DINING OPTIONS**   Food is a focus at Oceania, which offers menus overseen by celebrated chef Jacques Pépin and multiple gourmet eateries on every ship. Even Oceania's smallest vessels offer an Italian eatery and steakhouse in addition to a main restaurant, and the food at all three is superb. While you'll pay extra for drinks on Oceania, one of the premium aspects of a sailing with the line is that none of its restaurants come with an extra charge, in contrast to the norm on the ships operated by the likes of Princess, Holland America, and Royal Caribbean. Another nice feature of Oceania's longer sailings is that entrees and featured items are not repeated, allowing the galley staff to show off their skills with great variety. Pépin, the line's Executive Culinary Director, works with Oceania's chefs to develop exciting and exotic dishes as well as more traditional ones. For those who want more, Oceania's ships also offer afternoon pizza, ice cream and sundae bars, 24-hour complimentary room service, and afternoon tea. Alternatives include Canyon Ranch Spa Cuisine and vegetarian and kosher meals upon request.

**ACTIVITIES**   Oceania does not go out of its way to provide an extensive list of things for passengers to do, in keeping with its informal style and port-intensive sailings. It offers lectures on the destination and the ports of call. The beautiful library has lots of reading selections. Weather permitting, the private cabanas are a great place to hang out and watch the scenery unfold. Dance classes and cooking lessons are part of a sea-day's agenda. And there's plenty of live music around the ship to enjoy.

**CHILDREN'S PROGRAMS**   While kids may be on board, it's mostly up to their parents to entertain them. Oceania's ships have no facilities specifically for kids and really don't cater to them. That said, in 2013 Oceania introduced the Alaska Explorer Youth Program for select Alaskan sailings, a program designed for children ages 5 to 13 that is supervised by experienced youth counselors. It includes games, activities, and Alaska-inspired special events.

**ENTERTAINMENT**   Show lounges on Oceania ships, including the Alaska-based *Regatta*, are relatively small and limit what performers can do. But *Regatta* has an eight-piece orchestra for shows and musical entertainment, a small team of performers, and cabaret acts. Depending on the cruise, there may be a string quartet, flamenco guitarist, concert pianist, jazz combos, local and regional folk ensembles, and the occasional headline entertainers.

**SERVICE** The *Regatta's* crew complement of 400 (European officers and international crew) does a great job, and the passenger-to-crew ratio of 1.7 is right there with the top luxury lines. Service is warm and friendly without being overbearing. In the dining room and bars, staff is particularly skillful at getting to know passenger names. In the main dining room, service can be a bit rushed (they do need to turn over the tables) and, because many of the tables are a bit close to each other, a bit informal. It's a much more relaxed experience in the alternative restaurants. Cabin service is excellent, and those rooms with butler service get extra pampering.

**CRUISETOURS & ADD-ON PROGRAMS** For those who have never been to Alaska before, a land trip before or after the cruise is virtually a must. Oceania's brochure includes a 5-day pre-cruise tour package from Anchorage that includes a combination of rail and bus travel. All transfers and hotels as well as most meals are included in the pricing. The price for this 5-day program is $2,699 per person, double occupancy and $3,199 per person, single occupancy. Oceania also offers hotel packages in San Francisco, Vancouver, and Anchorage for pre/post stays. Prices depend on number of days booked.

# Oceania Regatta

### The Verdict

*Regatta* is a terrific midsize ship carrying 684 passengers in a decidedly deluxe/upscale, informal atmosphere. Dining and service are key elements in this non-glitzy ship, with very classy decor and features. The ship is a great midpoint between the more heavily populated premium ships and the more expensive luxury ships.

### Specifications

| | | | |
|---|---|---|---|
| Size (in tons) | 30,277 | Crew | 400 |
| Passengers (double occ.) | 684 | Passenger/Crew Ratio | 1.7:1 |
| Passenger/Space Ratio | 44 | Year Launched | 1998 |
| Total Cabins/Veranda Cabins | 342/232 | Last Refurbishment/Upgrade | 2011 |

### Frommer's Ratings (Scale of 1–5)                    ★★★★½

| | | | |
|---|---|---|---|
| Cabin Comfort & Amenities | 4 | Dining Options | 4.5 |
| Appearance & Upkeep | 5 | Gym, Spa & Sports Facilities | 4.5 |
| Public Comfort/Space | 4.5 | Children's Facilities | N/A |
| Decor | 4.5 | Enjoyment Factor | 4.5 |

**THE SHIP IN GENERAL** *Regatta,* a midsize 30,277-ton vessel, carrying only 684 passengers, is an upper premium vessel, offering a great compromise between the bigger premium ships and the more expensive luxury ships. The space ratio (the industry measure that tells you how spacious a ship is going to be based on the amount of inside room per person) is 44, a nice midpoint in today's market. It's a calm experience where passengers mostly fend for themselves without relying on the ship to keep them active every minute of every day. It's mostly a couples experience that is decidedly not for kids. The decor of the ship is old-world country-club classy in a mix of styles—with some public rooms such as the library, Grand Bar, and the simply gorgeous atrium/ staircase. The refurbishment scheduled for 2014 will really make a big difference: suites, cabins, and public rooms redone in the more current colors and decor of the line's newer ships; new bathrooms in the Owner's and Vista suites; expanded restaurants; the addition of a classic, Italian-style Baristas coffee bar (a staple of Oceania's newer ships); and new steam and changing rooms in the Canyon Ranch SpaClub. New original artwork, in line with the celebrated collection on *Marina* and *Riviera,* will be a nice addition as well.

**CABINS**   The 342 rooms break down into 16 different pricing categories. Realistically, however, there are eight types of rooms. At the top end of the spectrum are the six Owner's Suites and four Vista Suites, located fore and aft on decks 6, 7, and 8. Including their verandas, these rooms range from 786 to nearly 1,000 square feet. The 52 Penthouse Suites are all on deck 8 and measure 322 square feet including the veranda. These categories come with butler service.

The three categories of Concierge Level Veranda Staterooms on deck 7 and the two categories of Veranda Staterooms on deck 6 all measure 216 square feet including the veranda. The four categories of Deluxe Ocean View Staterooms on decks 3, 4, 6, and 7 are 143 or 165 square feet. The 28 Inside Staterooms measure 160 square feet.

Naturally, the larger rooms come with the most amenities. For example, butler service comes with penthouses on up; Jacuzzis, 42-inch plasma TVs, a laptop computer, and more are in the Owner's and Vista suites; living room area and bathtubs in the Penthouse Suites; and large flatscreen TVs and premier services (such as priority restaurant reservations and debarkation) in the concierge level rooms. The rooms were redone in 2011 to include custom-crafted fabric headboards, new lighting and wenge walnut paneling, queen or twin Tranquility Beds, vanity desk, breakfast table, 20" flatscreen TVs with DVD player, security safe, goose-down pillows, Egyptian-cotton linens, plush towels, Grohe handheld shower head, full length mirror, and more.

## CABINS & RATES

| CABINS | PER DIEMS FROM | SQ. FT. | FRIDGE | HAIR DRYER | SITTING AREA | TV |
|---|---|---|---|---|---|---|
| Inside | $350 | 160 | yes | yes | yes | yes |
| Outside | $400 | 165 | yes | yes | yes | yes |
| Outside w/ Veranda | $460 | 215 | yes | yes | yes | yes |
| Penthouses/ Suites | $600–$850 | 322–1,000 | yes | yes | yes | yes |

**PUBLIC AREAS**   Beyond the very attractive reception area on deck 4 with a reception desk, concierge, and shore excursion desk, the rest of the public areas cover deck 5 and 9 through 11. Deck 5 starts with the Lounge at one end, where all performances and most activities take place, including cooking demos, dance classes, lectures, and more. At the other end is the Grand Dining Room. Midship has the casino, shops, and two great bars—the martini bar and lounge, with an extensive list of beverage options and, often, live music before and after dinner; and the lovely Grand Bar, adjacent to

Oceania Cruises

THE CRUISE LINES: THE BIG SHIPS

the main dining room; comfy seating and excellent service make this a great spot before meals. Deck 9 has the Canyon Ranch SpaClub at one end with salon, fitness center, treatment rooms, and steam rooms/lockers. Tucked in nearby are the Internet facility and the card room. At the other end is the Terrace Cafe. In between, naturally, is the pool area. It's not a huge pool but it has two whirlpools, plenty of seating, and comfy loungers. On the side opposite the Grill is The Patio, a wonderful, relaxing space. Deck 10 offers up the forward-looking Horizons Bar at one end and Toscana/Polo Grill at the other. Just outside the alternative restaurants is the library, perhaps the most beautiful room of its kind to be found anywhere at sea. Forward on deck 11 is the sundeck; at the very front end are the private cabanas. They're a bit pricey, but for scenic days in Alaska, they're a sure bet to be booked early.

**DINING OPTIONS** *Oceania Regatta* features four primary places to dine. First is the Grand Dining Room on deck 5. It holds about 340 passengers, all open seating, for breakfast, lunch, and dinner. While there are plenty of tables for two, some of them are side by side, so it doesn't offer much privacy. For more intimacy, try and get a table along the wall or window. Table settings include Versace bone china, Riedel crystal, and Christofle silverware. Menus, all prepared under the auspices of famed chef Jacques Pépin, are a delight; not one of the nightly international-cuisine entrees and specialties is repeated during a cruise. In addition to the regular menu, Canyon Ranch Spa Cuisine as well as vegetarian and kosher options are available. The two alternative restaurants, Polo Grill, offering steaks, chops and seafood (98 seats), and Toscana (96 seats), for Italian dining, are terrific. There's no extra charge, but reservations are required. Casual dining is available for all meals in the Terrace Cafe, which has 154 seats inside and 186 seats outside. The eatery offers up buffets (with some custom-made items) for breakfast and lunch and converts to a really nice alternative for evenings, with tapas, pasta, sushi, and various other dishes. The aft, outdoor section is a great location for scenery watching on summer evenings in Alaska, when it stays light so late. In addition, there's 24-hour room service at no charge, sunrise continental breakfast in the Horizon lounge, and pizza.

**POOL, FITNESS, SPA & SPORTS FACILITIES** The Canyon Ranch SpaClub, a nautical branch of Arizona's famous Canyon Ranch, offers up a wide range of spa and salon services including its signature Canyon Stone Massage, Thai Massage, and Total Elegance Facial. Special treatments for men are on the menu. It also offers wellness lectures and lifestyle analysis, holistic sessions, a thalassotherapy pool, steam rooms, private spa deck with day beds, personal fitness training, yoga and Pilates, aerobics, and step and strength-training classes. The smallish pool is ship-center on deck 9, while the short jogging track goes around part of deck ten.

# PRINCESS CRUISES

2844 Avenue Rockefeller, Santa Clarita, CA 91355. ℂ **800/PRINCESS** (774-6237) or 661/753-0000. Fax 661/753-1535. www.princess.com.

## Pros

- **Good service.** The warm-hearted Italian, British, and Filipino service crew does a great job. On a Princess cruise a few years ago, one barman with a glorious cockney accent (which we noted he could mute or emphasize at will) was a huge hit with our group, dispensing one-liners, simple magic tricks, and drinks with equal facility. We've met others on Princess ships with the same gift for making passengers feel welcome without being overly familiar.

o **Private verandas.** Virtually all the line's Alaska ships have scads and scads of balconies, some of them in as many as 75 percent of the cabins.

## Cons

o **Average food.** The ships' cuisine is perfectly fine if you're not a foodie, but if you are, you'll find that it's pretty banquet-hall-esque.

**THE LINE IN A NUTSHELL**   The company strives, successfully, to please a wide variety of passengers. It offers more choices in terms of accommodations, dining, and entertainment than nearly any other line.

**THE EXPERIENCE**   If you were to put Carnival, Royal Caribbean, Celebrity, and Holland America in a big bowl and mix them all together, you'd come up with Princess Cruises' megaships. The *Coral, Island, Grand,* and *Crown Princess* are less glitzy and frenzied than the ships of, say, Carnival and Royal Caribbean; not quite as cutting-edge as Celebrity's *Solstice* and *Millennium;* and more exciting, youthful, and entertaining than Holland America's near-megas. The Princess fleet appeals to a wider cross-section of cruisers by offering loads of choices and activities, plus touches of big-ship glamour, along with plenty of the private balconies, quiet nooks, and calm spaces that characterize smaller, more intimate-size vessels. Aboard Princess, you get a lot of bang for your buck, attractively packaged and well executed.

Although its ships serve every corner of the globe, nowhere is the Princess presence more visible than in Alaska. Through its affiliate, Princess Tours, the company owns wilderness lodges, motorcoaches, and railcars in the 49th state, making it one of the major players in the Alaska cruise market, alongside Holland America and, increasingly, Royal Caribbean Cruises' two brands, Celebrity and Royal Caribbean International. Princess also operates spectacular wilderness lodges, including the River Princess Wilderness Lodge at Cooper Landing near Wrangell–St. Elias National Park.

In 2004, Princess became the first line to use the rather nondescript Whittier as the northern terminus for its Gulf cruises instead of the more commonly used Seward, and it has done so ever since. Whittier's primary advantage over Seward is that it's about 60 miles closer to Anchorage. Passengers bound for rail tours of Denali National Park are able to board their trains right on the pier instead of taking a bus to Anchorage and then embarking on their rail carriages. The inauguration of the service was yet another effort by a cruise line to gain a competitive edge over its Alaska rivals. The battle for the minds and wallets of the public is being fought as much on land as at sea these days. With so many ship lines striving to attract new passengers or persuade old ones to come back, every little bit helps. The competition goes on, to the benefit of the traveling public. Princess Cruises is now a member of the same group that owns Holland America and Carnival, both of them highly visible in the Alaska cruise market. That gives the parent, Miami-based Carnival Corp., control of no fewer than 15 ships in Alaska in 2014.

**THE FLEET**   Princess's diverse fleet in Alaska in 2014 comprises seven ships, all but two of which have entered service since the start of the millennium. The fleet includes the *Crown Princess,* completed in 2006; the *Coral* and *Island,* of 2002/2003 vintage; and the *Golden* and *Star,* built in 2001 and 2002, respectively; plus the *Grand Princess,* unveiled in 1998. The much smaller *Pacific Princess* (1999) completes Princess's Alaska fleet this year. The ships generally are pretty but not stunning, bright but not gaudy, spacious but not overwhelmingly so, and decorated in a comfortable, restrained style that's a combination of classic and modern. They're a great choice when you want a step up from Carnival, Royal Caribbean, and Norwegian but aren't interested in (or can't afford) the luxury of Regent Seven Seas or Silversea.

**PASSENGER PROFILE**   Typical Princess passengers are likely to be between about 50 and 65 and are often experienced cruisers who know what they want and are prepared to pay for it. But the line also is popular with families, particularly multi-generation families, thanks to its solid children's programs and a-little-something-for-everyone vibe.

**DINING OPTIONS**   In general, Princess serves meals that are good, if hardly gourmet. But you've got to give it points for at least trying to be flexible: About a decade ago, Princess implemented a new fleetwide dining option known as Anytime Dining. Basically, this plan allows passengers to sign up for the traditional first or second seating for dinner, or for a come-as-you-please restaurant-style dining option. The latter allows you to eat dinner anytime between 5:30pm and midnight, though you must be seated by 10pm. Passengers who choose the restaurant-style option may request a cozy table for two or bring along a half-dozen shipmates, depending on their mood that evening. It's also possible to eat all your meals in the Horizon Court cafe on all Princess ships in Alaska. If you don't go to the main dining room, though, you may miss one of Princess's best features: its pastas. The newest ships also have several alternative-dining restaurant options, including a steakhouse, and it's our experience that meals at these restaurants are well worth the price of admission, ranging from $15 to $25 per person.

**ACTIVITIES**   Princess passengers can expect enough onboard activity to keep them going from morning to night if they've a mind to, and enough hideaways to let them do absolutely nothing if that's their thing. The line doesn't go out of its way to make passengers feel that they're spoilsports if they don't participate in the amateur-night tomfoolery or learn to fold napkins. These activities are usually there, along with the inevitable bingo, shuffleboard, and the rest, but they're low-key. Internet access is provided on all the ships for 75¢ per minute. Various packages that bring the cost down are also available for those who use the Internet more—for instance, $55 for 100 minutes, $75 for 150 minutes, and $100 for 250 minutes. The line's ScholarShip@Sea program, which allows passengers to take classes in subjects as diverse as photography, computers, cooking, and even pottery, has been hugely popular since it was pioneered by Princess in 2003. All the Princess ships in Alaska also are equipped with Nintendo Wii Fit game systems, projected on a wide screen.

Specifically in Alaska, the line has naturalists and park rangers on board to offer commentary.

**CHILDREN'S PROGRAMS**   Supervised activities are held year-round for ages 3 to 17, clustered in three groups: Princess Pelicans for ages 3 to 7, Shockwaves for ages 8 to 12, and Remix for ages 13 to 17. For more than a decade now Princess has sought to broaden its appeal and distance itself from its old image as a staid, adults-only line, and all the ships are now well equipped for children and clearly intended to cater to

## Princess Fleet Itineraries

| SHIP | ITINERARIES |
| --- | --- |
| **Coral/Island/Crown** | 7-night Gulf of Alaska: North- and southbound between Vancouver, BC, and Whittier/Anchorage, visiting Ketchikan, Juneau, and Skagway, and cruising Glacier Bay and College Fjord or Hubbard Glacier (May–Sept) |
| **Grand/Golden** | 7-night Inside Passage: Round-trip from Seattle, visiting Ketchikan, Juneau, Skagway, Tracy Arm or Glacier Bay National Park, and Victoria, BC (May–Sept) |
| **Pacific** | 7-night Inside Passage with Glacier Bay: Round-trip from Vancouver, BC, visiting Ketchikan, Juneau, Skagway, Tracy Arm or Glacier Bay National Park (May–Sept) |
| **Star** | 10- and 11-night Inside Passage: Round-trip from San Francisco, visiting Juneau, Skagway or Icy Strait Point, Ketchikan, and Victoria, BC, plus cruising Tracy Arm or Glacier Bay (May–Sept) |

families. Each ship has a spacious children's playroom and a sizable area of fenced-in outside deck for kids only, with a shallow pool and tricycles. Teen centers have computers, video games, and a sound system. Wisely, these areas are placed as far away as possible from the adult passengers.

**ENTERTAINMENT**   From glittering Vegas-style shows to New York cabaret-singer performances to a rocking disco, this line provides a terrific blend of musical delights, and you'll always find a cozy spot where some soft piano or jazz music is being performed. You'll also find entertainers such as hypnotists, puppeteers, and comedians, plus karaoke for you audience-participation types. In the afternoons, there are always a couple of sessions of that ubiquitous cruise favorite, the Newlywed and Not-So-Newlywed Game. Each of the ships also has a wine bar selling caviar by the ounce and vintage wine, champagne, and iced vodka by the glass. The Princess casinos are sprawling and exciting places, too, and are bound to excite gamblers with their lights and action. Good-quality piano-bar music and strolling musicians, along with dance music in the lounge, are part of the pre- and post-dinner entertainment.

For years, Princess has had a connection to Hollywood—this is the *Love Boat* line, after all. It's the only line we know of where you can watch yesterday's and today's television shows on your in-room TV. Also shown are A&E, Biography, E! Entertainment TV, Nickelodeon, Discovery Channel, BBC, and National Geographic productions. Like several other lines, Princess also shows recently released movies.

**SERVICE**   Throughout the fleet, the service in all areas—dining room, lounge, cabin maintenance, and so on—tends to be of consistently high quality. An area in which Princess particularly shines is the efficiency of its shore-excursion staff. Getting 2,600-plus people off a ship and onto motorcoaches, trains, and helicopters—all staples of any Alaska cruise program—isn't as easy as this company makes it look. And a real benefit of the Princess shore-excursions program is that passengers are sent the options about 60 days before the sailing and can book their choices on an advanced-reservations basis before the trip (tickets are issued on board), either by mail or on the Internet at www.princess.com. The program improves your chances of getting your first choice of tours before they sell out. All of the Princess vessels in Alaska have laundry and dry-cleaning services, as well as their own self-service laundromats. On Princess ships, a $11.50 per-person per-day service charge ($12 for passengers in suites and

THE CRUISE LINES: THE BIG SHIPS

minisuites) is automatically added to your bill. If you want to raise or lower that amount, you can do so at the passenger services desk.

**CRUISETOURS & ADD-ON PROGRAMS**  Princess has an array of land packages this year in Alaska in conjunction with its Gulf of Alaska and Inside Passage voyages. Virtually every part of the state is covered—from the Kenai Peninsula to the Interior to the Far North. The land portions come in 3- to 8-night segments, all combinable with a 7-night cruise. Four types of land itineraries are offered in conjunction with Princess's five wilderness lodges—Denali Explorer, On Your Own, Off the Beaten Path, and Connoisseur (escorted).

## Coral Princess • Island Princess

### The Verdict

These two vessels are plenty big, but such is the sophistication of marine architecture nowadays that passengers don't feel as if they're living with a couple of thousand others. There are lots of places to get away from it all.

### Specifications

| Size (in Tons) | 92,000 | Crew | 900 |
|---|---|---|---|
| Passengers (Double Occ.) | 1,974 | Passenger/Crew Ratio | 2.2 to 1 |
| Space/Passenger Ratio | 44 | Year Launched | 2003/2003 |
| Total Cabins/Veranda Cabins | 987/727 | Last Major Refurbishment | 2013/2010 |

### Frommer's Ratings (Scale of 1–5)                                    ★★★★

| Cabin Comfort & Amenities | 4 | Dining Options | 4 |
|---|---|---|---|
| Ship Cleanliness & Maintenance | 4 | Gym, Spa & Sports Facilities | 5 |
| Public Comfort/Space | 4 | Children's Facilities | 4.5 |
| Decor | 4 | Enjoyment Factor | 4 |

**THE SHIPS IN GENERAL**  These two ships are essentially twins, with the same amenities and services, and nothing but relatively minor cosmetic differences between them. Roominess is the key here. The ships carry around the same number of passengers as, say, the *Sea Princess,* but have about 20 percent more public space—a noticeable difference.

The ships reflect the marine-design inventiveness that is becoming more obvious with the arrival of every new ship. Both have a 9-hole putting green, a world-class art collection, a spacious kids' and teens' center, a wedding chapel, a cigar lounge, a martini bar (the last two features have become almost standard on new ships), and much more. Decor is tasteful and rich, with a lot of teak decking, stainless steel and marble fittings, and prominent use of light shades of gray, blue, and brown in the soft furnishings.

**CABINS**  The two ships have a remarkable number of outside rooms (almost 90 percent) and a huge number of private balconies—727, or more than 7 out of 10 of the outside units. The smallest accommodations on either of the ships are about 160 square feet, and the largest, the 16 top suites, stretch to 470 square feet, including the veranda. In between, the *Coral* and *Island* offer rooms with square footage ranging from 217 to 248. Don't assume when making a reservation that a minisuite will necessarily come with a veranda; each of the ships has eight minisuites without that amenity, so if you want one, be sure to specify that when you make your reservation. Twenty of the cabins (16 outside, 4 inside) are configured for wheelchair use. They are very spacious—between 217 square feet and 248 square feet.

## CABINS & RATES

| CABINS | PER DIEM RATES | SQ. FT. | FRIDGE | HAIR DRYER | SITTING AREA | TV |
|--------|----------------|---------|--------|------------|--------------|-----|
| Inside | $109–$129 | 156–166 | yes | yes | no | yes |
| Outside | $139–$169 | 217–248 | yes | yes | no | yes |
| Suites | $185–$428 | 280–470 | yes | yes | yes | yes |

**PUBLIC AREAS**  In keeping with the trend these days, the *Coral* and *Island* each have a comfy cigar bar and a martini lounge—the Churchill Lounge and the Crooners Bar, respectively. The nautical-themed Wheelhouse Bars are warm, inviting places to spend time after-hours. Also appealing but more frenetic is the Explorers Lounge, which functions as the disco after dinner. The huge casinos on the *Coral* and *Island* are London- and Paris-themed rooms, respectively. An Internet cafe, a wedding chapel, children's and teens' centers, and a putting green are located on the top deck.

**DINING OPTIONS**  The ships have two main dining rooms and four smaller alternative dining areas—Sabatini's, an elegant Italian eatery found on the most recent vintage Princess ships for which there is a $25-per-head charge (well worth the price); a Creole restaurant called the Bayou Cafe and Steakhouse ($15 per head); the poolside hamburger grill; and the poolside pizza bar. In combination, they allow passengers to eat pretty much when they want and be as formal or as relaxed as they wish.

**POOL, FITNESS, SPA & SPORTS FACILITIES**  There are three pools and five whirlpool tubs. The fitness center is a large, well-stocked, airy room with absolutely the last word in equipment. The Lotus Spa has one of the widest arrays of massage and beauty treatments afloat, including oxygenating facials, an "aromaflex" package that combines the ancient healing therapies of massage and reflexology, and a treatment that involves the placing of heated, oiled volcanic stones on key energy points of the body to release muscular tension and promote relaxation.

# Golden Princess • Star Princess • Grand Princess • Crown Princess

## The Verdict

These four ships, all roughly the same size and similar in layout, are real winners. Despite their size and megacapacity (2,590–3,080 passengers!), you usually won't feel the crush of all those other guests, thanks to plenty of opportunities to "get away from it all."

## Specifications

| Size (in Tons) | 107,500 to 113,000 | Crew | 1,100 to 1,200 |
|----------------|--------------------|------|----------------|
| Passengers (Double Occ.) | 2,590 to 3,080 | Passenger/Crew Ratio | 2.4 to 2.6 to 1 |
| Space/Passenger Ratio | 38 to 42 | Year Launched | 1998/2001/2002/2006 |
| Total Cabins/Veranda Cabins | 1,301/710 | Last Major Refurbishment | 2009/2009/2011/2009 |

## Frommer's Ratings (Scale of 1–5)

★★★★½

| Cabin Comfort & Amenities | 4.5 | Dining Options | 4 |
|---|---|---|---|
| Ship Cleanliness & Maintenance | 4 | Gym, Spa & Sports Facilities | 4 |
| Public Comfort/Space | 4.5 | Children's Facilities | 4 |
| Decor | 4.5 | Enjoyment Factor | 4.5 |

**THE SHIPS IN GENERAL**   With more than dozen decks apiece, the *Golden, Star, Grand,* and *Crown* are taller than the Statue of Liberty (from pedestal to torch). In fact, they're so big that the *Pacific Princess* (take your pick: either the now-departed ship that inspired the original *Love Boat* series or the one of the same name that the company introduced into service a few years ago) could easily fit inside the hull of either of the ships with lots of room to spare.

Inside and out, the vessels—all similar in layout—are a marvel of size and design. They have massive white, boxy bodies, with two of the ships featuring a spoilerlike aft poking up into the air that offers a slightly bizarre, space-age profile (still on the *Golden* and *Star,* the feature was removed recently from the *Crown* and *Grand*). But the ships' interior designs are well laid out and easy to navigate. Amazingly, the ships seldom feel crowded—a tribute to the growing sophistication and creativity of the marine architecture community.

The ships provide an amazing variety of entertainment, dining options, and recreational activities. They have five restaurants each (plus a pizzeria and outdoor grill), four swimming pools, and three show lounges, as well as expansive deck space.

Even the ships' medical centers are grand, boasting high-tech "teleradiology" equipment that enables doctors to transmit X-rays to land-based experts.

**CABINS**   Even the smallest of these ships' inside cabins are quite adequate, at about 160 square feet; standard outside units, sans balcony, go from 165 to 210 square feet; and larger oceanview rooms run between 215 and 255 square feet, including the balcony. All the rooms have twin beds that easily convert to queens, along with refrigerators, televisions, spacious closets, robes, safes, and plenty of drawer space. The larger of the outside rooms comes with a small writing desk. Minisuites give you 325 square feet (including the balcony), and the suites range from 515 to about 800 square feet—again, including the balcony—and feature a tub and shower (regular balcony cabins and non-balcony cabins have only shower stalls). The rooms are tastefully decorated with subdued, hidden lighting, soft furnishings in quiet colors, and eye-catching (though not gallery-quality) art. The ships have 28 wheelchair-accessible cabins. (The Skywalkers disco on a couple of the ships has a wheelchair lift up to the elevated dance floor, too.)

Nearly two-thirds of each of the ships' cabins has balconies. But be forewarned: The verandas are tiered, as they are on so many new ships these days, so passengers in levels above may be able to look down on you. While they might be said to be private, they're really rather exposed. Don't do anything out there you wouldn't want the neighbors to see! TV stations available (geography permitting) include CNN, ESPN, Nickelodeon, BBC programming, and TNT (as well as the inevitable *Love Boat* reruns).

## CABINS & RATES

| CABINS | PER DIEM RATES | SQ. FT. | FRIDGE | HAIR DRYER | SITTING AREA | TV |
|---|---|---|---|---|---|---|
| Inside | $114–$135 | 160 | yes | yes | no | yes |
| Outside | $149–$182 | 168–257 | yes | yes | no | yes |
| Suites | $235–$422 | 323–800 | yes | yes | yes | yes |

**PUBLIC AREAS**  Hey, where'd everyone go? Thanks to the smart layout of the vessels, with lots of small rooms rather than a few large rooms, passengers are dispersed rather than concentrated into one or two main areas; you'll have no problem finding a quiet retreat.

The public areas have a contemporary and upscale appeal, thanks to pleasing color schemes and the well-designed use of wood, marble, and brass. Two full-time florists on each vessel create and care for impressive flower arrangements and a large variety of live plants.

A major overhaul of the *Golden Princess* in 2009 brought a new piazza-style atrium that serves as a central meeting point on the ship and is home to casual, cafelike seating. It's ringed by the International Cafe, where you can pick up a specialty coffee, a pastry, and more, and a wine bar called Vines.

Besides the three—count 'em—main dining rooms on each of the ships, there are two principal alternative eateries: Sabatini's, a fine Italian staple found on every new Princess ship, and the Crown Grill, for steaks and seafood. Other options include the casual Horizon Court and two spaces—the Trident Grill (poolside) and a pizza counter—both with limited hours and both serving snacks and light meals. The ships' restaurants are on the small side, designed that way so you don't feel like you're dining with a crowd and to maintain good acoustics (although you may also feel like the ceiling is closing in on you a bit).

Gamblers will love the sprawling and dazzling 13,500-square-foot casino, among the largest at sea. Near the casino, two lounge areas are ideal for whiling away a few moments before attacking the gaming tables.

The most striking design feature on the *Star* and *Golden* (once a staple of the *Grand*-class design) are their discos, which jut out over the stern and are suspended—scarily, in our opinion—some 155 feet above the water. It's really quite spectacular. If you're scared of heights, of course, don't even think of looking down; you're so far above the water that it's (literally!) breathtaking. Smoke machines and other high-tech gizmos add to the spooky effect at night. During the day, its banquettes make a particularly cozy spot to snuggle up with a good book.

All four of ships have an Internet cafe, and *Crown* also has a library.

**DINING OPTIONS**  The principal alternative eating areas are Sabatini's and the Crown Grill. At Sabatini's, the $25 cover charge gets you the finest Italian food at sea—and gobs of it. The $25-a-head Crown Grill is a traditional steakhouse with steaks and seafood.

**POOL, FITNESS, SPA & SPORTS FACILITIES**  The ships have something like 1.7 acres of open deck space apiece, so it's not hard to find a quiet place to soak in the sun. They each have four great swimming pools, including one with a retractable glass roof so it can double as a sort of solarium (of special importance in Alaska), another touted as a swim-against-the-current pool (although, truth be told, there really isn't enough room to do laps if others are in the water with you), and a third, aft under the disco, that feels miles from the rest of the ship (and is usually the least crowded). There are also nine whirlpool tubs up front.

On the forward sundeck on each of the vessels, surrounding the lap pool and its tiered, amphitheater-style wooden benches, is the large Lotus Spa, which almost appears to be separate from the rest of the ship. Personally, we find the layout to be a bit weird: For instance, there are no showers in the dressing area. The complex includes a very large oceanview salon and an oceanview gym, which is surprisingly small and cramped for a ship of this size (although it has an unusually large aerobics floor).

Other active diversions include basketball, paddle tennis, and a 9-hole putting green.

# Pacific Princess

## The Verdict

An outlier in the Princess fleet, this cozy, midsize vessel (a third the size of most other Princess ships) offers a more intimate version of the Princess experience in Alaska.

## Specifications

| Size (in Tons) | 30,200 | Crew | 373 |
|---|---|---|---|
| Passengers (Double Occ.) | 670 | Passenger/Crew Ratio | 1.8 to 1 |
| Space/Passenger Ratio | 45.2 | Year Launched | 1999 |
| Total Cabins/Veranda Cabins | 334/232 | Last Major Refurbishment | 2010 |

## Frommer's Ratings (Scale of 1–5)                            ★★★★

| Cabin Comfort & Amenities | 4 | Dining Options | 4 |
|---|---|---|---|
| Ship Cleanliness & Maintenance | 4 | Gym, Spa & Sports Facilities | 4 |
| Public Comfort/Space | 4.5 | Children's Facilities | N/A |
| Decor | 4 | Enjoyment Factor | 4 |

**THE SHIP IN GENERAL**   Far smaller than the typical Princess ship, this former Renaissance Cruises vessel is comfortable, traditional, and sedate, with an emphasis on intimate spaces. Like European boutique hotels, it's decorated mostly in warm, dark woods and rich fabrics and offers a small-scale, clubby feel that larger ships can only hope to mimic.

**CABINS**   Cabins are straightforward, no-nonsense spaces with a hint of modern European city hotel: plain off-white walls, tasteful wood trim and furniture, and cheery carpeting and bedspreads. The vast majority are oceanview doubles, some with a balcony and some without, and average about 165 square feet—neither tiny nor huge, but perfectly adequate for most people. All come with a sofa or sofa bed, a minifridge, TV, and vanity. Bathrooms in standard cabins verge on the cramped, with a fairly small shower stall. Balconies are on the small side, large enough for only a small table and chairs. Most cabins on Deck 9 are 322-square-foot minisuites with balconies, adding to the standard cabin amenities a bathtub and a larger seating area. Ten suites measure 786 to 962 square feet and are located at the ship's bow and stern. Five cabins are wheelchair accessible.

## CABINS & RATES

| CABINS | PER DIEM RATES | SQ. FT. | FRIDGE | HAIR DRYER | SITTING AREA | TV |
|--------|----------------|---------|--------|------------|--------------|-----|
| Inside | $109–$131 | 158 | yes | yes | no | yes |
| Outside | $149–$175 | 146-216 | yes | yes | no | yes |
| Suites | $269–$458 | 322-962 | yes | yes | yes | yes |

**PUBLIC AREAS**   Like other former Renaissance ships, the *Pacific Princess* is an elegant yet homey vessel, with classic styling that includes dark-wood paneling, fluted columns, ornate railings and faux fireplaces, gilt-framed classical paintings, Oriental-style carpets, frilly moldings, marble and brass accents, faux skylights and deep-hued upholstery. Think Edwardian sitting room, minus the palm trees. Passengers enter into a modest two-story reception Atrium that (intentionally or not—and we suspect the former) mimics the famous Grand Staircase from *Titanic*. In the bow on Deck 10, the spacious observatory lounge has floor-to-ceiling windows and cozy seating areas, and is used for dancing in the evenings and for various activities during the day. Farther astern on the same deck, the cozy library is decorated in a traditional English style, with high-back chairs and deep-cushioned couches, faux mahogany paneling, marble faux fireplace, and a trompe l'oeil garden skylight. Most of the other public rooms are on Deck 5. Up front, the Cabaret Lounge seats about 350 and offers performances on its floor-level stage. At midship, a smallish, but comfortable casino offers gaming tables and slots, while the attached Casino Bar offers musical entertainment in the evenings. A card room and Internet center on Deck 9 round out the public room offerings.

**DINING OPTIONS**   The main dining room is an elegant single-level space surrounded on three sides by windows. It's spacious and understated, with simple wood-veneer wall panels and lighting sconces. Just outside the maitre d's station is the cozy, country-club-esque Club Bar, the perfect spot for a pre-dinner drink. Up on Deck 10, in the stern, are the ships' two alternative restaurants: Sabatini's for Italian cuisine and the Sterling Steakhouse for slabs of beef. Intimately sized (seating only about 90 passengers each), they're decorated to match their cuisine: Mediterranean style for Sabatini's, dark woods for Sterling. The restaurants are open on alternating nights. In the stern on Deck 9 is a buffet restaurant that incorporates a pizzeria and barbecue. There's also a pool grill out on deck.

**POOL, FITNESS, SPA & SPORTS FACILITIES**   The ship has a central pool area with a small pool and two hot tubs, surrounded by wall-to-wall deck chairs. A short jogging track (11 laps makes a mile) wraps around the deck above, while one deck above that is additional sunning space, a golf practice cage, and shuffleboard. Just forward of the pool area, the smallish Lotus Spa offers massages, facials, and other treatments, while the next-door beauty salon makes you gorgeous. A decent-size oceanview gym with aerobics floor is attached. Just forward of the spa is a small outdoor lounging area with a hydrotherapy whirlpool overlooking the bow. It's probably the most private sunning spot on the ship, save for your private balcony.

# REGENT SEVEN SEAS CRUISES

8300 NW 33rd St., Suite 100 Miami, Fl. 33122. ☎ **866/217-1369.** www.rssc.com.

## Pros

o **Overall excellence.** The line has a no-tipping policy, excellent food, open seating for meals, generally fine service, great accommodations, and creative shore excursions. *Seven Seas Navigator*'s recent refurbishment really brought the ship up to date.

o **Great room service.** It's about the best we've found on a ship, with the food served promptly, fresh, and course-by-course or all at once—your choice (okay, so the room-service pizza isn't so great).

o **Liquor included in the price.** Regent has a fleetwide liquor-inclusive policy on all departures.

## Cons

o **Sedate nightlife.** Although the line recently upgraded its evening entertainment, many guests, exhausted after a full day in port, retire early, perhaps to watch a movie on their in-suite DVD player, leaving only a few night owls in the disco and other lounges. The ship does have some occasional late-night fun, though, for those with the energy to stay up that long.

**THE LINE IN A NUTSHELL**   Regent's guests travel in style and extreme comfort. Its brand of luxury is casually elegant and subtle, its cuisine among the best in the industry. The line operates three midsize ships geared toward affluent and worldly travelers. This year marks the line's 15th full season in Alaska, and it'll be deploying the refurbished, all-suite, 490-passenger *Seven Seas Navigator* to the region for the fifth year in a row.

**THE EXPERIENCE**   The Regent Seven Seas experience means outstanding food, service, and accommodations in an environment that's a little more casual than some of its luxury competitors; there is, for instance, no formal dress night during its 7-night Alaska program. The line also moved to being ultra-all-inclusive in 2009, with shore excursions included in the cruise fare (excluding the more exclusive Regent Choice tours). The *Navigator*—no stranger to Alaska, as it was deployed there in 2000, 2002, and again in 2010 through 2013—is one of the most intimate and comfortable ships at sea, providing its passengers with mostly large outside suites and spacious public areas.

**THE FLEET**   As we noted above, *Seven Seas Navigator* is not new to the Alaska market, having returned in 2010 and 2011 after an 8-year absence. It is the smallest ship in the Regent fleet, with an elegant yet comfortable modern design and a graceful yet casual onboard atmosphere. Nearly 9 out of 10 cabins on the ship have balconies, an advantage in stunning view-laden Alaska.

**PASSENGER PROFILE**   Regent tends to attract travelers from their 50s to their 70s (sometimes even in their 30s and 40s) who have a high household income but don't like to flaunt their wealth. The typical guest profile is that of an admirably well-educated, well-traveled, and inquisitive person. The travelers may also be a mixed bunch. On a recent cruise, passengers included an economist for an international financial

## Regent Seven Seas Cruises Fleet Itineraries

| SHIP | ITINERARIES |
|---|---|
| **Seven Seas Navigator** | 7-night Gulf of Alaska: North- and southbound between Vancouver, BC, and Seward/Anchorage, visiting Ketchikan, Juneau, Skagway, and Sitka, and cruising Tracy Arm and Hubbard Glacier (late May–Aug) |
| | 12-night Inside Passage: North- and southbound between San Francisco and Vancouver, BC, visiting Astoria, Ketchikan, Juneau, Skagway, Sitka, and Victoria, plus cruising Hubbard Glacier and Icy Strait (May and Aug) |

institution, a man who opens banks for a living, a retired auto-parts engineer, and an environmental lobbyist.

**DINING OPTIONS**   Regent's cuisine would gain high marks even if it were on land. Service by professional waiters adds to the experience, as do little touches such as fine china and fresh flowers on the tables. The complimentary wines served with meals are generally quite good; there's very little reason to want to trade up (however, the wines available at extra cost are actually fairly priced). On the *Seven Seas Navigator,* the attractive Compass Rose room's new table settings, window decor, and comfy chairs make dining a pleasure.

**ACTIVITIES**   The line assumes that, for the most part, guests want to entertain themselves on board, but that doesn't mean there isn't plenty to do on board the ships, considering their relatively small size. On the line's Alaska cruises, there are lectures by local Alaska experts and golf instruction. There are card and board games, art auctions, blackjack and Ping-Pong tournaments, bingo, and big-screen movies with popcorn. Bridge instructors are on board for select sailings; check when you make a reservation. Like other Regent ships, the Alaska-based *Seven Seas Navigator* has Wi-Fi throughout and offers great deals on Internet packages (an unlimited plan that is $29.99 per day, 500 minutes for $350, and pay-as-you-go for $0.99 a minute).

**CHILDREN'S PROGRAMS**   The line in general is adult-oriented, and the smaller *Navigator,* in any case, is not the perfect vehicle for kids.

**ENTERTAINMENT**   The small size of Regent ships limits the line's ability to provide entertainment as lavish as some of its big-ship competitors; however, the program in the *Seven Seas Navigator*'s two-tiered showroom, the South Seven Seas Lounge, includes well-presented, medium-scale production shows with high-quality performers, cabaret acts, and headliners including comedians and magicians, and sometimes members of symphony orchestras and other musical groups. New shows launched in 2013 include **Broadway Tonight** featuring music from hit Tony Award–winning musicals including *Book of Mormon, Spiderman, Mamma Mia!, Rock of Ages,* and *Les Miserables.* **The Dawning of Aquarius** showcases the music of the 1960s with favorite songs from The Four Seasons and The Rolling Stones to Sonny & Cher and The Beatles, and **Piano Men** is a celebration of the music of two industry giants—Sir Elton John and Billy Joel. The library stocks books and movies, which guests can play on their in-suite DVD player.

**SERVICE**   The senior dining room staff on Regent vessels generally has had experience at fine hotels as well as on ships. (They provide service so good that you don't really notice it.) A small point about bar service: During our last cruise, just about all the staff members in the public lounges remembered our favorite drinks after just one meeting. Excellent room stewards and butlers do a great job in the suites, and bar service is outstanding. The *Seven Seas Navigator* also provides dry cleaning and full- and self-service laundry. On Regent ships, gratuities for the staff are included in the fare and are not expected.

**CRUISETOURS & ADD-ON PROGRAMS** The Denali Corridor features prominently in Regent Seven Seas' land packages. The company's brochure includes 4-night packages originating in Anchorage. The rates start at under $2,184 depending on the itinerary chosen. The line also includes a free 1-night luxury hotel stay at the beginning of all Alaska cruises in Anchorage.

## Seven Seas Navigator

### The Verdict

*Seven Seas Navigator* is a true luxury leader among the medium-size ships in Alaska. All rooms are outside-facing, and 90 percent have balconies; the spacious public and deck areas make viewing easy and supremely comfortable. A recent multi-milliondollar refurbishment really spiffed up the ship nicely.

### Specifications

| | | | |
|---|---|---|---|
| Size (in Tons) | 28,550 | Crew | 345 |
| Passengers (Double Occ.) | 490 | Passenger/Crew Ratio | 1.5 to 1 |
| Space/Passenger Ratio | 58 | Year Launched | 1999 |
| Total Cabins/Veranda Cabins | 245/208 | Last Major Refurbishment | 2012 |

### Frommer's Ratings (Scale 1–5) ★★★★★

| | | | |
|---|---|---|---|
| Cabin Comfort & Amenities | 5 | Dining Options | 4.5 |
| Ship Cleanliness & Maintenance | 5 | Gym, Spa & Sports Facilities | 4.5 |
| Public Comfort/Space | 5 | Children's Facilities | N/A |
| Decor | 4.5 | Enjoyment Factor | 5 |

**THE SHIP IN GENERAL** The *Seven Seas Navigator* is a luxurious vessel that carries its 490 guests in extreme comfort. The amount of public space per person is enormous for a ship this size, and its roomy, all-outside accommodations design gives everyone lots of private space as well. The three dining rooms, plus poolside options, ensure that nobody on the *Seven Seas Navigator* ever goes hungry. Daytime activities are not extensive, but that seems to suit the clientele just fine. The company has made enormous strides in service and entertainment in recent years, putting this ship in the upper echelon of luxury cruises. It is arguably one of the most luxurious ships in Alaska this year.

**CABINS** All rooms are oceanview suites, more than 85 percent of them with private verandas, the remainder with huge picture windows. Even the smallest of the suites is a very large 301 square feet. The largest of the suites is a whopping 1,173 square feet, including a 106-square-foot balcony. All suites—even nonveranda units—have separate living room areas, and top levels of suites have dining areas as well. Every suite comes with queen-size beds that convert to twins, walk-in closets, tons of drawer space, marble-appointed bathrooms with shower and separate tubs (some have large shower stalls instead), TVs and DVD players, refrigerators stocked with complimentary bottled water and soft drinks, safes, phones, and 24-hour room service. You can order full meals from the dining room menu, served in-suite. The larger suites come with butler service and upgraded amenities, including such things as iPod players/speakers. Four of the suites are wheelchair-accessible. Some of the nonveranda rooms are very appealing to those who do not crave outside space; the space allocated to the veranda is part of the room itself, and there's a huge picture window.

## CABINS & RATES

| Cabins | Per Diem Rates | Sq. Ft. | Fridge | Hair Dryer | Sitting Area | TV |
|--------|----------------|---------|--------|------------|--------------|-----|
| Suites | $614–$2,499*/ $499–$1,333** | 301–1,173 | yes | yes | yes | yes |

*Rates based on 7-night cruise.*
**Rates based on 12-night cruise.*

**PUBLIC AREAS**    Italian-designed and -built, the *Seven Seas Navigator* has an eclectic interior that's elegant yet comfortable. *Seven Seas Navigator* guests may relax in a number of intimate evening bar/lounges, including Galileo's, with its live piano music; the Stars Lounge, with DJ-chosen dance tunes; the Navigator Lounge, popular all day long now that it's also a coffee bar; and the Connoisseur Bar, a haven for cigar smokers. The casino has blackjack, roulette, Caribbean stud poker, minicraps, and slots. Shoppers can indulge at a few small, classy boutiques selling clothes, jewelry, and your usual array of cruise-line logo items (but no alcohol). The library/computer area has books, games, and DVDs as well as nine new computer terminals. Guests only pay for transmission time and can use such programs as Word free of charge (a very nice feature).

**DINING OPTIONS**    The design of the main dining room, the Compass Rose, has a great open feeling so that passengers can see out both sides of the ship without straining, but it still gives one the impression of eating in a much smaller, more intimate facility. Compass Ross serves lavish breakfasts, lunches, and dinners. Its dinner menu has such yummy starter items as chilled kiwi and mango with apricot liqueur; napoleon of crabmeat, avocado, and black sesame crisp; and grilled calamari marinated with herbs. For entrees, choices include a fabulous grilled rib-eye steak, couscous Casablanca, baked fresh turbot fillet Viennoise, and much more. The addition of the magnificent steakhouse Prime 7 and the more casual La Veranda in recent years, meanwhile, has added a whole new dimension to the dining experience on the *Seven Seas Navigator*. Prime 7 has an extensive list of main courses, including beef cuts, chops, Alaska king crab, lobster, and more. Meals also come with a vast range of appetizers, side dishes, and desserts (there's no charge, but reservations are a must). La Veranda serves a breakfast and lunch buffet, and in the evening it is transformed into Sette Mari at La Veranda, the line's casual Italian restaurant. Buffets in La Veranda are not as lavish as they are on the line's *Seven Seas Voyager* and *Seven Seas Mariner,* but diners definitely will not go hungry. In the evening, the Sette Mari at La Veranda experience showcases authentic antipasti and Italian specialties served a la carte and paired with fine wines. Sette Mari at La Veranda is open for dinner only. As is typical for luxury lines, neither Prime 7 or La Veranda come with an extra charge. Room service also is readily available (if only the pizza were better). An enlarged and enhanced pool grill and bar serves a very nice range of lunch fare such as hot dogs, custom-made hamburgers, paninis, and salads.

**POOL, FITNESS, SPA & SPORTS FACILITIES**   When the ship was refurbished in late 2009, the spa was changed into a Canyon Ranch SpaClub. It's a classy operation, and there's virtually no product push either during or after treatments. The smallish gym and aerobics area do not seem to get crowded despite their size. The five treatment rooms and beauty salon offer the normal range of services (treatments aren't cheap though). The pool is flanked by heated whirlpools and surrounded by an enormous amount of open deck space (the pool area was actually reduced in favor of more comfy seats). Recreational facilities beyond the gym include a golf driving cage, a paddle tennis court, a jogging track, table tennis, and shuffleboard.

# ROYAL CARIBBEAN INTERNATIONAL

1050 Caribbean Way, Miami, FL 33132. ✆ **866/562-7625.** www.royalcaribbean.com.

## Pros

- **Great spas and recreational facilities.** Royal Caribbean's Alaska ships for 2014 all have elaborate health-club and spa facilities, a covered swimming pool, and large, open sundeck areas.
- **Great observation areas.** The Viking Crown Lounge and other glassed-in areas make excellent observation rooms for gazing at the Alaska sights.
- **Quality entertainment.** Royal Caribbean spends big bucks on entertainment, which includes high-tech show productions. Headliners are often featured.

## Cons

- **Crowds.** As with some other big ships, you almost need a map to get around, and you'll likely experience the inevitable lines for buffets, debarkation, and boarding of buses during shore excursions.

**THE LINE IN A NUTSHELL**   This bold, brash, innovative company now in its 44th year has the largest passenger capacity in the industry on the biggest ships. Royal Caribbean International introduced the concept of the megaship with its *Sovereign of the Seas* in 1988, and the industry hasn't been the same since. The mass-market style of cruising that Royal Caribbean sells aboard its megaships is reasonably priced and has nearly every diversion imaginable.

**THE EXPERIENCE**   The ships are more informal than formal and are well run, with a large team of friendly service employees paying close attention to day-to-day details. Dress is generally casual during the day and informal most evenings, with 2 formal nights on a typical 7-night cruise. The contemporary decor on Royal Caribbean vessels doesn't bang you over the head with glitz like, say, the Carnival line; it's more subdued, classy, and witty, with lots of glass, greenery, and art. All the Royal Caribbean vessels feature the line's trademark Viking Crown Lounge, an observation area located in a circular glass structure on the upper deck (in some cases, encircling the smokestack). Another popular trademark feature is the ships' nautically themed Schooner bars. The range of what's available on different Royal Caribbean ships does vary somewhat depending on age, size, and design.

**THE FLEET**  Royal Caribbean owns most of the largest ships in the world, including the recently introduced *Oasis of the Seas* and sister ship *Allure of the Seas*—the world's largest vessels at 225,282 gross registered tons. But don't expect to see the line's biggest vessels in Alaska. While *Oasis* and *Allure* have room for 5,400 passengers at double occupancy and several other Royal Caribbean ships can hold nearly 4,000, the largest vessel the line sends to Alaska is the 2,143-passenger *Radiance of the Seas*. Introduced in 2001 as a new category of ship for the line and revitalized in 2011, the vessel has many innovations, including a billiards room with self-leveling pool tables. The *Radiance* is in Gulf of Alaska service between Vancouver, BC, and Seward, Alaska. It's joined in Alaska in 2014 by a second ship that also recently has undergone a major revitalization—the 1,998-passenger *Rhapsody of the Seas,* sailing round-trip out of Seattle.

**PASSENGER PROFILE**  The crowd on Royal Caribbean ships, like the decor, tends to be a notch down on the flashy scale from what you'll find on Carnival and perhaps a notch up from those on, say, Princess or the Holland America Line. Guests represent an age mix from 30 to 60, and an increasing number of families are attracted by the line's well-established and fine-tuned kids' programs.

**DINING OPTIONS**  Food on Royal Caribbean has been upgraded and improved in recent years, and occasionally a dish will knock your socks off. The dining rooms have two seatings with assigned tables at dinner, as well as the more flexible My Time Dining program for dinner, and open seating at breakfast and lunch. Every menu contains selections designed for low-fat, low-cholesterol, and low-salt dining, as well as vegetarian and children's dishes. On the *Radiance,* you also have the option of dining on a reservations-only basis at Chops Grille, a classy steakhouse, or Giovanni's Table, an upscale Italian eatery. The line levies a cover charge of $20 per person at Giovanni's Table and $30 per person at Chops, but in our experience, the food soars above what's served in the dining room. Casual table-service dining is enjoyed at Rita's Cantina for dinner as an alternative for those who don't want to sit in the dining room. Buffet-style breakfast, lunch, and dinner are available in the Windjammer Café, on Deck 11. A basic menu is available from room service 24 hours a day, and during normal dinner hours, a cabin steward can bring you anything being served in the dining room that night. Royal Caribbean bans smoking in the dining rooms on all its vessels.

**ACTIVITIES**  On the activity front, Royal Caribbean has plenty of the standard cruise-line fare (crafts classes, horse racing, bingo, shuffleboard, deck games, line-dancing lessons, wine-and-cheese tastings, cooking demonstrations, and art auctions). But if you want to take it easy and watch the world go by or scan for wildlife, nobody will bother you or cajole you into joining an activity. Port lectures are given on topics such as Alaska wildlife, history, and culture. The ships also have an extensive fitness program called Vitality.

**CHILDREN'S PROGRAMS**  Children's activities are some of the most extensive afloat and include a teen disco, children's play areas, and the Adventure Ocean and teen programs, which have a full schedule of scavenger hunts, arts-and-crafts sessions,

## Royal Caribbean Fleet Itineraries

| SHIP | ITINERARIES |
| --- | --- |
| *Radiance of the Seas* | 7-night Gulf of Alaska: North- and southbound between Vancouver, BC, and Seward, visiting Ketchikan, Juneau, Skagway, Icy Strait Point, and Hubbard Glacier (May–Aug) |
| *Rhapsody of the Seas* | 7-night Sawyer Glacier: Round-trip from Seattle, visiting Juneau, Tracy Arm, Skagway, and Victoria, BC (May–Aug) |

and science presentations—so many activities, in fact, that kids get their own daily activities programs delivered to their cabins. Royal Caribbean also provides teen-only spaces on board every ship in its fleet. After *Radiance* and *Rhapsody* were revitalized as part of the line's fleetwide revitalization program, a Royal Babies and Tots nursery was added, designed by Fisher-Price and Crayola, for youngsters 6 to 36 months of age and up (for a fee of $8 per hour per child).

**ENTERTAINMENT**   Royal Caribbean's entertainment package, which incorporates sprawling, high-tech cabaret stages into each of its ships' showrooms, some with a wall of video monitors to augment live performances, is as good as any other mainstream line. *Rhapsody of the Seas* also features a spectacular aerial-acrobatic musical production called the Centrum Experience in the ship's four-deck-high atrium. Entertainment begins before dinner and continues late, late into the night. There are musical acts, comedy acts, sock hops, toga parties, talent shows, and that great cruise favorite, karaoke. The Vegas-style shows are filled with all the razzle-dazzle guests have come to expect, and these large-cast revues are among the best you'll find on any ship. Royal Caribbean uses 10-piece bands in its main showroom. Show bands and other lounge acts keep the music playing all over the ship.

**SERVICE**   Overall, service in the restaurants and cabins is friendly, accommodating, and efficient. You're likely to be greeted with a smile by someone polishing the brass in a stairwell. That said, big, bustling ships like Royal Caribbean's are no strangers to crowds and lines, and harried servers may not be able to get to you exactly when you'd like them to. Considering the vast armies of personnel required to maintain a line as large as Royal Caribbean, it's a miracle that staffers appear as motivated and enthusiastic as they do. Laundry and dry-cleaning services are available on both the ships, but neither has a self-service laundromat. Royal Caribbean automatically adds daily gratuities in folios of passengers who have not prepaid gratuities prior to boarding, although passengers can modify these payments at any time during the sailing. The line's recommended daily gratuities breakdown is $6.80 per person per day to the dining room staff and $5.20 per person per day to the cabin steward and housekeeping staff ($7.45 for suite attendant and housekeeping staff).

**CRUISETOURS & ADD-ON PROGRAMS**   Royal Caribbean International offers 10- to 13-night cruisetours in Alaska combining a 7-night cruise with a 3- to 6-night land package in the Denali Corridor, in conjunction with the northbound/southbound Inside Passage sailings on board *Radiance of the Seas*. All tours are escorted and spend at least 1 night in Denali National Park and one leg on the Wilderness Express—plush, glass-domed train cars that offer panoramic views of the grand Alaskan frontier. The 10-night Alaska cruisetour prices start at $1,594 per person, based on double occupancy, with package prices varying depending on cabin category, land package, and departure date. Additionally, Royal Caribbean offers pre- and post-cruise hotel stays in Anchorage (from $233 per person double, including transfers) and Vancouver (from $193 per person double, including transfers).

# Radiance of the Seas

## The Verdict

So what if you need a map to find your way around this large vessel? It's worth it if the map leads you to the superb spa, the self-leveling billiards tables, or the revolving bar in the disco.

## Specifications

| Size (in Tons) | 90,090 | Crew | 894 |
|---|---|---|---|
| Passengers (Double Occ.) | 2,143 | Passengers/Crew Ratio | 2.5 to 1 |
| Space/Passenger Ratio | 43 | Year Launched | 2001 |
| Total Cabins/Veranda Cabins | 1,056/577 | Last Major Refurbishment | 2011 |

## Frommer's Ratings (Scale of 1–5)                      ★★★★

| Cabin Comfort & Amenities | 4 | Dining Options | 4.5 |
|---|---|---|---|
| Ship Cleanliness & Maintenance | 4 | Gym, Spa & Sports Facilities | 4.5 |
| Public Comfort/Space | 4 | Children's Facilities | 4 |
| Decor | 4 | Enjoyment Factor | 4 |

**THE SHIP IN GENERAL**    *Radiance of the Seas* was one of Royal Caribbean's first ships of the 21st century, as well as being one of the first vessels in a new class that continues the line's tradition of being an innovator in the industry. Highlights include a billiards room with custom-made, self-leveling tables (in case there are big waves) and a revolving bar in the disco. The ship is designed to remind guests that they are at sea; with that goal in mind, it features huge expanses of glass (adding up to more than 3 acres) in some rooms through which to view the passing Alaska scenery. You won't even miss the views when you are in the 12-story lobby elevators because they, too, are made of glass and face the ocean. Even the Internet cafe has an ocean view! This ship is slightly more upscale than the line's other vessels—Royal Caribbean seems to have borrowed a page from sister company Celebrity. It features wood, marble, and lots of nice fabrics and artwork, adding up to a pretty, low-key decor that lets the views provide most of the visual drama.

**CABINS**    Rooms on *Radiance* are larger than on the *Rhapsody*—the smallest is 165 square feet—and more come with verandas than on the earlier vessels. All rooms are equipped with an interactive flat-panel TV, telephone, Wi-Fi service, vanity table, refrigerator/minibar, and hair dryer. Suites also come with a veranda, sitting area with a sofa bed, dry bar, stereo and DVD, and bathtub and double sinks. The Royal Suite has a separate bedroom (with a king-size bed) and living room, a whirlpool bathtub, and a baby grand piano. Family staterooms and suites can accommodate five. Fifteen rooms are wheelchair-accessible.

## CABINS & RATES

| CABINS | PER DIEM RATES | SQ. FT. | FRIDGE | HAIR DRYER | SITTING AREA | TV |
|--------|----------------|---------|--------|------------|--------------|-----|
| Inside | $111 | 165 | yes | yes | yes | yes |
| Outside | $143–$224* | 194 | yes | yes | yes | yes |
| Suites | $351–$1,070 | 299–952 | yes | yes | yes | yes |

*\* with balcony*

**PUBLIC AREAS**   The ship is full of little surprises. There's that billiards room we mentioned and a card club with five tables dedicated to poker. Of course, you can also find more gaming options in the ship's massive French Art Nouveau–inspired Casino Royale (although dice players will be disappointed by the less-than-friendly odds). Bookworms will want to check out the combo bookstore and coffee shop.

The numerous cushy bars and lounges include champagne and piano bars. If you tire of the ocean views, you can gaze into the atrium, eight decks below, from a portholelike window in the floor of the Crown and Anchor Lounge. The ship's Viking Crown Lounge holds the disco and its revolving bar, as well as an intimate cabaret area. The three-level theater recalls the glacial landscapes of not only Alaska, but the North Pole as well.

Wi-Fi throughout the ship was added as part of the 2011 refurbishment.

Other public rooms include a show lounge, a conference center, a library, a shopping mall, and a business center. For kids, there's a children's center equipped with computer and crafts stations; teens get their own hangout space. There's also a video arcade. Past passengers will enjoy the new Diamond Lounge.

**DINING OPTIONS**   The elegant two-level main dining room features a grand staircase, but is a rather noisy space. Casual buffet breakfasts and lunches are provided in the Windjammer Cafe, which also offers casual dinners with waiter service at night. The ship also features several reservations-only restaurants that come with a cover charge: Chops Grill, serving steaks and chops for $30 per person; and the newly added Chef's Table, Samba Grill, Rita's Cantina, Izumi Asian Cuisine, Boardwalk Dog House, Giovanni's Table, and Park Cafe, all of which are a big step up from the ship's regular dining. Park Cafe offers an assortment of gourmet deli selections in the solarium.

**POOL, FITNESS, SPA & SPORTS FACILITIES**   For the active sort, there's a rock-climbing wall and a 9-hole minigolf course designed as a baroque garden, of all things. There is a nice spa (including a sauna and steam rooms), an oceanview fitness center with dozens of machines (including 18 Stairmaster treadmills), a jogging track, a sports court (including basketball), golf simulators (for those who like to play virtual golf), and three swimming pools—one outside, one enclosed (the indoor pool has an African theme complete with 17-ft.-high stone elephants and cascading waterfalls), and the third a teen/kiddie pool with slide. Whirlpools can be found in the solarium and near the outdoor pool.

# Rhapsody of the Seas

## The Verdict

This ship has it all—a great spa, good shopping, and lots of glass for premium viewing of the passing Alaska scenery.

## Specifications

| | | | |
|---|---|---|---|
| Size (in Tons) | 78,491 | Crew | 765 |
| Passengers (Double Occ.) | 1,998 | Passenger/Crew Ratio | 2.6 to 1 |
| Space/Passenger Ratio | 39 | Year Launched | 1997 |
| Total Cabins/Veranda Cabins | 999/233 | Last Major Refurbishment | 2012 |

## Frommer's Ratings (Scale of 1–5)                                    ★★★½

| | | | |
|---|---|---|---|
| Cabin Comfort & Amenities | 3.5 | Dining Options | 3.5 |
| Ship Cleanliness & Maintenance | 4 | Gym, Spa & Sports Facilities | 4 |
| Public Comfort/Space | 3.5 | Children's Facilities | 4 |
| Decor | 3.5 | Enjoyment Factor | 3.5 |

**THE SHIP IN GENERAL**  The *Rhapsody* is a true floating city, with trappings from multimillion-dollar art collections to a wide range of onboard facilities. Plenty of nice touches—a sumptuous, big-windowed health club/spa with lots of health and beauty treatments, and loads of fine shopping, dining, and entertainment options—give the *Rhapsody* the feel of a top-flight shore resort. But just like a popular resort, the ship sometimes feels crowded.

**CABINS**  Staterooms are not large—inside rooms measure 142 square feet and outside ones with balconies 191 square feet—but do have small sitting areas. All staterooms have TVs, phones, twin beds that convert to queens, ample storage space, and well-lit, moderately sized bathrooms. TVs feature movies, news, and information channels, and excursion and debarkation talks are rebroadcast in-room just in case you missed any information. Nearly a quarter of the staterooms have private verandas, and about a third of the rooms are designed to accommodate third and fourth guests. For bigger digs, check out the Royal Suite—it measures a mammoth 1,140 square feet, not including a 131-square-foot balcony, and even has a grand piano. Fourteen rooms on the ship are wheelchair-accessible.

## CABINS & RATES

| CABINS | PER DIEM RATES | SQ. FT. | FRIDGE | HAIR DRYER | SITTING AREA | TV |
|---|---|---|---|---|---|---|
| Inside | $118 | 142 | no | yes | yes | yes |
| Outside | $146–$271* | 191 | some | yes | yes | yes |
| Suites | $290–$793 | 1,150 | yes | yes | yes | yes |

* with balcony

**PUBLIC AREAS**  The *Rhapsody* soars 11 stories above the waterline and features a three-story glass-walled atrium with glass elevators (a la Hyatt Regency) and a winding brass-trimmed staircase. At the top of the staircase, the Viking Crown Lounge affords a 360-degree view of the passing scenery. You'll also appreciate the view through the glass walls of the bi-level dining room, although the dining room has no stern views (the galley is placed behind the dining room). Actually, other than in the windowless casino and show lounge, there are great views to be found virtually everywhere on this ship—perfect for scoping glaciers.

A playroom, teen center, and video arcade provide plenty to keep kids happily occupied while parents relax, gamble, attend one of the many activities (there are dozens to select from each week, including informative nature lectures), take in a show, or dance the night away in the disco or one of numerous lounges and bars, which include the new R-Bar and signature Schooner Bar. Other rooms include a card room, a library, several shops, and a conference room.

**DINING OPTIONS**   Meals are served both in the windowed, two-story dining room and in the casual, open-seating Windjammer Cafe (an indoor/outdoor facility open for breakfast and lunch), so there's freedom as to when you dine and, since the menus in each venue are different, choices as to what you'll eat. Gourmet deli selections and other treats are served at Park Cafe in the solarium.

**POOL, FITNESS, SPA & SPORTS FACILITIES**   The spa on the ship is a soothing respite from the hubbub of ship life. It offers a wide selection of treatments, as well as the standard steam rooms and saunas. Adjacent to the spa, the spacious, adults-only solarium has a pool, lounge chairs, floor-to-ceiling windows, and a retractable glass ceiling. This is a peaceful place for repose before or after a spa treatment, or anytime at all. Surprisingly, the gym is small for the ship's size—and in comparison to those on the megaliners of Carnival, Holland America Line, and Celebrity—but it's well equipped.

The main pool area has four whirlpools, and there are two more in the solarium. The observatory on deck (complete with stargazing equipment) is protected from wind by glass windbreaks. The *Rhapsody* also has a cushioned jogging track and a basketball half-court.

# SILVERSEA

110 E. Broward Blvd., Fort Lauderdale, FL 33301. ℂ **877/276-6816** or 954/522-2299. Fax 954/356-5881. www.silversea.com.

## Pros

o  **All-around excellence.** A no-tipping policy is always a hit, and the cuisine, open seating for meals, exemplary service, and great accommodations make Silversea well worth the money for those who want something special.
o  **Surprisingly little formality.** Considering the economic status of most of the passengers, there's very little stuffiness.
o  **A huge number of private verandas.** More than 80 percent of the suites on the *Silver Shadow* have this desirable feature.

## Cons

o  **Not a great deal of nightlife.** Although the ship has a show lounge, it's not really big enough for anything overly lavish. The line in recent years has been de-emphasizing production-type shows in favor of more low-key performances by vocalists and other musicians.

## Silversea Fleet Itineraries

| SHIP | ITINERARIES |
| --- | --- |
| *Silver Shadow* | 7- to 11-night Inside Passage: North- and southbound between Vancouver, BC, and Seward, Alaska, or round-trip from Vancouver, visiting Ketchikan, Sitka, Sawyer Glacier, Hubbard Glacier, Juneau, and Skagway (May–Sept) |

**THE LINE IN A NUTSHELL**    There's no argument: Silversea is a very worthy member of the small number of operators of truly luxurious small-to-midsize ships. The only rival to its *Silver Shadow* in that category in Alaska this year is Regent's *Seven Seas Navigator.* Silversea isn't in Alaska every year, though this will mark its sixth year in a row in the market. It likes to give past passengers as much variety as possible, so some years it chooses to move from the 49th State to deploy its ships in more exotic trades—Southeast Asia, South America, and the like.

**THE EXPERIENCE**    Silversea represents the last word in elegance and service. Spacious accommodations, all oceanview suites, no tipping expected, free beverages (alcoholic and otherwise), swift and caring baggage handling—these are the hallmarks of the Silversea product.

**THE FLEET**    The 382-passenger *Silver Shadow,* which joined the fleet in 2000, is one of seven Silversea ships, and it's the only one that cruises to Alaska. Its twin, the *Silver Whisper,* entered service the following year. The others are the smaller and virtually identical *Silver Cloud* (1994) and *Silver Wind* (1995), as well as *Silver Explorer,* the company's expedition ship (2008), and the somewhat bigger *Silver Spirit* (2009). Late in 2013, the company also rolled out a small, 100-passenger expedition ship in the Galapagos, the *Silver Galapagos.*

**PASSENGER PROFILE**    Guests tend to be in their mid-40s and up. They are generally well educated, with definite ideas on just what luxury means in accommodations, cuisine, and service. And they have the means to pay for it!

**DINING OPTIONS**    Food is one of Silversea's greatest strengths—both in preparation and in presentation—not only in the main dining room (known simply as The Restaurant), but also in the breakfast/lunch buffets in La Terrazza. That room doubles as a low-capacity candle-lit Italian restaurant with a "slow-food" philosophy in the evening.

Silversea serves very acceptable complimentary wine with dinner (and at other meals), but if you must upgrade to something really, really expensive (Opus One and Dom Perignon are a couple of tipples that come to mind), you should expect to pay the going rate. There are many mid-priced options by the bottle as well.

**ACTIVITIES**    In the past couple of years, Silversea has significantly enhanced its onboard enrichment program. Naturalists, historians, well-known authors, award-winning chefs, and wine experts host excellent sessions, often targeted for the specific cruising location. The line has also introduced a Cooking School with state-of-the-art cooking theaters that allow chefs to present a variety of specialized cooking classes and demonstrations on every cruise.

**CHILDREN'S PROGRAMS**   There are youth counselors on Silversea ships based on the number of children on board, and activities are defined accordingly.

**ENTERTAINMENT**   It's just not possible to stage extravagant song-and-dance presentations on ships of the small size that Silversea operates, but the Alaska-based *Silver Shadow* sails with a team of six vocalists and musicians who do an excellent job nonetheless as they put on several shows every week in the main theater. Outside the main showroom, there's usually a small combo for dancing (no disco, please!). The library has an ample supply of books.

**SERVICE**   This is uniformly of the highest order. These people could take their places in the finest restaurants and hotels ashore—from where, in fact, many of them came. The finest compliment that anybody can pay the Silversea staff is that they provide the kind of service that you just don't notice. It has a self-service laundry and remarkably speedy valet service, including laundry and dry cleaning. On Silversea ships, gratuities for the staff are included in the fare and not expected.

**CRUISETOURS & ADD-ON PROGRAMS**   Silversea offers a small number of pre- and post-cruise land packages ranging from 3 to 6 nights. The shortest, least-expensive one is a 3-night trip to Denali National Park, which starts at $1,739 per person. The most elaborate outing: a 6-night trip that includes a visit to the Eskimo settlement of Barrow above the Arctic Circle, which starts at $3,169 per person.

## Silver Shadow

### The Verdict

If this ship had a movie equivalent, it would have to be Jack Nicholson's *As Good as It Gets*.

### Specifications

| | | | |
|---|---|---|---|
| Size (in Tons) | 28,258 | Crew | 295 |
| Passengers (Double Occ.) | 382 | Passenger/Crew Ratio | 1.3 to 1 |
| Space/Passenger Ratio | 74 | Year Launched | 2000 |
| Total Cabins/Veranda Cabins | 194/168 | Last Major Refurbishment | 2011 |

### Frommer's Ratings (Scale of 1–5)   ★★★★★

| | | | |
|---|---|---|---|
| Cabin Comfort & Amenities | 5 | Dining Options | 5 |
| Ship Cleanliness & Maintenance | 5 | Gym, Spa & Sports Facilities | 4 |
| Public Comfort/Space | 4.5 | Children's Facilities | N/A |
| Decor | 4.5 | Enjoyment Factor | 5 |

**THE SHIP IN GENERAL**   This ship has one of the highest space-to-passenger ratios in the industry—technically, determined as 74. That's a rather esoteric measurement that's arrived at by dividing the ship's gross tonnage (the volume of its interior space) by the lower berth capacity. It's complicated, but take our word for it—this ship is plenty spacious. The *Silver Shadow* takes Silversea's concept of luxury cruising to exceptional heights, with walk-in closets, dressing table with hair dryer close at hand, real marble, double-vanity basin, bathtubs and separate showers, and DVD units in

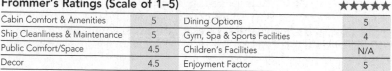

every stateroom. Butler service is provided for all suites (in other words, in all rooms). Wi-Fi access is available throughout the ship. A major refurbishment in 2011 brought additional features and amenities, including an upgraded show lounge sound system, new balcony furniture, and new design themes.

**CABINS**  All outside, all suites. All but a few of them have private verandas; the smallest of the units—there are only a handful—have none. But they're a roomy 287 square feet, with picture windows. From there the sizes go up and up, ranging from 345 square feet to 1,435 square feet. Every suite comes with convertible twin-to-queen beds, a minibar (stocked), and safes.

Two of the suites are wheelchair-accessible.

## CABINS & RATES

| CABINS | PER DIEM RATES | SQ. FT. | FRIDGE | HAIR DRYER | SITTING AREA | TV |
|--------|----------------|---------|--------|------------|--------------|-----|
| Suites | $508–$1,725 | 287–1,435 | yes | yes | yes | yes |

**PUBLIC AREAS**  The *Silver Shadow*'s two-level showroom is not the biggest we've ever seen, but it has good sightlines, and it's a good place to while away an hour after dinner. There is a small cigar bar, known as the Connoisseur's Corner. The casino provides the usual array of money-speculating ventures—roulette, blackjack, and a few slots. You can have a drink in the casino or in a bigger room simply called The Bar that is a great gathering spot, with live music in the evening. The best place for a drink may well be the really small Lampadina, just off the casino. The rear-facing Panorama Lounge has dancing to a range of musical styles, from ballroom and dinner dancing to rock-'n'-roll favorites to the latest club mixes. The ship's forward-facing Observation Lounge on the top deck is a quiet sanctuary for a game of chess or backgammon, conversation, reading, or watching the scenery. There's also a fully equipped eight-computer Internet center, a card room, an upscale boutique, and an H. Stern jewelry store.

**DINING OPTIONS**  Thanks to recent changes, there are now four dining venues on *Silver Shadow*. The Restaurant, the main dining room, serves breakfast, lunch, and dinner in elegant style. A more casual, buffet-style breakfast and lunch are served at the indoor/outdoor La Terrazza—and in the evening, this spot becomes a lovely specialty Italian restaurant. (The dinner menu no longer rotates among different regions; rather, there's one menu with a very extensive list of offerings. Reservations are required, no cover charge). The third location, Le Champagne, was developed in collaboration with Relais & Châteaux. The eatery offers seasonally inspired menus showcasing regional specialties prepared with fresh, locally sourced items in an intimate setting on Deck 7 next to La Terrazza (reservations are absolutely necessary, and there's a cover charge of $30 per person). The fourth dining venue is The Grill, the ship's outside poolside cafe, for burgers, sandwiches, and salads at lunchtime; it turns into a wonderful outside grill restaurant at night. The Grill features an interactive Black Rock experience: A preheated volcanic rock is brought to your table, allowing you to cook such delicacies as steak, veal, pork, lamb, salmon, fish, or prawns exactly to your liking right in front of you. Of course, there's 24-hour room service, and meals can be served course-by-course if so desired.

**POOL, FITNESS, SPA & SPORTS FACILITIES** The spa is, like most of the other public rooms, small when measured alongside its megaship competition. But even with just four treatment rooms, it provides the same range of hydrotherapy, massage, and beauty treatments; men's and women's saunas; and more. The line recently introduced a Wellness Program that combines daily activities, including yoga, Pilates, and meditation classes, with suggestions from its light and low-carb lunch and dinner menus. For fitness buffs, there is a newly expanded fitness center and a small jogging track. The beauty shop provides pedicures, manicures, and facials as well as hair styling. The one pool and two hot tubs are just right for a ship this size, and they are surrounded on two levels by lots of lounge chairs.

# THE CRUISE LINES: THE SMALL SHIPS

Big ships show you Alaska from a vibrant, resortlike atmosphere; small ships let you see it from the waterline, with no distraction from anything un-Alaskan—no glitzy interiors, no big shows or loud music, no casinos, no crowds. The largest of these ships (the *American Spirit*—more on that later) carries only 100 passengers. On the small ships, you're immersed in the 49th State from the minute you wake up to the minute you fall asleep, and for the most part, you're left alone to form your own opinions, although there invariably will be a naturalist, a historian, or some such expert along to provide a running commentary en route.

The vessels listed in this chapter allow you to visit more isolated parts of the coast. Thanks to their smaller size and shallow draft (the amount of hull below the waterline), they can go places larger ships can't, and they have the flexibility to change their itineraries as opportunities arise—say, to go where whales have been sighted or to watch black bears on the shore. (Keep in mind, though, that ships are prohibited from "stalking" wildlife for too long: They must keep their distance and break off after a relatively short while.) Depending on the itinerary, small-ship ports of call might include popular stops such as Juneau, Sitka, or Ketchikan; lesser-visited areas such as Elfin Cove or Warm Springs Harbor; or a Tlingit Native village such as Kake. The one thing you can be confident of is that all itineraries will include **glacier viewing** and **whale-watching.** Most of the itineraries also have time built in for passengers to explore the wilder parts of Alaska and for ferrying passengers ashore for hikes in wilderness areas. In some cases, the ships also carry **sea kayaks** and **Zodiac** inflatable boats for passenger use—allowing a type of exploration not available on big ships in Alaska.

Rather than glitzy entertainment, you'll likely get informal and informative **lectures** and sometimes video presentations on Alaskan wildlife, history, and Native culture. In most cases, some shore excursions are included in the cruise fare. Meals are served in open seatings, so you can sit where and with whom you like—and time spent huddled on the outside decks scanning for whales fosters great camaraderie among passengers. It must be noted, though, that the size of the ships precludes any kind of spacious dining rooms. Generally, they're quite small—some would say cramped. And on most of the smaller ships, room service is not an option (unless you are sick, of course).

Cabins on these ships don't always have TVs or telephones, and they tend to be tiny and sometimes spartan. (See individual reviews below for exceptions.) Most don't have e-mail access. There are no stabilizers on most small ships, so the ride can be bumpy in rough seas. Because the vessels tend to spend most of their time in the somewhat protected waters of the Inside Passage, this is not usually a major concern. But it can be a problem when the vessels ply open seas.

Another drawback of small ships is that they generally are not wheelchair-friendly; small ships are not a good choice for travelers with mobility issues. Small ships also may not be the best choice for families with children, unless those kids are avid nature buffs and able to keep themselves entertained without a lot of outside stimuli.

## Reading the Reviews

In this chapter, you'll also see the following terms used to describe the various small-ship experiences:

- **Soft adventure:** These ships don't provide on-board grandeur, organized activities, or entertainment, but instead give you a really close-up Alaska experience. These ships often avoid large ports.
- **Active adventure:** These ships function less like cruise ships than like base camps. Passengers use them only to sleep and eat, getting off the ship for hiking and kayaking excursions every day.
- **Port-to-port:** These ships are for people who want to visit the popular Alaska ports (and some lesser-known ones), but also want the flexible schedules and maneuverability of a small ship and a more homey experience than you would find aboard a glitzy big ship.

## Rates

Cruise rates in these reviews are brochure rates. Some discounts may apply, including early-booking and last-minute offers (see more in chapter 3), although small-ship lines do not traditionally discount their fares as much as bigger ship lines. As in chapter 5, all rates have been calculated by nights spent on ship, based on 7-night sailings, unless otherwise indicated. Note that, in general, small ships are more expensive—often significantly so—than the large ships operating in Alaska. It costs more to provide the more intimate experience of small ships, and that extra cost is passed on to passengers.

## Tipping

Tipping on small ships is not exactly standardized, as it tends to be on the big ships. None of the small lines operating in Alaska automatically adds gratuities to passenger bills. Instead, they suggest amounts that would be appropriate to leave for crew, while leaving the decision of how much to tip—or whether to tip at all—to the customer. Gratuities then are pooled among all the staff on board, from the room cleaners to the deck hands. Below is a rundown of the amount the companies suggest for a 1-week cruise:

- **Alaskan Dream Cruises:** $105 ($15 per day).
- **American Cruise Lines:** $125
- **Lindblad Expeditions:** $98 to $112 ($14 to $16 per day).
- **Un-Cruise Adventures:** 5 percent to 10 percent of the cost of the cruise.

## A NOTE ON SHIP ratings

Because the small-ship experience is so completely different from the megaship experience, we've had to adjust our ratings. For instance, because all but a tiny fraction of these ships have just one dining room for all meals, we can't judge them by the same standard we use for ships with 5 or 10 different restaurants. So we've set the default **Dining Options** rating for these ships at 3, or "good," with points deducted if a restaurant is particularly uncomfortable and points added for any options above and beyond. Similarly, we've changed the "Pool, Fitness, Spa & Sports Facilities" rating to **Adventure & Fitness Options** to reflect the fact that on small ships the focus is what's outside, not inside. Options covered in this category include kayaks, trips by inflatable Zodiac, and frequent hiking trips.

When reading the reviews in this chapter, bear in mind, too, that small-ship lines often measure their ships' gross register tonnage, or GRT (a measure of internal space, not actual weight), differently than the large lines. Some use an international standard, others a U.S. standard, so to compare ship sizes it's best to just look at the number of passengers aboard. Also note that where GRT measures are done using the U.S. standard, passenger/space measurements are impossible or meaningless.

## Dress Code

The word is *casual.* You're fine with polo shirts, jeans, khakis, shorts, a fleece pullover, and a Gore-Tex shell. Having a pair of rubber sandals or old sneakers is handy, since going ashore in rubber landing crafts might require you to step out into the surf. Hiking boots are also recommended.

# ALASKAN DREAM CRUISES

1512 Sawmill Creek Rd., Sitka, AK 99835. © **855/747-8100.** Fax 907/747-4819. www.alaskan dreamcruises.com.

### Pros

o **Off-the-beaten-path itineraries.** With a mantra of showing customers the "true Alaska," Alaskan Dream has built itineraries around such little-visited Southeast Alaskan outposts as the Native village of Kake and normally-off-limits Hobart Bay, as well as such iconic attractions as Glacier Bay National Park.
o **Local Alaskan flavor.** Alaskan Dream is locally owned by a family in Sitka, Alaska, and its staff is mostly made up of resident Alaskans who are proud to show off their home.

### Cons

o **Tough to reach.** Most of Alaskan Dream Cruises' itineraries begin and end in Sitka, which only gets a few flights a day.

**THE LINE IN A NUTSHELL**   Run by a local Southeast Alaska family, Alaskan Dream promises a glimpse of the "true Alaska" away from the tourist hordes, with local Alaskans as your guide. Its growing fleet of recently refurbished small ships take vacationers to off-the-beaten path Native villages and little-visited natural areas across Southeast Alaska in addition to such classic hotspots as Glacier Bay.

**THE EXPERIENCE**    Launched in 2011 by the Allen family of Sitka, Alaska, Alaskan Dream focuses on small-ship cruises in Southeast Alaska with a local twist. The line has taken great pains to hire local Alaskans to staff its vessels, who bring an insider's knowledge of the region, and its itineraries include stops at several little-visited, "locals only" destinations in the region such as the Native village of Kake. In addition, many itineraries include a stop at scenic Hobart Bay, an off-the-beaten-path gem of a wilderness area that is within Native lands and is normally off-limits to tourists. Alaskan Dream operates a private adventure camp within the Bay that has kayaks, motorized Zego boats, and ATVs that passengers can take out exploring. Other Alaskan touches on Alaskan Dream trips include local Alaska products prominently featured on board vessels, from fresh Alaskan seafood and other local ingredients used by the chefs for meals to the Alaska beer and spirits offered at the bar to the Alaska-crafted soaps and shampoos in every cabin. While the line is new, the Allens are no strangers to the boat-and-ship business in Alaska, having owned and run Sitka-based boat building company Allen Marine since 1967, as well as Allen Marine Tours, which offers day cruises across Alaska's Inside Passage. The family also owns Southeast Alaska's Windham Bay Lodge, a wilderness resort. As is typical with most of the small-ship lines in Alaska, Alaskan Dream includes all excursions in the base cost of its sailings, including adventure tours in Hobart Bay. The cruising atmosphere on the line's ships is casual, as also is typical of small ships in Alaska.

**THE FLEET**    While the line is new, its ships aren't. Alaskan Dream Cruises launched in 2011 with two vessels that had sailed before in Alaska, but had been out of commission for several years, and it has since added two more older vessels to its fleet. New for 2014 is the 88-passenger *Chichagof Dream*, originally built in 1984. It joins the 58-passenger *Admiralty Dream* (built in 1979), the 49-passenger *Baranof Dream* (1980), and 38-passenger *Alaskan Dream* (1986). All four of the ships received major overhauls before going into service for Alaskan Dream Cruises and are well maintained by the Allen family's shipyard.

**PASSENGER PROFILE**    Alaskan Dream Cruises passengers tend to be well-traveled, well-educated people (most hold a bachelor's degree or higher) in search of an authentic Alaska experience. Often they're semi-retired or retired, and they come from all over the world. In addition to the United States, passengers from Australia, the United Kingdom, and Germany are fairly common. The line also is drawing a growing number of multigenerational families, which led to the development of new family cruises in 2013.

**DINING OPTIONS**    All of the line's ships have a single communal dining room where meals are served three times a day. As is often the case on vessels with fewer than 100 passengers, there is no fixed seating, allowing passengers to sit with different people at different times. In the morning, in addition to a full breakfast, an early morning Continental breakfast is put out for early risers, and you'll always find snacks available at other times, whether it be a batch of muffins whipped up by the pastry chef or afternoon cookies. All of the food aboard the ship is sourced locally when possible,

## Alaskan Dream Cruises Fleet

| SHIP | ITINERARIES |
|------|-------------|
| **Baranof Dream** | 7-night Glacier Bay and Island Adventure: Roundtrip from Sitka with stops in Metlakatla, Misty Fjords, Kasaan, Wrangell, Petersburg, Tracy Arm, Hobart Bay, Juneau, and Glacier Bay National Park (July–Sept) |
| | 10-night Admiralty, Baranof, and Chichagof Explorer: Roundtrip from Sitka with stops in Juneau, Skagway, Icy Strait, Tracy Arm, Hobart Bay, Petersburg, Kake, and Red Bluff Bay (Aug) |
| | 8-night Alaska's Inside Passage Sojourn: One-way between Ketchikan and Sitka with stops in Skagway, Petersburg, Wrangell, Kasaan, Misty Fjord, Tracy Arm, Hobart Bay, Juneau, and Glacier Bay National Park (Aug) |
| **Admiralty Dream** | 7-night Glacier Bay and Island Adventure: Roundtrip from Sitka with stops in Metlakatla, Misty Fjords, Kasaan, Wrangell, Petersburg, Tracy Arm, Hobart Bay, Juneau, and Glacier Bay National Park (July–Sept) |
| | 12-night Alaska's Glacier Bay & Inside Passage Voyage: One-way from Sitka to Ketchikan with stops in Skagway, Gustavus, Glacier Bay, Juneau, Tracy Arm, Hobart Bay, Kake, Petersburg, Wrangell, Kasaan,and Misty Fjords (Aug) |
| **Alaskan Dream** | 10-night Alaska's Dream Southeast Explorer: One-way between Ketchikan and Sitka with stops in Kake, Petersburg, Tracy Arm, Hobart Bay, Juneau and Glacier Bay National Park (Aug) |
| | 8-night Alaska's Inside Passage Sojourn: One-way between Ketchikan and Sitka with stops in Skagway, Petersburg, Wrangell, Kasaan, Misty Fjord, Tracy Arm, Hobart Bay, Juneau, and Glacier Bay National Park (Aug) |

and in Alaska meals focus on locally inspired dishes, including locally caught salmon and other seafood. In addition, beer from the Alaskan Brewing Company and Alaskan Distillery spirits are prominent on all four vessels. Passengers with dietary restrictions and allergies will find that the line's head chefs and crew make a great effort to be accommodating. Don't be shy about asking!

**ACTIVITIES**   Whether it be a kayak trip across a remote bay or a walk around a Native village, most of the activities in which passengers participate take place off the ship—and they're all included in the base price of the trip. Led by naturalist guides who travel with passengers on the vessel, daily outings on a typical cruise in Alaska will include a mix of outdoorsy pursuits such as riding an ATV through a forest and visits to some of Southeast Alaska's small fishing towns. During some port calls, there's time for two excursions, though one is typical. Examples of popular outings on Alaska trips is a king salmon and king crab dinner at a lodge near Juneau; sea kayaking, all-terrain vehicle tours, and small Zego sports-boat excursions at Hobart Bay, home to an adventure base camp visited exclusively by Alaskan Dream Cruises; and visits to historically and culturally significant sights in the Alaskan towns of Sitka and Petersburg.

**CHILDREN'S PROGRAM**   While most Alaskan Dream sailings have no formal children's program, the line in 2013 added dedicated family cruises that include daily excursions aimed at kids, young adults, and families. Activities on these trips range from classes in traditional arts to geo-caching expeditions in the rain forest, with dedicated youth leaders. When not leading a family-friendly expedition off the ship, youth leaders coordinate onboard activities and crafts aimed at children and families.

**ENTERTAINMENT** There are no shows in the traditional sense, but in the evenings, after dinner, the ships' lounges often are the site of onboard presentations and discussions led by scientific and cultural expedition leaders. Passengers also gather in the lounge before dinner for hors d'oeuvres, drinks, and a recap of the day from the ship's expedition leader. Books are available for passengers to borrow from a small onboard library.

**SERVICE** Alaskan Dream prides itself on hiring local Alaskans to work on its ships, and much of the crew comes from Southeast Alaska and other parts of the state. Naturalists and other English-speaking crew members facilitate all off-ship and onboard activities, as well as serve meals and perform housekeeping duties. *Note:* While gratuities are not mandatory, the line suggests that passengers leave $15 per person per day to be shared among the crew.

**CRUISETOURS & ADD-ON PROGRAMS** Alaskan Dream Cruises passengers can pair a cruise with a stay at Alaska's **Windham Bay Lodge,** also owned by parent company Allen Marine. Located about 65 miles from Juneau at the end of a 6-mile bay, the lodge lies within the Chuck River Wilderness and Tongass National Forest and accommodates up to 16 people at a time in three guest cabins and two bedrooms in the main lodge. The main lodge is also equipped with a full-size kitchen, bar, living room, and dining room. Excursions available from Windham Bay Lodge include visits to Frederick Sound, Endicott Arm, Sawyer Glacier, and Dawes Glacier. Activities include wildlife watching on Admiralty Island, kayaking along Endicott Arm, exploring Windham Bay by skiff, and a visit to the company's exclusive adventure camp at Hobart Bay.

# Admiralty Dream • Baranof Dream • Chichagof Dream

## The Verdict

Small, Alaskan-run ships that show you to the "true Alaska," including colorful Native villages.

## Specifications

| | | | |
|---|---|---|---|
| Size (in U.S. reg. GRTs) | 95/97/95 | Crew | 21/19/30 |
| Passengers (Double Occ.) | 58/49/88 | Passenger/Crew Ratio | 2.8/2.6/2.9 |
| Passenger/Space Ratio | N/A* | Year Launched | 1979/1980/1984 |
| Total Cabins | 29/25/44 | Last Major Refurbishment | 2012/2013/2014 |

## Frommer's Ratings (Scale of 1–5)                    ★★★½

| | | | |
|---|---|---|---|
| Cabin Comfort & Amenities | 3.5 | Dining Options | 3.5 |
| Ship Cleanliness & Maintenance | 4 | Adventure & Fitness Options | 3.5 |
| Public Comfort/Space | 3.5 | Children's Facilities | NA |
| Decor | 3.5 | Enjoyment Factor | 4 |

**THE SHIPS IN GENERAL**    Built between 1979 and 1984, these three similar vessels are among the oldest sailing in Alaska, and their accommodations and public areas are relatively simple by today's standards (some might even call them spartan). That said, they all were significantly renovated before going into service for Alaskan Dream over the past 3 years, and they're well maintained. Just don't expect a lot of bells and whistles in cabins (there are no TVs, for instance, and bathrooms are tiny) or elaborate gathering areas (the single lounge and dining room on each vessel is relatively basic). Still, small-ship cruising in Alaska isn't about the ship. It's about exploring the state's spectacular scenery and wildlife in a way that big ships can't. These vessels have a shallow draft that's perfect for navigating intimate coves and passages, a spacious bow deck for viewing fjords and glaciers, a covered outside deck, and a relaxed cruising speed for optimum viewing of wilderness and wildlife. While simple, the vessels' lounges and dining rooms offer an intimate venue for getting to know your fellow travelers.

**CABINS**    With the exception of a few large "deluxe" cabins on each of the vessels, accommodations are relatively small and simple. The typical cabin has two twin beds or a double bed that takes up a good portion of the room, a closet, built-in storage drawers under beds, and in some cases a desk with chair. Bathrooms are tiny and, in the style of expedition ships of old, often combine the toilet and shower in the same small dual-purpose space (the largest cabins have separate toilet areas as well as a desk area). In keeping with the line's "true Alaska" focus, soaps and shampoos all are locally made in the state. Rooms have no TVs, and none come with balconies (windows are the norm), but passengers will find high-powered binoculars for spotting wildlife. An intercom system in the cabins allows passengers to hear expedition leaders talking about the passing scenery.

### CABINS & RATES

| CABINS | PER DIEM RATES | SQ. FT. | FRIDGE | HAIR DRYER | SITTING AREA | TV |
|---|---|---|---|---|---|---|
| **Admiralty Dream/Baranof Dream/Chichagof Dream** | | | | | | |
| Outside | $271–$785* | 74–135/85-117/ 105-155 | no | no | some | no |

*Rates are per day based on 7-night cruises.

**PUBLIC AREAS**    The vessels all have a similar layout, with cabins spread out among three to four passenger decks including a few at the front of an open-air top deck. Activity on board all three ships revolves around a single lounge at the front (home to a daily pre-dinner social hour with hors d'oeuvres and recap from the expedition leader), and all have a main dining room toward the back of the same level. Still, in Alaska at least, the place to be often is on the ships' bow viewing decks, just below the bridge, where passengers gather to watch for whales, seals, and sea otters and to gaze at the lush green forests, soaring, snow-covered mountains, and calving glaciers of Southeast Alaska. Also offering great views is the open-air sundeck on each of the ships.

**POOL, FITNESS, SPA & SPORTS FACILITIES**    The top decks of the vessels feature several exercise machines. There are no hot tubs, pools, or other sports facilities.

# Alaskan Dream

## The Verdict

An intimate, yacht-like vessel for vacationers who want a truly small-scale experience.

## Specifications

| Size (in U.S. reg. GRTs) | 93 | Crew | 18 |
|---|---|---|---|
| Passengers (Double Occ.) | 38 | Passenger/Crew Ratio | 2.1 |
| Passenger/Space Ratio | N/A* | Year Launched | 1986 |
| Total Cabins | 19 | Last Major Refurbishment | 2011 |

## Frommer's Ratings (Scale of 1–5)                          ★★★½

| Cabin Comfort & Amenities | 3.5 | Dining Options | 3.5 |
|---|---|---|---|
| Ship Cleanliness & Maintenance | 4 | Adventure & Fitness Options | 3.5 |
| Public Comfort/Space | 3.5 | Children's Facilities | NA |
| Decor | 4 | Enjoyment Factor | 4 |

**THE SHIP IN GENERAL**  Smaller than Alaskan Dream Cruises' three other vessels, the 38-passenger Alaskan Dream looks more like a large yacht than a small cruise ship—a funny-looking one, to boot, as it seems unusually tall for its length, giving it a top-heavy look. Technically, the vessel is a catamaran, with two parallel hulls, which means it has unusually good stability for its size. Its small footprint (of major overnight cruise operators, only Un-Cruise Adventures has a smaller vessel in Alaska) also means the Alaskan Dream can get into narrow bays and other natural areas that other vessels can't visit. Alaskan Dream has three indoor passenger levels that contain its 19 cabins and a handful of public areas, and an open-air Observation Deck at its top.

**CABINS**  The Alaskan Dream's 19 cabins are split into four categories that range notably in size. All but six of the cabins fall within Category A, which has the least square footage; expect twin beds that take up a large portion of the room, a closet, a sink in the main part of the cabin and a separate toilet. Slightly longer due to their location on the bottommost deck are the three Category AA cabins, and two significantly larger Vista View Suites come with a small sitting area. Even bigger is the vessel's single Owner's Suite, which measures up at exactly twice the size of standard cabins.

## CABINS & RATES

| CABINS | PER DIEM RATES | SQ. FT. | FRIDGE | HAIR DRYER | SITTING AREA | TV |
|---|---|---|---|---|---|---|
| **Alaskan Dream** | | | | | | |
| Outside | $271–$780* | 104–416 | some | no | some | no |

*Rates are per day based on 7-night cruises.

**PUBLIC AREAS**  The biggest of the Alaskan Dream's three interior passenger decks is the bottommost Main Deck, which is home to the forward-facing Vista View Lounge and the nearby Sitka Rose Dining Room (with three passenger cabins squeezed in between the two venues). When not in one of these two areas, passengers can be found up top on the vessel's large observation deck, and there's also a small covered opened deck one floor below at the rear of the Bridge Deck (the Bridge and four more passenger cabins also are on this level).

**POOL, FITNESS, SPA & SPORTS FACILITIES**   There are no pools, hot tubs, or sports facilities.

# AMERICAN CRUISE LINES

741 Boston Post Rd., Ste. 200, Guilford, CT 06437. ℂ **800/460-4518.** Fax 203/453-0417. www. americancruiselines.com.

## Pros

o **Spacious, upscale cabins.** At more than 200 square feet, cabins on American Cruise Lines vessels are the most spacious in small-ship cruising and feature large bathrooms and picture windows.
o **Balconies.** Unlike most small ships in Alaska, American Cruise Lines' Alaska-based *American Spirit* offers a large number of cabins with balconies—a real plus in such a scenic region.
o **Modern amenities.** Newer than other small ships in Alaska, the *American Spirit* also boasts satellite TV, DVD players, and complimentary Wi-Fi in every cabin.

## Cons

o **The cost.** Starting at more than $5,000 per person per week for the smallest cabins, cruises on the *American Spirit* are among the most expensive in the region.

**THE LINE IN A NUTSHELL**   Still relatively unknown to many Americans, 14-year-old American Cruise Lines is a niche operator of upscale small-ship voyages on America's waterways from the Chesapeake Bay to Puget Sound and Alaska.

**THE EXPERIENCE**   Founded in 1999 by Connecticut entrepreneur Charles A. Robertson, family-run American Cruise Lines offers a true slice of Americana: Sailing exclusively in the United States, its ships are U.S.–built, U.S.–flagged, and staffed by an all American crew. Robertson's original vision of offering gracious hospitality and personalized service in an intimate, small-ship setting remains the line's mantra, and the line's vessels are relatively new, modern, and environmentally friendly, with lots of upscale amenities. In addition to Alaska, American Cruise Lines vessels sail to 27 other U.S. states on 35 different itineraries. Hallmarks of the line include elegant cuisine, nightly entertainment (something not always found on small ships), and daily lectures from historians, naturalists, and local experts.

**THE FLEET**   American Cruise Lines owns and operates six small U.S.–flagged cruise ships, only one of which—the 100-passenger *American Spirit*—sails in Alaska. The vessels range in size from the 49-passenger *American Glory* to the 150-passenger *Queen of the Mississippi,* and nearly all are less than a decade old, giving the line one of the youngest fleets in small-ship cruising. In addition to Alaska, the vessels operate in the U.S.'s Pacific Northwest, New England, mid-Atlantic, Southeast, and Mississippi River complex.

**PASSENGER PROFILE**   The line tends to attract experienced travelers who are mostly well educated, professional, and over 50 years old. In the mix are some singles and a smattering of younger passengers who share a common interest in history and

## American Cruise Lines Fleet

| SHIP | ITINERARIES |
|------|-------------|
| *American Spirit* | 7-night Southeast Alaska: Roundtrip from Juneau visits to Haines, Skagway, Petersburg, Icy Strait/Hoonah, and Glacier Bay (June–Aug) |
| | 11-night Alaska Inside Passage: One-way between Seattle and Juneau with visits to Anacortes and Friday Harbor, Wash.; Strait of Georgia; Ketchikan, Wrangell, Petersburg, Frederick Sound, and Tracy Arm (June and Aug) |

cruising (and the money to afford American Cruise Lines' high rates). They also like to socialize, and if you do, too, you'll find plenty of fun and interesting people who make for excellent company.

**DINING OPTIONS** As is typical with small ships, American Cruise Lines' vessels have a single main restaurant that's the site of breakfast, lunch, and dinner daily. Each evening before dinner passengers enjoy complimentary cocktails and hors d'oeuvres in a lounge as they mingle with other passengers to exchange tales of the adventures of the day. Then it's off to the dining room, where every meal is open seating—there are no table reservations. This gives passengers an opportunity to move from table to table making new friends. The system works perfectly. As for the food, all meals are served by waiters. There are no buffets, although when you enter the dining room you'll see a table offering a variety of tasty selections such as fruit, veggies, and assorted muffins. Still, for the most part, breakfast, lunch, and dinner are ordered off a menu. There is no midnight buffet, but you can go to the main lounge anytime and find soft drinks, coffee, tea, and snacks. Food in the dining room is well prepared and presented by waiters eager to please. Generally the menu offers a choice of a couple of appetizers, two or three entrees, and a few dessert selections. At both lunch and dinner, wine is always on the table, included at no extra charge, and beer is also available at no charge. You won't go hungry!

**ACTIVITIES** During days in port most activities take place off the ship. American Cruise Lines includes shore excursions in its trips, and many passengers take advantage of them. Some are quite elaborate, such as the Stikine River Tour on jet boats offered during visits to Wrangell, Alaska. You'll talk about that one for a long time. In Glacier Bay, where American Cruise Lines has a highly-sought-after permit to cruise, an official park ranger and native interpreter come on board in the morning and stay all day offering information, folklore, and stories about Alaska in addition to pointing out sites. If you're staying on board during a port call you can relax on deck or in one of the library-lounges socializing, reading, or getting together for a friendly game of chess or bridge. Up on the top deck you can relax or work out on one of several exercise machines. On the *American Spirit*, there's even a small putting green. At the cruise director's discretion, additional activities such as wine tastings or a hot chocolate bar are arranged for passengers.

**CHILDREN'S PROGRAMS** Children aren't a huge market for American Cruise Lines, and its ships don't offer programs for Junior Cruisers. Still, if you notify the company in advance that you will be bringing children on board, they will prepare special activities of interest and fun.

**ENTERTAINMENT**   American Cruise Lines is unusual among small-ship companies in that it always offers nightly entertainment in the main lounge of its vessels. In Alaska, the offerings can range from lectures and slide presentations covering Alaska's wildlife, geography, and history to a talk from the captain followed by a tour of the bridge to see how the ship navigates. More lightweight evenings might include activities such as bingo complete with silly prizes. In addition, on some nights, singers and musicians perform classic songs that everyone knows, prompting passenger sing-alongs. In an American Cruise Lines tradition, at some point during the evening's program, a waiter makes his way through the audience with a tray full of ice cream sundaes.

**SERVICE**   American Cruise Lines prides itself on its gracious hospitality, offered from an all-American crew, and passengers can expect warm, personal service. While the line says tipping is left to the discretion of its customers, passengers on weeklong cruises leave about $125 per person, on average, to be shared among the crew.

**CRUISETOURS & ADD-ON PROGRAMS**   American Cruise Lines doesn't offer land-and-sea cruisetours in Alaska, but all Alaska sailings do include a 1-night stay at the **Goldbelt Hotel** in Juneau the day before the cruise departs.

## American Spirit

### The Verdict

Looking for a relatively new, upscale small vessel with all the latest amenities, including large cabins with balconies? The *American Spirit* is your ship (assuming you can afford it).

### Specifications

| Size (in GRTs) | 1,933 | Crew | 31 |
|---|---|---|---|
| Passengers (Double Occ.) | 100 | Passenger/Crew Ratio | 3 |
| Passenger/Space Ratio | 19.3 | Year Launched | 2005 |
| Total Cabins | 47 | Last Major Refurbishment | N/A |

### Frommer's Ratings (Scale of 1–5)                                     ★★★★★

| Cabin Comfort & Amenities | 5 | Dining Options | 4 |
|---|---|---|---|
| Ship Cleanliness & Maintenance | 5 | Adventure & Fitness Options | 3.5 |
| Public Comfort/Space | 5 | Children's Facilities | NA |
| Decor | 4 | Enjoyment Factor | 5 |

**THE SHIP IN GENERAL**   In a market where most small ships are 20 or even 30 years old, with tiny cabins and limited on-board features, the *American Spirit* stands out. Built in 2005, it has all the modern amenities, including relatively large cabins that in many cases have balconies. Activity on board revolves around the main Chesapeake Lounge, at the front of the vessel's aptly-named Lounge Deck. One deck below, at the back, is the Main Dining Salon, where most meals take place. Still, in Alaska at least, the place to be often is the ship's top Observation Deck, where passengers gather to watch for whales, seals, and sea otters and gaze at lush green forests, snow-covered mountains, and calving glaciers.

**CABINS**  At 200 to 400 square feet, the *American Spirit's* cabins are quite spacious for small ships and—notably—many come with balconies (a rarity on small ships in Alaska). Each room has twin or double beds, a closet, a desk, dresser, and two chairs. Cabin bathrooms have a full-size shower and enough room to do everything you've got to do without feeling claustrophobic. While fairly narrow, cabin balconies are wide enough to enjoy sunsets and the spectacular vistas of Alaska's Inside Passage.

## CABINS & RATES

| CABINS | PER DIEM RATES | SQ. FT. | FRIDGE | HAIR DRYER | SITTING AREA | TV |
|---|---|---|---|---|---|---|
| *American Spirit* | | | | | | |
| Outside | $764–$1,083* | 200–400 | no** | yes | yes | yes |

*Rates are per day based on 7-night cruises.*
**Fridges can be placed in cabins upon request*

**PUBLIC AREAS**  The *American Spirit* has three passenger decks, not including the open-air top deck, all accessible via stairs or one small elevator. In addition to cabins, each deck has a small but comfortable library lounge stocked with books and magazines. There's also a computer in each lounge for those passengers who must stay in touch with the world. As mentioned above, the dining room is on the first deck, toward the back. The second deck has the forward-facing main lounge for socializing and evening activities. There's always coffee, tea, soft drinks, and snacks in the main lounge. The third deck is home to the ship's bridge. The top deck offers lounge chairs, exercise equipment, and lots of fresh Alaskan air.

**POOL, FITNESS, SPA & SPORTS FACILITIES**  The top deck of the *American Spirit* harbors several exercise machines and a small putting green. There are no pools or hot tubs on the vessel.

# LINDBLAD EXPEDITIONS— NATIONAL GEOGRAPHIC

96 Morton St., 9th Floor, New York, NY 10014. ℂ **800/397-3348** or 212/765-7740. Fax 212/265-3770. www.expeditions.com.

## Pros

- **Great expedition feeling.** Lindblad's programs have innovative, flexible itineraries; outstanding lecturers/guides; and a friendly, accommodating staff.
- **Built-in shore excursions.** Rather than relying on outside concessionaires for their shore excursions (which is the case with most other lines, big and small), Lindblad Expeditions runs its own. These excursions are an integral part of its cruises and included in the cost of the cruise fare.
- **Highly knowledgeable experts on board.** The partnership with *National Geographic* has resulted in many top *National Geographic*–affiliated photographers, explorers, scientists, and researchers joining the line's voyages. Six naturalists are on board every expedition, for a 10-to-1 passenger-to-naturalist ratio.

## Cons

- **Cost.** Cruise fares tend to be a little higher than similar adventure-focused sailings on competing lines.

**THE LINE IN A NUTSHELL**  In 1979, Sven-Olof Lindblad, son of adventure-travel pioneer Lars-Eric Lindblad, followed in his father's footsteps by forming Lindblad Expeditions, which specializes in providing environmentally sensitive, soft-adventure/educational cruises to remote places in the world, with visits to a few large ports. In 2004, Lindblad Expeditions entered into an alliance with *National Geographic*. As pioneers of global exploration, the organizations work in tandem to produce innovative marine expedition programs and to promote conservation and sustainable tourism around the world. The venture lifts Lindblad's educational offerings out of the commonplace.

**THE EXPERIENCE**  Lindblad's expedition cruises are explorative and informal, designed to appeal to the intellectually curious traveler seeking a vacation that's educational as well as relaxing. Passengers' time is spent learning about life above and below the sea (from *National Geographic* experts and high-caliber expedition leaders and naturalists trained in botany, anthropology, biology, and geology) and observing the world either from the ship or on shore excursions, which are included in the cruise package. Lindblad Expeditions' crew and staff emphasize respect for the local ecosystem—the company's literature calls it "Responsible Travel"—and the company has won many awards for its commitment to conservation. Flexibility and spontaneity are keys to the Lindblad experience, as the route may be altered anytime to follow a pod of whales or school of dolphins. Depending on weather and sea conditions, there are usually two or three excursions every day.

**THE FLEET**  The 62-passenger *National Geographic Sea Lion* and *National Geographic Sea Bird* (built in 1981 and 1982, respectively) are nearly identical in every respect. Both are basic vessels built to get you to beautiful spots and have a minimum of public rooms and conveniences: one dining room, one bar/lounge, and lots of deck space for wildlife and glacier viewing. There are no inside cabins or suites.

**PASSENGER PROFILE**  Lindblad Expeditions tends to attract well-traveled and well-educated, professional, 55-plus couples who have "been there, done that" and are looking for something completely different in a cruise experience. The passenger mix may also include some singles and a smattering of younger couples. Although not necessarily frequent cruisers, many passengers are likely to have been on other Lindblad Expeditions programs, and they share a common interest in history and wildlife.

**DINING OPTIONS**  Hearty buffet breakfasts and lunches and sit-down dinners include a good variety of both hot and cold dishes with plenty of fresh fruits and vegetables. Many of the fresh ingredients are obtained from ports along the way, and meals may reflect regional tastes. (In Alaska, Lindblad chefs will search out sustainably caught local fish as part of an overall commitment to promoting sustainable cuisine.) Although far from haute cuisine, dinners are well prepared and well presented, served at single open seatings, which lets passengers get to know one another by moving around to different tables. Lecturers and other staff members dine with passengers.

**ACTIVITIES**  During the day, most activity takes place off the ship, aboard Zodiac boats or kayaks and/or on land excursions. While on board, passengers entertain

# Lindblad Expeditions Fleet Itineraries

| SHIP | ITINERARIES |
| --- | --- |
| *Sea Bird/Sea Lion* | 14-night "Remarkable Journey to Alaska, British Columbia & Haida Gwaii" North- and southbound between Seattle and Sitka visiting Gulf Island, BC; Alert Bay and Johnstone Strait, BC; Inside Passage, BC; Haida Gwaii; Misty Fjords; Frederick Sound; Petersburg; Tracy Arm/Fords Terror Wilderness Area; Juneau; Glacier Bay; and Sitka (May and Sept) |
| | 7-night Coastal Wilderness: North- and southbound between Juneau and Sitka, visiting Tracy Arm, Petersburg, Frederick Sound, Chatham Strait, Glacier Bay, Point Adolphus, and Inian Pass (May–Aug) |

themselves with the usual small-ship activities: wildlife watching, gazing off into the wilderness, reading, and chatting. Shore excursions are included in the cruise fare. Lindblad also has an open-bridge policy—rare in the cruise industry—that gives travelers the opportunity to spend time on the bridge to observe and interact with the captain and staff.

**CHILDREN'S PROGRAM**   Family cruising to Alaska is big business, and Lindblad has stepped up to the plate and now has special family activities led by specially trained staff on all sailings. Activities have a nature slant, such as exploring an Alaskan rain forest or meeting with a local ranger in Glacier Bay National Park to work toward earning a "Junior Ranger" badge. Don't expect such big-ship features as a video arcade or playroom for the little ones, however.

**ENTERTAINMENT**   Lectures and slide presentations are scheduled throughout the cruise, and documentaries or movies may be screened in the evening in the main lounge. Many voyages also have a special photo element that provides opportunities for travelers to learn from *National Geographic* photographers on board, and the line's ships now feature a Lindblad–*National Geographic* Certified Photo Instructor on every departure to help passengers take their photography skills to the next level. In 2011, Lindblad also began bringing a native Huna/Tlinglit interpreter on board its vessels in Glacier Bay to offer a local perspective on Alaska's indigenous people. The interpreter will share local stories that date back before written history that have been passed down through oral traditions and arts. Also new on Lindblad's Alaska sailings is the Alaska Undersea Program, which brings an undersea specialist on board who makes regular dives up to 80 feet below the vessel with high-intensity lighting and a video camera to capture Alaska's underwater wonders. The fascinating footage is viewed by passengers on a plasma screen in the lounge, often in real time. Books about Alaska are found in each ship's small library.

**SERVICE**   Dining-room staff and room stewards are affable and efficient and seem to enjoy their work. As with other small ships, there's no room service unless you're ill and unable to make it to the dining room. The line suggests passengers leave a gratuity of $14 to $16 per person per day at the end of the voyage to be shared among crew.

**CRUISETOURS & ADD-ON PROGRAMS**   The company is offering no land packages in 2014.

# Sea Bird • Sea Lion

## The Verdict

Get up close and personal in Alaska on these comfortable small ships, and expect excellent commentary from knowledgeable naturalists along the way.

## Specifications

| | | | |
|---|---|---|---|
| Size (in U.S. reg. GRTs) | 100 | Crew | 29 |
| Passengers (Double Occ.) | 62 | Passenger/Crew Ratio | 2.1 |
| Passenger/Space Ratio | N/A* | Year Launched | 1981 |
| Total Cabins | 31 | Last Major Refurbishment | N/A |

*\* These ships' sizes were measured using a different scale than the others in this book, so comparison is not possible.*

## Frommer's Ratings (Scale of 1–5)     ★★★★

| | | | |
|---|---|---|---|
| Cabin Comfort & Amenities | 3.5 | Dining Options | 3.5 |
| Ship Cleanliness & Maintenance | 4 | Adventure & Fitness Options | 5 |
| Public Comfort/Space | 3.5 | Children's Facilities | N/A |
| Decor | 3.5 | Enjoyment Factor | 4.5 |

**THE SHIPS IN GENERAL**   The shallow-draft *National Geographic Sea Lion* and *National Geographic Sea Bird* are identical twins, right down to their decor and furniture. Not flashy at all, each ship has just two public rooms that are utilitarian but comfortable.

**CABINS**   Postage-stamp cabins are tight and functional rather than fancy. Each has twin or double beds, a closet (there are also drawers under the bed for extra storage), and a sink and mirror in the main room. Behind a folding door lies a Lilliputian bathroom with a head-style shower (toilet opposite the shower nozzle, all in one compact unit). All cabins are located outside and have picture windows that open to fresh breezes. The vessels have no wheelchair-accessible cabins.

## CABINS & RATES

| CABINS | PER DIEM RATES | SQ. FT. | FRIDGE | HAIR DRYER | SITTING AREA | TV |
|---|---|---|---|---|---|---|
| Outside | $898–$1,572*/ $713–$1,210** | 90–120 | no | no | no | no |

*\* Rates are based on 7-night cruises; includes shore excursions.*
*\*\* Rates are based on 14-night cruises; includes shore excursions.*

**PUBLIC AREAS**   Public space is limited to the open sundeck and bow areas, the dining room, and an observation lounge that serves as the nerve center for activities. In the lounge, you'll find a bar; a library of atlases and books on Alaska's culture, geology, history, plants, and wildlife; a gift shop tucked into a closet; and audiovisual aids for the many presentations by naturalists.

**POOL, FITNESS, SPA & SPORTS FACILITIES**   While there is no formal gym space, the ships have two outdoor exercise machines (bicycle and treadmill) and a 30-minute stretching class every morning on the top deck led by the wellness specialist. In addition, Lindblad's style of soft-adventure travel means you'll be taking frequent walks or hikes in wilderness areas (usually accessed via inflatable expedition landing craft) and kayaking excursions. The ships offer a full line of wellness treatments through the LEXspa.

# UN-CRUISE ADVENTURES

3826 18th Ave. W., Seattle, WA 98119. ℭ **888/862-8881.** Fax 206/283-9322. www.un-cruise.com.

## Pros

- **Intimate experience.** With just 22 to 88 passengers, Un-Cruise vessels are the antithesis of the crowded mega-ships that dominate Alaska tourism.
- **Built-in shore excursions.** Most off-ship excursions and activities (such as kayaking and skiffing) are included in the cruise fare, as is an open bar on Un-Cruise's Luxury and Heritage Adventures vessels.
- **Night anchorages.** A great boon to light sleepers is that the routes taken allow time for the vessels to often anchor overnight, making for quiet nights and gorgeous mornings in coves and inlets.
- **Time to explore.** Some Un-Cruise vessels spend as much as 3 days exploring Glacier Bay National Park—allowing time for hiking with a park ranger on a glacier or into the rain forest, and even kayaking.

## Cons

- **The price.** On Un-Cruise's Luxury Adventures and Heritage Adventures, in particular, the least expensive accommodations can start at more than $600 per person per night. At a recommended 5 percent to 10 percent of the tariff, gratuities also can add mightily to the outlay. In short, you pay for all the privacy and pampering you get.

**THE LINE IN A NUTSHELL**  Looking for an off-the-beaten-path adventure in Alaska? That's what it's all about at Un-Cruise Adventures.

**THE EXPERIENCE**  Un-Cruise Adventures fills a distinct niche in waterborne travel, offering vacationers the chance to explore remote areas by luxury yacht, small expedition ship, or small coastal steamer. None of the company's eight vessels holds more than 88 passengers, and it prides itself on offering intimate, un-rushed getaways into spectacular wilderness areas where close-up encounters with wildlife are a focus along with scenery, history, and culture. In Alaska, the philosophy has translated into sailings through the most beautiful and wildlife-filled corners of Southeast Alaska's Inside Passage. With the exception of the line's Heritage Adventures, offered on a single vessel, Un-Cruise itineraries mostly forego calls in Southeast Alaskan towns such as Skagway and Haines, allowing for more time to explore the many remote (and little-visited) bays, fjords, and glaciers of the region. A key element of Un-Cruise trips is unraveling the tradition of rigid cruise-ship schedules. Itineraries are flexible, and getting off the ship and interacting with the landscape in a meaningful way is a focus. In short, it's not a typical cruise, hence the line's name, Un-Cruise. The idea is that this is a vacation to the outdoors of Southeast Alaska that is on a ship only because that's the easiest way to get people into the region's remote back bays and hidden areas. It's not about cruising but about getting out into the wilderness. Nearly all itineraries include kayaking from kayaks carried on board, exploring for wildlife in motorized Zodiac boats (also carried on board), and hiking. Still, the cruises are designed so passengers who don't want to participate in the most active adventure activities aren't left out, and sailings also offer all the creature comforts for which cruising is known, including gourmet cuisine, fine wines, and craft beers. Un-Cruise's offerings are broken down into three categories: High-priced **Luxury Adventures** where the outdoor exploring is leavened with no shortage of pampering; similar but less-expensive **Active Adventures;** and history- and culture-focused **Heritage Adventures.**

**THE FLEET**   Expanding rapidly in recent years, the line now operates eight vessels that carry from 22 to 88 passengers. Four of the vessels, all with "safari" in their names—the *Safari Endeavour, Safari Explorer, Safari Quest,* and *Safari Voyager*—focus on the line's most upscale offerings, called Luxury Adventures (longtime cruise fans will recognize this segment of the company as what used to be called American Safari Cruises). Three other ships, all sporting the word "wilderness" in their names—the *Wilderness Adventurer, Wilderness Discoverer,* and *Wilderness Explorer*—operate the company's less-expensive Active Adventures. A single ship, a replica coastal steamer called S.S. *Legacy,* is dedicated to what the line calls Heritage Adventures—trips focused on history and culture

**PASSENGER PROFILE**   For the most part, the company targets young-at-heart, outdoorsy types who typically range from 40 to 70 years old—or, in the words of one manager, the kind of people who shop at outdoor store REI. Multigenerational families are a solid market, and Un-Cruise's focus on wildlife and scenery on many itineraries can be appealing to teens and even young children, although those 13-and-under aren't allowed on the line's Luxury Adventures ships except on select family departures. Un-Cruise often attracts people who have not cruised before and who are not particularly interested in a big-ship experience. Ages skew a bit younger on the line's Active Adventure trips, which typically feature more activities each day as well as a lower price point. The line's Luxury Adventures often draw a slightly older crowd, as one might expect given the higher price point. The outliers among the line's offerings are its Heritage Adventures, which debuted in 2013 on the S.S. *Legacy* and appeal to those interested in discovering the history of a destination and visiting ports rather than exploring wilderness in a kayak.

**DINING OPTIONS**   On Luxury Adventures, shipboard chefs delight guests with multicourse meals and clever snacks (such as, fresh halibut ceviche, outstanding fresh muffins every morning, smoked salmon). Given the opportunity, chefs barter with nearby fishing boats for the catch of the day and raid local markets for the freshest fruits and vegetables. Passengers on Luxury Adventures also can serve themselves from the well-stocked bar, which during our recent visit had two kinds of sherry and four brands of gin alone, all of them premium; there were also a variety of Alaskan beers to savor. On Active Adventures, the dining is simpler though still scrumptious. Passengers assemble in a single dining room for breakfast, lunch, and dinner, with breakfast and lunch buffet style (call it gourmet buffet) and plated service for dinner. A typical dinner might include a main course of roasted Pacific cod topped with ceviche and paired with a side dish of sautéed chayote and fire-roasted tomatoes, or a filet mignon with shallot tart tatin and roasted asparagus paired with an arugula salad with a preserved lemon vinaigrette and Parmesan fricco. The ships' galleys also work wonders when it comes to desserts, baking such items as a citrus tart or a pavlova with kiwi and strawberry sauce from scratch on a daily basis.

| SHIP | ITINERARIES* |
|---|---|
| **Safari Explorer/Safari Endeavour/Safari Quest** | 7-night Glacier Bay: Round-trip from Juneau, with an extended, 2-day visit to Glacier Bay, plus Icy Strait, Frederick Sound, Endicott Arm/Dawes Glacier, and Admiralty Island (May–Aug) |
| **Wilderness Discoverer/ Wilderness Adventurer** | 7-night Inside Passage: One-way from Juneau to Ketchikan with a half-day stop in Wrangell and visits to Tracy Arm Wilderness, Frederick Sound, Thomas Bay, Ideal Cove, Behm Canal, and Misty Fjords National Monument (May–Sept) |
| **Wilderness Explorer/ Wilderness Discoverer/ Wilderness Adventurer** | 7-night Glacier Bay: One-way between Juneau and Sitka with 3 days exploring Glacier Bay National Park and visits to Icy Strait, Chichagof Island, Baranof Island, Peril Strait and Sergius Narrows (May–Sept) |
| | 14-night Inside Passage that combines the 7-night Inside Passage and Glacier Bay itineraries above |
| | 21-night Inside Passage: that combines the three 7-night itineraries above. |
| **S.S. Legacy** | 7-night Inside Passage, one-way between Ketchican and Juneau with visits to Wrangell, Petersburg, Haines/Skagway, Sitka, Glacier Bay, and Icy Strait (June–Aug) |

*\* In addition to the itineraries above, many of the ships offer repositioning cruises between Seattle and Juneau. Also, Un-Cruise itineraries are designed to be flexible, and it's not uncommon for the ship to make a detour from one cove or bay to another as the ship's captain seeks out the best wildlife viewing opportunities.*

**ACTIVITIES** Getting outdoors is what it's all about on Un-Cruise's Luxury and Active Adventures. When passengers aren't eating or drinking, an expedition leader is helping them into motorized rubber rafts or kayaks to explore glaciers and icebergs and to look for wildlife such as whales, bears, and sea lions. Other activities include landings by raft for guided hikes through remote forests, paddleboarding, snorkeling, "polar bear club" swims, birding, and glacier walks. The line even offers optional (extra charge) overnight camping trips from its ships.

By foregoing calls in Southeastern Alaska towns such as Skagway and Haines, Un-Cruise ships on Luxury and Active Adventures offer much more time to explore rarely visited and sparsely populated parts of the region. Caving is offered on Prince of Wales Island during one itinerary (Forest Service guides lead passengers into remote El Capitan cave, the largest mapped cave in North America). Extended days in Glacier Bay National Park allow guests on board the rare opportunity to explore the park off the boat hiking and kayaking. Many itineraries explore remote areas along Chichagof and Baranof Islands.

Luxury and Active Adventures do occasionally include a stop in a town such as Wrangell or the Native community of Klawock. Billed as nontraditional port calls, these aren't the typical cruise stop where a bus awaits to take people around. Instead, in the case of Klawock, passengers can take a boat ride to a landing area near the totem carving shed just outside of Klawock, where elders will be instructing Native teens how to carve and restore ancient totem poles; others may choose to stroll over to the totem park, still others to make their way through town. In Wrangell passengers similarly can experience the Native tribal house on Chief Shakes Island by skiff; elders will be there to interpret the totems. Or they can visit the town and explore the petroglyphs.

The Un-Cruise ships carry high-quality equipment to use during outings, including top-of-the-line sea kayaks; trekking poles; some backpacks and day packs; binoculars; rain pants and slickers; mud boots; paddle boards; and wet suits (some, but not enough for all guests) for water activities.

The exception to all of the above are the history- and culture-focused Heritage Adventures that Un-Cruise offers on a single ship, the S.S. *Legacy,* which have a greater emphasis on Southeast Alaska's historic port towns. On these trips, a shore excursion to a point of historical interest is included during each port call, and crew in period costumes bring the history of the Klondike Gold Rush to life through onboard skits and character reenactments.

**CHILDREN'S PROGRAMS**   Un-Cruise ships have no formal children's program, but the outdoorsy focus of the line's Luxury and Active Adventures make them a natural for animal-loving kids, and activities such as kayaking and hiking are tailored for all ages. Children ages 12 and under receive a discount of 25 percent off the regular cruise fare on select "Kids in Nature" sailings aimed specifically at families. In 2014, six such voyages were planned on the *Safari Endeavour, Safari Quest,* and *Wilderness Adventurer. Note:* Children ages 13 and under are not allowed on Luxury departures that are not designated as "Kids in Nature" sailings, nor are they allowed on Heritage Adventures.

**ENTERTAINMENT**   In the evening, after dinner, passengers will often gather in a lounge to share discoveries made during the day. Many of Un-Cruise's vessels feature a small but often lively bar that serves local Alaskan craft beers on tap as well as wine and mixed drinks. Flatscreen TVs in the lounge/bar area are used to show educational videos and movies—and sometimes even videos shot by passengers. Educational presentations are provided by onboard naturalists on select nights, with topics such as whales, glaciers, and Native cultures. Passengers can also relax in the evening under the Alaska night sky in the top-deck hot tubs or saunas found on most Un-Cruise ships. Some may choose to schedule a massage with the onboard wellness director/licensed masseuse (an extra charge on Active Adventures). Passengers can also view the world below from new bow-mounted underwater cameras on most ships that stream video into all TVs on board. DVDs are available for passengers to watch in their cabins.

**SERVICE**   All of the line's ships offer top-notch service, with the most pampering coming on Luxury Adventures, where the staff-to-passenger ratio is the highest. Naturalists and English-speaking crew members facilitate all off-ship and onboard activities, as well as serve meals and perform housekeeping duties. *Note:* The company suggests passengers leave an end-of-voyage tip for the crew of 5 percent to 10 percent of the cruise fare paid, which works out to around $200 to $400 per person for the typical cabin on an Active Adventure during the peak summer months (more for passengers on higher-priced Luxury Adventures).

**CRUISETOURS & ADD-ON PROGRAMS**   The line offers land-tour add-on packages into Denali National Park and Glacier Bay National Park and Preserve; self-drive adventures to Wrangell–St. Elias National Park, the Kenai Peninsula, and Chugach National Forest; and a river rafting/camping trip. The line also offers pre- and post-cruise stopover packages in Ketchikan, Sitka, and Juneau.

# Safari Explorer • Safari Quest

## The Verdict

Excellent adventure cruising at a relaxed, flexible pace; aah, a decidedly different Alaska experience.

## Specifications

| Size (in GRTs) | 695/345 | Crew | 15/11 |
| --- | --- | --- | --- |
| Passengers (Double Occ.) | 36/22 | Passenger/Crew Ratio | 2 |
| Passenger/Space Ratio | 19.3/15.7 | Year Launched | 1998/1992 |
| Total Cabins/Veranda Cabins | 18/2; 11/4 | Last Major Refurbishment | 2008/2006 |

*\* These ships' sizes were measured using a different scale than the others in this book, so comparison is not possible—nor are they realistically applicable.*

## Frommer's Ratings (Scale of 1–5)                    ★★★★½

| Cabin Comfort & Amenities | 4.5 | Dining Options | 4 |
| --- | --- | --- | --- |
| Ship Cleanliness & Maintenance | 4 | Adventure & Fitness Options | 5 |
| Public Comfort/Space | 4 | Children's Facilities | N/A |
| Decor | 4 | Enjoyment Factor | 5 |

**THE SHIPS IN GENERAL**   More private boat than cruise ship, these two vessels are an oddity in the cruise community, and as far from the Alaska norm as it's possible to get. The bigger of the two, the *Safari Explorer,* is just 145 feet long. Inside virtually no area is out of bounds, including the bridge; the captain will welcome your visit, provided he's not involved in some critical nautical maneuver at the time. It all leads to the feeling that you're vacationing on a friend's private floating home. Used exclusively for Un-Cruise's Luxury Adventures, these two vessels promise an intimate, virtually all-inclusive cruise to more out-of-the-way parts of the Inside Passage—and succeed admirably. The price for these Luxury Adventures is not inexpensive, but the items included and the degree of pampering make it a worthwhile investment for those seeking an "uncruise." With just 24 to 36 guests, the vessels guarantee flexibility, intimacy, and privacy. Once passenger interests become apparent, the expedition leader shapes the voyage around them. Black-bear aficionados can chug off in a Zodiac boat for a better look, active adventurers can explore the shoreline in one of the yacht's kayaks, and slacker travelers can relax aboard the ship. A crew-to-passenger ratio of about one to two ensures that a cold drink, a good meal, or a sharp eagle-spotting eye is always nearby on the line's comfortable vessels, which range in length from 120 to 232 feet.

**CABINS**   Sleeping quarters aren't large, but they are comfortable and clean, with beds outfitted with memory-foam Tempur-Pedic® mattresses, adequate light, and art (of varying quality, if hardly museum-standard) on the walls. Bathrooms are fine, even in the standard cabins; cabins on the *Safari Quest* have showers only. On the *Safari Explorer,* six premium cabins have a combination Jacuzzi tub/shower. The top-category cabins have sliding glass doors and a step-out balcony, a small sitting area, and even a separate living room. Down below, deluxe rooms are tidy, filled with a surprising amount of natural light, and fairly spacious. All staterooms have iPod docking stations, binoculars, hair dryers, automatic nightlights and heated tile floors in the bathrooms, robes, slippers, and flatscreen TV/DVDs. There are no special facilities for travelers with disabilities. Both the *Safari Explorer* and *Safari Quest* have cabins designed specifically for single occupancy and are priced accordingly. Those looking for posh accommodations and over-the-top amenities should look elsewhere.

## CABINS & RATES

| CABINS | PER DIEM RATES | SQ. FT. | FRIDGE | HAIR DRYER | SITTING AREA | TV |
|--------|----------------|---------|--------|------------|--------------|-----|
| **Safari Quest** | | | | | | |
| Outside | $914–$1,242*/ $692–$850** | 125–168 | no | yes | some | yes |
| **Safari Explorer** | | | | | | |
| Outside | $856–$1,542/ $*675–$1,008** | 133–275 | some | yes | some | yes |

*Rates are per day based on 7-night cruises.*
**Rates are per day based on 14-night cruises*

**PUBLIC AREAS** Sitting rooms are intimate and very comfy, almost as if they've been transported intact from a spacious suburban home. Four or five prime vantage points for spotting wildlife (one is a hot tub!) ensure as little or as much privacy as you desire. As an example, the back area of *Safari Quest* has a great sitting nook to get away from the "masses," and the aft outside area is great for enjoying early morning coffee. In an upscale touch, meals are served fully plated for breakfast, lunch, and dinner (a breakfast buffet is also put out for early risers). There's a sense of communal dining, with one seating in a casual room. Ships have 24-hour espresso/coffee/tea facilities, a fully stocked open bar, and a small book/DVD library.

**POOL, FITNESS, SPA & SPORTS FACILITIES** There are stair-steppers and elliptical machines on both vessels; sea kayaks and stand-up paddleboards for passenger use (15 on *Safari Explorer*, 8 on *Safari Quest*). Both ships have hot tubs on the top deck; the *Safari Explorer* also has a sauna. The best equipped is the *Explorer*, which also has a small dedicated fitness area. The wellness director/licensed masseuse on the *Safari Explorer* leads yoga classes in the early mornings and provides each passenger with a complimentary massage.

# Safari Endeavour

## The Verdict

The same pampering as Un-Cruise's other Luxury Adventures vessels, but in a somewhat bigger ship with more amenities.

## Specifications

| | | | |
|---|---|---|---|
| Size (in GRTs) | 1425 | Crew | 34 |
| Passengers (Double Occ.) | 86 | Passenger/Crew Ratio | 2.5 |
| Passenger/Space Ratio | 16.6 | Year Launched | 1983 |
| Total Cabins | 43 | Last Major Refurbishment | 2012 |

## Frommer's Ratings (Scale of 1–5)                              ★★★★½

| | | | |
|---|---|---|---|
| Cabin Comfort & Amenities | 4 | Dining Options | 5 |
| Ship Cleanliness & Maintenance | 4.5 | Adventure & Fitness Options | 4.5 |
| Public Comfort/Space | 4.5 | Children's Facilities | NA |
| Decor | 4 | Enjoyment Factor | 4.5 |

**THE SHIP IN GENERAL**    *Safari Endeavour* is the largest of Un-Cruise's three Luxury Adventures vessels and offers more onboard amenities than the smaller *Safari Quest* and *Safari Explorer,* including two hot tubs overlooking the back of the vessel that are hot spots, literally, for watching wildlife and passing scenery. Significantly renovated in 2012, it has room for more "toys" than the smaller Un-Cruise vessels, including a small armada of inflatable motorized boats and sea kayaks used for off-ship adventure touring, and it has its own massage suite (where every passenger gets a complimentary massage once per voyage). "Casual elegance" is the phrase to describe the onboard ambience. In addition to a stylish forward-facing lounge called the Salon where passengers congregate for pre-dinner happy hours and post-dinner lectures, the ship has a small self-serve Wine Bar (carved out of the dining room in the 2012 renovation), a sauna, and a small library. Overall, this is one of the more comfortable small ships in the Alaska market. In part, that's because Un-Cruise doesn't pack in the passengers. The *Safari Endeavour*'s last owner, now-defunct Cruise West, carried up to 102 passengers on the vessel, but Un-Cruise had it reconfigured for just 86 people, resulting in a lot more room per person.

**CABINS**    The *Safari Endeavour* offers five categories of well-appointed cabins that vary significantly in size (and pricing). All offer views of the ocean through outward-facing windows, and the four biggest cabins, labeled Commodore Suites, also have step-out balconies (as well as Jacuzzi tubs). All cabins have private bathrooms. Depending on the room, beds may be configured as twin, double, or queen, and in many cases are convertible. All rooms include an iPod docking station, flatscreen TV with DVD player, desk with chair, and hair dryers.

### CABINS & RATES

| CABINS | PER DIEM RATES | SQ. FT. | FRIDGE | HAIR DRYER | SITTING AREA | TV |
|---|---|---|---|---|---|---|
| **Safari Endeavour** | | | | | | |
| Outside | $556–$1,428*/ $475–$833** | 100–240 | no | yes | some | yes |

*Rates are per day based on 7-night cruises.
**Rates are per day based on 12-night cruises.

**PUBLIC AREAS**    For a small ship, the Safari Endeavour has a lot of outdoor public space, including an ample outdoor bow viewing area where passengers often congregate during wildlife sightings and a partially covered outdoor Sun Lounge deck atop the vessel. In short, you won't find yourself elbowing fellow passengers for a deck-top spot for wildlife watching. On the inside, the ship has a spacious forward-looking lounge with a bar called the Salon that is hopping at happy hour and also is the hub for after-dinner presentations. One deck below, the Main Dining Room is where all meals are served. The same deck is also home to a small library that's an intimate place to tuck yourself away with a good book or a friend for a chat. A new self-serve Wine Bar built into the main dining room is quite elegant. You can do a tasting while standing at the Wine Bar or pour a glass and head up to the lounge.

**POOL, FITNESS, SPA & SPORTS FACILITIES**    The wellness program on board consists of a smattering of fitness equipment on the top deck of the vessel (open to the air), two hot tubs, and a sauna, which is a lot more than you'll find on most small ships in Alaska. In addition, in one of the vessel's luxury touches, there's a small massage room where a certified massage therapist provides a complimentary massage for every passenger during cruises (the therapist also does impromptu sessions in a massage chair set up in the lounge). Each morning, weather permitting, free yoga classes also are held on deck. Of course, the highlight of a trip on this vessel is the adventure available with its wide array of adventure equipment. A custom-made kayak launch platform is attached at the stern of the vessel, and four kayaks at a time can quickly be launched. This is also a stable platform for departing on tours on Zodiac boats carried on the ship, and on single-person paddleboards. You'll always find crew on hand to help you in and out of the equipment and make you feel comfortable. The platform also is a jumping-off point for passengers who want to take the "polar bear" plunge into Alaska's icy water during the cruise (there always are a few).

# Wilderness Discoverer • Wilderness Adventurer • Wilderness Explorer

## The Verdict

Looking for a way to get off the beaten path in Alaska's Inside Passage? These three small ships will bring you right into the wilderness, where bears and eagles outnumber humans.

## Specifications

| Size (in U.S. reg. tons) | 99/89/94 | Crew | 26/25/27 |
|---|---|---|---|
| Passengers (Double Occ.) | 76/60/76 | Passenger/Crew Ratio | 2.9/2.4/2.8 |
| Passenger/Space Ratio | N/A* | Year Launched | 1992/1984/1976 |
| Total Cabins | 38/30/38 | Last Major Refurbishment | 2011/2011/2012 |

## Frommer's Ratings (Scale of 1–5)                              ★★★★

| Cabin Comfort & Amenities | 3 | Dining Options | 4 |
|---|---|---|---|
| Ship Cleanliness & Maintenance | 4 | Adventure & Fitness Options | 5 |
| Public Comfort/Space | 4 | Children's Facilities | NA |
| Decor | 3.5 | Enjoyment Factor | 4.5 |

**THE SHIPS IN GENERAL**  Built as expedition ships, the similar-sized *Wilderness Discoverer, Wilderness Adventurer,* and *Wilderness Explorer* (the *Adventurer* is slightly shorter) are capable of nimble exploration through nature's most dramatic hideaways. The shallow draft and hull design allow easy access to Southeast Alaska's wildlife-rich shores and glacially fed inlets, and they serve as ideal launching pads for an array of daily adventure excursions. Each of the vessels carries several dozen kayaks that passengers can use to explore the glacier-carved coves and fjords where the ships often anchor, as well as several motorized rubber rafts (deployable by a large mechanical arm built at the rear of the ships). The rubber rafts are used daily to take small groups of passengers on waterborne tours to view wildlife, waterfalls, glaciers, and other natural wonders, and the boats also are used to land passengers on shore for such activities as guided hikes and tidal-zone walks. Completely gutted and rebuilt in either 2011 or

2012, the interior spaces of the ships offer contemporary colors and simple furnishings.

**CABINS**   As is typical on small expedition ships, the cabins on these vessels are relatively spartan, though not uncomfortable. All face outward and have view windows that slide open to allow in a breeze. Four large cabins added to the top deck of the *Discoverer* (labeled the Explorer category) offer a premium location for wildlife viewing and privacy as well as significantly more space—unlike standard cabins, there's room for relatively normal-size bathrooms with full-size showers. Three out of four of the Explorer cabins also have a daybed that can be made up for sleeping, turning what is normally a cabin for two into a triple. All cabins have a large closet as well as multiple wall hooks for storing adventure gear; soft overhead lighting; bedside reading lamps; a compact corner sink located on the outside of the bathroom; and functional if not luxurious beds and bedding. Hair dryers, iPod docks, and flatscreen TVs with built-in DVD players round out the amenities (a small DVD library is available for passenger use at no charge). *Note:* The ships don't get a television satellite signal, so there are no cable or broadcast stations on the TVs, just a handful of internal ship stations. With the exception of the Explorer category, cabins on the *Wilderness Adventurer* and *Wilderness Discoverer* have compact, expedition-ship-style bathroom facilities that combine the shower and toilet in the same small compartment (a shower curtain pulls across the toilet to keep it dry while you shower).

## CABINS & RATES

| CABINS | PER DIEM RATES | SQ. FT. | FRIDGE | HAIR DRYER | SITTING AREA | TV |
|---|---|---|---|---|---|---|
| **Wilderness Discoverer** | | | | | | |
| Outside | $285–$856* | 81–180 | no | yes | some | yes |
| **Wilderness Adventurer** | | | | | | |
| Outside | $256–$585* | 60–101 | no | yes | no | yes |
| **Wilderness Explorer** | | | | | | |
| Outside | $256–$585* | 90–125 | no | yes | some | yes |

*\* Rates are per day based on 7-night cruises.*

**PUBLIC AREAS**   All three vessels offer plenty of open deck space from which to watch for wildlife, including an open sundeck with tables and chairs and a bow observation area. In the ships' interiors, public space is limited to a main salon and adjacent dining area that fills part of a single deck (the two areas blend into one). The salons serve as the ships' hubs and offer lounge seating and bars serving local Alaskan craft beers, wine, and mixed drinks (the bars, notably, were handmade from Alaskan yellow cedar during the ships' renovation); large flatscreen TVs; small libraries of DVDs and books on Alaska wildlife, plants, history, and culture; and a collection of games.

**POOL, FITNESS, SPA & SPORTS FACILITIES**   Each ship has a hot tub (two hot tubs on *Wilderness Discoverer*) on an outside deck overlooking the back of the ship, a deck-top sauna, and several elliptical cross trainers and exercise bikes for passenger use (also located on an outdoor deck in a covered area). The ships also offer complimentary yoga classes, with yoga mats on board, and a masseuse offers Swedish massage daily (for an extra charge).

# S.S. Legacy

## The Verdict

A charming replica coastal steamer that brings Southeast Alaska's history and culture alive.

## Specifications

| Size (in GRTs) | 1472 | Crew | 35 |
| Passengers (Double Occ.) | 88 | Passenger/Crew Ratio | 2.5 |
| Passenger/Space Ratio | 16.7 | Year Launched | 1984 |
| Total Cabins | 44 | Last Major Refurbishment | 2013 |

## Frommer's Ratings (Scale of 1–5)                ★★★★½

| Cabin Comfort & Amenities | 4.5 | Dining Options | 4.5 |
| Ship Cleanliness & Maintenance | 4.5 | Adventure & Fitness Options | 3.5 |
| Public Comfort/Space | 4.5 | Children's Facilities | NA |
| Decor | 4.5 | Enjoyment Factor | 4.5 |

**THE SHIP IN GENERAL**  Designed to resemble a coastal steamer from the gold-rush era, this charming, well-maintained vessel features turn-of-the-century decor and period furniture that sets the mood for cruises where history and culture are the focus. An outlier among Un-Cruise's ships, which normally revolve around outdoorsy adventure, the S.S. *Legacy* is dedicated to the line's history-heavy Heritage Adventures and features such unusual twists as crew in period costumes. Instead of expedition guides, there are "Heritage Guides" who bring history to life by occasionally appearing as historic characters—conservationist John Muir, say—and the ship's Alaska itineraries revolve around stops in historic port towns such as Skagway, the gateway to the Klondike Gold Rush of the late 1890s. Significantly renovated in 2013, the S.S. *Legacy* is in sparkling condition, despite dating back to the 1980s, and features a high crew-to-passenger ratio. Like Un-Cruise's Luxury Adventures vessels, it's designed as a premium product in the small-ship category (and is priced accordingly, with rates starting at more than $700 per person per day). Fine wines, craft beers, and premium spirits are included in the fare, as are such upscale touches as a massage for every passenger once per cruise. Shore excursions at every port also are part of the experience at no extra charge (including some big-ticket items such as a ride on the White Pass & Yukon Route railway in Skagway).

**CABINS**  The S.S. *Legacy* offers six categories of cabins that vary widely in size, including a 600-square-foot Owner's Suite that takes up a sizeable chunk of the top deck. None of the cabins have balconies, but many open onto balcony-like exterior walkways that circle the ship, and all have windows. The cabin decor gives a nod to the gold-rush era with ornamented wooden beds, small dressers, and stand-alone closets; green-shaded brass light fixtures; and maroon fabric curtains. The well-maintained rooms also feature iPod docking stations that double as alarm clocks, and wall-mounted flat-screen televisions for playing DVDs (a wide selection of movies on DVD are available at no extra charge in the Grand Salon). Some rooms also have writing desks topped with binoculars for wildlife viewing. Cabin bathrooms have showers, toilets, and Victorian-style sinks (in some cabins, the sink is on the outside of the bathroom). Overall, cabins are quite comfortable compared to many small ships in Alaska.

## CABINS & RATES

| CABINS | PER DIEM RATES | SQ. FT. | FRIDGE | HAIR DRYER | SITTING AREA | TV |
|--------|----------------|---------|--------|------------|--------------|-----|
| **S.S. Legacy** | | | | | | |
| Outside | $742–$1,999* | 110–600 | no | yes | some | yes |

*\* Rates are per day based on 7-night cruises.*

**PUBLIC AREAS**    The hub of the vessel is the elegant Grand Salon, a spacious lounge designed to evoke the gold-rush era. Located at the front of the ship overlooking the bow, it features comfortable furnishings including several sofas, fabric-covered chairs, and granite-topped lounge tables as well as a lovely wood-and-granite bar, an upright piano and even a small dance floor. The Grand Salon is home to a lively happy hour with hors d'oeuvres each evening before dinner and after-dinner presentations that sometimes include actors taking on the roles of historic characters from Alaska's history. One deck down from the Grand Salon is the 1890s-style Klondike Dining Room, where all meals are served, and—through swinging wooden doors of the kind seen in Old West movies—a small but atmospheric self-serve beer-and-whiskey lounge called the Pesky Barnacle Saloon. Overlooking the aft of the ship, the latter is a cozy, wood-trimmed hideaway with mismatched antique tables and chairs, and moose antlers on the wall where one can "STEP INTO THE WORLDS OF JACK LONDON, SAM HILL, (AND) ELIZA SKIDMORE," according to a sign near the entrance. Passengers can pour themselves a beer or whiskey and enjoy a card game at the round poker table at the room's center. Outdoor areas of the ship include a bow viewing area in front of the Grand Salon that is bustling when wildlife is sighted and a sundeck with tables and chairs and two hot tubs.

**POOL, FITNESS, SPA & SPORTS FACILITIES**    In addition to the two hot tubs, the top deck of the vessel harbors two sit-down bicycle machines in a covered area and is the site of daily yoga classes that are available to all passengers at no charge. There's also a small sauna tucked into a nook one deck below the main sundeck, and a massage room is located on the Lounge Deck. Passengers can sign up for one complimentary, 45-minute massage per sailing.

# ALASKA MARINE HIGHWAY SYSTEM

7559 N. Tongass Hwy., Ketchikan, AK 99901. ✆ **800/642-0066** or 907/465-3941. Fax 907/465-8824. www.ferryalaska.com.

In Alaska, which has fewer paved roads than virtually any other state, getting around can be a problem. There are local airlines, of course, and small private planes—lots and lots of small private planes, some with wheels, some with skis, some with floats for landing on water. (In fact, there are more private planes per capita in Alaska than in any other state in the union.) But given the weather conditions in many northland areas for large parts of the year, airplanes are not always the most reliable way of getting from Point A to Point B.

That's why the Alaska Marine Highway System (aka the Alaska Ferry, or AMHS) is so important. Sometimes in inclement weather even the state capital, Juneau, cannot be reached by air (there are no roads of any consequence linking it with the rest of the state) and relies heavily on the ferryboats of the AMHS to bring in visitors, vehicles, supplies, and even, now and then, the legislators who run the state. (Although the

AMHS relocated its administrative headquarters to Ketchikan in 2005, its reservations center remains in Juneau.)

Although the ferry system was originally created more than 50 years ago with the aim of providing Alaska's far-flung, often inaccessible smaller communities with essential transportation links with the rest of the state and with the Lower 48, the boats have developed a following in the tourism business as well. Every year, thousands of visitors eschew luxury cruise ships in favor of the more basic services of the 11 vessels of the AMHS. The service is of particular value to independent travelers, enabling visitors to come and go as they please among Alaska's outposts. All the AMHS ferries carry both passengers and vehicles.

In 2005, AMHS was officially designated an "All American Road" by the U.S. Department of Transportation, and it remains the only marine route with such a designation. To qualify for such recognition, according to federal rules, a road must have qualities that are nationally significant and contain features that do not exist elsewhere—it must be "a destination unto itself." AMHS definitely fits the bill.

The AMHS's southernmost port is Bellingham, Washington. Its network stretches throughout Southeast and Southcentral Alaska and out to the Aleutian island chain to the west of Anchorage.

### Pros

o **Unique way to travel.** The ferry system allows the chance for adventuresome travel that is not too taxing.

o **Lots of flexibility.** Passengers can combine the various itineraries that the ferry system has scheduled to customize their vacation package.

### Cons

o **No doctor on board.** None of the vessels carry a doctor, so this may not be a good way to travel if you have health concerns.

o **Space books up quickly.** The only way you will be able to find a space on most of the ferries is by booking promptly. Don't call in May and expect to get what you want in June. It ain't gonna happen! If you're serious about experiencing Alaska by ferry, book now. Call them at ✆ **800-642-0066** or book electronically through the website at **www.ferryalaska.com**.

o **Spartan cabins.** Sleeping accommodations, when available, are basic, to say the least—no fridge, no telephone, and so on. (One traveler was overheard to say, "I've known Trappist monks with more luxurious quarters!")

**THE LINE IN A NUTSHELL** The ferries operate in three distinct areas. Year-round service is offered in the Southeast, or Inside Passage, from Bellingham to Skagway/Haines; in Southcentral, which includes Prince William Sound, the Kenai Peninsula, and Kodiak Island; and, in the summer months, the Southwest region, which includes the Aleutian chain. The Aleutian's service is not offered during the winter due to the extreme weather of the region. The seas become too rough, the fog too thick, and the cold too intense in this region for the ferries to operate safely or profitably in the winter. One of the newest ports added to the system is Gustavus, the town recognized as the gateway to Glacier Bay National Park & Preserve. Another popular summer route connects the southernmost community of Bellingham, through the Inside Passage and across the Gulf of Alaska, to Whittier, located only 60 miles south of Anchorage. See the website (www.ferryalaska.com) for more details on the many routes that the AMHS operates.

**THE EXPERIENCE** It must be stressed that ferry-riding vacations are different from cruise vacations. Don't even think about one if you're looking for a lot of creature comforts—fancy accommodations, gourmet food, spa treatments, Broadway-style shows, and the rest. You won't find any of the above on the sturdy vessels of the AMHS. In fact, not all ferry passengers get sleeping berths—5 of the 11 ferries in the fleet are considered day boats and have no bedroom accommodations at all.

It's in the lounges or on deck that riders may encounter the only entertainment on board, all created by passengers on a strictly impromptu basis. It might be a back-packer strumming a guitar and singing folk songs, or a father keeping his children occupied by performing magic tricks. Occasionally, spirited discussion groups will form in which all are welcome to participate. The subject might be the environment (always a hot topic in Alaska, especially now with talk of opening up the Alaska Wild-life Preserve for oil exploration), politics (Alaskan or federal), the effect of tourism on wildlife (as much a hot-button issue as the environment), or any of a thousand other topics. (It's tempting to suggest—tongue slightly in cheek—that the entertainment on many Alaska Ferry boats is better than on some cruise ships we've been on, but that wouldn't be kind!) Occasionally, sports will be discussed—but don't look for the locals to want to talk about anything as much as dog sledding. It's almost a religion in the 49th State—their World Series, Super Bowl, and Stanley Cup rolled into one.

**THE FLEET** All nine of the traditional AMHS boats are designated M/V, as in motor vessel. The two newer, catamaran-style vessels are designated FVF, for fast vehicle ferries. Below is a thumbnail description of each one:

The 382-foot-long *Kennicott,* in service since 1998, operates some of the longest runs in the system, connecting Bellingham with the towns of the Southeast before continuing on across the Gulf of Alaska as far north and west as Seldovia. The *Kenn-icott* holds up to 499 passengers and 80 vehicles, and it has 109 cabins: 51 four-bed rooms with private bathrooms containing toilets and showers; 34 two-bed rooms with sinks but no showers or toilets (public facilities are down the hall); and 24 super-small, two-bunk "roomettes" that don't even have sinks but are far less pricey. Five of the cabins are wheelchair-accessible.

The 418-foot-long *Columbia,* the largest of the AMHS vessels, connects Belling-ham with the towns of the Southeast only (unlike the *Kennicott,* it doesn't continue across the Gulf of Alaska). It holds up to 600 passengers and 134 vehicles, and it has 44 four-berth cabins and 59 two-berth cabins. Three cabins are suitable for wheelchair users. The vessel has a dining room for fine dining, a cafeteria, and a cocktail lounge.

Also sailing between Bellingham and the towns of the Southeast is the 499-pas-senger, 88-vehicle *Malaspina.* It has 46 four-berth cabins, 27 two-berth cabins, a caf-eteria, a cocktail lounge, and a solarium.

The 499-passenger, 88-vehicle *Matanuska* sails between Prince Rupert, B.C., and the towns of the Southeast (including Juneau, Ketchikan, Wrangell, Petersburg, and Skagway). It has 23 three-bunk cabins and 81 two-bunk cabins (one of which can accommodate a wheelchair user) as well as a cafeteria and cocktail lounge.

One of the newest and fastest vessels in the AMHS fleet is the fast ferry *Fair-weather,* which operates strictly in the Southeast, mostly between Juneau and Sitka (about a 4½-hour trip; slightly longer when it stops in Angoon along the way). The 235-foot-long catamaran also makes a weekly Juneau-to-Petersburg run (a 4-hour trip). The *Fairweather* can hold 250 passengers and 35 vehicles but has no sleeping quarters; it is designed purely to provide fast access between the above-mentioned

Southeast towns. Its value to locals in Sitka and Petersburg is immense; they now can get to the stores and government offices of Juneau twice as fast as once was possible. Its value to tourists is that it enables them to spend less time in transit.

A sister high-speed vessel that debuted in 2005, the *Chenega,* similarly provides speedy service between the communities of Prince William Sound. It also has no sleeping accommodations.

Also sailing between the towns of Prince William Sound is the *Aurora,* which has room for 300 passengers and 34 vehicles but no cabins. It has a cafeteria and solarium.

The 352-foot-long *Taku,* meanwhile, is an additional option for travelers who want to get between the towns of the Southeast. It carries 370 passengers and 69 vehicles, and it has 44 cabins (mostly with two bunks; a few have four). The ship has a cafeteria, cocktail lounge, observation lounge, and solarium.

The *Lituya,* the smallest and slowest of the ferries, has operated exclusively between Ketchikan and the nearby Native village of Metlakatla since joining the fleet in 2004. The 8-mile trip takes just 45 minutes, and the cabin-less vessel carries 149 passengers and 18 vehicles. Although built with a specific local market in mind, it offers tourists an easy way to visit the off-the-beaten-path outpost.

Another vessel that will get you off the-beaten path is the 300-passenger, 34-vehicle *Le Conte.* It connects Juneau with such small Southeast communities as Angoon, Gustavus (gateway to Glacier Bay National Park), Pelican, and Hoonah. It has a cafeteria, but no cabins.

The 174-passenger, 36-vehicle *Tustumena,* in Alaska since 1964, connects the towns of the Southwest from Seldovia all the way west to Dutch Harbor in the Aleutian Islands. It has 26 cabins (one of which is adapted for wheelchair use), a fine dining room, and a cocktail lounge.

**PASSENGER PROFILE**   More than half of the passengers on the Alaska ferry system are locals traveling between towns for everything from work to sporting events (remember that many towns in rugged Alaskan such as Ketchikan and even state capital Juneau lack roads to the outside world). But you'll also find a healthy mix of vacationers from the Lower 48 and beyond, everything from young and adventurous backpackers to retirees (who just might have their RV parked down below in the ship's hold). It's a fairly laid-back crowd and totally casual. Jeans and hiking boots (sometimes not removed for days), anoraks and backpacks—these are the basic accessories of ferry travelers in the 49th State. They are definitely not looking for luxury.

The ferries have become extremely popular with RVers, who use them to move their vehicles into and out of the state, saving thousands of miles of driving.

**CABINS**   Booking passage on the AMHS can be a complicated affair. First, you'll pay for a spot on the ship, which can be as little as $31 for the 1-hour trip between Skagway and Haines or as much as $547 for the 1,629-mile, 4-day voyage between Bellingham and Whittier. Then you'll pay extra if you want a cabin for the sailing, which can add hundreds of dollars more for a multi-day trip. Children between the ages of 6 and 11 are charged roughly half the adult fare throughout the system, and children 5 and under travel free. Once you've booked basic passage and paid for a cabin, assuming you want one, you'll then have to account for what you're taking along. A kayak? A motor vehicle? A motorcycle? An inflatable boat? All of these, and more, are an additional cost. Only in Alaska! You'll want to be careful when you make a reservation. Be sure to disclose all information about what you are bringing on board and the overall length of your vehicle so that there are no surprises when you get to the ferry terminal.

In general, cabins are small and spartan, coming in two-, three- and four-bunk configurations, and either inside (without windows) or outside (with windows). For a premium, you can reserve a more comfortable sitting-room unit on some vessels. Some cabins have tiny private bathrooms with showers and toilets; others have sinks only, with showers and toilets located down the hall. Cabins can be stuffy, and the windowless units can be claustrophobic as well, so try to get an outside one. (If you're insistent on a balcony with your cabin when sailing in Alaska, forget about traveling on the AMHS!)

Travelers who do not book ferry passage in time to snag a cabin—or purposely eschew one in an effort to save money—must spend nights curled up in chairs in lounges or in the glass-enclosed solariums found on some vessels. This being Alaska, where the frontier spirit is alive and well, some hearty travelers without cabin reservations will bring tents and sleeping bags and "camp" in the solariums or even out on deck—a phenomenon that not only is allowed but encouraged. If you plan on setting up outside, just be sure to bring duct tape to secure your tent to the deck in case you can't find a sheltered spot, as the wind blows like an endless gale over a ship in motion. If the vessel looks crowded, grab your spot fast to get a choice location. No matter whether you have a cabin or not, public showers are available, although there may be lines. Lock valuables in the coin-operated lockers.

**DINING OPTIONS** Only 2 of the 11 AMHS ferries (*Columbia* and *Tustumena*) have a full-service, sit-down dining room. The others have cafeteria-style facilities that serve hot meals and beverages. There are also vending machines on all the boats, which dispense snacks and drinks. Priced from $1 for a vending machine snack to $8 and up for hot meals, food is not included in the fares. The ships take cash and credit cards.

**ACTIVITIES** There are no organized activities but lots of scenic viewing—and good listening on most sailings. Some vessels have small theaters that show films of general interest and documentaries on Alaska and the outdoors. Small gift shops sell magazines, books, toiletries, and Alaska souvenirs. In addition, some vessels have card rooms, reading rooms, small video game arcades, and/or toddler play areas. Be sure to stay a day or two in the port communities visited by the ferries to experience true Alaska activities.

**CHILDREN'S PROGRAMS** None.

**ENTERTAINMENT** None.

**SERVICE** Service is not one of the things for which the AMHS is noted. The small American staff on each vessel works enthusiastically, but without a great deal of distinction.

**CRUISETOURS & ADD-ON PROGRAMS** None. However, those seeking a change from the more popular and frequently congested, larger Inside Passage and Gulf ports find that the ferries are an ideal way to get around the less-visited parts of Alaska, where paved roads are in short supply and reliable air connections—especially when the weather turns ugly—are nonexistent. A trip on one of the ferries can deposit you in, say, Pelican, on Chichagof Island, where you can enjoy fishing and scenery and join in the banter of the local fisherfolk in Rosie's Bar, the center of activity in town. A trip on another ferry will transport you to Tenakee Springs, a popular hot springs as far back as the gold-rush days, where you can "take to the waters" and also take advantage of saltwater fishing and brown bear viewing opportunities in the area. The ferry will get you to Port Lions, which is on the northeast coast of Kodiak Island at the eastern end of the Aleutian Chain, or to other areas of the Aleutians—False Pass and King Cove, for instance; to Chenega Bay, in Prince William Sound; to the Native settlements at Kake, on Kupreanof Island; and to Metlakatla on Annette Island, among many other destinations. These are not, and never will be, ports with mass appeal. No giant cruise liner will ever unload 3,000 passengers in any of them. But those who seek a taste of down-home spirit, Alaskan style, find these ports to be attractive destinations. In short, the AMHS can get you to places where cruise ships just don't go. Of course, the ferry system also can get you to big-ship cruise ports such as Ketchikan, Juneau, and the rest, but much of the system's appeal, to many visitors, is its ability to transport travelers to lesser-known outposts. It also allows you to take a vehicle, so you can explore the interior of Alaska without driving the entire Alcan Highway both directions. Riding on a ferry, as opposed to a cruise ship, allows you the flexibility to explore the communities for several days (as opposed to only a few hours) at your leisure. It gives you time to meet real Alaskans in large and small communities and enjoy a variety of activities such as fishing, hiking, kayaking, biking, hunting, skiing, and much, much more.

**PUBLIC AREAS**   All the ferries have warm, if somewhat sparse, interiors, with room for all when the weather is foul. They often have solariums with high windows for viewing the passing scenery.

**POOL, FITNESS, SPA & SPORTS FACILITIES**   Are you kidding?

# THE PORTS OF EMBARKATION

Most Alaska cruises operate either round-trip from Vancouver or Seattle, or one-way northbound or southbound between Vancouver or Seattle and Seward/Anchorage. Whittier, an unprepossessing little place that has the advantage of being 60 miles closer to Anchorage, has become the northern turnaround port for Princess's cruises in the Gulf of Alaska, and more recently also Norwegian Cruise Line. Another U.S. city, San Francisco, also is growing as a home port for voyages to Alaska, with round-trip and one-way sailings, including from Princess. The small adventure-type vessels sail from popular Alaska ports of call such as Juneau, Ketchikan, and Sitka (as well as Seattle). In this chapter, we'll cover the most common of these home ports: Anchorage, Seward, Vancouver, Seattle, Juneau, and Whittier.

Consider traveling to your city of embarkation at least a day or two before your cruise departure date. You can check out local attractions, and if you're traveling from afar, give yourself time to overcome jet lag.

## ANCHORAGE

Anchorage, which started as a tent camp for workers building the Alaska Railroad in 1914, stands between the Chugach Mountains and the waters of upper Cook Inlet. It was a remote, sleepy railroad town until World War II, when a couple of military bases were located here and livened things up a bit. Even with that, though, Anchorage did not start becoming a city in earnest until the late 1950s, when oil was discovered on the Kenai Peninsula, to the south.

The place still feels like a backwater town, but as Alaska's only cosmopolitan city, Anchorage now boasts good restaurants, fine museums, and a nice little zoo. There's even a Nordstrom store. The city is surrounded by wilderness, and moose regularly annoy gardeners. Bears occasionally show up in the streets too—though it's unlikely you'll run into the critters in the height of the cruise season. You're more likely to see bald eagles as they fly around the office buildings.

Anchorage's downtown area, near Ship Creek, is about 8 by 20 blocks wide, but the rest of the city spreads some 5 miles east and 15 miles south. The city center is pleasant, but we recommend you try to see more than just the streets of tourist-oriented shops. Check out the **coastal trail** and the

**museums,** and if you have time, plan a day trip about 50 miles south along **Turnagain Arm** to explore the receding **Portage Glacier** and visit the mountains.

# Getting to Anchorage & the Port

Most cruise ships dock not in the city but in Seward or Whittier on the east coast of the Kenai Peninsula, to avoid the extra day that cruising around the peninsula to Anchorage adds to Gulf of Alaska itineraries. It's quicker to transport passengers between the towns in motorcoaches or by train than it is to sail all the way around the peninsula. Holland America's *Amsterdam* in 2010 became the first major cruise ship to dock in Anchorage proper in 25 years. Most visitors will use Anchorage as a hub because, thanks to the international airport, it's where Alaska connects to the rest of the world. We recommend spending a day or two in Anchorage before or after your cruise.

**BY PLANE**   If you're arriving or leaving by plane, you'll land at the **Ted Stevens Anchorage International Airport.** The facility is located within the city limits, a 15-minute drive from downtown. Taxis run about $27 for the trip downtown; many hotels also have free shuttles.

**BY CAR**   There is only one road into Anchorage from the rest of the world: the Glenn Highway. The other road out of town, the Seward Highway, leads to the Kenai Peninsula.

# Exploring Anchorage

**INFORMATION**   The **Anchorage Convention and Visitor Bureau** (© **907/276-4118;** www.anchorage.net) maintains five information locations. The main one is the Log Cabin Visitor Information Center at 4th Avenue and F Street (© **907/257-2363;** www.anchorage.net). It's open daily 8am to 7pm June through August, and 8am to 6pm in May and September. Visit the bureau's website for everything you need to know before you go.

**GETTING AROUND**   Most car-rental companies maintain a counter at the airport. A compact car costs from about $55 a day, with unlimited mileage. (There aren't many of those $30-a-day specials that you see advertised in some other states!) Advanced bookings are strongly recommended in midsummer. Anchorage's bus system, **People Mover** (www.peoplemover.org), is an effective way of moving to and from the top attractions and activities. The buses operate between around 6:30am and 9pm daily, with limited service on weekends and holidays, and passage costs $1.75 for adults, 50¢ for seniors, and $1 for ages 5 to 18 (4 and under free).

## ATTRACTIONS WITHIN WALKING DISTANCE

With its old-fashioned grid of streets, Anchorage's downtown area is a fun place to wander, if a bit touristy. The 1936 **Old City Hall,** at 4th Avenue and E Street, has an interesting display on city history in its lobby, including dioramas of the early streetscape. For a better sense of what Alaska's all about, though, you'll want to check out the heritage museums or take a ride outside the city to the Chugach Mountains. You can also take a walk or bike on the **Tony Knowles Coastal Trail,** which comes through downtown and runs along the water for about 11 miles, from the western end of 2nd Avenue to Kincaid Park (keep an eye out for wildlife including moose). You can hop onto the trail at several points, including Elderberry Park, at the western end of 5th

# Anchorage

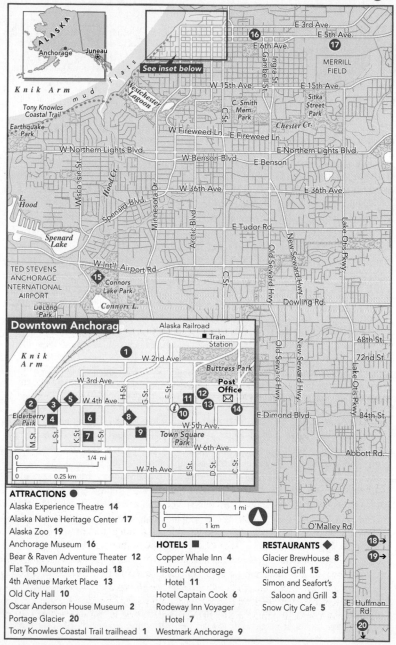

## Downtown Anchorage

**ATTRACTIONS** ●
Alaska Experience Theatre **14**
Alaska Native Heritage Center **17**
Alaska Zoo **19**
Anchorage Museum **16**
Bear & Raven Adventure Theater **12**
Flat Top Mountain trailhead **18**
4th Avenue Market Place **13**
Old City Hall **10**
Oscar Anderson House Museum **2**
Portage Glacier **20**
Tony Knowles Coastal Trail trailhead **1**

**HOTELS** ■
Copper Whale Inn **4**
Historic Anchorage
   Hotel **11**
Hotel Captain Cook **6**
Rodeway Inn Voyager
   Hotel **7**
Westmark Anchorage **9**

**RESTAURANTS** ◆
Glacier BrewHouse **8**
Kincaid Grill **15**
Simon and Seafort's
   Saloon and Grill **3**
Snow City Cafe **5**

Avenue. And if you're in the mood for some free music, local musical acts perform at Peratrovich Park on 4th Avenue every Wednesday, Thursday, and Friday at noon during the summer as part of the Music in the Park program.

**The Alaska Experience Theatre ★**   Think Alaska, think big. This popular attraction features Alaska-themed movie presentations shown in a 96-seat domed theater with a wraparound, planetarium-style screen that stands nearly three stories high. It is a cool introduction to some of the places you'll be touring, but be aware the format (like IMAX) may cause motion sickness in some people. A smaller Safe-Quake Theatre shows a video about the 1964 Alaska earthquake—and seating shakes to simulate an earthquake.

333 W. 4th Ave. (at C St.). ℂ **907/272-9076.** www.alaskaexperiencetheatre.com. Admission movies $9.95 ($1 off for kids), earthquake video $6.95, combo tickets $12.95. Daily 10am–6pm.

**Anchorage Museum ★★★**   The largest museum in Alaska was expanded in 2010 (to the tune of $107 million) and now serves up everything from a chance to experience the depths of the ocean and outer space (at the Thomas Planetarium) to a large collection of Native Alaskan artifacts. The history of Alaska and its people include a whole exhibit on Arctic aviation, the displays highlighted by photography and artifacts. In the contemporary art galleries it's fun to see what's happening in the state's art scene today, but the must-do is the Smithsonian Arctic Studies Center. Here you can view everything from waterproof clothing made from seal intestines, intricate baskets, and fascinating masks to weapons and drums. It even has historic kids' games. Much of the collection was under lock and key in Washington and is displayed here for the first time anywhere. If you're traveling with kids, make a beeline for the Imaginarium Discovery Center, where learning is enhanced by such attractions as a saltwater touch tank (stocked with critters that include starfish). The museum's hip **cafe** serves up surprisingly creative cuisine (such as a fig and goat cheese salad) plus a kids' menu. Special exhibits are frequent.

625 C St. (at the corner of 7th Ave). ℂ **907/929-9200.** www.anchoragemuseum.org. Admission $15 adults, $10 seniors and students, $7 for children 3–12. Mid-May–mid-Sept 9am–6pm; mid-Sept–mid-May Tues–Sat 10am–6pm, Sun noon–6pm.

**Bear & Raven Adventure Theater ★★**   This 35-seat theater screens locally produced movies about Alaska while providing visitors with state-of-the-art virtual experiences, including full sensory effects and surround sound. Learn about the Iditarod Trail while the lights of the aurora borealis dance on the ceiling and snow falls over the audience, or brush up on some bear smarts while your seat rumbles right along with the on-screen grizzlies. After the show, hook some virtual fish or take a virtual hot-air balloon ride in the lobby. The theater is located in Bear Square, which also features a restaurant, a used bookstore, a Scandinavian fashion store, and a panning-for-gold attraction. You can bring the gold you panned to the Alaska Mint jewelry store to trade or make into a keepsake.

315 E. St. ℂ **907/277-4545.** www.bearsquare.net. Admission both movies plus lobby experience $15 adults, $13 children; 1 movie $10 adults, $8 children.

**The Oscar Anderson House Museum ★**   Back in 1915 when Anchorage was a big tent city, butcher Oscar Anderson decided to build his family a real wood-frame house. Today the small house is listed on the National Register of Historic Places.

House tours—which last about 45 minutes—give a glimpse into what Anchorage life was like in the early 20th century, with period furnishings, historic photos, and a chance to hear a tune on Oscar's player piano.

420 M St. (in Elderberry Park). ℭ **907/274-2336.** www.aahp-online.net. Admission $10 adults (13 and up), $5 children 5–12, children under 5 free. Summer Tues–Sat noon-4pm; closed in winter except for Swedish Christmas (1st and 2nd weekends in Dec).

## ATTRACTIONS OUTSIDE THE DOWNTOWN AREA

**The Alaska Native Heritage Center ★★★** Come to this 26-acre center to learn about 11 distinct Alaska Native cultures. It has a small museum and a theater showing an introductory film on the different cultures in the Welcome House. The building's rotunda serves as a venue for lively Native song and dance performances, held throughout the day—you will be invited to join in for the last number. Also check out the center's workshop where Native craftspeople demonstrate such traditional crafts as kayak making. Outdoors, along a small lake, a walking trail takes visitors to six life-size dwellings showcasing the traditional way of life of various groups including the Athabascans and Tlingits. Cultural representatives are on hand to answer questions and share stories.

8800 Heritage Center Dr. ℭ **800/315-6608** or 907/330-8000. www.alaskanative.net. Admission $25 adults, $21 seniors and military, $17 children 7–16, free for children 6 and under; family rate (2 adults, 2 children) $71.50; combined Anchorage Museum/Native Heritage Center culture pass $30; dog cart ride $10. Summer daily 9am–5pm. Closed in winter. From the Glenn Hwy., take the Muldoon Rd. N. exit.

**The Alaska Zoo ★★** Don't expect a big city zoo. Instead, come to experience a little Eden complete with Alaskan bears, seals, otters, musk oxen, mountain goats, caribou, moose, and waterfowl. One of two resident adult polar bears was elected animal president of the zoo in 2012, in an effort to promote Arctic conservation. A bear cub rescued and brought to the zoo in March 2013 is not expected to be a permanent resident. You'll also see decidedly non-Alaskan elephants, tigers, and the like here.

4731 O'Malley Rd. ℭ **907/346-2133.** www.alaskazoo.org. Admission $12 adults, $9 seniors, $6 children 3–17, free children 2 and under. Summer daily 9am–9pm. New Seward Hwy. to O'Malley Rd., then turn left and go 2 miles; it's 20 min. from downtown, without traffic.

**4th Avenue Market Place ★** Located in the heart of downtown, this small mall has a number of stores and restaurants—some quite touristy—and houses the Alaska Experience (see above). Go if you want trinkets, but also check out the permanent art exhibit featuring 63 Alaska-themed prints by the late Alaskan artist Fred Machetanz (1908–2002). It also has Alaskan native cultural demonstrations and live musical events in summer. While on 4th Ave., check out the various food carts selling reindeer sausage on a bun—toppings include hot chili sauce, pineapple, or caramelized onions (yummy!).

433 W. 4th Ave. ℭ **907/278-3263.** Summer daily 9am–7pm.

**Flattop Mountain ★★★** Rising right behind Anchorage, this mountain is a great and easy climb, perfect for an afternoon or early evening hike. The parking area at Glen Alps, above the tree line, is a good starting point. You can sign your name on a plank at the summit.

In the Chugach Mountains. From the New Seward Hwy., drive east on O'Malley Rd., turn right on Hillside Dr. and left on Upper Huffman Rd., then right on the narrow, twisting Toilsome Hill Dr.

# THE iditarod

Few things fire up Alaska's residents like the **Iditarod Trail Sled Dog Race,** a grueling, nearly 1,000-mile run from Anchorage to Nome that takes place in mid-March, across frozen tundra and rivers, through dense forest, over mountains and along windy coastline. Winners cover the distance in 9 or 10 days (the record as of press time was 8 days, 18 hours, 46 minutes and 39 seconds set by commercial pilot John Baker in 2011), which includes mandatory stopovers to rest the dogs. In 2013, at the 41st Iditarod, Mitch Seavey (age 53) became the oldest musher to ever win the race, and he did it in just over 9 days, 7 hours. His son, Dallas, in 2012 became the youngest winner ever at age 25. The event is big news here—TV anchors speculate on the mushers' strategies at the top of the evening news, and schoolchildren plot the progress of their favorite teams on maps.

The start of the race in downtown Anchorage is covered by network TV too. The number of teams varies per year—in 2013, 68 mushers were on the roster, most from Alaska but also from places including Brazil and Jamaica. Each musher handles a team of 12 to 16 dogs. When the event hits Nome, the town overflows with visitors kept busy by the many local events and activities that coincide with the race. Even if the first team of man or woman led by dogs crosses the finish line at 3am—in 30°F (–34°C) weather, a huge crowd turns out to congratulate the musher.

This is Alaska's Super Bowl, its World Series. Recent competitors have included a mortician, a former fashion model, a dentist, teachers, contractors, a fur trapper, and even married couples and other family members competing against each other. Some are professional mushers (who get endorsement deals), others run kennels, and some do dog sledding as a hobby. To qualify, you need to compete in three smaller races—of which there are many in Alaska.

The victors are feted and admired throughout the state as much as any sports star ever is in the Lower 48. They're not compensated quite as well, mind you: First prize in the grueling event varies, but Seavey took home $50,000 and a new truck last year. The lead dogs are celebrated, too. The cruise lines long ago recognized the significance of the Iditarod, even to non-Alaskans. Princess, for instance, has a contract with Libby Riddles, the first woman to win the race, in 1985. She comes aboard in Juneau with a slide show to talk about her mushing experience. The *Riverboat Discovery* is a popular day sternwheeler cruise on the Chena River in Fairbanks, an outing cruise lines include in their cruisetour itinerary if they have programs in the Denali Corridor. The boat stops on each sailing at the dog yard where the late Susan Butcher—an Alaska legend who won the Iditarod four times (1986, 1987, 1988, and 1990)—kept some of her champion dogs. The Iditarod Trail Sled Dog Race headquarters (with a small museum) is located in Wasilla, a city near Anchorage made famous by its former mayor, Sarah Palin, and is also a part of the shore-excursion schedule of virtually all Gulf of Alaska cruise operators.

Cruise aficionados may never be in the state to see the race itself, as it takes place off cruise season—way off-season. But they are likely to see and hear plenty about it during their summer vacations.

You will have opportunity to meet sled dogs on tours offered in several ports including in Juneau, Seward (where Mitch Seavey has an operation), and Skagway, with opportunity too to ask Iditarod racers why the heck they do it.

**Portage Glacier** ★★★  In 1985, the National Forest Service spent $8 million building the Begich-Boggs Visitor Center at Portage. Imagine its chagrin when the glacier then started receding, moving away from the center so fast that at this point, you can't even see one from the other. You must now board a tour boat to get close to the glacier face. Portage is not the best glacier in Alaska—it's relatively small—but if you haven't had enough of them after your cruise (or want a preview beforehand), it's well worth a tour. The visitor center itself is worth a stop; it's a sort of glacier museum and an excellent place to learn about what you'll be seeing (or saw) on your cruise. Many bus tours are offered (your cruise line may give one, too), including a 5½-hour **Gray Line of Alaska** (✆ 888/452-1737; www.graylinealaska.com) trip from Anchorage, which involves a motorcoach ride to the glacier and a 1-hour cruise across Portage Lake. On the way back, stop for lunch at Hotel Alyeska and take an optional tram ride to the top of Mount Alyeska. The cost is $79 for adults and $39 for children, and the trip is offered daily at 1:30pm in the summer.

About 50 miles south of the city on the Seward Hwy. (toward Seward). Admission $5 adults, free for children 15 and under. May–Sept daily 9am–6pm. Closed in winter.

## BEST CRUISE-LINE SHORE EXCURSIONS

**Anchorage Flightseeing Safari** (1½ hr.; $149): See Anchorage surroundings by air as a bush pilot takes you on an exciting seaplane ride to explore the Chugach Mountain Range, where views include secluded valleys and slopes with Dall sheep, and over the Cook Inlet in search of beluga whales.

**McKinley/Denali National Park Flightseeing** (4 hr.; $449): View some of Alaska's most spectacular views and wild settings. The bush pilot will follow the spine of the Alaska Range, with its walls of rock and ice, to the awesome sight of the south face of Mount McKinley, where climbers summit.

**Portage Cruise and Alaska Wildlife Conservation Center** (5½ hr.; $99): Travel by bus on the Seward Highway to visit the Conservation Center, a refuge for wildlife including moose, bears, and caribou. Then board the MV *Ptarmigan* for a cruise across Portage Lake to the Portage Glacier, narrated by a U.S. Forest Service representative.

**Redoubt Bay Lodge Bear Viewing** (7 hr.; $599): See black and brown bears in their natural habitat. Includes a flight to the Redoubt Bay Lodge, at the entrance to the Lake Clark Wilderness Preserve, where you get on a covered pontoon boat to view bears without disturbing them. A naturalist accompanies the trip; lunch is included.

## EXCURSIONS OFFERED BY LOCAL AGENCIES

**Scenic City Tour**  Locally owned and operated Salmon Berry Tours offers a variety of different excursions, including a 2-hour scenic drive through the city and up Flat Top Mountain for stunning photo opportunities of the Chugach Mountains as well as Anchorage itself. Other tours include the 2-hour Chocolate City Circuit, during which you'll check out local chocolate boutiques as well as the world's largest chocolate waterfall; and the Big Rig Experience, highlighting the Ice Road Truckers of Alaska, which includes a visit to Anchorage's trucking terminal and the chance to try out a truck-driving simulator.

515 W. 4th Ave. (✆ **907/278-3572.** www.salmonberrytours.com. 2 hr. scenic city tour $49  Apr–Oct.

# Where to Stay

Rooms can be hard to come by in Anchorage in summer, so try to arrange lodging as far in advance of your trip as possible, whether through your cruise line or on your own. It's not a cheap city: Room rates in Anchorage, before discounts, often range upward of $200. In addition to the more moderately priced properties listed below you might try the luxurious **Hotel Captain Cook ★★,** 939 W. 5th Ave. (© **800-843-1950** or 907/276-6000; www.captaincook.com); the **Westmark Anchorage ★★,** 720 W. 5th Ave. (© **800 544-0970** or 907/276-7676; www.westmarkhotels.com); or the small and charming **Historic Anchorage Hotel ★★** at 330 E. St. (© **800/544-0988** or 907/272-4553; www.historicanchoragehotel.com). The town also has chain hotels.

**Copper Whale Inn ★★★**    This quaint bed & breakfast overlooks both the water and Elderberry Park. Inside the duo of clapboard houses are casually charming rooms of every shape and size—some in the newer building have nice high ceilings. Rent a bike through **Lifetime Adventures** (www.lifetimeadventures.net; $30/day), and hit the coastal trail after breakfast.

440 L St. © **866/258-7999** or 907/258-7999. www.copperwhale.com. 14 units, 12 with bathroom. $185 double w/out bathroom; $220 double w/bathroom. Extra person $20. Lower rates in winter and shoulder seasons. Special packages available. Rates include continental breakfast. Parking $15. *In room:* TV, hair dryer, Wi-Fi (free).

**Rodeway Inn Voyager Hotel ★★★**    This small property serves up big rooms, all with kitchens. While the property might be categorized as a boutique hotel, don't expect anything fancy. Still, it's a nice, casual place with warm hospitality and modern conveniences, perfect for a few nights. No smoking allowed.

501 K St. (at W. 5th Ave.). © **800/247-9070** or 907/277-9501. www.rodewayinn.com. 40 units. $185–$205 double. Lower rates in winter and shoulder seasons. Rates include continental breakfast. Limited free parking. *In room:* A/C, TV, hair dryer, kitchenette, Wi-Fi (free).

# Where to Dine

**Glacier BrewHouse ★★** GRILL/SEAFOOD    The lodge decor will remind you that you're in the frontier, and so will the menu, with such tasty options as reindeer sausage and fresh fish prepared on a wood-fired grill. The place is large and lively, and most diners accompany their meal with one of the hearty beers brewed behind a glass wall. Even if you've vowed to go low carb, try the bread, made with spent brewery grain and served with olive oil for dipping.

737 W. 5th Ave. © **907/274-BREW** (2739). www.glacierbrewhouse.com. Reservations recommended for dinner. Main courses $10–$37 lunch and dinner. Mon 11am–9:30pm; Tues–Thurs 11am–10pm; Fri 11am–11pm; Sat 10am-11pm; Sun 10am–9:30pm.

**Kincaid Grill ★★★** REGIONAL/SEAFOOD    A local foodie favorite, this small restaurant is about 5 minutes from the Ted Stevens International Airport and serves up everything from excellent lobster risotto to the must-have dessert of pumpkin bread and butter pudding. Chef Al Levinsohn is well-known in town for his appearances on local TV and on the Food Network.

6700 Jewel Lake Rd. © **907/243-0507.** www.kincaidgrill.com. Main courses $28–$36. Tues–Sat 5–10pm.

**Simon and Seafort's Saloon and Grill ★★★** STEAK/SEAFOOD    The amazing views of Cook Inlet and mountains in the distance is worth the visit, but so is

## SHOPPING SMART FOR native art

If you're interested in Native Alaskan art, know that there is a large market in fakes: More than one shopkeeper's assistant has been spotted removing MADE IN TAIWAN stickers from supposedly Native art objects.

Before you buy a piece of Native art, ask the dealer for a biography of the artist and whether the artist actually carved the piece (rather than just lending his or her name to knockoffs). Most dealers will tell you where a work really comes from—you just have to ask. Price should also be a tip-off to fakes, as real Native art is pricey. An elaborate mask, for instance, should be priced at $3,000, not $300. Be particularly wary of soapstone carvings—most are not made in Alaska.

There are two marks used for Alaska products: a MADE-IN-ALASKA polar bear sticker, which means the item was at least mostly made in the state, and a silver hand sticker, which indicates authentic Native art. An absence of the label does not necessarily mean the item is not authentic; it may just mean the artist doesn't like labels. So just ask if you're curious about a piece of artwork lacking a sticker.

the food. Sockeye salmon is the star of the show, along with other seafood specialties, but the prime rib will keep meat-lovers well satisfied. Locals come here, as do smart tourists—the friendly atmosphere and warm service enhance the experience. Light meals are available in the bar.

420 L St. (✆) **907/274-3502.** www.simonandseaforts.com. Reservations recommended (days in advance in summer). Main courses $13–$23 lunch, $17-$65 dinner. Mon–Fri 11am–2:30pm and 4–10pm; Sat-Sun 10am-3pm (for brunch) and 4:30–10pm.

**Snow City Cafe ★★★** REGIONAL/AMERICAN   Don't let the snowman with a fork and spoon for arms logo (or the diner ambience) fool you. There's great stuff cooking at this favorite local breakfast/brunch spot. Sit at the counter and dive into such treats as Kodiak Benedict (poached eggs on Alaska Red King Crab cakes) or the Ship Creek Benedict (eggs on salmon cakes), both topped with house-made hollandaise. Can't decide? Try The Deadliest Catch Benedict and get both. It also serves reindeer sausage and such classics as pancakes, omelets (the Crabby is made with crab, Swiss cheese, green onions, and avocado), French toast, as well as smoothies and decent coffee. Photos of the Iditarod sled dogs decorate the walls. Make reservations, come early, or be prepared for lines that often snake out the door.

1034 W 4th Ave. (✆) **907/272-CITY** (2489). www.snowcitycafe.com. A limited number of reservations available on the website. Main dishes $10–$13. Mon–Sun 7am–4pm (open breakfast and lunch only).

# SEWARD

Since Seward is the northern embarkation and debarkation port for many Gulf of Alaska cruise operators, passengers can almost be forgiven if they sometimes think the correct name of this Resurrection Bay community is "Seward-the-port-for-Anchorage." Although the majority of 7-day Gulf cruises are advertised as "Vancouver to Anchorage" (or the reverse), the ships don't actually sail to Anchorage. Instead, they dock in Seward or Whittier, and guests are carried by motorcoach or train to or from Anchorage. Why? Because Seward—and Whittier—lie on the south side of the Kenai Peninsula, while Anchorage is on the north. Sailing around the peninsula would add another day to the cruise.

As such, most people pass through Seward on their way to or from their ship, but they never really see much of the town. That's a pity. Seward, which traces its history back to 1793 when Russian pooh-bah Alexander Baranof first visited, is an attractive little town rimmed by mountains and ocean, with streets lined with old wood-frame houses and fishermen's homes. It's also home to the spectacular **Alaska SeaLife Center** (a marine research, rehabilitation, and public education center where visitors can watch scientists uncovering the secrets of nearby **Prince William Sound**). Seward is an ideal spot from which to take wildlife-watching day trips by boat into the sound or begin one of a variety of road and rail trips through the beautiful **Kenai Peninsula.**

Seward was hit hard on Good Friday 1964 when a massive earthquake rattled Anchorage, the peninsula, and everything in between. The villagers (there were only about 2,500 of them) watched the water in the harbor drain away after the shaking stopped and realized immediately what was about to happen: a tidal wave. Because they were smart enough to read the signs and run for high ground, loss of life was miraculously slight when the towering 100-foot wall of water struck. The town itself, however, was heavily damaged, so many of the buildings that visitors see today are of a more recent vintage than might be expected. However, care has been taken to rebuild them in the style of the town's earlier days. One of the more interesting facilities in town is the **Resurrect Art Coffee House & Gallery** (© **907/224-7161;** www.resurrectart.com), located in a converted church, built in 1916, at 320 3rd Ave. It's a neat place to buy art or just schmooze with the residents over coffee. Seward isn't exactly a shopping mecca. But given the arty nature of the place, there are some local products to be found.

## Getting to Seward

Most cruise passengers arrive at Seward either by ship (at the end of their cruise) or by bus.

**BY PLANE**    The nearest major airport, Ted Stevens Anchorage International Airport, is 130 miles away.

**BY BUS**    The bus trip from the airport takes about 3 hours, passing through the beautiful Chugach National Forest. If you haven't made transportation arrangements through your cruise line, **Seward Bus Line** (© **907/224-3608;** www.sewardbuslines. net) has one trip a day (leaving at 9:30am and 2pm) from Anchorage for $40 one-way from May 1 through September 15.

**BY CAR**    For those arriving by car, Seward and the Kenai Peninsula are served by a single major road, the Seward Highway.

**BY TRAIN**    The train ride to or from Anchorage with a stop at Seward goes through some truly beautiful scenery; it costs $79 one-way for adults ($125 round-trip) and $40 one-way for kids ($63 round-trip) on the **Alaska Railroad** (© **800/321-6518** or 907/265-2494; www.alaskarailroad.com). The route is prettier than going by road; you'll see gorges, rushing rivers, and tunnels cut through mountains. Be aware you may have to schlep your own bags when you arrive in Seward, though some cruise lines offer buses for the short distance to the pier.

# Seward

ATTRACTIONS ●
Alaska SeaLife Center **8**
Caines Head State
   Recreation Area **7**

HOTELS ■
Breeze Inn **3**
Hotel Seward **6**
Van Gilder Hotel **5**

RESTAURANTS ◆
Chinooks Waterfront **2**
Resurrect Art Coffee House
   & Gallery **4**
The Smoke Shack **1**

## Exploring Seward

**INFORMATION** The **Seward Chamber of Commerce** (© **907/224-8051;** www.
seward.com) operates an information booth right on the cruise-ship dock; it's open
8am to noon and 3 to 7pm daily. If you have time, stop by **Kenai Fjords National
Park Visitor Center,** near the waterfront at 1212 4th Ave. (© **907/224-7500**), to learn
about what's in the area, including nearby hiking trails. It's open daily May through
Labor Day 8:30am to 7pm; off season Monday through Friday 9am to 5pm.

**GETTING AROUND** The downtown area is within walking distance of the cruise-
ship dock, and you can easily cover downtown Seward on foot. For motorized transport, the city operates a complimentary shuttle from 8am to 8pm daily during the
summer (look for a big yellow school bus) on cruise days. The route loops from the
cruise-ship terminal through the small boat harbor and then downtown. The trip isn't
much more than a mile, though, so it's a pleasant walk if the weather cooperates.

### ATTRACTIONS WITHIN WALKING DISTANCE

Downtown Seward can be explored with the help of a **walking-tour map,** available
from the Chamber of Commerce visitor center near the cruise-ship docks and at estab-
lishments throughout town.

**The Alaska SeaLife Center** ★★★ Alaska's only public aquarium and ocean wildlife rescue center offers up-close encounters with puffins, octopus, sea lions, and other sealife, as well as the chance to observe ocean scientists at work. It should be on every visitor's must-see list. Steller sea lions, porpoises, sea otters, harbor seals, fish, and other forms of marine life abound in the area, as well as umpteen species of local seabirds. The ground-floor fish lab is a rehabilitation facility for sea otters, which visitors can observe being cared for. At the Discovery Pool, kids will enjoy a close encounter with sea creatures in open pools, while at the Steller Sea Lion Habitat, you can watch the playful sea lions swim and sun themselves on the rocks in a 162,000-gallon habitat resembling sea lion haulouts found in Resurrection Bay.

301 Railway Ave. (at milepost 0 of the Seward Hwy.). © **800/224-2525** or 907/224-6300. www. alaskasealife.org. Admission $20 adults, $15 children 12–17, $10 children 4–11, free for children 3 and under; special programs (include a Puffin Encounter, minimum age 12, and an Octopus Encounter; 1 hr., minimum age 6) $79 adults, $59 students. Reservations suggested. Summer Mon–Thurs 9am–9pm, Fri–Sun 8am–9pm; winter daily 10am–5pm.

## ATTRACTIONS BEYOND THE PORT AREA

**Caines Head State Recreation Area** ★★ Parts of this 7-mile coastal trail, south of town, are accessible only at low tide, so it's best done with someone picking you up and/or dropping you off by boat beyond the beach portion; **Miller's Landing water taxi** (© **866/541-5739** or 907/224-5739; www.millerslandingak.com) offers this service for $38 per person one-way, $48 round-trip. The trail has some gorgeous views, rocky shores, and the concrete remains of Fort McGilvray, a World War II defensive emplacement. Take flashlights and you can poke around in the spooky underground corridors and rooms. For an easy 2-mile hike to Fort McGilvray, start with a boat ride to North Beach. The main trail head is on Lowell Point Road. Stop at the Kenai Fjords National Park Visitor Center at the boat harbor for tide conditions and advice. Check out **www.alaskastateparks.org** for more about these local trails.

## BEST CRUISE-LINE SHORE EXCURSIONS

**Kenai Fjords/Resurrections Bay Wildlife Cruise** (8 hr.; $129 adults, $69 children): Board a day boat for a 5-hour cruise in Kenai Fjords National Park, narrated by a park ranger. Cruise past Bear Glacier and the hanging glaciers of Thumb Cove as you look for wildlife, including puffins and bald eagles, whales, and Dall's porpoises. Lunch included. Some tours also visit the Seward Sealife Center.

## EXCURSIONS OFFERED BY LOCAL AGENCIES

**Alaska Railroad** (© **800/544-0552** or 907/265-2494; www.alaskarailroad.com) has a variety of day tours from Seward, including a 5-hour cruise (offered with Major Marine Tours) that explores Resurrection Bay. The cruise is narrated by a park ranger and costs $232 per person; advance reservations are suggested.

**Kenai Fjords Tours** (© **877/777-4051**; www.kenaifjords.com) has a variety of land excursions and day cruises in Resurrection Bay and the Kenai Fjords National Park. A 6-hour cruise is priced at $144 for adults and $72 for children, while an 8½-hour, 150-mile cruise, including an all-you-can-eat wild Alaska salmon and prime rib dinner, is priced at $164 for adults, $82 for children 12 and under. The company also offers full- or half-day cruises combined with kayaking packages at Fox Island for $189 or $139, respectively, for adults and children 12 and older.

**IdidaRide dog-sled tours,** 12820 Old Exit Glacier Rd., 3¾ miles off the Seward Hwy. (© **800/478-3139** or 907/224-8607; www.idadaride.com), is Iditarod champion Mitch Seavey's racing kennel. Visitors can pet a lot of cute puppies and take 1½-hr. tours that include dog-sled demonstrations and rides on a wheeled dog sled ($69 for adults, $34.50 for kids). IdidaRide also offers a **summer glacier dog-sledding adventure.** After your 15-minute scenic flight to the top of Punch Bowl Glacier, you'll meet your musher and an enthusiastic team of huskies ready to let you take the reins or simply sit back and enjoy the ride. Each 2-hour tour costs $479 for adults and $459 for children, with flights leaving from Girdwood Airport every 1 hour and 45 minutes between 8:30am and 5:15pm.

In addition to these tours, **fishing charters** are available from various operators in the harbor.

## Where to Stay

**The Breeze Inn** ★ This large property, located right at the boat harbor, offers decent standard accommodations at reasonable rates—just don't expect anything fancy. The "classic rooms" are motel-like, with exterior entrances. Book one of the 22 executive-style rooms in the North Addition for mountain views and added amenities—including refrigerators and coffeemakers. Rooms in the Harbor View Annex indeed have Resurrection Bay views, plus interior corridors. Some rooms have a Jacuzzi and a king-size bed, for those looking for romance. Chocolate-chip cookies are an added perk.

303 North Harbor Dr. © **888/224-5237** or 907/224-5237. Fax 907/224-7024. www.breezeinn.com. 100 units. $149–$279 double. Free parking. **Amenities:** Restaurant; bar. In room: A/C, TV (w/free HBO), fridge (in some), hair dryer, Wi-Fi (free).

**Hotel Seward** ★★ Alaskan-family-owned and right in the heart of downtown, the Seward Hotel is within walking distance of the Alaska Sea Life Center, restaurants, and shopping. Some rooms have large bay windows overlooking Resurrection Bay (ask what the views are when you book). Amenities in the Alaskan Wing include pillow-top beds, flatscreen TVs, microwaves, and refrigerators. The **Historic Wing** has smaller rooms with similar amenities, but no elevator. Other facilities include an espresso bar.

221 5th Ave. (P.O. Box 2288). © **800/440-2444** or 907/224-8001. www.hotelsewardalaska.com. 62 units. $159–$279 double; $109 economy rooms. Extra person $10. Special packages available. Free parking. **Amenities:** Restaurant; lounge. In room: TV, hair dryer, kitchenette, laundry, Wi-Fi (free).

**The Van Gilder Hotel** ★ This 1916 hotel, listed on the National Register of Historic Places, is a charming place to stay, but be aware that authenticity means rooms tend to be small. Most rooms have antique-style brass beds, lace curtains, and pedestal sinks. Bathrooms are small and some are shared—one bathroom per two bedrooms.

308 Adams St. (P.O. Box 609). © **800/478-0400** or 907/224-3079. Fax 907/224-3689. www.vangilder hotel.com. 24 units. $79 double w/shared bathroom; $149–$199 double w/private bathroom. Extra person $10. In room: TV, Wi-Fi (free).

## Where to Dine

**Chinooks Waterfront** ★★ STEAK/SEAFOOD Chinook's is a lively, noisy place, with big windows looking out across the small-boat harbor. If you ask a local where to eat, this is where he'll send you. The menu is sourced locally, with fresh halibut, salmon, king crab, spot shrimp, and scallops. Order the Alaskan Fisherman's Stew and a local brew and enjoy the scene.

1404 4th Ave. ℭ **907/224-2207.** www.chinookswaterfront.com. Main courses $15–$32. Daily 11am–11pm.

**The Smoke Shack** ★★★ AMERICAN    Smoked meats are the calling card at this tiny restaurant, with tables outside and inside an old rail car. For breakfast, go with the eggs Benedict, which come with house-smoked ham. At lunch, order the ribs or smoked green-chili burrito, or dive into a smoked burger such as the Black & Blue, which is topped with blue cheese. It has a few chicken and veggie options as well.

411 Port Ave. (at the small-boat harbor). ℭ **907/224-7427.** Main courses $9–$13; breakfast $6–$12. Wed–Sun 7am–3pm.

# VANCOUVER

Located in the extreme southwestern corner of British Columbia, Vancouver has the good fortune to be surrounded by both mountains and ocean. The city has been expanding and growing rapidly, thanks to an influx of foreign money (especially from Hong Kong), and has undergone a major construction boom. But the development has not diminished the quality of life in Vancouver, which has a rich cultural heritage that includes Northwest Coast Native tribes and a flourishing Asian community. As part of the push for the 2010 Winter Olympics and Paralympic Games, Vancouver saw a host of developments, including a 12-mile rapid transit line connecting the Vancouver National Airport to downtown and the opening of the luxury Shangri-La Hotel Vancouver, part of a 62-story mixed-use skyscraper, the tallest building in the city.

The city has a thriving **arts** scene, including numerous summertime festivals focusing on various forms of entertainment such as folk music, jazz, comedy, and fireworks displays. Residents and visitors alike relish the proximity to **outdoor activities:** You can sailboard, rock-climb, mountain-bike, wilderness-hike, kayak, and ski on a world-class mountain here. For day-trippers the city offers easily accessible attractions, including the historic **Gastown district,** with its shops and cafes, and a bustling **Chinatown.**

Those traveling with teenagers will likely know Vancouver as the place where the movie *Twilight* and sequels were filmed.

Shopping on Robson Street and Granville Island may not be the bargain it once was, but the shops are still enticing. You'll probably visit Vancouver at the beginning or end of your Alaska cruise, since it's the major southern transit point. We recommend that you try to spend at least a day here before or after your cruise to have time to explore.

*Note:* Rates below are in Canadian dollars. At press time, the conversion was C$1 = US $0.97 and may change based on the exchange rate at the time of your trip.

## Getting to Vancouver

Most cruise ships dock at **Canada Place** (ℭ **604/775-7200**) at the end of Burrard Street. A landmark in the city, the pier terminal is noted for its five-sail structure, which reaches into the harbor. It's located at the edge of the downtown district and is just a quick stroll from the **Gastown** area (see below), filled with cafes, art galleries, and souvenir shops; and **Robson Street,** a mecca for trendy clothing stores. Right near the pier are hotels, restaurants, and shops, as well as the **Tourism Vancouver Infocentre.**

# Downtown Vancouver

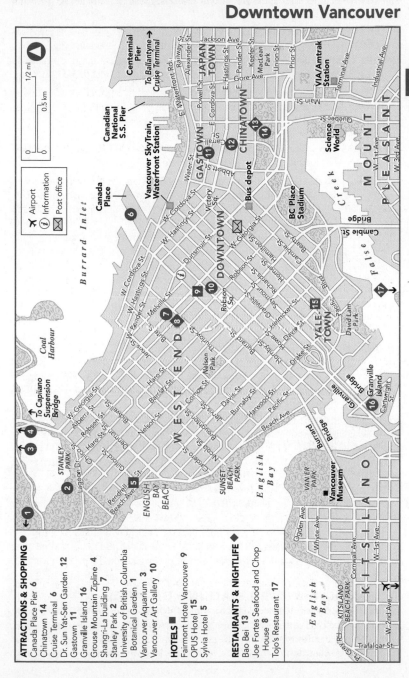

**ATTRACTIONS & SHOPPING** ●
Canada Place Pier **6**
Chinatown **14**
Cruise Terminal
Dr. Sun Yat-Sen Garden **12**
Gastown **11**
Granville Island **16**
Grouse Mountain Zipline **4**
Shangri-La building **7**
Stanley Park **2**
University of British Columbia
  Botanical Garden **1**
Vancouver Aquarium **3**
Vancouver Art Gallery **10**

**HOTELS** ■
Fairmont Hotel Vancouver **9**
OPUS Hotel **15**
Sylvia Hotel **5**

**RESTAURANTS & NIGHTLIFE** ◆
Bao Bei **13**
Joe Fortes Seafood and Chop
  House **8**
Tojo's Restaurant **17**

Ships also sometimes dock at the **Ballantyne** cruise terminal, a 5-minute cab ride from Canada Place.

**BY PLANE**  **Vancouver International Airport** is 13km (8 miles) south of downtown Vancouver. The average taxi fare from the airport to downtown is about $30. **LimoJet Gold** (© **604/273-1331;** www.limojetgold.com) offers flat-rate limousine service at $80 total for up to three passengers. **Trans Link** (© **604/953-3333;** www.translink.ca) offers service to the waterfront between 5am and 1am.

**BY CAR**  Take Granville Street in and hope that the traffic's light.

# Exploring Vancouver

**INFORMATION**  The **Tourism Vancouver Infocentre,** 200 Burrard St. (© **604/683-2000;** www.tourismvancouver.com), is open from 8:30am to 6pm.

**GETTING AROUND**  Because of its shape and setting, Vancouver has lots of bridges—Burrard Bridge, Granville Bridge, Cambie Street Bridge, and, of course, Lions Gate Bridge. Cruise ships pass under the Lions Gate Bridge on their way to and from Canada Place. The bridges sometimes make driving in Vancouver a slow endeavor. The **Aquabus ferries** shuttle visitors from Granville Island and elsewhere. Fares are $3.25 to $5.50 for adults (depending on destination) and $1.75 to $3.50 for seniors and children (© **604/689-5858;** www.theaquabus.com). A water taxi service called the **Bowen Island Express** runs between Granville Island and Bowen Island. There are six sailings per weekday from 6am to 7pm, and 9am to 7pm on weekends, and the trip takes 35 minutes. Bowen Island makes for a perfect Vancouver day trip, with opportunities for hiking, kayaking, golf, dining, and shopping. One-way fares are $20 for adults ($35 roundtrip), and $10 children; reservations are recommended (© **604/484-8497;** http://www.eblaunch.com).

Car-rental agencies with local branches include Avis, Budget, Hertz Canada, and Thrifty. You can easily walk the downtown area of Vancouver, but if you want transportation, you've got a few options. The **Translink system** (schedules and trip info © **604/953-3333** [6:30am–11:30pm daily]; www.translink.ca) includes electric buses, ferries, and the magnetic-rail SkyTrain. On the main routes, it runs from 5am to 1am daily. Schedules are available at many hotels and online. **Taxis** are available through **Black Top** (© **604/731-1111;** www.btccabs.ca), **Yellow Cab** (© **604/681-1111;** www.yellowcabonline.com), and **MacLure's** (© **604/831-1111;** www.maclurescabs.ca); call them by phone or look for them around the major hotels.

You can rent a bicycle from **Bayshore Bicycle Rentals** (which also rents in-line skates), 745 Denman St. (© **604/688-BIKE** [2453]; www.bayshorebikerentals.ca), or **Spokes Bicycle Rentals,** 1798 W. Georgia St. (© **604/688-5141;** www.vancouverbikerental.com); rates start at about $6 per hour, $20 for a half-day, and $28 for a full day. Helmets (required by law) and locks are included in the rate. The city has several great bicycle runs, including Stanley Park, the Seawall Promenade on the park's north end, and Pacific Spirit Park.

## ATTRACTIONS WITHIN WALKING DISTANCE

**Canada Place Pier** ★★★  Hands down, Vancouver's most distinctive landmark is Canada Place Pier, with its five gleaming white Teflon sails that recall a giant sailing vessel. The pier houses the Vancouver Convention and Exhibition Centre as well as the Alaska cruise-ship terminal. Check out Canada's Storyboard, a 14×25-foot

LED high-definition video screen featuring iconic Canadian content. Walk along the waterfront behind the western building of the Convention Centre, and there are markers showing Vancouver Island history, such as the time an explosion caused a river to clog, trapping 30 million salmon. The Olympic Flame also has a permanent memorial in front of the Convention Centre.

At foot of Howe and Burrard sts., next to the Waterfront SkyTrain Station. www.canadaplace.ca.

**Chinatown ★★★**   Vancouver has one of the largest Chinatowns in North America (though it doesn't hold a candle to those in New York and San Francisco), and, like Gastown, it's also a historic district. Chinese architecture and the **Dr. Sun Yat-Sen Garden,** 578 Carrall St. (© **604/662-3207;** www.vancouverchinesegarden.com; admission $14 adults, $11 seniors, $10 students, free for children 5 and under; daily May 1–June 14 10am–6pm; June 15–Aug 31 9:30am–7pm; Sept 1–30 10am–6pm; Oct 1–Apr 30 10am–4:30pm; closed Mon Nov–April), are among the attractions, along with great food and shops selling Chinese wares. Take the 45-minute tour (included with admission) to learn about the significance of each element in the gardens. Along with the photogenic Chinese gates, bright red buildings, and open-air markets, don't miss the amazing 6-foot-wide **Sam Kee Building** at 8 W. Pender St., which holds the record for being the narrowest commercial building in the world.

In the area bordered by E. Pender and Keefer sts., from Carrall St. to Gore Ave.

**Gastown ★★★**   In 1867, "Gassy" Jack Deighton built a saloon in Maple Tree Square (at the intersection of Water, Alexander, and Carrall sts.) to serve the area's loggers and trappers. Today, the area named for him, Gastown, boasts cobblestone streets, historic buildings, gaslights, a steam-powered clock (near the corner of Water and Cambie sts.), street musicians, and a hipster vibe. It's so close to the ship pier that it's a must-see and an easy outing. Boutiques, including several home-design shops, antiques stores, and art galleries, stand beside touristy shops, restaurants, clubs, and cafes. Our coauthor, Fran Golden, can attest to the fine offerings at **Hill's Native Art,** 165 Water St. (© **604/685-4249;** http://hillsnativeart.com/); a raven totem pole in her living room is from the shop. Hill's has five outlets in British Columbia, but this was the first and features more than 1,200 Native artists, representing every Tribe and Nation of the Northwest Coast.

In the area bordered by Water and Alexander sts., from Richard St. east to Columbia St.

**Granville Island ★★★**   A hearty walk from downtown (you may want to take a cab or water taxi), Granville is a delight for shoppers, with its vibrant daily market and streets lined with art studios and boutiques. Once an industrial center, where ironworks, sawmills, and slaughterhouses were the norm, today it's home to more than 300 businesses, studios, and the immensely popular public market, a foodie's paradise. Take time to explore and chat with the local artists.

http://granvilleisland.com.

**Stanley Park ★★★**   Designated a national historic site of Canada, Stanley Park is the country's largest urban park and the green-space pride of the city. Best of all, it's just outside of downtown (about a 20-min. walk from Canada Place), attracting more than 8 million visitors a year. Its 1,000 acres contain rose gardens, totem poles, a yacht club, a kids' water park, beaches, miles of wooded hiking trails, a scenic 5-mile bike path along the waterfront, great views of Lions Gate Bridge, and the outstanding **Vancouver Aquarium** (© 604/659-FISH [3474]; www.vanaqua.org; admission $30 adults, $23 seniors/students/children 13–18, $19 children 4–12, free children 3 and under; daily summer 9:30am–7pm; winter 9:30am–5pm). Check out short movies in the 4D Theatre, which combine 3-D imagery with in-theatre effects; catch one of the three daily dolphin shows or four daily beluga shows; or try to be around when some of the penguins take a daily walk (or waddle) with a trainer for an up-close and hilarious experience.

Downtown Vancouver, NW of the cruise-ship terminal. http://vancouver.ca/parks/parks/stanley. Park open daily sunrise–sunset.

**Vancouver Art Gallery** ★★★   With a permanent collection of more than 10,000 artworks, including an impressive number by British Columbia artist Emily Carr and the Canadian Group of Seven, the Vancouver Art Gallery is a must-do for those interested in the region's art. Only about 5 percent of the collection is on display at any given time in the impressive 1906 building, built as a courthouse. It's within easy walking distance of the cruise pier. International works including paintings, sculptures, graphics, photography, and video art are also on display. The Annex Gallery has rotating exhibits focused on art education.

750 Hornby St. © **604/662-4719.** www.vanartgallery.bc.ca. Admission $20 adults, $15 seniors and students, $6 children 5–12, free for children 4 and under. Daily 10am–5pm; Tues 10am–9pm.

## ATTRACTIONS BEYOND THE PORT AREA

**Capilano Suspension Bridge** ★★   It may be touristy, but it's still a treat to walk across the narrow, historic, 137m (449-ft.) bridge, located 70m (230 ft.) above the Capilano River in North Vancouver (about a 10-min. drive, or a $17 cab ride, from downtown), which has been drawing visitors since 1889. More than 700,000 other people who visit annually agree. From the high vantage point, even the towering evergreens below look tiny (this attraction is not for those with a fear of heights). The adjacent park has hiking trails, history and forestry exhibits, a carving center, and Native American dance performances (only in summer), as well as restaurants and a gift shop. The Treetops Adventure (included in admission price) lets you walk across 197m (646 ft.) of cable bridges high in the forest, while the Cliffwalk leads those brave enough to take it across a series of suspended and cantilevered walkways that jut out above the Capilano River.

3735 Capilano Rd.. © **604/985-7474.** www.capbridge.com. Admission $35 adults, $33 seniors, $29 students 17 and older with ID, $16 youths 13–16, $12 children 6–12, free for children 5 and under. May–June 9am–7pm; June–Sept 8:30am–8pm; Sept–Oct 9am–6pm; Oct–Dec 9am–5pm; Dec 10am–9pm (Canyon Lights 5–9pm); Jan–Mar 9am–5pm; Mar–Apr 9am–6pm.

**Grouse Mountain Zipline** ★★   Grouse Mountain is a ski and year-round mountain resort with a thrilling zipline high above the rainforest. On the five-line adventure circuit, you whip along at more than 40 mph, and if you can take a look, you'll see Blue Grouse Lake and other views whizzing by. Along the 2-hour ride, guides will tell you about the indigenous flora and fauna and its significance to the First Nations people (a three-line course is available late fall through spring). The **Grouse Mountain All Experience Skyride** is a more restful way to view your surroundings, by way of North America's largest aerial tramway. You can also check out shows at the **Theatre in the Sky,** attend a birds-of-prey demonstration at the "Birds in Motion" amphitheatre, and take in a 45-minute live lumberjack show (included in the ticket price).

6400 Nancy Greene Way. ℭ **604/980-9311.** www.grousemountain.com. Zipline $70, including aerial tramway up mountain. Daily 10am–10pm (time of last departure). All Experience tickets, $40 adults, $36 seniors, $24 children 13–18, $14 children 5–12.

## BEST CRUISE-LINE SHORE EXCURSIONS

**Capilano Canyon Nature Tour** (4 hr.; $99 adults, $49 children 12 and under): Walk alongside the canyon and through a rainforest with 500-year-old trees as guides describe the ecosystem and wildlife habitats. Then cross the Lions Gate Bridge, with its spectacular views of the skyline, and eat a picnic lunch before returning to the air-port or your downtown hotel.

**City Tour** (2½–3½ hr.; $49 adults, $29 children): This bus tour covers major sights such as Gastown, Chinatown, Stanley Park, and high-end residential areas. You'll also visit Queen Elizabeth Park, the city's highest southern vantage point and home of the Bloedell Conservatory, which commands a 360-degree city view and features an enclosed tropical rainforest complete with free-flying birds; the tour may also include Granville Island.

*Note:* This tour is usually offered after the cruise and is available only to passengers with late-afternoon or evening flights. At the end of the tour, you are dropped off at the airport for your flight home.

## EXCURSIONS OFFERED BY LOCAL AGENCIES

**Stanley Park Horse-Drawn Tours** (ℭ **604/681-5115;** www.stanleyparktours.com) has offered horse-drawn-trolley tours of the 405-hectare (1,000-acre) Stanley Park for more than a century. The narrated 1-hour tours depart from the Coal Harbour parking lot beside the Stanley Park information booth on Park Drive. Tickets are $29 for adults, $27 for seniors and students, $16 for children 3 to 12, and free for children 2 and under. March 15 to Oct 31.

The **Vancouver Trolley Company** (ℭ **888/451-5581** or 604/801-5515; www. vancouvertrolley.com) has old-fashioned (engine-powered) San Francisco–style trol-leys with narrated tours on a circuit that includes Gastown, Chinatown, Granville Island, Stanley Park, and other areas of interest. You can get off and on as you like. Stop number one is in Gastown. Tickets are $38 for adults, $35 for seniors and stu-dents, and $20 for children. Summer sunset tours to Grouse Mountain and the Cap-ilano Suspension Bridge are also offered.

**A Wok Around Chinatown** (ℭ **604/736-9508;** www.awokaround.com) is a 4-hour walking tour that takes visitors around the colorful and flavorful neighborhood. The tour is given Friday through Monday at 10am and leaves from Dr. Sun Yat-Sen Garden (see listing for "Chinatown" in "Attractions Within Walking Distance," above); the tour costs $68 and includes a dim sum lunch.

For a great day trip, take a ride on the **Rocky Mountaineer** (ℭ **877/460-3200;** www.rockymountaineer.com). You'll be picked up at your hotel around 7am and board the train at 8am, where you'll enjoy breakfast and the scenery, then have a chance to tour the charming alpine village of Whistler for 3 hours as part of the Sea to Sky Climb package. En route back to Vancouver, afternoon tea and sandwiches are served. The Mountaineer departs daily from May through October; a round-trip ticket costs $199 for adults and $109 for children 2 to 11 (free for kids 1 and under).

If you'd prefer to stay on the water, the **Prince of Whales** marine adventure com-pany (ℭ **888/383-4884;** www.princeofwhales.com) offers harbor tours, day trips to Victoria, and whale-watching from its floating offices adjacent to the Westin Bayshore

Hotel. Passengers don red cruiser suits and then climb aboard for the chance to see harbor seals, sea lions, eagles, and maybe even bears, in addition to beautiful scenery. Prices range from $35 to $235, depending on the tour.

A more unusual way of seeing the city is urban kayaking. Paddle down False Creek (actually an inlet), which threads past up-market Yaletown condos and the bustle of Granville Island, and float under the Granville and Burrard street bridges. If you have time, take a few hours to explore the rugged coastline of Stanley Park, Vancouver's 1,000-acre nature reserve. **Ecomarine Ocean Kayak Centre** (✆ **604/689-7575;** www. ecomarine.com) is the place to go for rentals, sales, and guided tours from Granville Island and English Bay, with prices starting at $59 per person. Rainforest and night-time paddles are also available.

## Where to Stay

Almost all of Vancouver's downtown hotels are within walking distance of shops, restaurants, and attractions, although you might want to avoid places around Hastings and Main after dark. Granville Street downtown is an area that has been "cleaned up" and is now home to some lower-end, boutique-type hotels.

**The Fairmont Hotel Vancouver ★★★**  The grande dame of Vancouver's hotels is sometimes referred to as the "Castle in the City," its impressive copper roof a highly visible city landmark. Inside the marble interiors are public rooms of massive proportions—you know you are in a special place. Stop by for afternoon tea and you will be immersed in luxury and tradition. Reflecting the same luxe sensibility, guest rooms feature marble bathrooms and mahogany furnishings and serve up stunning views of the city, harbor, and/or mountains.

900 W. Georgia St. ✆ **866/540-4452** or 604/684-3131. www.fairmont.com/hotelvancouver. 556 units. $279–$322 double; from $319 suite. Children 17 and under stay free in parent's room. Valet and self-parking $39 (plus tax). **Amenities:** 2 restaurants; lounge; babysitting; concierge; state-of-the-art health club & spa. *In room:* A/C, ceiling fans, TV, hair dryer, high-speed Internet ($15/24 hr.).

**The Sylvia Hotel ★★**  This 1912 building started out as an apartment building and was turned into a hotel in 1936. Several rooms and suites have kitchens, a nice touch if you're staying for more than a day or two. The location can't be beat: across the street from English Bay and just a short walk to Stanley Park, Robson Street, a shopping mecca, and the Vancouver Art Gallery are also close by. The staff is super-friendly and the rates are quite reasonable. You need to book pretty far in advance: The Sylvia has a loyal clientele who return year after year.

1154 Gilford St. on English Bay. ✆ **877/681-9321** or 604/681-9321. www.sylviahotel.com. 120 units. Doubles $135–$229; Suites $219–$450. Parking $15. **Amenities:** Restaurant; lounge; Wi-Fi throughout hotel (free). *In room:* TV, hair dryer.

**OPUS Hotel ★★★**  Renovated in 2013, this hotel is about as cutting-edge and trendy as it gets. Every room is stocked with an iPad for guest use and decorated in eye-catching colors. The funky hotel also features lots of avant-garde artwork and a whimsical sensibility, the perfect complement for the chic neighborhood of Yaletown where it's located (just a few blocks from the cruise ship terminal).

322 Davie St. ✆ **866/642-6787** or 604/642-6780. vancouver.opushotel.com. 96 units. $299–$399 double; from $499 suite. Parking $35. **Amenities:** Restaurant; lounge; babysitting; concierge; fitness center, use of mountain bikes. *In room:* A/C, TV, iPad, hair dryer, free high-speed wireless Internet, minibar.

## Where to Dine

**Bao Bei** ★★★ CHINESE   It can be hard to choose a restaurant to dine at in Vancouver's vibrant Chinatown, but Bao Bei, a "Chinese Brasserie," stands out from the crowd. It's been a crowd-pleaser since it opened a few years ago, and its popularity has never waned. The menu is designed around small plates to share, but when you find one you like, such as the steamed truffled pork dumplings or octopus salad, you'll end up ordering one just for yourself. No reservations are accepted, so prepare to wait at the bar, which serves up creative cocktails like Cheung Po the Kid, a concoction of rum, Dubonnet, pomegranate molasses, and homemade Chinese plum bitters.

163 Keefer St. ℂ **604/688-0876.** www.bai-beu.ca. Tues–Sun 5:30–midnight. Main dishes $9–$18.

**Joe Fortes Seafood and Chop House** ★★★ SEAFOOD   Twenty-seven years and going strong, Joe Fortes is a landmark in Vancouver, garnering awards—for its food, its wine list, and its oysters—year after year. The bar here is hugely popular and attracts a young and prosperous local crowd, some of whom come to smoke cigars in the covered rooftop garden, high above Robson Street (an excellent spot for people-watching). Inside it's all about dark wood and seafood—including up to a dozen types of oysters on the menu daily (order them raw or cooked). Joe's Seafood Tower on Ice, with oysters, lobster, crab, clams, mussels, tuna, prawns, and scallops, is a thing of beauty.

777 Thurlow St. ℂ **604/669-1940.** www.joefortes.ca. Reservations recommended. Most main courses $23–$48. Daily 11am–11pm.

**Tojo's Restaurant** ★★ JAPANESE/SUSHI   Hidekazu Tojo is a cult figure in Vancouver, and the accolades and awards his restaurant has received from around the globe are well-earned. A diner's best bet is to choose the *omakase* and let the chefs show off their creativity using the day's fresh ingredients. If you can't handle the price tag—unlike the occasional Hollywood celebrities, Japanese businesspeople, and well-heeled local crowd that frequent the place—you can still see what the fuss is about by choosing a la carte offerings.

1133 W. Broadway. ℂ **604/872-8050.** www.tojos.com. Reservations required for sushi bar. Omakase meals $80–$120 and up. A la carte menu of hot dishes $28–$55, sushi $3–$9 per piece. Mon–Sat 5 11pm.

# SEATTLE

Americans now have more opportunities than ever to begin and end their Alaska-bound cruises on U.S. soil. In recent years, Americans' growing interest in the 49th State and their clear preference for American gateways and destinations has had the cruise lines falling over themselves to deploy more of their Alaska ships in Seattle. Seattle has become an attractive alternative home port to Vancouver for large oceangoing passenger liners bound for the Northland. In 2000, only one major ship was based in Seattle for the Alaska cruise season; in 2014, 10 big ships will cruise from the city, as will some smaller ships.

As cruise ports go, Seattle has no reason to bow to any other. Known as the Emerald City for the abundant greenery found in every direction, it is every bit as scenically appealing as Vancouver. Its skyline is dominated by the 607-foot-high revolving Space Needle, built in 1962 for the World's Fair (known at the time as the Century 21

Exposition). It's linked to the heart of downtown by a monorail. Seattle has shopping, fine restaurants, attractions galore, good air service, culture, a wide range of accommodations, internal transportation—everything you need, in fact, to enjoy a day or two before or after your cruise.

Seattle is very much a water-oriented city, set between Puget Sound and Lake Washington, with Lake Union in the center. Practically everywhere you look, the views are of sailboats, cargo ships, ferries, windsurfers, and anglers—and trees and parklands, of course. One of our favorite pastimes on nice days in Seattle is to take one of the local ferries—to anywhere, just for the fun of it.

The **Seattle Waterfront,** along Alaskan Way from Yesler Way North to Bay Street and Myrtle Edwards Park, is one of the city's most popular attractions, and much like San Francisco's Fisherman's Wharf area, this can be both good and bad. It incorporates the north side of Pier 57, all of Pier 58, and the southern part of Pier 59. Major seawall construction in this area was set to begin in 2013. It may be very touristy, with tacky gift shops, saltwater taffy, T-shirts galore, and lots of overpriced restaurants, but it's also home to the Seattle Aquarium and the Pike Place Market. Companies located here offer sailboat and sea-kayak tours.

At Pier 55, Argosy Cruises departs for 1-hour harbor cruises, 2½-hour cruises through the locks to Lake Union, and 4-hour trips to Tillicum Village (see "Attractions Beyond the Port Area," below). At Pier 57, you'll find the **Bay Pavilion,** which has a vintage carousel and a video arcade to keep the kids busy. Pier 57 is also called "Miners Landing"—said to be the landing point where the schooner *Portland* arrived with a ton of gold from the Klondike.

At Pier 59, you'll find the **Seattle Aquarium** and a waterfront park. Meanwhile, Pier 69 is the dock for the ferries that ply the waters between Seattle and Victoria. Sunset and jazz cruises leave from this pier. It's home of the *Victoria Clipper,* offering daily trips to Victoria, B.C. (year-round) and Friday Harbor on San Juan Island (summer only).

If you are in the city for a day or two, you may want to venture 20 minutes from downtown (by car, cab, or bus) to **Ballard,** a waterfront area that has moved from blue collar to trendy with a variety of boutiques, hip eateries, and nighttime spots.

## Getting to Seattle

**BY PLANE** **Seattle-Tacoma International Airport** (✆ 800/544-1965 or 206/787-5388; www.portseattle.org/seatac), also known as **Sea-Tac,** is located about 14 miles south of Seattle. It's connected to the city by I-5. Generally, allow 30 minutes for the trip between the airport and downtown. Because the **Bell Street passenger ship pier,** also known as Pier 66, where Norwegian Cruise Line and Celebrity ships depart, is superbly located a few minutes' walk from the heart of downtown, airport taxis will drop you at the terminal for about the same price as they would charge to go to any of the major Seattle hotels. Other lines depart from the **Smith Cove Cruise Terminal** at Terminal 91, opened in 2009, just north of downtown but not within walking distance.

A **taxi** between the airport and downtown will cost you between $35 and $40; to Terminal 91, it's about $50. **Seattle Downtown Airporter** (✆ 800/426-7532 or 206/626-6088; www.shuttleexpress.com/hotels) provides service between all the airport terminals and eight downtown hotels, with the first hotel pickup at 4:55am and then every half-hour through the day until the last pickup at 10:00pm. The fares are

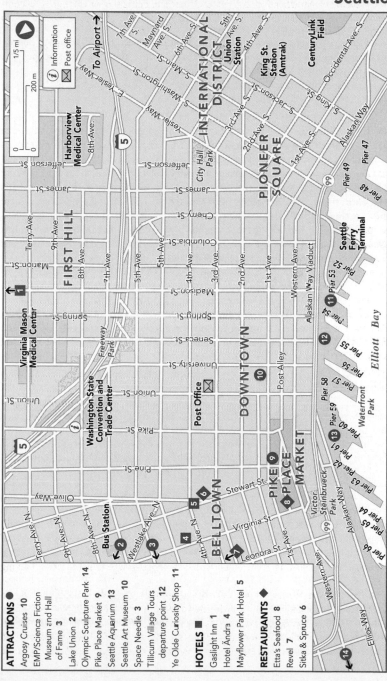

# Seattle

**ATTRACTIONS** ●
Argosy Cruises 10
EMP/Science Fiction Museum and Hall of Fame 3
Lake Union 2
Olympic Sculpture Park 14
Pike Place Market 9
Seattle Aquarium 13
Seattle Art Museum 10
Space Needle 3
Tillicum Village Tours departure point 12
Ye Olde Curiosity Shop 11

**HOTELS** ■
Gaslight Inn 1
Hotel Ändra 4
Mayflower Park Hotel 5

**RESTAURANTS** ◆
Etta's Seafood 8
Revel 7
Sitka & Spruce 6

ⓘ Information
☒ Post office

1/5 mi
200 m

To Airport →

Harborview Medical Center

FIRST HILL

Virginia Mason Medical Center

Washington State Convention and Trade Center

Freeway Park

INTERNATIONAL DISTRICT

Union Station

King St. Station (Amtrak)

CenturyLink Field

PIONEER SQUARE

City Hall Park

Seattle Ferry Terminal

Elliott Bay

Waterfront Park

DOWNTOWN

Post Office

PIKE PLACE MARKET

BELLTOWN

Bus Station

Steinbrueck Park

Pier 47
Pier 48
Pier 49
Pier 52
Pier 53
Pier 54
Pier 55
Pier 56
Pier 57
Pier 58
Pier 59
Pier 60
Pier 61
Pier 62
Pier 63
Pier 64
Pier 65
Pier 66

181

$18 one-way, $31 round-trip; children 17 and under free, one with each paying adult. **Shuttle Express** (© 425/981-7000; www.shuttleexpress.com) also gets you between Sea-Tac and downtown. The company's check-in desk is in the center of the third floor of the parking garage at the airport, next to the Ground Transportation Office, and a one-way fare for up to two people is $32 to most downtown areas. The public **Seattle Metro** (© 800/542-7876 or 206/553-3000; http://metro.kingcounty.gov) operates service from the airport to downtown for as little as $2.25 in the off-peak hours, clearly the least expensive transportation. But the bus drops passengers only at the Seattle Convention Center, not at the hotel of their choice, so it's not necessarily the most convenient.

**BY CAR**    The major freeway running through Seattle is I-5. Follow it south from downtown to Sea-Tac. I-5 runs north to the Canadian border, which leads, ultimately, to the road to Vancouver. Alaskan Way, a busy street, runs along the waterfront and past the Bell Street cruise-ship terminal. For Terminal 91, you'll head toward Magnolia Bridge. It's only a very short car or cab ride from any city hotel to the cruise terminals, which are no more than 10 minutes from even the most distant of the hotels listed here. If you're driving, parking is available at both terminals. Bell Street parking is $17.21 per day (plus tax), with a $1 discount per day if you book online (**https://www.rpnw. com/seattle/fuel**). Smith Cove is $21.31 per day (plus tax), with $1 off per day if you book online at **https://www.rpnw.com/seattle/fuel**.

## Exploring Seattle

**INFORMATION**    Seattle's visitors' bureau, **Visit Seattle,** operates a visitor information center in the Washington State Convention Center, 800 Convention Place, Galleria Level, at the corner of 7th Avenue and Pike Street (© 206/461-5840; www. visitseattle.org). It's open 9am to 5pm Monday through Friday and summer weekends.

**GETTING AROUND**    Nearly every major car-rental company has an outlet at Sea-Tac, and many companies also have offices in downtown hotels. Prices depend on the season and even on the day of the week (rentals on Fri, for example, when cruise passengers are likely to arrive in large numbers, will probably cost more than on, say, Wed). That said, if you're staying within the confines of downtown, a car is more of a liability than a plus because parking is very expensive. **Seattle Metro** (© 800/542-7876 or 206/553-3000; http://metro.kingcounty.gov) operates buses in the downtown area and throughout King County. The standard fare is $2.25 to $3 for adults, 75¢ for seniors.

### ATTRACTIONS WITHIN WALKING DISTANCE

**EMP Museum** ★★    In a building designed by Frank Gehry, this museum pays homage to rock-and-roll and serves as a memorial to Seattle native Jimi Hendrix. Come here to learn both about the Northwest rock scene and the history of popular contemporary music. Check out the guitar gallery and other rock artifacts. A fun attraction is the interactive Sound Lab, where you can play a bunch of instruments. Temporary exhibits, like 2013's "Women Who Rock," keep things fresh. In the same building (admission covers both museums), fans of science and fantasy fiction—especially blockbuster movies—will want to visit the **Science Fiction Museum and Hall of Fame** (© 206/724-3428; www.empsfm.org), the world's first. Included in displays are *The Hobbit* and *Doctor Who*.

325 5th Ave. N. ℭ **206/770-2700.** www.empsfm.org. $20 adults ($15 if you buy them online), $17 seniors and students with ID (or $15 online) and $14 children 5–17 (or $12 online), free for children 4 and under. Summer daily 10am–7pm; winter daily 10am–5pm.

**Nordstrom** ★★ Shoppers from around the world come to Seattle to pay homage to the original Nordstrom department store in the heart of downtown, founded in 1901. It's actually the second-biggest attraction for tourists in town—after Pike Place Market—and worth a visit for its historical significance. It was financed, incidentally, with money earned by founder John W. Nordstrom in the Klondike gold rush. The women's shoe selection, if that's your goal, is sublime.

500 Pine St. ℭ **206/628-2111.** http://shop.nordstrom.com. Mon–Sat 9:30am–9pm; Sun 10am–7pm.

**Pike Place Market** ★★★ Begun in 1907 by just eight farmers selling produce from their wagons, Pike Place Market is one of Seattle's most enduring institutions and a major tourist draw. Now spanning 9 acres, the market is still the best place in the city to find fresh produce and seasonal specialties such as Rainier cherries, Washington asparagus, fresh king salmon, and Northwest hazelnuts. Make sure you go there hungry: You won't want to miss the multiple chances to snack. We highly suggest that you don't leave without trying a Dungeness crab cocktail, a fresh-baked cinnamon roll or *piroshki* (Russian meat pie), and, of course, coffee from any number of vendors, including the *original* Starbucks. Explore the shops underground. Wonderful specialty stores, including one of the best places to find magic and old magic posters in the country, abound. At night the vendors clear out, but several excellent restaurants, bars, and theaters in the market keep it hopping. A 60-minute **Market Heritage Tour,** which meets near the corner of Western Avenue and Virginia Street, at the tree surrounded by a low brick wall, is offered daily at 10am and 2pm (walk-up price is $19 adults; $17 seniors/youth ages 11–17, $14 children ages 6–10; $4 off all tickets if purchased in advance); make reservations at **www.publicmarkettours.com**, or call ℭ **206/209-5488.**

Btw. Pike and Pine sts. at 1st Ave. ℭ **206/682-7453.** Mon–Sat 9am–6pm; Sun 9am–5pm.

**The Seattle Aquarium** ★★ In 2013, the Seattle Aquarium unveiled a new harbor seal exhibit, which offers a 180-degree view of the Aquarium's three harbor seals Barney, Q, and Siku in a naturalistic habitat against the backdrop of Pier 60's panoramic views of Puget Sound. It's immensely popular, but the aquarium's interactive tide pool is a perennial favorite, especially for kids. A variety of other exhibits describe Puget Sound's underwater world. Each September, visitors can watch salmon return up a fish ladder to spawn, an amazing sight.

1483 Alaskan Way, Pier 59, Waterfront Park. ℭ **206/386-4300.** www.seattleaquarium.org. Admission $22 adults, $15 ages 4–12, free for children 3 and under. Daily 9:30am–6pm (last entry 5pm).

**Seattle Art Museum and Olympic Sculpture Park** ★★★ Art fans will want to devote many hours to this top-flight museum, known as "SAM," where the collections include everything from African masks to Old Masters to Andy Warhol. Plan to devote at least some of your stay to the museum's impressive collection of Northwest Coast Native art. If the weather is nice, check out the free outdoor **Olympic Sculpture Park** (2901 Western Ave.; open 30 min. before sunrise to 30 min. after sunset). Paths here zigzag along the waterfront and through four ecosystems, displaying the art of such contemporary sculpture masters as Alexander Calder, Louise Bourgeois, Richard Serra, and Teresita Fernandez. Enjoy views of water, mountains, and art, and best of all, admission to the park is free.

1300 1st Ave. © **206/654-3137.** www.seattleartmuseum.org. Admission (suggested donation) $17 adults, $15 seniors, $11 students and youths 13–17, free for children 12 and under; free to all 1st Thurs of month. Wed, Fri–Sun 10am–5pm. Thurs 10am–9pm. Closed Mon and Tues.

**The Space Needle ★★**    Seattle's iconic landmark, the Space Needle, offers stunning views 518 feet above ground level from its observation deck, where high-powered telescopes let you focus in on distant sights. But even if you don't go up to the top, the building is still an eye-catching attraction. Built for the 1962 World's Fair to suggest the future in architecture, it looks like a flying saucer on top of a tripod. Inside is a lounge and a very expensive restaurant.

6th Ave. and Broad St. © **206/905-2100.** www.spaceneedle.com. Admission $21 adults, $18 seniors, $12 children 4–12, free for children 3 and under. $1 discount if booked online; early and late admission discounts available in summer. Daily 8am–midnight.

**Ye Olde Curiosity Shop ★**    If you crossed a souvenir store and Ripley's Believe It or Not!, what you'd end up with is something like the Ye Olde Curiosity Shop. It's a quirky assortment of stuff that began with Joe Standley, an avid collector, who opened up shop in 1899. Among the curiosities are shrunken heads, Siamese-twin calves, a natural mummy, the Lord's Prayer on a grain of rice, a narwhal tusk, shrunken heads, a four-legged chicken, fleas in dresses, and other oddities.

1001 Alaskan Way, Pier 54. © **206/682-5844.** www.yeoldecuriosityshop.com. Free admission. Summer daily 9am–9:30pm; winter Sun–Thurs 10am–6pm, Fri–Sat 9am–9pm.

## ATTRACTIONS BEYOND THE PORT AREA

**Tillicum Village/Tillicum Village Tours ★**    **Tillicum Village** was built in conjunction with the 1962 Seattle World's Fair. The "village" is actually a large restaurant and performance hall fashioned after a traditional Northwest Coast Indian longhouse. Though it sounds cheesy, totem poles stand vigil out front, the forest encircles the longhouse, the waters of Puget Sound stretch out into the distance, and it's simply a beautiful spot. Since it's located at Blake Island State Marine Park across Puget Sound from Seattle, it's only accessible by tour boat or private boat. **Tillicum Village Tours** operates trips that include the scenic boat ride to and from the island, a lunch or dinner of alder-smoked salmon, and a performance by traditional masked dancers—members of 11 Northwest tribes. After the meal and the dance performance, you can wander along forest trails to explore the island.

1101 Alaskan Way, Pier 55. © **206/623-1445.** www.tillicumvillage.com. Admission/4-hr. tour $80 adults, $73 seniors, $30 children 4–12, free for children 3 and under.

## BEST CRUISE-LINE SHORE EXCURSIONS

**Seattle City Tour** (3½ hr.; $69 adults, $35 children): A basic spin around Pike Place Market, the World's Fair site, downtown Seattle, Lake Union, and more, offered by virtually all cruise lines. May include a stop at the Space Needle.

**Seattle Underground Tour** (4 hr.; $69 adults, $42 kids): A little history and a good share of tall tales are presented on this fun tour. It starts at a restored 1890s saloon, takes you literally under the streets of Pioneer Square, and includes a view of an original Crapper (toilet) imported from England. See what remained after the Great Seattle Fire of 1889; learn how mud on city streets was sometimes deep enough to consume dogs and small children; and hear about how the Yukon Gold Rush brought 100,000 adventurers to town. The tour ends at an underground gift shop.

**Woodinville Wine Country** (5 hr.; $79): Visit the renowned Columbia Winery for a behind-the-scenes tour and tasting, and then take a quick drive to Château Ste Michelle for a look at the winemaking process and more tasting. You'll sample both red and white selections. Minimum age for this tour is 21.

## EXCURSIONS OFFERED BY LOCAL AGENCIES

**Argosy Cruises** (© 888/623-1445; www.argosycruises.com) offers a variety of short cruises around the Seattle area, including a **Seattle harbor cruise** (for the best views, sit on the starboard side!), a cruise through the **Hiram Chittenden Locks to Lake Union,** and cruises around **Lake Washington** (which, among other things, take you past the fabled Xanadu, built by Bill Gates on the shore of Lake Washington). Cruises depart from Pier 55. Tickets for the 1-hour Harbor Cruise are $23 for adults, $20 for seniors, $10 for children 5 to 12, and free for children 4 and under; the 2-hour Lake Cruise costs $33 for adults, $29 for seniors, $12 for children 5 to 12, and free for children 4 and under. **Gray Line of Seattle** (www.graylineseattle.com) offers a 4-hour tour that takes visitors 30 miles from downtown to the **Future of Flight: Aviation Center and Boeing Tour** at Paine Field Airport in Everett, a cutting-edge facility with interactive aviation exhibits (you also visit the Boeing factory), for $55 for adults and $45 for children.

# Where to Stay

**Hotel Ändra** ★★★   This Art Deco hotel is located in the trendy Belltown neighborhood, within minutes of Pike Place Market, the Seattle Art Museum, and downtown shopping. The 1926 classic brick and terra-cotta building has been updated to contemporary environs via a combination of traditional Northwest style (lots of wood and stone) and high-tech comforts. Frette towels and plump goose-down pillows and comforters are welcome luxuries. Not one, but two amazing restaurants call the hotel home. **Lola,** run by top chef Tom Douglas, features the classic produce of the Pacific Northwest mixed with cooking styles of Greece, while **Assaggio** offers bold, robust central and northern Italian cuisine.

2000 4th Ave. © **877/448-8600** or 206/448-8600. www.hotelandra.com. 119 units. $269–$389 double. Valet parking $39. **Amenities:** 2 restaurants; concierge; exercise room; room service. *In room:* A/C, TV, hair dryer, minibar, Wi-Fi (free).

**Gaslight Inn** ★★★   This cozy eight-room Capitol Hill B&B, built in 1906, is a nice alternative to a big, bustling hotel and offers a chance to unwind before or after your cruise. Rooms are comfortably appointed (though two do share a bath), with lots of wood and eclectic artwork collected over the years by the innkeepers. Enjoy a continental breakfast before heading out for the day to Pike Place Market and other Seattle sites. Come evening, a dip in the heated pool (in season) or a glass of wine in the living room makes you feel as if you're staying at a good friend's house.

1247 15th Ave. © **206/325-3654.** www.gaslight-inn.com. 8 units. $108–$168 (2 rooms have shared bath). **Amenities:** Seasonal heated pool; Wi-Fi throughout hotel (free). *In room:* TV, hair dryer, Wi-Fi (free).

**Mayflower Park Hotel** ★★★  This stately Seattle classic was built in 1927. It serves up a trip to the past, a glamorous and beautiful past, that is. Shoppers appreciate the fact that it's connected to the upscale shops of Westlake Center and is flanked by the Nordstrom and Bon Marché department stores, while cocktail connoisseurs swear by the martinis served at Oliver's Lounge. Rooms are done up in a funky blend of contemporary Italian and traditional European furnishings. The smallest rooms are cramped, so if you need space to spread out ask for a larger corner room.

405 Olive Way. © **800/426-5100** or 206/623-8700. Fax 206/382-6997. www.mayflowerpark.com. 160 units. $179–$239 double; $249–$405 suite. Valet parking $35. **Amenities:** Restaurant; bar; concierge; exercise room; room service. *In room:* A/C, TV, hair dryer, Wi-Fi (free).

## Where to Dine

**Etta's Seafood** ★★★  SEAFOOD  Fresh, fresh, fresh. With picture windows looking out at Pike Place Market, you'll probably be able to see some of the vendors from whom this seasonal menu is sourced. Chef/owner Tom Douglas serves what is arguably the best seafood in town—his signature crab cakes (crunchy on the outside, creamy on the inside) are worth the trip alone. The Etta's Salmon dish was so popular it has inspired its own line of spice rub and sauce now sold in markets. If you're not a seafood lover, other options include lamb T-bone, burgers, and salads.

2020 Western Ave. © **206/443-6000.** www.tomdouglas.com/restaurants/ettas. Reservations recommended. Main courses $14–$32. Mon–Thurs 11:30am–9:30pm; Fri 11:30am–10pm; Sat 9am–3pm and 4–10pm; Sun 9am–3pm and 4–9pm.

**Revel** ★★★ ASIAN  They had us at "Asian street food," but the husband-and-wife team of Rachel Yang and Seif Chirchi (also of Joule fame), who met while cooking at Alain Ducasse at the Essex House in New York, manage to transcend any one category. The dumplings certainly are divine (try the pork, green curry, and coconut), but short ribs with mustard greens; buckwheat noodles with maitake mushrooms and foie gras cream; and Dungeness crab with seaweed noodles will have you talking about your meal long after you've left Seattle. The icing on the cake? Revel has very reasonable prices, if you can restrain yourself. No reservations are taken for parties less than six, so prepare to belly up to the bar and enjoy a creative cocktail like a Brown Derby or Montauk Punch.

403 N. 36th St. (about 2½ miles from the Port of Seattle). © **206/547-2040.** www.revelseattle.com. Main courses $7–$16. Mon–Sat 11am–2pm; Sun 10am–2pm; daily 5pm–close.

**Sitka & Spruce** ★★ ECLECTIC  Chef Matt Dillon combines his love of local with playful touches of whimsy and cutting-edge technique, is an enormously popular Capitol Hill spot. Its location inside Melrose Market is a bonus. Eggs, meat, and produce come from the restaurant's own farm on Vashon Island. Since the restaurant only takes a limited number of reservations, walk-ins have a good chance of scoring a table, though waits can be long. No matter, walk around the market or relax with a drink while you wait. On Monday nights, Dillon gives the kitchen over to Alvaro Candela-Najera, who cooks dishes from his native Mexico. The tacos fly out the door.

1531 Melrose Ave. © **206/324-0662.** www.sitkaandspruce.com. Main courses $14–$32. Mon–Fri 11:30am–2pm; Tues–Thurs. 5:30–10pm; Fri–Sat 5:30–11pm; Sun 4:30–9pm. Brunch Sat–Sun. 10am–2pm.

# JUNEAU

Because Juneau is also a major port of call, see the Juneau section in chapter 8 for a map and information on attractions and tours.

## Getting to Juneau

**BY PLANE**   Juneau is served by **Alaska Airlines** (𝒸 **800/252-7522;** www.alaskaair.com) with daily nonstop flights from Seattle and Anchorage. Because weather can wreak havoc with landing conditions, it's especially advisable, if you're flying to Juneau, to get there a day or two before your embarkation date.

**BY BOAT**   The vessels of the **Alaska Marine Highway** (commonly known as the **Alaska Ferry;** www.dot.state.ak.us/amhs) link Juneau with Alaska, British Columbia, and U.S. gateways as far south as Bellingham, Washington, but unless you have 2 or 3 days to spare, you probably won't use that service to get to your ship.

**BY CAR**   You can't drive to Juneau (there are no roads to the outside world) or get there by train. That leaves you with airplanes or long boat trips, period.

## Exploring Juneau

**INFORMATION**   The brand-new **Visitor Information Center** is right at the ship pier and boasts exterior tiles designed to resemble fish scales and an inside designed to look like a fishing ship (𝒸 **888/581-2201** or 907/586-2201; www.traveljuneau.com). It's open May through September daily 8:30am to 5pm and October through April Monday through Friday 9am to 4:30pm. There is also a visitor center midway down the cruise-ship pier that's open when ships are in.

**GETTING AROUND**   A cab from the airport to downtown will cost about $35. The **Capital Transit city bus** (𝒸 **907/789-6901**) comes to the airport at 11 minutes past the hour on weekdays from 7:11am to 5:11pm and costs $2 for adults and $1 for children; your luggage has to fit under your seat or at your feet. Ask the driver for the stop closest to your hotel; you may need a short cab ride from there. The public bus can also get you to the city's top visitor attraction, Mendenhall Glacier (p. 219). The passenger cruise-ship pier is right in town and an easy walk. However, with baggage it might be necessary to take a taxi, which shouldn't cost more than $8. Major car-rental companies have offices at the airport.

## Where to Stay

**Goldbelt Hotel Juneau ★★**   A $2-million redo has this hotel on the waterfront boasting contemporary guest rooms with amenities that include flatscreen TVs, iPod docking stations, and Keurig coffee machines. The rooms were already good-sized, and the ones in front serve up views of the Gastineau Channel (less-expensive rooms have mountain views). The renovation also brought a smallish fitness center. The lobby is decorated with museum-quality Native art. **Zen,** the hotel restaurant, serves Asian-fusion dishes at lunch and dinner (open for breakfast, too). An Avis car-rental booth is located in the lobby.

51 Egan Dr. 𝒸 **888/478-6909** or 907/586-6900. www.goldbelthotel.com. 104 units. $189–$299 double. Free parking. **Amenities:** Restaurant; free airport transfers; room service. *In room:* TV, hair dryer, coffee machine, Wi-Fi (free).

**Prospector Hotel ★** It's nothing fancy, but the Prospector is a comfortable hotel on the waterfront right next to the new Alaska State Museum. This is good and bad news, because construction at the museum is expected to be ongoing (during limited hours) until it reopens in 2016. Still, the hotel serves up affordable rates on large standard rooms and suites, some with views of the water and small-ship pier, many with kitchenettes. It has a friendly staff and a fun pub called **T.K. Maguire's** serving steaks, seafood, and bottomless portions of fries.

375 Whittier St. ℂ **800/331-2711** or 907/586-3737. www.prospectorhotel.com. 62 units. $159–$209 double. Free parking. **Amenities:** Restaurant; bar. *In room:* TV, hair dryer, kitchenette (in some), Wi-Fi (free).

**The Silverbow Inn ★★★** Next door to the **Silverbow Bakery & Cafe,** the oldest operating bakery in Alaska, this boutique hotel is run by the same owners (a husband-and-wife team). The highlight is a hot tub on a deck overlooking downtown Juneau. The building dates to mid-1914, but it's gotten a very contemporary redo. Guests are treated to a complimentary breakfast that befits the bakery connection—including fresh baked scones and yummy banana bread. You can also meet other travelers at a nightly wine tasting. Guest rooms are done up in a cheerful modern decor. Bathrooms are oversize, and beds have 400-thread count sheets. The top-end Mount Jumbo Room comes with a private whirlpool tub; the Large Family Room sleeps four. The bakery is a popular gathering spot; in the back is an arthouse movie theater.

120 Second St. (a hike uphill into downtown from the pier). ℂ **907/586-4146** or 800/586-4146. www.silverbowinn.com. 11 rooms. $149–$249. Rates include breakfast. Off-street parking (on a limited basis). **Amenities:** Hot tub; nightly wine tasting; 24-hour coffee, service, and snacks. *In room:* TV, hair dryer, CD player, iPod docking station, Wi-Fi (free).

# Where to Dine

See also **Tracy's King Crab Shack** in Chapter 8.

**Red Dog Saloon ★** BREWPUB Past the "GENTS CHECK YOUR SIDE ARMS, LADIES WELCOME" sign and the red swinging doors is a rowdy, fun atmosphere and decent pub grub (including Angus beer burgers and Alaskan clam chowder). The history of this place dates to the city's mining heyday. The Red Dog Saloon has sawdust on the floor and a frontier atmosphere complete with ragtime music and tall tales. Just don't expect a quiet meal. Recently added around the corner (on Manila Square) is a huge Red Dog souvenir shop.

278 S. Franklin St. ℂ **907/463-3777.** www.reddogsaloon.com. Main courses $10–$15. AE, MC, V. Summer daily 11am–11pm.

**Twisted Fish Company ★★** SEAFOOD/GRILL/PIZZA Cruise passengers flock to this casual restaurant, probably because it's right at the cruise-ship pier. But the lively place also does a great job with dishes like salmon tacos and pizzas topped with salmon. If you want to get fancy, order the salmon on a silver plank. Steak is on the menu too. Try to snag one of the tables with views of the Gastineau Channel. Beer selections from the Alaskan Brewing Company are on tap.

550 S. Franklin St. (behind Taku Smokeries). ℂ **907/463-5033.** http://twistedfish.hangaron thewharf.com. Main courses $14–$38 dinner. Daily 11am–10pm.

# WHITTIER

Some 700,000 tourists pass through this tiny city each year. But unless you're getting on or off a cruise ship or are going sightseeing in Prince William Sound, there's little reason to go here—unless, that is, you're on a quest to find America's oddest towns. Most of the townspeople (just over 200 at last count) live in a 14-story concrete building, **Begich Towers,** built by the U.S. Army. It has a grocery store on the first floor, and medical clinic on the third. The police department and post office are located in the building too. The idea is, you need never leave—especially during the harsh winters.

Begich Towers was built during the 1940s, when Whittier's strategic location on the Alaska Railroad and at the head of a deep fjord made it a key port in the defense of Alaska. The City of Whittier was incorporated in 1969. Today, with its barren gravel ground and ramshackle warehouses and boat sheds, the town maintains a stark military-industrial character. The pass above the town is a funnel for frequent whipping winds, it always seems to rain, and the glaciers above the town keep it cool even in summer. The official boosters look on the bright side: With nearly everyone living on one place, it saves on snow removal in a town that gets an average of 20 feet every winter. The kids don't even have to go outside to get to school—a tunnel leads from the tower to the classroom. It's a crazy setup even for Alaska.

No matter how odd or dreary Whittier may seem, it has assumed huge importance to Princess—and vice versa. The line's Gulf ships do their turnarounds here, exposing tens of thousands of visitors to the city. How much money any of those thousands of passengers actually spend on goods and services here is open to question. But the cruise lines' docking fees alone are worth big bucks to Whittier. An **ATM** is located at the liquor store near the boat harbor, but Whittier lacks a bank and other services, so bring what you need.

## Getting to Whittier

**BY PLANE**    Fly to the **Ted Stevens International Airport** in Anchorage, then drive for about 1½ hours. You're best off booking a transfer through the cruise line to get there.

**BY BUS**    The **Magic Bus** departs from the Anchorage Museum of History and Fine Art (at 7th and A sts.) at 3pm on Monday, Wednesday, and Saturday, and arrives in Whittier some 90 minutes later. Luggage is limited to two bags per passenger (extra luggage is allowed on a space-available basis, for an extra fee). The trip costs $65 for adults, $32.50 for kids, each way. For reservations, call © **800/208-0200** or go to www.alaskatravel.com/bus-lines/anchorage-whittier.html.

**BY CAR**    It's possible to drive to Whittier from Anchorage by way of the Portage Glacier Highway through the Anton Anderson Memorial Tunnel at Whittier. *Be forewarned:* Although, theoretically, Whittier is only a couple hours' drive or train ride from Anchorage, the journey can take much, much longer. That's because the tunnel on the outskirts of town is shared by both automobiles and trains, and while one is using it, the other can't. They switch every half-hour or so, but it can make for some frustrating waits. Get the schedule through the tunnel's website (http://www.dot.state.ak.us/creg/whittiertunnel/schedule.shtml), through its phone recording (© **877/611-2586** or

907/566-2244), or by tuning to 1610AM in Portage or 530AM in Whittier. The toll for cars is $12. Overnight parking in Whittier is $10 per day.

**BY RAIL**   You can get to Whittier from Anchorage on the Alaska Railroad (© **800/ 544-0552** or 907/265-2494; www.alaskarailroad.com). The fare is $74 for adults and $37 for children ages 12 and under. The dock is near the mouth of Whittier Creek. Nothing in Whittier is more than a 5-minute walk away. Don't look for taxi ranks or free shuttles—you won't need them.

## Exploring Whittier

**INFORMATION**   Probably because it doesn't have much to promote, Whittier has no tourist board, per se, and there is no visitor center, but you can contact the city offices at © **907/472-2327,** ext. 101 (or by e-mail at admin@ci.whittier.ak.us). A Greater Whittier Chamber of Commerce lists "attractions" on its website (www.whittier alaskachamber.org). The people at the harbormaster's office are also helpful and maintain public toilets and showers; it's the only two-story building at the harbor (© **907/ 472-2327,** ext. 110 or 115). Inside the cruise terminal, brochures promote area tour operators and the like.

**GETTING AROUND**   You can walk everywhere, but there's also a cab or two in town. Look for them when you get off the boat or train.

### ATTRACTIONS WITHIN WALKING DISTANCE

Everything is easily accessible on foot, but there just isn't much to see. Visit the yacht harbor and the town's apartment building, and stop by the **Prince William Sound Museum** at the **Anchor Inn** (see listing under "Where to Dine," below), for a few exhibits highlighting the city's military and civilian history; (suggested donation $3 for adults, $1.50 for children 12 and under).

### ATTRACTIONS BEYOND THE PORT AREA

You can take the **Alaska Railroad ★★** train (© **800/544-0552** or 907/265-2494; www.alaskarailroad.com) straight to Anchorage. It's a fun scenic ride (one-way for $74 for adults, $37 children 2 to 11, free for kids 1 and under).

### BEST CRUISE-LINE SHORE EXCURSIONS

The following excursion is offered only to passengers with a pre- or post-cruise stay in Anchorage or those with departing flights after 5pm.

**Kayaking in Prince William Sound** (3 hr.; $99): Learn the basics, and then follow your guide into the pristine waters of Prince William Sound. He or she will point out the native flora, fauna, and marine life.

### EXCURSIONS OFFERED BY LOCAL AGENCIES

Several companies offer day trips to Prince William Sound's western glaciers. Besides the incredible scenery, the water is calm, making seasickness unlikely—for the queasy, this is a much better choice than Kenai Fjords National Park. Departures are timed with the daily Alaska Railroad train from Anchorage, described above, which means you'll have up to 6 hours for the trip. Some visitors see as much as possible, while others savor the scenery and wildlife sightings.

**Phillips Cruises and Tours** (© **800/544-0529** or 907/276-8023; www.phillips cruises.com) has 2 day-cruise options out of Whittier on three-deck, high-speed

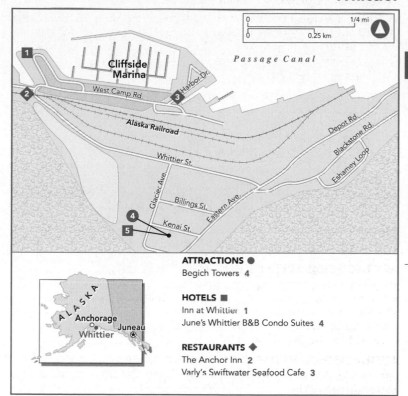

**ATTRACTIONS** ●
Begich Towers **4**

**HOTELS** ■
Inn at Whittier **1**
June's Whittier B&B Condo Suites **4**

**RESTAURANTS** ◆
The Anchor Inn **2**
Varly's Swiftwater Seafood Cafe **3**

catamarans. A 26-glacier cruise of the sound on the 338-passenger Klondike Express is for 4½ hours and costs $139 for adults, $89 for children 12 and under. A 3¾ hour cruise to the giant waterfalls of beautiful Blackstone Bay on the 149-passenger Glacier Quest costs $99 for adults, $58 for kids. Both cruises are narrated by rangers from the U.S. Forest Service and hot lunch is included.

**Major Marine Tours** (© **800/764-7300** or 907/274-7300; www.majormarine.com) operates a 149-passenger vessel at a slower pace than Phillips' catamarans—it visits just 10 glaciers, but spends more time waiting for them to calve. The route goes up Blackstone Bay, and the boat is comfortable, with reserved table seating. Food costs extra; the all-you-can-eat salmon and prime rib buffet is $19 ($9.50 for children). The trip lasts 5 hours; the price is $149 for adults, $74.50 for children 12 and under.

**Sound Eco Adventures** (© **907/242-0637**; www.soundecoadventure.com) is operated by a retired wildlife biologist who spent years researching the waterfowl and ecology of Prince William Sound. The 30-foot wheelchair-accessible boat carries up to six passengers at a time on wildlife, whale, and glacier tours and does kayak drop-offs as well. Prices range from $199 per person for an up-to-8-hour wildlife-viewing cruise to $234 per person for a whale and wildlife adventure. Lunch and a snack are included. Open scheduling is available.

## Where to Stay

**Inn at Whittier** ★★★   This 25-room property is as good as it gets in Whittier; it's the fancy place in town, complete with 150-seat restaurant. The timber-framed structure has a lighthouse design in the center—presumably to remind you you're on the harbor. Pick the view you want, whether the waters of Prince William Sound or a backdrop of mountains; both are impressive. You'll have the modern comforts: TV and free Internet access, and junior suites come with Jacuzzi tubs. If you splurge on one of the two-story townhouse suites, you get both a Jacuzzi and a fireplace (perfect for those seeking a romantic interlude). The restaurant serves three meals a day, lighter fare including sandwiches at lunch with a seafood focus (including Alaska crab and salmon) at dinner. With fishing a popular visitor pastime, the chef is ready, willing, and able to prepare your catch on request.

P.O. Box 773. © **907/472-3200.** www.innatwhittier.com. 25 units. $169–$249 double; $249–$299 suite. Free parking. **Amenities:** Restaurant; bar. *In room:* TV, high-speed Internet (free).

**June's Whittier Bed and Breakfast Condo Suites** ★   These condo units are in the Begich Towers, the concrete building that dominates Whittier. Stay here and you can sample what life is like for those who live in this unusual town. The units all come with views of water or mountains and full kitchens. Because you are staying in condos, features vary (check descriptions online). One unit comes with a desktop computer you can use, another has a sauna. Some have Wi-Fi. Most units sleep up to six people. It has a free shuttle to the harbor. Also in the building are a laundry, a grocery store, a nondenominational church, a video rental place, and even a tanning bed.

P.O. Box 715. © **888/472-6001** or 907/472-6001. http://whittiersuitesonline.com. 12 units. $155–$265 double. Rates include continental breakfast. Free parking. *In room:* TV/VCR, kitchen, Wi-Fi (in some; free).

## Where to Dine

Most dining spots in Whittier are for people who just want to grab a sandwich while passing through.

**The Anchor Inn** ★ AMERICAN   You will rub shoulders with fishermen and other colorful locals when you visit this casual spot, a combination restaurant, grocery store, laundromat, and bar (with live entertainment). The menu is simple: burgers, seafood, fried chicken, and steak. It has a few rooms available for overnight guests and also houses the small **Prince William Sound Museum** ★, highlighting the history of Whittier.

100 Whittier St. © **907/472-2354** or 877/870-8787. www.anchorinnwhittier.com. Main courses lunch $6–$12, dinner $12–$21. Open daily 7am–11pm.

**Varly's Swiftwater Seafood Cafe** ★★★ SEAFOOD   This small, friendly seafood shack on the water—across from the ferry dock in the area known as The Triangle—has been known to draw visitors to Whittier. The menu features freshly caught halibut, cod, and shrimp straight from Prince William Sound, hand-battered, fried to perfection, and served with fries in plastic baskets. Ship and other maritime photos adorn practically every inch of the walls. Casual and kid-friendly, the place is run by the Varlamos family, operator as well of the town's pizza shop and ice cream parlor—you can even have a handmade pizza delivered here. Start your meal with homemade clam chowder or tomato-based seafood chowder and finish off with amazing rhubarb crisp. Choose from a selection of 30 imported and domestic beers or wine. Grab a seat outdoors on the deck to watch the goings-on in the harbor.

Across from the ferry dock, at the Triangle. (©) **907/472-2550.** www.swiftwaterseafoodcafe.com. Main courses $10–$18. Sun–Thurs 11:30am–9pm; Fri–Sun 11:30am–10pm.

# THE PORTS & GLACIERS

Whether you are on an Inside Passage or Gulf itinerary, you will likely call at two or more of the most popular Alaskan ports—Ketchikan, Juneau, and Skagway. You will also find yourself staring in awe at a glacier, either in Glacier Bay, Hubbard Glacier, or College Fjord. All are magnificent. Your itinerary may also include the Russian-heritage town of Sitka, just outside the Inside Passage, and the lovely Canadian city of Victoria.

Some of the big-ship cruise lines offer longer cruises (for more details, see chapter 5) that allow additional exploration to less-visited areas—such as the classic Alaskan town of Haines. Small-ship lines can access certain regions more easily, thanks to their shallow drafts, and they also have the flexibility to visit smaller towns and wilderness areas, including on shorter itineraries (for more details, see chapter 6).

See chapter 4 for information on shore excursions and tips on debarkation, what to bring along with you while ashore, and little matters such as not missing the boat.

*Note:* Shore excursion prices for children apply to age 12 and under unless otherwise noted.

## VICTORIA, BRITISH COLUMBIA

Yes, we know it's in Canada, not Alaska, but cruises that start in Seattle or San Francisco typically include Victoria (on Vancouver Island) as a port of call while traveling northward. This lively city, the capital of British Columbia, has Victorian architecture and a very proper British atmosphere—some say it's more British than Britain itself—with main attractions that include high tea and a visit to **Butchart Gardens** with its incredible botanical displays.

A former British outpost, Victoria has a history filled with maritime lore. Whalers and trading ships once docked in the city's harbors, transporting Vancouver Island's rich bounty of coal, lumber, and furs throughout the world. One of the great sights on any visit to Victoria is its Inner Harbour, framed by the venerable (ca. 1908) Fairmont Empress Hotel and the British Columbia Parliament Building. It is, by any yardstick, a panorama of great beauty. The big ships don't dock there (see "Coming Ashore," below).

There are tangible attractions right on the harbor too. For souvenirs of a crafts variety, check out the **Night Market,** outdoors at Ship Point (open

# Victoria, British Columbia

Butchart Gardens **1**
Craigdarroch Castle **7**
Cruise Terminal **8**
Fairmont Empress Hotel **5**
Miniature World Museum **5**
Royal British Columbia
  Museum and National
  Geographic IMAX Theater **6**
Ship Point Night Market **3**
Spinnakers Gastro
  Brewpub **2**
Victoria Bug Zoo **4**

Fri and Sat evenings, June–Sept), just past the visitor's center. For photographic opportunities—not to mention stalls selling tasty fish and chips—stop by Fisherman's Wharf, a neighborhood of colorful floating homes and buildings. Or stop by the Steamship Terminal, where the brand-new **Robert Bateman Centre** houses galleries devoted to the work of acclaimed Canadian wildlife artist Robert Bateman (✆ **250/ 940-3630;** http://batemancentre.org; admission $13 adults, $8.50 seniors, $6 youth 6–18, children 5 and under free).

Take a tour around the island and you'll see gorgeous homes and gardens, with views that include the snowcapped mountains of Washington State.

**COMING ASHORE**  Spectacular as it would be to dock in Victoria's Inner Harbour, it's too small for major cruise ships, which park instead at the recently upgraded and expanded Ogden Point terminal on Juan De Fuca Strait. It's about a mile into town, so if you don't mind a stretch of the legs, walk west along Dallas Street from the dock and north on Oswego Street or Menzies Street, and you'll find yourself in the heart of the action—right on the Inner Harbour. Or do the Harbour Walk (well marked from the ship terminal), which takes about 40 minutes, but follows the water the whole way. Shuttle buses from the cruise pier to the Empress Hotel are $10 round-trip. There, on the waterfront, flowers, milling crowds, and street performers—including, usually, a lone bagpiper—enliven the scene.

Beautifully maintained, old wooden water taxis operated by **Victoria Harbour Ferry** ($5 each way; ℭ **250/708-0201;** www.victoriaharbourferry.com) ply the harbor. Catch one at Fisherman's Pier, about a 10-minute walk from the Ogden point terminal (with a stop near the Empress Hotel). It's worth taking a jaunt, even if you're going nowhere! Be sure you (and your camera) are prepared to take lots of pictures: Victoria's Inner Harbour is one of the most photogenic sights on the planet.

*Note:* Rates below are in Canadian dollars. At press time, the conversion to U.S. dollars was C$1 = US$.97. Shore excursions are priced in U.S. dollars.

**INFORMATION** You'll typically see cruise-ship greeters handing out maps at the pier, but if not, pick up a map of the city at the **Tourism Victoria Visitor Information Centre** (ℭ **250/953-2033;** www.tourismvictoria.com), on the waterfront at 812 Wharf Street; it's open daily 8:30am to 8:30pm May to September.

## Best Cruise-Line Shore Excursions

Note that shore excursion prices quoted here are representative of what's available, but may differ slightly among cruise lines.

**English Tea at Butchart Gardens** (4 hr.; $119 adults, $79 children): The bus makes the 13-mile trip from the ship to world-renowned Butchart Gardens along Brentwood Bay. There you'll have time to explore the 131-acre grounds and enjoy an elegant, traditional afternoon tea with finger sandwiches, scones, and cream, and all kinds of goodies, along with honest-to-goodness brewed English tea.

**Victoria by Horse-Drawn Trolley** (1½ hr.; $60 adult, $30 children): It's a romantic way to see the sights of the city: the Inner Harbour, Chinatown, the historic James Bay residential area, and much more.

**Victoria Pub Crawl** (3½ hr.; $96 adults only): Flowers and greenery may be what most people envision when they think of Victoria, but the city also boasts some fabulous English-style pubs. The tour, mostly on foot, takes visitors to several of them to sample the local brews. *Note:* Minimum age is 19.

## Excursions Offered by Local Agencies

Several local operators greet passengers right at the pier, offering rides into the city and longer tours using various modes of transportation. **Classic Car Tours** (ℭ **250/383-2342;** www.classiccartours.com) gives tours in classic convertibles (perfect on a sunny day), with commentary that is both colorful and delightful. Fares are $80 an hour per car, for up to four passengers. The bicycle rickshaws operated by **Victoria Pedicab Company** (ℭ **250/884-0121;** www.victoriatours.net) are an unusual way to get around the city for about $60 per hour (for two people); from the ship pier to the downtown area, the standard charge is about $30 (for two people). **Gray Line Victoria** (ℭ **855/ 385-6553** or 250/385-6553; www.graylinevictoria.com) provides a shuttle to Butchart Gardens (including admission), leaving from near the Fairmont Empress Hotel, six times a day beginning at 8:55am, for $53 adults, $40 children 13 to 17, and $19 children 5 to 12 (free for children 4 and under). The company also operates a hop-on, hop-off double-decker bus that makes a number of stops in and around the city including at Craigdarroch Castle, for $28 adults, $25 youth, $9 kids. Whale-watching cruises are another popular Victoria diversion; you can book one with Prince of Whales (© **888/383-4884;** www.princeofwhales.com). A 3-hour tour in an open, Zodiac-style boat is $110 for adults, $100 for seniors, $95 students 13 to 17, and $85 children 8 to 12 (tour not available for kids 7 and under), with departures every half-hour in summer.

## On Your Own: Within Walking Distance

**The Fairmont Empress Hotel ★★★** It's a splurge, but afternoon tea at this classic, ivy-covered 1908 hotel has become a time-honored tradition. Dress up a bit (the dress code bans torn jeans, short shorts, jogging pants, and tank tops) and head into the opulent **Tea Lobby,** overlooking the Inner Harbour, for a spread that includes—in proper British style—little tea sandwiches, raisin scones with heavy cream and strawberry preserves, and extravagant pastries (from the hotel's award-winning pastry chef). There's even a secret Empress tea blend. It's all served with pomp and circumstance, as befitting a price tag of $51 per person (half-price for children 12 and under).

721 Government St. © **250/384-8111,** or 250/389-2727 for tea reservations. www.fairmont.com/empress. Daily seatings noon–5:15pm.

**Miniature World Museum ★** Marketed as "The World's Greatest Little Show on Earth," this quirky museum offers the world in miniature—as in dollhouse size. The collection has been continually updated over the museum's 40-plus years, and displays include the building of the Canadian railway, the world's smallest sawmill, and the World of Dickens. It's located around back of the Fairmont Empress Hotel.

649 Humboldt St. © **250/385-9731.** www.miniatureworld.com. Admission $12 adults, $11 seniors, $10 youths 12–18, $8 children 5–12 (under 5 free). Summer daily 9am–9pm (until 5pm in September).

**Royal British Columbia Museum ★★★** The Royal title of this major provincial museum was approved by Queen Elizabeth II and bestowed by Prince Philip in 1987. But the museum was first established in 1868. The collection, now in a modern, three-story building, covers everything from British Columbia's recent past to Native cultures to natural history (prehistoric to present day). Spend time checking out the extensive collection of artifacts, masks, and carvings in the First People's Galleries. A special exhibit in 2014 will highlight the 34 languages of the First Peoples of British Columbia. The Old Town exhibit in the Modern History Gallery has walk-through examples of old Victoria. The museum complex includes Thunderbird Park, with totem poles and a ceremonial house; Helmecken House, once the home of a pioneer doctor and one of the oldest houses in B.C.; and a Native Plant Garden, featuring more than 400 species. There's also an **IMAX theater.**

675 Belleville St. © **888/447-7977** or 250/356-7226. www.royalbcmuseum.bc.ca. Admission museum $22 adults, $16 seniors and youths 6–18, free for children 5 and under, $62 family admission (2 adults, 2 kids 18 and under). IMAX admission is extra. Museum Mon–Wed and Sun 10am–5pm, Thurs–Sat 10am–10pm in summer.

**Spinnakers Gastro Brewpub ★★★** Victoria's oldest brewpub is a must for microbrew fans but also a decent spot for non-drinkers—especially given its waterfront deck. In addition to making handcrafted ales, the gastropub makes its own malt vinegar (delicious on the flaky halibut or salmon fish-and-chips) and soda creations. Victoria's beer history, which dates to the early 1840s, can be traced via a self-guided Ale Trail map (available around town) that also takes you to other stops including the **Canoe Brewpub & Restaurant,** 450 Swift St. (© **250/361-1940;** www.canoebrewpub.com), an easy walk from the harborfront and featuring live music at night; and **Buckerfield's Brewery** at the Swans Suite Hotel, 506 Pandora Ave. (© **250/361-3310;** www.swans hotel.com), especially for their summer Raspberry Ale made with local berries.

308 Catherine St. © **877/838-2739** or 250/386-2739. www.spinnakers.com. Daily 11am–11pm.

**Victoria Bug Zoo ★** If you are traveling with kids or just really into creepy-crawly things, this attraction takes you into the world of spiders and insects. Exhibits come from around the world and include giant walking sticks, alien-eyed praying mantises, hairy tarantulas, and glow-in-the-dark scorpions. It's all safe and fun. The zoo also features Canada's largest ant farm. Knowledgeable "bug guides" are on hand.

631 Courtney St. © **250/384-2847.** www.bugzoo.bc.ca. Admission $10 adults, $9 seniors, $8 youths 11–18, $6 children 3–10, free for children 2 and under. Mon–Sat 10:30am–5:30pm; Sun 11am–5pm.

## On Your Own: Beyond the Port Area

**Butchart Gardens ★★★** A ride by cab, public bus, or other transportation (see "Excursions Offered by Local Agencies," below) and several free hours are required for a visit to this world-renowned attraction. The gardens lie 13 miles north of downtown Victoria on a 131-acre estate and feature English-, Italian-, and Japanese-style plantings, as well as water gardens and rose beds. There are also restaurants and a gift shop on-site. *Note:* You can catch a public bus from downtown Victoria for less than $5.50 each way. A cab will cost you about $55 each way.

800 Benevenuto Ave., Brentwood Bay. © **250/652-5256.** www.butchartgardens.com. Admission from June 15–Sept 30 $30 adults and seniors, $15 children 13–17, $3 children 5–12, free for children 4 and under. Mid-June to Labor Day daily 9am–10pm; hours vary rest of year.

**Craigdarroch Castle ★★** Climb the 87 steps to the tower at this Victorian-era castle and you'll be rewarded with excellent views of Victoria. The elaborate Scottish Highlands–style castle was built by in the 1880s by Scottish immigrant Robert Dunsmuir, who made his fortune in coal. The 39-room mansion is topped with stone turrets, has nice examples of stained glass, and is lavishly furnished with Victorian goods. The location is about a half-hour walk from the inner harbor (you may want to take a cab from the pier).

1050 Joan Crescent. © **250/592-5323.** www.craigdarrochcastle.com. Admission $14 adults, $13 seniors, $9 students with valid ID, $5 children 6–12, free for children 5 and under. Mid-June to Labor Day daily 9am–7pm; rest of year 10am–4:30pm.

# CANADA'S INSIDE PASSAGE

Canada's Inside Passage is simply the part of an Inside Passage cruise that lies in British Columbia, south of the Alaskan border and running to Vancouver. On big ships, the first day out of Vancouver (or the last day going south) is usually a day at sea. Passengers get the chance to enjoy the coastal beauty of the British Columbia mainland to the east and Vancouver Island to the west, including some truly magnificent scenery in Princess Louisa Inlet and Desolation Sound.

In most cases, that's all the ships do, though: Go past the scenery—much of it at night. In their haste to get to Ketchikan, the first stop in Alaska, they invariably sail right past much of the Canadian Inside Passage.

One of the Canadian Inside Passage's loveliest stretches is **Seymour Narrows,** 5 or 6 hours north of Vancouver, just after the mouth of the Campbell River. It's so narrow that it can be passed through only at certain hours of the day, when the tide is right, often late in the day or in the wee hours of night. On the long days of summer, it's often possible to enjoy Seymour Narrows if you're prepared to stay up late.

The U.S./Canada border lies just off the tip of the Misty Fjords National Monument, 43 sailing miles from Ketchikan (and 403 miles from Glacier Bay, for those who are keeping count).

# KETCHIKAN

Ketchikan is the southernmost port of call in Southeast Alaska. Its 14,000 residents sometimes refer to it as "the first city." That's not because it's the most important city to the region's economy, or that it's the biggest, or even that it was literally the first built. The name comes from the fact that Ketchikan is usually the first city visited by cruise ships on the Inside Passage when ships are running northbound out of Vancouver or Seattle.

Upon arrival at the dock, look for the Liquid Sunshine Gauge, which the city put up to mark the cumulative rainfall for the year, day by day. We once checked and saw that the mark showed over 36 inches—and it was only June. Even at that, the gauge had a long way to go. The average annual rainfall is about 160 inches (more than 13 ft.!) and has topped 200 inches in the rainiest years. Precipitation is so predictable here that the locals joke that if you can't see the top of nearby Deer Mountain, it's raining; if you can see it, it's going to rain!

Still, we have a soft spot for this place. Climate notwithstanding, it's a fun port to visit—a glorified fishing village with quaint architecture, history, salmon fishing, the great scenery found in just about every Inside Passage community, and **totem poles**— lots and lots of totem poles. However, we have to admit concern that the place has gotten touristy and overcrowded. About 70 jewelry stores and dozens of what locals call "trinket shops" cater to cruise-ship passengers. Much of the character we loved has vanished in favor of such touristy attractions as the Great Alaskan Lumberjack Show and Duck Tours (which take you on land and into the water on amphibious vehicles).

That said, from up close—say, on the sidewalk of Stedman Street—the main thoroughfare, historic **Creek Street,** the centerpiece of downtown, still presents a very photogenic side. It's often said (perhaps only by the Ketchikan Chamber of Commerce!) that it's the most photographed street in Alaska.

Creek Street comprises a row of historic buildings on pilings over a stream up which salmon swim in their spawning season. Today the narrow wooden sidewalk is lined mostly with funky restaurants, such as the Creek Street Cafe, and boutiques and galleries specializing in offbeat pieces, many by local artists. In the early 1900s, this was Ketchikan's redlight district, with more than 30 brothels lining the waterway; a small sign at the head of the street notes that it was where both the fishermen and the fish went up the stream to spawn. The most famous of the courtesans (or, at least, the most enduring) was Dolly Arthur (born Thelma Dolly Copeland). Not the most successful—nor, according to pictures we've seen, the prettiest—working girl, she nevertheless outlived the rest. **Dolly's House,** 24 Creek St. (© **907/617-1433;** www.dollyshouse.com), is now a small museum with a hokey "Red Light" video tour. Just like the house's old clientele, you have to pay to get inside. We don't know what they used to pay, but today it'll cost you $10.

Ketchikan is still a strong center of the Tlingit, Tsimshian, and Haida cultures. These proud Southeast Alaska Native peoples have preserved their traditions and kept their icons intact over the centuries. They've also re-created **clan houses** and made replicas of totem poles that were irretrievably damaged by decades of exposure to the elements. The tall hand-carved poles are everywhere—in parks, in the lobbies of buildings, in the street. It should be no surprise to anyone that there are more totems in Ketchikan than in any city in the world.

While many of the shops in town are operated by out-of-towners who only come here for the summer, there are still some hidden gems, our favorite being a friendly hole-in-the-wall called **Salmon, Etc.** (© **800/354-7256** or 907/225-6008; www.salmon etc.com), a few blocks from the ship pier at 322 Mission St., where you can buy cans of yummy smoked salmon. The shop has been in town since the early 1980s and is locally owned. Its smoked-fish products are so good, we always make a beeline here to buy a few cans to take home—at prices cheaper, by the way, than at the shops at Salmon Landing, a mini-mall closer to the ship pier. Ketchikan has a decent arts scene, and a good place to check out what's new is the Main Street Gallery of the **Ketchikan Area Arts and Humanities Council,** 330 Main St. (© **907/225-2211;** www.ketchikan arts.org). Shows change monthly.

One of our favorite things to do in Ketchikan, besides booking a shore excursion and getting into the gorgeous surrounding natural areas, is to walk the few blocks from the ship, past Creek Street, and take the **funicular railway** ($2) to the **Westcoast Cape Fox Lodge,** for views of the city, Tongass Narrows, and Deer Mountain (if you want to linger you can get a decent lunch at the hotel restaurant). It's also an easy walk from here to Totem Heritage Center (see below). Up on the top of the mountain is the **Deer Mountain Tribal Hatchery & Eagle Center,** a Native-run operation that was unfortunately closed for the 2013 cruise season due to funding issues. If it is open in 2014, it's a good place to see where salmon come from and to meet some rescued eagles.

If you prefer to stay down by the pier, walk along the waterfront to see the fishing boats. Ketchikan claims to be the "Salmon Capital of the World," and in fact, five species of wild Pacific salmon return from the ocean to creeks and streams near the town each year. The saltwater fishing is some of the best anywhere, and it's fun to watch the fishing boats unload their catch.

**COMING ASHORE**  Ships dock right at the pier in Ketchikan's downtown area. Because the pier was recently expanded and a half-dozen ships can be in port at one time, guard rails have been installed, and you need to cross to the town's main areas with a crossing guard.

**INFORMATION**  Our first stop in Ketchikan is usually the **Ketchikan Visitors Center,** right on the dock, at 131 Front St. (© **907/225-6166;** www.visit-ketchikan. com), near Berth 2 (with a summer satellite office also near Berth 3), to pick up literature (including walking maps) and information on what's new in town (and discount coupons for attractions). A city-operated free shuttle bus visits sights around town,

Cruise Ship Dock
(i) Information
✉ Post Office
▓▓▓ Stairs

*Ketchikan Creek*

Woodland Ave.

Park Ave.

Summit Terrance

Miller Ridge Rd.

Harris St.

Venetia Ave.

Funicular

Forrest Ave.

Park Ave.

Creek St.

**To Saxman Native Village Totem Pole Park** →

Bawden St.

Stedman St.

Revilla St.

Pine St.

Grant St.

Edmond St.

Main St.

Mission St.

Mill St.

Spruce Mill Way

*Thomas Basin*

Pine St.

Water St.

Tunnel

Front St.

Dock St.

East St.

Deermount St.

*Tongass Narrows*

← To Airport,
Totem Bight State
Historical Park
and Salmon Falls

0 ____ 1/10 mi
0 ____ 100 m

*A L A S K A*

○ Fairbanks

○ Anchorage    Juneau ✦

Ketchikan

Creek Street **4**
Deer Mountain Tribal Hatchery
& Eagle Center **1**
Dolly's House **3**
St. John's Church **7**
Salmon Ladder **5**
Southeast Alaska Discovery
Center **8**
Tongass Historical Museum **6**
Totem Heritage Center **2**

including the Totem Heritage Center, which otherwise is about a 15-minute uphill walk.

## Best Cruise-Line Shore Excursions

**Alaska Duck (Amphibious) Tours** (1½ hr.; $41 adults, $25 children): See Ketchikan by both land and sea. This fun outing, in a high-riding "duck" vehicle, takes you through rustic streets (past the salmon ladder, Creek Street, and Totem Heritage Center) and into the harbor, where you can eye the aquatic wildlife, check out the leisure and fishing boats, and get an up-close look at the floatplanes taking off. Be forewarned that, as you hit the water, there may be splashes (which typically elicit squeals of delight).

**Bear Country & Wildlife Expedition** (3½ hr.; $199): This extraordinary naturalist-led tour brings only 12 guests at a time to a relatively new rainforest trail that leads to a creek frequented by black bears, who come there in search of salmon. Viewing is from elevated areas that include a suspension bridge and tree platforms. You'll likely see bald eagles, too. Minimum age 12.

**Bering Sea Crab Fishermen's Tour** (3½ hr.; $179 adults, $119 children): This tour is a must-do for fans of the Discovery Channel's *Deadliest Catch*. Real fishermen share their tales and exploits as you travel on the F/V *Aleutian Ballard,* the same vessel featured on the show (though without the rough seas, cold conditions, and other dangers the show highlights). Plenty of crabs and other marine life are on view.

**Great Alaskan Lumberjack Show** (1 hr. 10 min.; $36 adults, $25 children 2–10): Chopping, sawing, speed climbing, log rolling, and more—and all within a short walk of the cruise-ship pier. Kids will love this show—and while the performers are in the open air, spectator seats are warm and dry.

**Misty Fjords Flightseeing** (2 hr.; $269 adults, $219 children): Everyone gets a window seat aboard the floatplanes that run these quick flightseeing jaunts over Misty Fjords National Monument. There are no ice fields and glaciers on this trip, but Misty Fjords has another kind of majesty: You'll see sparkling fjords, cascading waterfalls, thick forests, and rugged mountains dotted with wildlife. Then you'll come in for a landing on the fjord itself, or on a nearby wilderness lake. Once you've landed, you can get out and stand—carefully—on the pontoons to take pictures.

**Mountain Point Snorkeling Adventure** (3 hr.; $109): Believe it or not, you can snorkel around Ketchikan, where the climate is warm for Alaska. It's not the Caribbean, but the water isn't as cold as you think, and wet suits are provided on this excursion, as well as hot beverages for when you get out of the water. Undersea are amazing kelp with large fluttering leaves, fish, colorful starfish, sea urchins, sea cucumbers, and more.

**Rain Forest Ropes & Zip Challenge** (3 hr. 25 min.; $179): This tour allows guests to traverse a zipline in harnesses between trees before rappelling to the ground. It's a new way to appreciate the Alaskan rainforest. This is real ziplining (unlike the offering in Icy Strait Point, which is more of a ride than ziplining). Instruction is given, and only minimal skill is required. A similar option is available in Juneau.

**Saxman Native Village & Ketchikan City Tour** (2½ hr.; $69 adults, $29 children): This modern-day Native village, situated about 3 miles outside Ketchikan, is a center for the revival of Native arts and culture. The tour includes either the telling of a Native legend or a performance by the Cape Fox dancers in the park theater, plus a guided walk through the grounds to see the totem poles and learn the stories behind them. Craftspeople are sometimes on hand in the working sheds to demonstrate totem-pole carving.

**Tatoosh Island Sea Kayaking** (4 hr.; $159 adults, $109 children 8–12): There are typically two kayaking excursions offered in Ketchikan: this one (which requires you to take a van and motorized boat to the island before starting your 90-min. paddle) and a trip that starts from right beside the cruise-ship docks. Of the two, this one is far more enjoyable, getting you out into a wilder area rather than just sticking to the busy port waters. The scenery is incredible, and you have a good chance of spotting bald eagles, seals (whether swimming around your boat or basking on the rocks), and leaping salmon.

**Totem Bight State Historical Park & City Tour** (2–2½ hr.; $45 adults, $29 children): This tour takes you by bus around Ketchikan and through the Tongass National Forest to see the historic Native fish camp, where a ceremonial clan house and totem poles sit amid the rainforest. There's a fair amount of walking involved and a lot of lecturing about the meaning of totem poles.

## Excursions Offered by Local Agencies

A bevy of tour operators sell their excursions at the **Ketchikan Visitors Center,** on 131 Front St. (© **907/225-6166**), right at the dock (near Berth 2). Schoolteacher Lois Munch of **Classic Tours** (© **907/225-3091**; www.classictours.com) makes her tours fun: She wears a poodle skirt to drive visitors around in her '55 Chevy, accompanied by '50s mood music. A 2-hour tour to the Saxman totem poles is $109 (two-person minimum, five-person maximum); a 3-hour tour adds a natural-history stop and costs $139. Lois is happy to customize a tour (price based on itinerary) for you as well, if you call in advance and tell her what you want. **Allen Marine Tours** (© **877/686-8100** or 907/225-8100; www.allenmarinetours.com) has cruises from Ketchikan to Misty Fjords National Monument on a high-speed catamaran built at the company's own boatyard in Sitka. A 4½-hour tour is $179 for adults, $115 for children 3 to 12. **Alaska Travel Adventures** (© **800/323-5757** or 907/789-0052; www.bestofalaskatravel.com) operates several tours, including a Rain Forest & Canoe Adventure (3½ hr.; $99 adults, $66 children), where you board a 37-foot, 20-passenger canoe and paddle under the direction of an experienced guide on a secluded mountain lake, surrounded by Tongass National Forest. The tour also includes a nature walk highlighting flora and fauna. **Southeast Sea Kayaks,** at Fish House Marina, 2 Salmon Landing (© **800/287-1607** or 907/225-1258; www.kayakketchikan.com), has guided paddle excursions (2½ hr.; $89 adults, $59 children) as well as rentals.

## On Your Own: Within Walking Distance

**Creek Street ★★★** This former redlight district is now arguably Ketchikan's number-one tourist attraction, jewelry stores and tourist shops aside. The view of Creek Street from the bridge over the stream on Stedman Street (the main thoroughfare) is striking, to say the least. It lays claim to the title "Most photographed street in the world" and, even allowing for a little Chamber of Commerce hyperbole, it just might be!

Off Stedman St., along Ketchikan Creek.

**St. John's Church ★** St. John's Church is the oldest place of worship in town. Both the church (Episcopal, by the way) and its adjacent Seaman's Center—built in 1904 as a hospital and now a commercial building—are interesting examples of local architecture in the early 1900s.

On Bawden St., at Mission St.

**The Salmon Ladder ★★★** We could spend hours on the observation deck at the artificial salmon ladder just off Park Avenue, watching these determined fish make their way from the sea up to the spawning grounds at the top of Ketchikan Creek. How these creatures can keep throwing their exhausted bodies up the ladder at the end of their long journey from the ocean, never giving up though they fail in three out of four leaps, is one of those mysteries of nature we never tire of observing.

Off Park Ave., in Ketchikan Creek.

**Southeast Alaska Discovery Center ★★★** Operated by the National Park Service, this museum is an easy walk from the ship pier and has impressive exhibits on the area's fishing, mining, and timber industries, ecosystems, and Tlingit, Haida, and Tsinshian culture—including some colorful totem poles at the entrance. An 18-minute film gives an introduction to the Tongass National Forest. Throughout the museum, videos amp up displays and feature rangers, Native storytellers, and other experts. It also serves as an information center for exploration of the Tongass, and has a decent bookstore.

50 Main St. © **907/228-6220.** www.alaskacenters.gov/ketchikan.cfm. Admission $5, free for children 15 and under. May–Oct daily 8am–3pm.

**Tongass Historical Museum ★**    Previously combined with Ketchikan's public library (which moved to a brand-new building last year), this small, city-run museum focuses its displays on the history, art, and culture of the area. It has some Native artifacts in the permanent collection along with a bunch of oddball donated relics including the skull of Old Groaner, a brown bear who was shot for attacking humans. Changing exhibits sometimes feature the personal collections of locals.

In the Centennial Building, 629 Dock St. © **907/225-5600.** www.ketchikanmuseums.org. Admission $2 for adults, free for children 12 and under. Summer daily 8am–5pm.

**Totem Heritage Center ★★★**    Built by the city, this museum houses a collection of rare 19th century totem poles, mostly unpainted, that were recovered from remote Tlingit and Haida villages. While they would traditionally have been left to rot on the ground where they fell, these poles—from a period that is considered carving's heyday—have been preserved with the permission of Native elders. Unfortunately, most of the stories associated with the poles have been lost. Newer works at the museum include an impressive Eagle Transformation dance rattle by Tlingit artist Norman Jackson, and the works of students and teachers involved with the center's traditional arts programs.

*Note:* The museum is at least a 15-minute uphill walk from the pier, so you may want to take the funicular or the free shuttle bus from the ship pier (which stops at key sights around town).

601 Deermount St. © **907/225-5900.** Admission $5, free 12 and under. May–Sept daily 8am–5pm; Oct–Apr Mon–Fri 1–5pm.

## On Your Own: Beyond the Port Area

In Ketchikan, we strongly recommend that you leave the out-of-port tours to either the cruise lines or tour operators in town.

# MISTY FJORDS NATIONAL MONUMENT

The 2.3-million-acre, Connecticut-size area of Misty Fjords starts at the Canadian border in the south and runs along the eastern side of the Behm Canal. Revillagigedo Island, where Ketchikan is located, is on the western side of the canal. It is topography, not wildlife, that makes a visit to Misty Fjords worthwhile. Among the prime features of Misty Fjords are New Eddystone Rock, jutting 237 feet out of the canal, and the Walker Cove/Rudyerd Bay area, a prime viewing spot for marine life, eagles, and other wildlife. Volcanic cliffs (up to 3,150 ft. high), coves (some as deep as 900 ft.), and peace and serenity are the stock-in-trade of the place.

Only passengers on small ships will see Misty Fjords close up—its waterway is too narrow in most places for big ships. The bigger ships pass the southern tip of the Misty Fjords National Monument and then veer away northwest to dock at Ketchikan. Unfortunately, this means that large-ship passengers miss one of the least spoiled of all wilderness areas—unless, that is, you book a flightseeing trip to see the place (see the sections on Ketchikan excursions, above).

Archaeologists believe local Indian tribes (Haida, Tlingit, and Tsimshian, primarily) lived here as far back as 10,000 years ago. The only way you're likely to see any trace of their existence now, though, is from a kayak or small boat that can get close enough to the rock face to let you see the few remaining pictographs etched into the stone along the shore.

Anglers in Misty Fjords are liable to think they've died and gone to heaven. The pristine waters yield a rich harvest of enormous Dolly Varden, grayling, and lake trout. It is possible to walk in the park, but only the hardy and the experienced are advised to do that. And it is necessary to follow some simple rules: Let somebody know where you are going and when you expect to return; keep to the trails (the wildlife—especially bears—don't always appreciate intruders); and carry out everything you carried in. That's the law.

By the way, the name Misty Fjords comes from the climatic conditions. Precipitation tends to leave the place looking as if it were under a steady mist much of the time. It also gives the waterway an almost spooky look. President Jimmy Carter named it a national treasure in 1978.

# ADMIRALTY ISLAND NATIONAL MONUMENT

About 15 miles due west of Juneau, this monument comprises almost 1 million acres and covers about 90 percent of Admiralty Island. It's another of those Alaska areas that cruise passengers on the bigger ships will never see. The villages here, some of them Native, have recently begun to attract some small-ship operators. The Tlingit village of **Angoon,** for example, welcomes small groups of visitors off ships. Small ships may also ferry passengers ashore in a more remote area of the island for a hike.

Admiralty Island is said to have the highest concentration of **bears** on earth. Naturalists estimate that there may be as many as four of these creatures per square mile. Bears, though, don't have a monopoly on the island. Also plentiful are **Sitka black-tailed deer** and **bald eagles,** and the waters around teem with **sea lions, harbor seals,** and **whales.** One of the largest concentrations of **bald eagles** in Southeast Alaska (second, perhaps, only to that in Haines in the fall) is found in the bays and inlets on the east side of the island. An estimated 4,000 eagles congregate there for the abundant and more easily accessible food supply.

# TRACY ARM & ENDICOTT ARM

Located about 50 miles due south of Juneau, these long, deep, and almost claustrophobically narrow fjords are a striking feature of a pristine forest and mountain expanse with a sinister name: **Tracy Arm–Ford's Terror Wilderness.** The place came by its name honestly after an 1889 incident in which a crewman from a U.S. naval vessel (name: Ford; rank: unknown) rowed into an inlet off Endicott Arm and found himself trapped for 6 hours in a heaving sea as huge ice floes bumped and ground against his flimsy craft. He survived, but the finger of water in which he endured his ordeal was forever after known as Ford's Terror. The banks were so close on a recent Disney Cruise Line sailing that we spotted a bear through our binoculars. We also saw humpbacks as we entered the area, so keep your eyes peeled for wildlife.

The Tracy and Endicott arms, which reach back from Stephens Passage into the Coastal Mountain Range, are steep-sided waterways, each with an active glacier at its head—the **Sawyer Glacier** and **South Sawyer Glacier** in Tracy Arm and **Dawes Glacier** in Endicott. These calve constantly, sometimes discarding ice blocks of such impressive size that they clog the narrow fjord passages, making navigation difficult. When the passage is not clogged, ships can get close enough for incredible sights and the sounds of calving glaciers (the sound of white thunder is amazing!). On a Regent Seven Seas cruise, we were thrilled when the captain ordered the tenders out at Sawyer Glacier for a great photo op.

A passage up either fjord allows eye-catching views of high cascading waterfalls, tree- and snow-covered mountain valleys, and wildlife that might include **Sitka black-tailed deer, bald eagles,** and possibly even the odd **black bear.** Around the ship, the animals you're most likely to see are whales, sea lions, and harbor seals.

# BARANOF ISLAND

Named after the Russian trader Alexander Baranof, Russian America's first appointed honcho, the island's main claim to fame is **Sitka,** on the western coast, the center of Russian-era culture and the seat of the Russian Orthodox Church in Alaska. (The island name, by the way, is often spelled Baranov, which some people contend is the way Alexander himself spelled it.) **Peril Straits,** off the northern end of the island, separating Baranof from Chichagof Island, is a scenic passageway too narrow for big cruise ships, but some of the smaller ones can get through.

# SITKA

Sitka differs from most ports of call on the Inside Passage cruises in that, geographically speaking, it's not on the Inside Passage at all. Rather, it stands on the outside (or western) coast of Baranof Island. Its name, in fact, comes from the Tlingit Indian *Shee Atika,* which means "people on the outside." For the relatively short time it takes ships to get to Sitka, they must leave the protected waters of the passage and sail with nothing between them and Japan but the sometimes turbulent Pacific Ocean. If you're going to run into heavy seas at any point on an Inside Passage cruise, this is where you'll most likely find them. This has been one of the only ports in Alaska where passengers on big ships had to tender to shore in small boats rather than dock (Icy Strait is another), which some considered a downside. A few years ago a new dock opened near the town's ferry terminal, built by a private developer, that allows big ships to tie up—if they choose to; most prefer to still tender right into downtown.

For us, this port is a must-do. Backing us up: The town was declared one of the 2010 Dozen Distinctive Destinations by the National Trust for Historic Preservation, in recognition of its historical architecture, cultural diversity, and commitment to historic preservation.

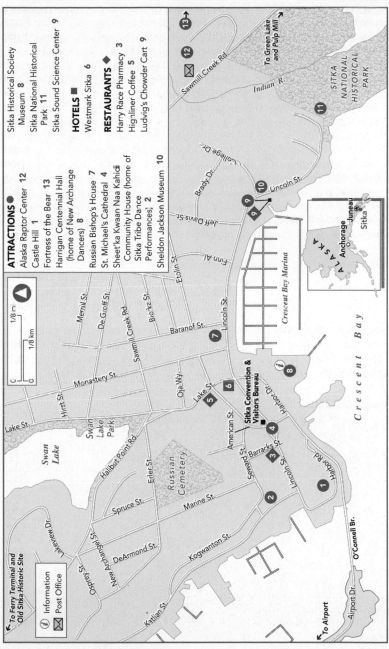

**ATTRACTIONS** ●
Alaska Raptor Center **12**
Castle Hill **1**
Fortress of the Bear **13**
Harrigan Centennial Hall
(home of New Archange
Dancers) **8**
Russian Bishop's House **7**
St. Michael's Cathedral **4**
Sheet'ka Kwaan Naa Kahidi
Community House (home of
Sitka Tribe Dance
Performances) **2**
Sheldon Jackson Museum **10**

Sitka Historical Society
Museum **8**
Sitka National Historical
Park **11**
Sitka Sound Science Center **9**

**HOTELS** ■
Westmark Sitka **6**

**RESTAURANTS** ◆
Harry Race Pharmacy **3**
Highliner Coffee **5**
Ludvig's Chowder Cart **9**

Step off your cruise ship here, and you step into the Russian Alaska of yesteryear. This is where, in 1799, trader Alexander Baranof established a fort in what became known as New Archangel. Today **St. Michael's Cathedral,** with its striking onion-shaped dome and ornate gilt interior, reflects that heritage, as does the all-female troupe the **New Archangel Dancers,** who perform during the cruise season in **Harrigan Centennial Hall.** The colorfully costumed, 30-strong troupe performs a program of energetic Russian folk dances several times a day. The New Archangel Dancers sometimes get together with a Tlingit dance troupe for a joint performance in the Sheet'ka Kwaan Naa Kahidi Community House on Katlian Street.

Most attractions in Sitka are within walking distance of the passenger docks. The **Sitka National Historical Park,** a must-do attraction with its impressive (mostly reproduction) totem poles and excellent views, is about a 10-minute walk from the passenger docks. One attraction that's a bit of a hike (just over a mile from downtown), but should not be missed, is the **Alaska Raptor Rehabilitation Center.** A nonprofit venture, the center opened in 1980 to treat sick or injured birds of prey (primarily eagles) and to provide an educational experience for visitors. We don't mind admitting that the sight of our majestic national bird close up, with its snowy white head and curved beak, gives us goosebumps. Go as part of a shore excursion or on the visitors' shuttle bus (See "Coming Ashore," below).

Every year from early June to early July, this town of just under 9,000 year-round residents hosts a celebration of chamber music, performed by world-class practitioners of the art in various halls throughout the town. The **Sitka Summer Music Festival** has been held since 1972. Performances are day and evening; admission prices vary. We recommend it as a perfect complement to the more frenzied, more modern entertainment found on cruise ships. All this culture is particularly impressive when you consider Sitka has as many boats as people.

Despite visits by big cruise ships several times a week (the town also serves as an embarkation point for small ships like those of Alaskan Dream Cruises), Sitka somehow manages to keep a quaint, small-town ambience. Walking along the harbor filled with fishing boats (and pleasure boats, too) you can catch conversations about the weekly fish count.

If you get the munchies, stop by **Ludvig's Chowder Chart,** a street cart located in the Mill Building adjacent to the Sitka Sound Science Center and serving Ludvig's fantastic spicy clam chowder (spicy sausage is the "secret" ingredient). **Harry Race Pharmacy,** 106 Lincoln St., has a cool 1950s-style soda fountain (and also serves ice cream). At the **Westmark Sitka,** at 330 Seward St., you can get a fancier restaurant meal (such as crab mac & cheese) inside or on the sea-view deck. **Highliner Coffee,** in the backside of Seward Square Mall (327 Seward St.), has lattes, other coffee drinks, and excellent baked goods (try the giant oatmeal cookies); it also has computers you can use (for a fee) to e-mail your friends back home. You'll also find free Wi-Fi at the public library across the parking lot from the pier (next to Centennial Hall).

Nearly all the shops in Sitka are locally owned, or at least owned by Alaskans. One of Fran's favorite shops on the whole Southeast route is the locally owned **Sitka Rose Gallery** (*©* **888/236-1536** or 907/747-3030; www.sitkarosegallery.com), in a pretty Victorian house at 419 Lincoln St. The gallery features the works of more than 100 Alaskan artists (no made-in-Taiwan merchandise here) at prices that are more reasonable than at bigger ports such as Ketchikan. The **Winter Song Soap Company** shop (© **888/819-8949** or 907/747-8949; www.wintersongsoap.com) sells soaps in such fragrances as Alaskan Herbs & Flowers from a new location at 321 Lincoln Rd. (if you like what you buy here, you can replenish your supplies online). Also new as of last year, Tlingit woodcarver Tommy Joseph (© **907/623-0705** or 907/738-3856) has opened **Raindance Gallery,** selling his and other artist's works, at his studio at 205 Monastery St. (behind the Russian Bishop's House).

For those who need to know such things, although the Sandra Bullock/Ryan Reynolds movie *The Proposal* was supposed to be set in Sitka, it was mostly shot in Maine.

**COMING ASHORE** If you arrive by tender, you'll be dropped off within walking distance of the downtown area. Sitka is so small and the heart of town so close to the passenger pier that it's ideal for exploring on foot. But shuttle buses (all-day pass $10) are also available to ferry you to local sights—such as the Raptor Center, for instance, which is not within walking distance. If you arrived at the ferry dock, it's about 3 miles from downtown. You can hop a bus into town, and taxis are also available.

**INFORMATION** Volunteers staff kiosks when cruise ships are in town at the O'Connell Bridge tendering area and at the city-operated **Harrigan Centennial Hall Visitor Center,** next to the Crescent Boat Harbor at 330 Harbor Dr. (© **907/747-3225**). The hall is open Monday through Friday 8am to 10pm, Saturday 8am to 5pm, and sometimes Sunday. Stop by the small museum operated by the Sitka Historical Society to see a scale model of how Sitka looked in 1867 at the time of the Alaska Purchase (when land was transferred from Russia to the United States).

## Best Cruise-Line Shore Excursions

**Artist Walk** (2½ hr.; $60; minimum age 14): Go with a guide to several galleries for demonstrations in woodcarving, jewelry making, and ceramics. Includes time at Wild Arts Gallery & Studio, where glassblowers show you how to make a take-home souvenir.

**Dry Suit Snorkel** (2½ hr.; $135; $89 children; minimum age 12): Keep your street clothes on, strap on a dry suit, and get in the water to view colorful starfish, crabs, and sea anemones. Time in the water is less than an hour (maximum weight 240 lbs.).

**4×4Wilderness Adventure** (4½ hr.; $243): Board a boat for a ride through the islands of Sitka Sound, and then, on Kruzof Island, drive yourself off-road (following a guide) on a two-person Yamaha Rhino. You'll explore temperate rainforest and may spot brown bears.

**Russian Sitka & New Archangels Dance Performance** (3½ hr.; $49 adults, $34 children): This motorcoach excursion hits all the historic sites, including St. Michael's Cathedral, the Russian Cemetery, Castle Hill, and Sitka's National Historical Park, with its totem poles and forest trails, and returns for the dance extravaganza at Harrigan Centennial Hall.

**Salmon or Halibut Fishing** (4 hr./7½; $250/$485): An experienced captain guides your fully equipped boat to a good spot for halibut and salmon; the rest is up to you. Your catch can be frozen or smoked and shipped to your home if you wish. *Note:* A $10 fishing license and a $10 king salmon tag are extra.

**Sea Otter & Wildlife Quest** (3 hr.; $128 adults, $87 children): A naturalist accompanies passengers on this jet-boat tour to point out the various animals you'll encounter and explain the delicate balance of the region's marine ecosystem. They're so sure you'll see a whale, bear, or otter that they offer partial cash refunds if you don't. A 4½-hr. version of the tour adds a visit to the Alaska Raptor Center ($142 adults, $103 children).

## Excursions Offered by Local Operators

Owned by the Sitka Tribe of Alaska, **Tribal Tours** (© **907/747-7290;** www.sitkatours. com) offers a cultural tour program that relates the history of Sitka, with an emphasis on Native history and culture. Tickets can be purchased at the pier (they try to have a staffer there when ships come in) or at the **Sheet'ka Kwaan Naa Kahidi Community House,** at 200 Katlian St. (near the tender docks). A 2½-hour comprehensive tour, priced at $58 for adults and $47 for children, includes a 45-minute narrative drive, a half-hour stop at the Sheldon Jackson Museum, a stop at the Sitka National Historical Park, and a performance by the Tlingit Indian Dance Troupe (not to be confused with the New Archangel Dancers).

**Sitka Sound Ocean Adventures** (© **907/752-0660;** www.ssoceanadventures.com) provides rentals for those experienced in sea kayaking ($50 single or $65 double for a half-day) and tours for beginners or advanced kayakers ($79 adults, $49 children 6–12 for a 2½-hr. tour; longer tours also available) and will pick you up at the pier.

## On Your Own: Within Walking Distance

**Castle Hill ★★★** At first we found the prospect of a climb up to the top of the hill—by way of a lengthy flight of stairs from the western end of Lincoln Street—a little daunting, but after climbing to the top, we have two words of advice: Do it. The reward is panoramic views of downtown Sitka. This is where the first post–Alaska Purchase U.S. flag was raised, in 1867. It was also on this site, in the 1830s, that the marauding Russians drove off the resident Kiksadi clan of Tlingit Indians and built a stronghold from which to conduct their fur-trading business. The last of the buildings within the walls of the stronghold was used by the first Russian American governor and was called Baranof's Castle (hence: Castle Hill). The structure burned some 60 years later, and its remains can still be seen, along with a lot of other reminders of those pre-Purchase days. Castle Hill is a National Historic Landmark, managed by the Alaska State Parks Department.

Climb stairs near intersection of Lincoln and Katlian sts.

**New Archangel Dancers ★★** Just watching the way these Russian folk dancers throw themselves around the stage makes us tired. Where do they get the energy? The dancers are all women—they even play the men's parts, complete with false beards if the dance requires it. When the troupe was organized in 1969, the men of the town pooh-poohed the idea. It'll never work, they said. Later, when the original handful of women proved that it could work, some of the men expressed the feeling that they wouldn't mind joining in. Too late, guys: The founders decided to keep the show all-female. The 30-minute show is presented at least twice a day and sometimes as often as four times most days in the summer, largely determined by the number of cruise ships in town.

In Harrigan Centennial Hall, 330 Harbor Dr., near the tender docks. (C) **907/747-5516.** www. newarchangeldancers.com. Admission $10 adults, $5 for children 12 and under. Check online or call for performance times, which change daily. Tickets go on sale about a half-hour before each show.

### Russian Bishop's House ★★

Owned and operated by the National Parks Service, this is the house where Bishop Innocent Veniaminov, born in 1797, translated scriptures into Tlingit and trained deacons to carry Russian Orthodoxy back to their Native villages. Veniaminov and his followers allowed parishioners to use their own language, a key element to saving Native cultures. The house was built in 1842, and a lot of history is shared on ranger-led tours. Exhibits downstairs trace the development of New Archangel into Sitka.

Lincoln and Monastery sts. No phone; call Sitka National Historical Park Visitor Center. (C) **907/ 747-0110.** www.nps.gov/sitk. Admission free to first floor; ranger-led tours (offered ever 30 min.) $4 per person, free for children 15 and under. Mid-May–Sept daily 8:30am–5pm; Oct–mid-May by appointment only.

### St. Michael's Cathedral ★

Even if you're not a fan of religious shrines, you'll be impressed by the architecture and finery of this rather small place of worship. One of the 49th State's most striking and photogenic structures, the current church is actually a replica; the original burned to the ground in 1966. So revered was the cathedral that Sitkans formed a human chain and carried many of the cathedral's precious icons, paintings, vestments, and jeweled crowns from the flames. Later, with contributions of cash and labor from throughout the land, St. Michael's was lovingly re-created on the same site and rededicated in 1976. A knowledgeable guide is on hand to answer questions. Sunday services are sung in English, Slavonic, Tlingit, Aleut, and Yupik.

At Lincoln and Cathedral sts. (C) **907/747-8120.** Admission $5. May–Sept Mon–Fri 9am–4pm; Sat–Sun varies (call in advance). Call ahead for hours other times of year.

### The Sheldon Jackson Museum ★★★

On the former campus of Sheldon Jackson College (which closed in 2007), this museum houses one of the finest collections of Native Alaskan art and artifacts anywhere. It's named for Presbyterian missionary Sheldon Jackson, who helped fund construction of the museum building—the first concrete structure in Alaska when it opened in 1897. Jackson also collected most of the artifacts, which date between 1888 and 1900. The glass cases in the main gallery house such treasures as a helmet worn by local Tlingit battle leader Katian, who fought off Russians in 1804—the helmet is covered in bearskin with a copper-eyed eagle on top. There are intricate beaded bags, impressive masks, amazing examples of prized Aleut baskets (so tightly woven they can carry water), and of waterproof gut and fish skin clothing from Northwest Alaska. If you have time, look for more in the exhibit drawers, which display smaller items such as ivory carvings. The museum is operated by the state. It also has a decent gift shop.

104 College Dr. (at Lincoln St.). (C) **907/747-8981.** www.museums.state.ak.us. Admission museum $5 adults, $4 seniors, free for youths 18 and under. In summer 9am–5pm. Closed holidays.

### Sitka Sound Science Center ★

In a rustic building across the street from the Sheldon Jackson Museum, the Sitka Sound Science Center, which also used to be affiliated with the college, is a research and learning facility that includes aquarium and touch tanks filled with local marine creatures. Kids especially will enjoy handling the brightly colored anemone and starfish. Outside is a salmon hatchery, and next door is an expansive gift shop and a stand selling **Ludvig's** signature clam chowder (see above) and sandwiches.

834 Lincoln St. ☏ **907/747-8878.** www.sitkasoundsciencecenter.org. Admission $5. Mon–Fri 9am–4pm, Saturday 10am–2pm.

### Sitka National Historical Park ★★★

At just 107 acres, this is the smallest national park in Alaska, but don't let that discourage you—the place breathes history. This is where the Russians and the Tlingits fought a fierce battle in 1804. Within the park are a beautiful totem-pole trail (which you can visit on your own or on a ranger-led tour) and a visitor center, where exhibits explain the art of totem carving and a 12-minute film talks about Sitkans past and present. The park is about a 20-minute walk from the farthest tender pier.

106 Metlakatla St. ☏ **907/747-6281.** www.nps.gov/sitk. Free admission. Visitor center mid-May–Sept daily 8am–5pm; Oct–mid-May Mon–Sat 8am–5pm. Park trails mid-May–Sept daily 6am–10pm; Oct–mid-May daily 8am–7pm.

### Sitka Tribe Dance Performances ★★

The Sheet'ka Kwaan Naa Kahidi, Sitka's Community House, stands on the north side of the downtown parade ground. It is a modern version of a Tlingit clan house, with an air-handling system that pulls smoke from the central fire pit straight up to the chimney. The magnificent house screen at the front of the hall, installed in 2000, is the largest in the Pacific Northwest. Performances last 30 minutes and include three dances and a story. It's entirely traditional and put on by members of the tribe. You can also sign up for tours and activities in the lobby.

200 Katlian St. ☏ **888/270-8687** or 907/747-7290. Admission $10 adults, $5 children 3–12 (2 and under free). Call for times.

## On Your Own: Beyond the Port Area

### Alaska Raptor Center ★★★

Local informational literature claims that the center is 20 minutes on foot from town, but these must be special Chamber of Commerce minutes, because it seems to take at least that long by bus. However you get there, though (and every cruise line offers it as a shore excursion), the center is well worth seeing. It's not a performing-animal show with stunts and flying action, but a place where injured raptors (birds of prey) are brought and, with luck, healed to the point whereby they can be returned to the wild. Some eventually can; those that cannot are housed permanently at the center or sent to zoos. Very few are euthanized. A flight-training center re-creates a little bit of rainforest in an aviary where recuperating birds learn to fly again. Visitors walk through in a tube with one-way glass so they can watch the birds without disturbing them. The tour through the center and on a wheelchair-accessible nature trail in the surrounding rainforest takes about an hour.

1000 Alaska Raptor Way (milepost 0.9), just across Indian River. ☏ **800/643-9425** or 907/747-8662. www.alaskaraptor.org. Admission $12 adults, $6 children 3–12. May–Sept daily 8am–4pm; Oct–Apr call for hours of operation.

### Fortress of the Bear ★★

This one-of-a-kind sanctuary opened in 2010 for orphaned Southeast Alaska Brown Bears—also known as grizzlies—provides visitors with a chance to view the creatures up close, in a ¾-acre re-created natural habitat. The organization is nonprofit, with an education and protection mission. A viewing area allows visitors to look into two holding tanks. The first residents were two male cubs found in a residential neighborhood, picking through trash, and three more young bears were later rescued (and cutely pose on cue). Research at the facility, which is about 5 miles from the tender pier (there's a shuttle), has been conducted by the Alaska Department of Fish and Game. The philosophy of project officials: Studying the bears in captivity can help wild grizzlies. For visitors, it's your best shot at seeing a grizzly in Alaska. The sanctuary also has a small gift shop.

Sawmill Cove Industrial Park. © **907/747-3032.** www.fortressofthebear.org. Admission $10 adults, $4 children 6–12, free for children 5 and under. Shuttle from the pier an additional $3. In the summer season daily from 9am–6pm.

# JUNEAU

Quick quiz: Can you name a state capital that cannot be reached by road from anywhere else in the state? Juneau, it is! Fronted by the bustling Gastineau Channel and backed by Mount Juneau (elevation 3,819 ft.) and Mount Roberts (elevation 3,576 ft.), the city is on the mainland of Alaska but is cut off by the Juneau Icefield to the east and wilderness to the north and south. To be sure, there are roads—150 miles of them, in fact—but they all dead-end against an impenetrable forest or ice wall.

In 1900, Congress moved the territorial capital to Juneau from Sitka, which had fallen behind in the flurry of gold-rush development. Not all Alaskans believe Juneau is the right and logical place for a legislative center. Its inaccessibility, some argue, disenfranchises many voters, and every few years somebody puts a "move the capital" initiative on the ballot. So far, all the proposals have been defeated. Among Juneau's 33,000 residents, government is the city's biggest industry. However, tourism is not far behind: Besides the thousands of independent visitors who arrive by air and ferry, many more thousands more come ashore during the 500 or so passenger-ship port calls made here each summer.

On any given day, four or five cruise ships might be in port, ranging from the biggest in the fleets of Princess, Celebrity, Holland America, and others, to the small ships. The small ships and most of the large ships usually find a dock, but depending on how many large ships are in port on any given day, some might have to anchor in the channel and tender their guests ashore.

While the city is dependent on tourism, not everyone loves the crowds, and it's easier to grasp the residents' unhappiness when you think of the number of cruise passengers who pour into the city. We were in Juneau once on a day when there were so many ships in port—four of the biggest plus two smaller vessels, as we recall—that there might have been as many as 10,000 cruise visitors in town.

This may explain why plans to expand with floating docks to handle more ships have been the subject of great debate and keep getting delayed. Other construction projects are flourishing, however. On a visit last year it seemed like half the city was under construction—including the **Alaska State Museum,** which is getting a huge addition and will be closed until 2016.

Juneau is a product of Alaska's golden past. It was no more than a fishing outpost for local Tlingit Indians until 1880, when gold was discovered in a creek off the Gastineau Channel by two prospectors, Joe Juneau and Richard (Dick) Harris. To be accurate, the gold was discovered first by Chief Kowee of the Auk Tlingit clan, who, in return for 100 warm blankets (more important to him than gold) passed on the information to a German engineer named George Pilz. Surveying sites around the Inside Passage for mineral deposits, Pilz gave the hitherto unsuccessful Juneau and Harris directions to the spot described by Chief Kowee—and they couldn't find it! Only when Kowee accompanied them on a second expedition did they succeed in pinpointing the source of the precious metal—and the rush was on. Mines sprang up on both sides of the channel. So rich was the area's gold yield that mines continued to open for the next 3 decades, including the most successful of them all, the **Alaska-Juneau Mine** (aka the A-J), which produced a whopping 3.5-million ounces of gold before it closed in 1944. Head to **Perseverance National Recreation Trail** (the trailhead is about 1½ miles from downtown) to see remaining mine buildings.

Today Juneau is arguably the most handsome of the 50 state capitals, despite a glut of souvenir shops near the pier (where you can buy anything from "I Love Alaska" backscratchers to fur coats). The city runs with a mix of quiet business efficiency and easygoing informality. It has a good deal more sophistication to it than any city in Alaska outside of Anchorage.

Yet there is still the frontier-style **Red Dog Saloon,** 278 S. Franklin St. (© **907/463-3658**), with its sawdust floor and swinging doors, a memorabilia-filled pub (serving food and drink including Alaskan Brewing Company selections) whose old-time raucousness may be tempered by its pursuit of the tourist buck (and a location adjacent to the Juneau Police headquarters). Another place to enjoy a not-so-quiet drink is the bar of the **Alaskan Hotel,** nearby at 167 S. Franklin St. (© **800/327-9347**), built in 1913. On the National Register of Historic Sites, the Alaskan is Juneau's oldest operating hotel.

Juneau's must-do attraction, the **Mendenhall Glacier,** is at the head of a valley a dozen miles away. The glacier is one of Alaska's most accessible and most photographed ice faces. If your tummy is growling after a glacier hike, try the fish tacos or pizza topped with smoke salmon (or fancier salmon served on a cedar plank) at **Twisted Fish Company** (p. 188), right near the ship pier, behind **Taku Smokeries** (where you can purchase take-home salmon products). For something more casual, check out the bevy of outdoor stands in the pier-side parking lot near the public library. Or head to the increasingly famous **Tracy's King Crab Shack ★★★,** in a new location right on the ship pier, behind the **Trove** store. This is the place to try giant boiled crab legs and Tracy's famous crab bisque (so popular that she now provides ship-home service). When "Top Chef" filmed Season 10 in Alaska, the hosts couldn't get enough of Tracy's delectable crab, even waiting in line with the rest of her fans.

While a lot of the shops in downtown are clearly geared towards capturing the tourist buck, the **Juneau Artists Gallery,** in the Senate Building, at 175 S. Franklin St. (© **907/586-9891;** www.juneauartistsgallery.com), is staffed by a co-op of local artists and shows only the members' work: paintings, etchings, photography, jewelry, fabrics, ceramics, and other media. **Hearthside Books,** at 254 Front St. (© **907/586-1726;** www.hearthsidebooks.com), is locally owned and has a friendly staff that can help you pick a novel to read on sea days. It also has a good selection of Alaska books, including those on the gold rush and Native culture.

*Note:* Free public Internet access is available at the Juneau Public Library, the big concrete building on the left past the ship pier but before you get to the Red Dog. You can also get free Wi-Fi when you purchase something at the Silverbow Bakery, the oldest continuously operating bakery in Alaska, 120 Second St., next to the Silverbow Inn (p. 188).

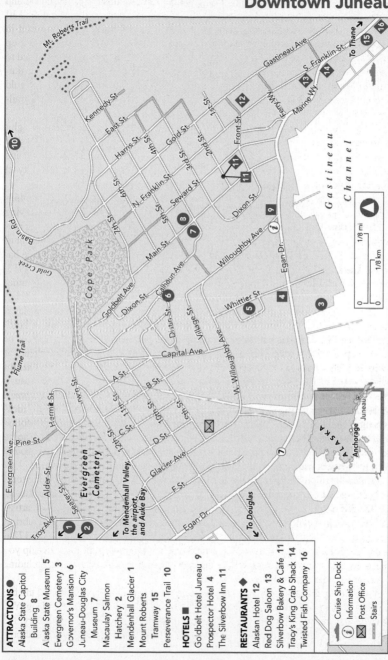

**ATTRACTIONS** ●
Alaska State Capitol
  Building **8**
Alaska State Museum **5**
Evergreen Cemetery **3**
Governor's Mansion **6**
Juneau-Douglas City
  Museum **7**
Macaulay Salmon
  Hatchery **2**
Mendenhall Glacier **1**
Mount Roberts
  Tramway **15**
Perseverance Trail **10**

**HOTELS** ■
Goldbelt Hotel Juneau **9**
Prospector Hotel **4**
The Silverbow Inn **11**

**RESTAURANTS** ◆
Alaskan Hotel **12**
Red Dog Saloon **13**
Silverbow Bakery & Cafe **11**
Tracy's King Crab Shack **14**
Twisted Fish Company **16**

Cruise Ship Dock
ⓘ Information
☒ Post Office
▨ Stairs

**COMING ASHORE**   Unless you arrive on one of the busiest days of the year, your ship will dock right in the downtown area, along Marine Way. The pier is directly adjacent to the downtown area, but shuttle bus service travels back and forth along the waterfront road. If you are at the far end of the pier, it is about a 20-minute walk to downtown, but you may find yourself even closer.

**INFORMATION**   Contact **Travel Juneau,** 800 Glacier Hwy., #201 (© **888/581-2201;** www.traveljuneau.com). A brand-new and impressively modern visitor center—with colorful tiles to resemble the scales of a salmon on the outside and a tall wooden ceiling resembling a fishing boat—is inside the cruise wharf. Stop in to pick up a walking-tour map and visitor's guide before striking out to see the sights. A smaller kiosk at Marine Park is open May through September daily from 8:30am to 5pm. The visitor center at the cruise-ship dock is open during the summer when the ships come in.

## Best Cruise-Line Shore Excursions

**Deluxe Mendenhall Glacier & City Highlights Tour** (4 hr; $99 adults, $59 children): Twelve miles long and 1½ miles wide, Mendenhall is the most visited glacier in the world and the most popular sight in Juneau. This trip will take you by bus to the U.S. Forest Service Observatory, from which you can walk up a trail to within a half-mile of the glacier (which feels a lot closer), or take one of the nature trails if time allows. After this you will visit Juneau's historic highlights; on some tours, you might also visit the Macaulay Salmon Hatchery, the Alaska State Museum, and other local attractions.

**Evening Whale-Watching Quest** (3½ hr.; $169 adults, $129 children): Combine whale-watching from a jet-powered catamaran in Stephen's Passage with an evening buffet and a chance to enjoy Alaska's summer twilight. You are guaranteed to see whales or you get your money back. Humpbacks are likely—this is a known breeding area—and orcas possible.

**Four Glacier Helicopter** (3½ hr.; $369): This thrilling trip is definitely not for those who are faint of heart or out of shape. The excursion involves a flight to the Juneau Icefield and to four glaciers found there. Some walking is involved (always in the company of a trained mountain guide). Accommodations may be made in advance for wheelchair-bound passengers, but generally a certain level of fitness is recommended—check with your cruise line for advice. An even more amazing version of the tour includes a dog-sled ride on the Icefield and costs $579.

**Glacier Flightseeing by Floatplane** (1¼ hr.; $215 adults, $179 children): Seeing the grand glaciers of Alaska is a thrill, and so is taking off and landing in the water in a floatplane. On this once-in-a-lifetime flight, you'll see five majestic glaciers of the Juneau Icefield. From your window seat, you'll also catch views of waterfalls and lush green rain forests. Expanded floatplane tours visit a remote, log-cabin-style lodge for lunch (3½ hr.; $299 adult, $255 child) or take fishing fans to a remote creek for fly-fishing (5 hr.; $429).

**Gold-Mine History Tour** (4 hr.; $59 adults, $35 children): Juneau's gold-rush history comes to life (especially for kids) as you visit the ruins of the Alaska Gastineau mine. Don a hard hat for a walk along a 360-foot tunnel and a demonstration of early-20th-century mining equipment and methods.

**Golf in Juneau** (5 hr.; $70): Golf at the private Mendenhall Golf Course, a 9-hole course designed by Tom File (and opened in 1986). The course serves up views of Mendenhall Glacier. Wildflowers add color in summer, and you can spot spawning salmon in a stream that runs through the course. Deer sometimes stroll across the green, and it's not unusual to spot eagles overhead. It offers challenges and bragging rights—you can say you golfed in Alaska.

**Mendenhall River Float Trip** (3½ hr.; $129 adults, $99 children): Board a 10-person raft on the shore of Mendenhall Lake, and an experienced oarsman will guide you out past icebergs and into the Mendenhall River. You'll encounter moderate rapids and stunning views and be treated to a snack of smoked salmon and reindeer sausage somewhere along the way.

**Whales & Glaciers Citizen Science Adventure** (5 hr.; $199 adult, $149 children): One of the coolest new offerings (particularly for science geeks) on this tour is getting a taste of what it's like to be a research scientist in the wilds of Alaska. You'll participate in a GPS time-lapse photo project documenting climate change at Mendenhall Glacier and then board a marine observation vessel to help record humpback whale and other marine-life behavior (whale sightings guaranteed; tour limited to 16 participants).

## Excursions Offered by Local Operators

At the pier, you'll find booths operated by various independent tour operators selling city and glacier tours starting at about $35 per person.

Ziplining in Juneau is provided through locally owned **Alaska Zipline Adventure** (𝕔 **907/321-0947;** www.alaskazip.com), which will harness you up to fly above the treetops for $149 for adults, $99 for children 10 and 11 (minimum age 10), for a 3½-hour excursion, including the ride. The company also offers combo zipline and mountain-bike tours and ziplining combined with an Alaskan feast.

## On Your Own: Within Walking Distance

**Alaska State Capitol Building** ★★★   We've often wondered how so lovely a capital city could come up with such an unprepossessing legislative home (ca. 1931), though the building is undergoing an extensive 4-year restoration expected to be completed around 2016. The interior is worth a visit to see the old-fashioned woodwork and interesting decorative details, especially in the lobby and legislative chambers. The governor's offices are on the third floor.

4th St. btw. Main and Seward sts. 𝕔 **907/465-3800.** Free admission. Summer Mon–Fri 9am–4:30pm (tours every half-hour).

**Evergreen Cemetery** ★   At this beautiful cemetery, which slopes toward the ocean, you can view the gravesites of Joe Juneau, Richard Harris, and other pioneers. The old Alaska Native graves are located in the wooded area on the far side of the cemetery.

12th St., just west of the downtown area.

**Governor's Mansion** ★   The six-pillar, 35-room mansion, also referred to as Governor's House, is located near the State Office Building, about 2 blocks from the State Capitol. The mansion was built and furnished in 1912 (at a cost of $40,000). The design is an interpretation of the New England style. The totem pole outside was carved in 1940 by Tlingit Indians and tells the story of the origin of the mosquito. The mansion is not open to the public; you can only drive past it. Local residents complain about bus-tour traffic near the mansion, which increased after Gov. Sarah Palin ran as vice president in 2008 and became a household name.

716 Calhoun Ave.

**Juneau-Douglas City Museum** ★ A Native basketry fish trap found in 1989 in the Montana Creek, about 13 miles from Juneau, and believed to be the oldest fish trap in existence, is the star attraction at this city museum. Exactly how it works is subject to debate. Other exhibits focus on the city's beginnings and industries, including mining and include a 30-minute video presentation. Hands-on exhibits are targeted to kids. A new gallery area highlights the works of Juneau artists.

Corner of 4th and Main sts. ⓒ **907/586-3572.** www.juneau.org/parkrec/museum. Admission $6 adults and age 13 and up, free for children 12 and under. Summer hours Mon–Fri 9am–6pm, Sat–Sun 10am–5pm.

**Mount Roberts Tramway** ★★★ The best place to take in Juneau's lovely position on the Gastineau Channel is an easy 6-minute ride in the comfortable 60-passenger cars of the Mount Roberts Tramway. Operated by Goldbelt, a Tlingit corporation, the tramway rises from a base alongside the cruise-ship docks and whisks sightseers 2,000 feet up to a center with a restaurant/bar, a gift shop, a museum, cultural film shows, a series of nature trails (bring mosquito repellent!), and a fabulous panorama. Don't miss it—but on the other hand, don't bother if the day is overcast: Some visitors have paid the fees for an all-day pass, reached the top, and been faced with a solid wall of white mist.

At the cruise-ship docks. ⓒ **888/820-2628** or 907/463-3412. www.goldbelttours.com. All-day pass $31 adults, $16 children 6–12, free for children 5 and under. May–Sept Mon noon–9pm; Tues–Fri 8am–9pm; Sat–Sun 9am–9pm.

## On Your Own: Beyond the Port Area

**Glacier Gardens Rainforest Adventure** ★★ Opened in 1998, this botanical garden was created in an area that had been decimated in a landslide. Privately owned, the garden has since expanded to 50 acres of landscaped gardens with alpine and other flowers and lush rainforest, including an eagle viewing area. A golf-cart shuttle takes you past the blooming flowers as you travel up Thunder Mountain, high above Gastineau Channel and past trees, waterfalls, and ponds. You can get to the gardens by city bus ($1.50 per ride) or cab (about $18 each way from downtown). There is also a greenhouse area with beautiful hanging plants, a gift shop, and a small cafe serving beverages and sandwiches (locals winter their plants here). Ships also sell prebooked tours to Glacier Gardens for those who prefer not to travel on their own.

7600 Glacier Hwy. ⓒ **907/790-3377.** www.glaciergardens.com. Admission $26 adults, $17 children 6–12, free for children 5 and under (includes guided 1½-hr. golf-cart tour). May–Sept daily 9am–6pm.

**Macaulay Salmon Hatchery** ★★★ About 2½ miles from downtown Juneau, the nonprofit Douglas Island Pink and Chum hatchery operates this visitor center to educate the public about Alaska's wild salmon. Catch a bird's-eye view of outdoor hatchery operations, with brief commentary by local guides, and then head inside the facility to see impressive saltwater aquariums filled with more than 150 species of local marine life, including a 5,000-gallon tank and touch tanks for those who want to get up close and personal with sea creatures. A new deluxe tour takes visitors to an incubation room where salmon eggs are hatched and a "raceway room" where hundreds of thousands of tiny king salmon mature before they're ready for saltwater. The museum gift shop sells both local art and salmon products.

2697 Channel Dr. (*) **907/463-4810** or 877/463-2486. Admission $3.25 adults, $1.75 children 2–12; "Nooks and Crannies" Deluxe Tour $11 adults, $5.25 children 11 and under. May–Sept Mon–Fri 10am–6pm, Sat–Sun 10am–5pm.

### Mendenhall Glacier ★★★
Mendenhall is the easiest glacier to get to in Alaska and the most visited glacier in the world. Its U.S. Forest Service visitor center has glacier exhibits, a 12-minute movie called *Magnificent Mendenhall,* and rangers who can answer any questions. Check out the trail descriptions and choose from several that'll take you close to the glacier and Nugget Falls. The easiest ones are the .3-mile **photo trail** (which takes about 20 min. and provides an excellent glacial photo op) and the .5-mile **Trail of Time,** a self-guided nature path (which takes about 1 hr. to complete). The 3.5-mile **Eastern Glacier Loop** follows the glacial trim line, with a lot of time in the forest. It takes about 2 hours and includes some moderate uphill climbing. If you hike, bring water, sunscreen, and bug spray. Bears occasionally are spotted in the forest; if you do encounter one, stand still but make a lot of noise.

Mendenhall is about 12 miles from downtown, and taxis and local bus services are readily available in town (the bus costs $1.50 each way; taxis about $25) for those who want to visit independently of a tour. If you take a taxi out, make arrangements with the driver to also pick you up—and negotiate a round-trip price before you leave. Or take the **MGT (Mighty Great Trips) Mendenhall Glacier Express,** a bus that offers roundtrip service between the pier and the door of the glacier visitor center for $16 adults, $8 kids 11 and under. No reservation is needed; just walk off the ship and get on one of the buses parked 50 yards away (just past the Mount Roberts Tramway). It's an old school bus painted bright blue—not necessarily the most comfortable way to go—but it has an advantage over city transportation in that it really takes you to Mendenhall Glacier, as opposed to dropping you off at the bus stop more than a mile away. Since it doesn't stop to embark and disembark riders en route, the MGT Mendenhall Glacier Express gets you there in 25 minutes; although the city bus is cheaper, the ride takes closer to an hour. The MGT bus also comes with commentary. Fran once had a Native American driver who shared such wisdom as: "Why does the bald eagle have a white head? Because the raven flies above."

Off Mendenhall Loop Rd. (*) **907/586-8800.** www.fs.fed.us/r10/tongass/districts/mendenhall. Admission to visitor center $3 adults, free for children 12 and under. May–Sept daily 8am–7:30pm.

# ICY STRAIT POINT, ICY STRAIT & HOONAH

Icy Strait Point wasn't on the map until 2004. The name was coined to describe a restored 1912 salmon cannery modified to handle cruise-ship traffic. It's located near the Tlingit city of Hoonah, the largest Tlingit settlement in Alaska with a population of about 800. Now with increasing attractions in the area—including one of the world's longest and highest ziplines—the once nonexistent place is getting visits from non-cruise travelers, too. The *Anchorage Daily News* named the Icy Strait Point ZipRider—an amusement park ride where you zip a mile down a mountain in 90 seconds—as a must-do attraction in the state. Cruise passengers who are on ships not calling at Icy Strait have the option of flying here on a shore excursion from Juneau. The place has become downright popular.

The concept is similar to what the cruise lines did in the Caribbean—with traditional ports (including Juneau) getting full to the gills, they encouraged the creation of new venues to get passengers off the ship and onto shore excursions.

Hoonah happens to be strategically located about 22 miles southeast of Glacier Bay National Park. Nature is the calling card here. We're talking prime whale-watching waters. Passengers aboard large ships may well be fortunate enough to see whales on their journey. Those in small ships or whale-watching excursions will have an even better chance, since the small ships have the luxury of going places where the bigger vessels can't, and their size and maneuverability make it possible for them to get closer to the whales.

Onshore around Hoonah is old-growth rain forest, and brown (grizzly) bear sightings are common. Bald eagles are frequently spotted overhead. Fishermen here angle for halibut and five species of salmon.

Blue-collar Hoonah may have just been "discovered," but the Huna Tlingit have resided here for thousands of years. Development-wise, the Northwest Trading Company came to town and opened a store in 1880. A mission and school were created shortly thereafter. The city got its first post office in 1901. Fire destroyed much of the city, including Tlingit artifacts, in 1944. The federal government led a rebuilding effort, and the city was incorporated in 1946.

The cruise dock, which receives tenders (small boats) from the big ships—which anchor nearby—was built by a 40-year-old Tlingit Indian corporation, Huna Totem Corp., owned by about 1,350 Alaska Natives with ancestral ties to Hoonah and Glacier Bay. It is now being visited on a regular basis (albeit one shipload at a time), by Royal Caribbean, Celebrity, Holland America, Princess, Regent Seven Seas, Oceania, and Norwegian.

The historic cannery dates to 1912 and operated up through the 1950s as a salmon processing facility—Hoonah was once one of the most productive salmon cannery towns in the state. Fishing and fish processing, along with logging, are still the mainstays of the economy in these parts, and tourism is catching on. If you find your tummy rumbling and seafood on your mind, indulge at the **Crab Station,** where you can eat fresh Dungeness crab that's come straight out of the water and into a pot; or at the new **Landing Zone Grill,** an outdoor spot offering wild Alaska salmon cooked to order—with views of people landing on the ZipRider.

**COMING ASHORE**   Cruise passengers are tendered into the dock right at **Icy Strait Point Cannery,** with its shops and restaurants. A new offering: Passengers stepping ashore are handed a wood chip and invited to place it in a fire on the beach, where a Huna Tlingit storyteller shares stories and local history.

**INFORMATION**   There is an information booth (no phone; www.icystraitpoint. com) at the dock. If you're a hiker, this is the place to ask for directions to local beach and forest trails.

# Best Cruise-Line Shore Excursions

**ATV Expedition** (2½ hr.; $159 adults and children; minimum age 8): Traverse the mountains of Chichagof Island in rugged fashion on a 4×4 expedition. You start high in the majestic mountains of Chichagof Island (after a drive by motorcoach through Hoonah). Your guide will provide a little area history and a brief orientation. Then you board a 4×4 Kawasaki Mule off-road vehicle and ride along a trail, taking in the Alaska wilderness, rain forest, and tremendous views of Icy Strait.

**Hoonah Sightseeing & Tribal Dance Combo** (2½ hr.; $79 adults, $39 children): Tour the quaint Alaska village, the largest Tlingit settlement in the 49th State. Your guide will explain the village's history, including how the Huna Tlingits had to flee advancing glaciers, and describe modern Native life. Then see dancers perform in full regalia at the Native Theater, telling the story of the Tlingits. Learn about the ancient significance of the raven and the eagle.

**Remote Wildlife & Brown Bear Search** (2½ hr.; $110; minimum age 10): Explore the wilds of Chichagof Island in search of grizzlies. Your motorcoach travels through Hoonah en route to the bush country of the Spasski River Valley. Learn about the local flora and fauna on a short hike along gravel and boardwalk-lined paths through a rainforest to viewing platforms overlooking the Spasski River. Keep your eyes out for bears, salmon, bald eagles, and more, though sightings, of course, are not guaranteed.

**Whales & Marine Mammals** (2½ hr.; $168 adults, $105 children): Whale sightings are actually guaranteed on this boat cruise to St. Adolphus, about 12 miles from Icy Strait Point. The area is considered one of the best locations for humpback-whale-watching in Alaska, if not the world. The operators are so sure you'll see whales (and maybe even orcas), they offer a return of $100 per guest if you don't (but that's never happened, at least not in the first 6 years of operation). A naturalist is on board to point out other wildlife, including sea lions, eagles, and porpoises.

**Ziprider Adventure** (1½ hr.: $129; weight restricted to between 90–275 lbs.): Ride on the world's longest zipline, 5,330 feet long with a 1,300-foot vertical drop, at speeds of up to 60 miles per hour. The highest point is 300 feet above the ground. If you dare to look down, you'll enjoy views of Port Fredrick, Icy Strait, and your cruise ship. You're harnessed in a seat for this ride; no skill is required.

## Excursions Offered by Local Agencies

The setup in Icy Strait Point is tightly controlled by the Hoonah Totem Native Corporation. Tours are offered only in advance, through the cruise lines.

## On Your Own: Within Walking Distance

**Icy Strait Point Cannery** ★★★ Beautifully restored and reopened in 2004, the historic cannery, located right where you get off the tender, once was one of the most productive salmon canneries in the state. Its halls are filled with family-owned shops and a museum with a 1930s cannery display, as well as a cultural center. Tlingit carvers can be observed working on carvings for a longhouse. The original cookhouse is open for family-style dining. All the shops are owned by Alaskans, and you can find local crafts and clever tourist items like handmade soaps and candles. You even can have a message canned and shipped to friends back home. A local Native craft market features a number of artisans.

## On Your Own: Beyond the Port Area

Hoonah, meaning "village by the cliff," is the largest Tlingit Indian village in Alaska, and it's just about a mile from the pier. It's an unspoiled little town that sustains itself mostly on fishing and logging. The wilderness is so close that, as you walk along the bay, you'll likely see eagles flying overhead; you may even spot whales from the pier. The town has grocery and hardware stores catering to locals. The atmosphere is much different than in ports used for the tourist trade. Some visitors may like that; others may not. But this is a chance to catch a glimpse of real Alaskan life.

# GLACIER BAY NATIONAL PARK & PRESERVE

Alask has an estimated 100,000 glaciers, 616 officially named. So what's all the fuss about Glacier Bay? Theories on its popularity abound. Some think it's the wildlife, which includes humpback whales, bears, Dall sheep, seals, and more. Some think it's the history of the place: It was frozen behind a mile-wide wall of ice until about 1870; a mere 55 years later, it was designated as a national park, along with its 3.3-million surrounding acres. The glaciers are thought to be some of the fastest-moving in the world, some retreating and others advancing. Whatever the reason, Glacier Bay has taken on an allure not achieved by other glacier areas.

The first white man to enter the vast (60-plus-mile) Glacier Bay inlet was naturalist **John Muir** in 1879. Just 100 years earlier, when Capt. James Cook and, later, George Vancouver sailed there, the mouth was still a wall of ice. Today all that ice has ebbed back, leaving behind a series of inlets and glaciers whose calving activity entertains hundreds of cruisers lining the rails as their ships sit for several hours. It can take 200 years for ice to reach the point where it falls off the face of a glacier.

Each ship that enters the bay takes aboard a park ranger. The ranger provides commentary about glaciers, wildlife, and the bay's history over the ship's PA system throughout the day. On large ships, the ranger may also give a presentation in the show lounge about conservation; on small ships, he or she will often be on deck throughout the day, available for questions.

Glacier Bay is the world's largest protected marine sanctuary. The bay is so vast that the water contained within its boundaries would cover the state of Connecticut. The bay is a source of concern for environmentalists, who would like to see cruise ships banned from entering or at least have their access severely curtailed. Ship operators, on the other hand, argue that no evidence shows that their vessels have any negative impact on the wildlife.

The park has numerous glaciers: 16 major tidewater glaciers (those that go all the way to the water) and 30 valley or alpine glaciers (those that compress between two hills but don't extend all the way to the water). In Tarr Inlet, at the Alaska/Canada border, two notable glaciers meet—Margerie and Grand Pacific. Margerie, on the Alaska side, is pristine white and very active, calving frequently; Grand Pacific, on the Canadian side of the line, is black, gritty and not particularly active.

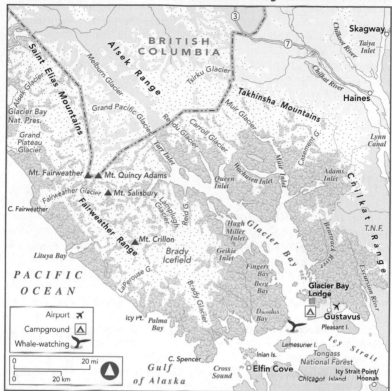

Visible from much of the bay (on a clear day) is massive Mount Fairweather (elevation 15,320 ft.). Although Fairweather is taller than any mountain in the Lower 48, it ranks no higher than 19th among Alaska's peaks.

# HAINES

This pretty, laid-back port is an example of Alaska the way you probably thought it would be. It's a small, scenic town with wilderness at its doorstep and only two stop signs. If you're not on one of the few ships that regularly visit Haines (pop. 2,600), you can easily reach the port on a day excursion from **Skagway.** The two communities lie at the northern end of the Lynn Canal, just 17 miles apart by water (350 miles by driving). The trip takes only about 45 minutes by fast ferry and is priced round-trip at $68 for adults, $34 for children (© **888/766-2103;** www.hainesskagwayfastferry.com). It's well worth taking, especially for those who have "done" Skagway before. But make sure to check return times so you get back to your ship on time.

The thing that's immediately striking about Haines is its setting, one of the prettiest in Alaska. The village lies in the shadow of the Fairweather Mountain Range, about 80 or so miles north of Juneau and on the same line of latitude as the lower reaches of Norway. Framed by high hills, it is more protected from the elements than many other Inside Passage ports.

Haines was established in 1879 by Presbyterian missionary S. Hall Young and naturalist John Muir as a base for converting the Chilkoot and Chilkat Tlingit tribes to Christianity. They named the town for Mrs. F. E. Haines, secretary of the Presbyterian National Committee, who raised the funds for the exploration. The natives called it *Da-Shu*, the Tlingit word for "end of the trail." Traders knew the place as Chilkoot. The military, which came later and built a fort here in 1903, knew it as Fort Seward or Chilkoot Barracks. In 1897 and 1898, the town became one of the lesser-known access points (it was less popular than Skagway and Dyea) to a route to the Klondike; it was located at the head of what became known as the Jack Dalton Trail into Canada. At about the same time, gold was discovered much closer to home—in Porcupine, just 36 miles away—drawing even more prospectors to Haines. The gold quickly petered out, though, and Porcupine is no more.

The **old fort** still stands. After World War II, and 42 years of service, it was decommissioned, but a group of veterans once stationed at Chilkoot Barracks would not let the fort die. In 1947 they bought the 85 buildings standing on 400 acres. They built a salmon smokehouse, a furniture-making plant, and other business ventures. They built the **Hotel Hälsingland,** established art galleries, and funded Indian arts training programs for local youngsters.

The **Officers' Club Lounge** in the Hotel Hälsingland is a nice place to stop for a libation. It serves Alaskan and Yukon beers and a house special known as the Fort Seward Howitzer. The descendants of some of these modern-day pioneers still live in homes that their fathers and grandfathers built on the fort grounds. Designated a National Historic Site by the U.S. government in 1972, **Fort William Seward** should be a must-see on your list.

Haines is so small that it can be covered on foot. You can see almost everything in 1 to 2 hours of reasonably flat walking. A few shops are worth a diversion, including **Fun Guy Foraged Products** at 121 2nd Ave. (© **907/766-2992**), operated by a California transplant and featuring such gourmet items as dried Chilkat Valley mushrooms (including porcini and chanterelles) and local honey.

In addition to gold, military history, and Native heritage, the thing drawing visitors to Haines is eagles. The area is a magnet for these magnificent creatures—a couple hundred are year-round residents. Unfortunately, cruise passengers are unable to experience the annual **Gathering of the Eagles,** which occurs in winter (usually Oct until mid-Feb) and brings as many as 4,000 birds from all over the Pacific Northwest to the area in search of salmon. During this time, trees along a 5-mile stretch of the river (in an area known as the **Alaska Chilkat Bald Eagle Preserve**) are thick with these raptors—often a dozen or more sharing a limb. But even during the cruise season, you're likely to spot at least an eagle or two. We once spotted eight in various swooping and tree-sitting poses on a bike ride out to Chilkoot Lake (about 10 miles from the cruise-ship pier).

**COMING ASHORE**   Haines has a fairly new dock for ships. Some smaller ships also come into the Native American–owned ferry terminal, which has a small shop selling souvenirs. A long-discussed plan to add more bathroom and parking facilities to the terminal has been hotly contested by local residents who don't want to give up

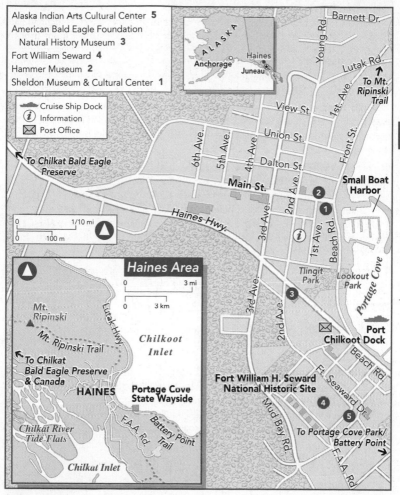

# Haines

Alaska Indian Arts Cultural Center **5**
American Bald Eagle Foundation
  Natural History Museum **3**
Fort William Seward **4**
Hammer Museum **2**
Sheldon Museum & Cultural Center **1**

Cruise Ship Dock
(i) Information
⊠ Post Office

To Chilkat Bald Eagle Preserve

Barnett Dr.
Young Rd.
Lutak Rd.
To Mt. Ripinski Trail
View St.
1st. Ave.
Front St.
Union St.
6th Ave
5th Ave
4th Ave
Dalton St.
Main St.
2nd Ave.
3rd Ave.
Small Boat Harbor
1st Ave
Beach Rd.
Haines Hwy.
(i)
**2**
**1**
Tlingit Park
Lookout Park
Portage Cove
3rd Ave
2nd Ave
**3**
⊠
Port Chilkoot Dock
Beach Rd.
Fort William H. Seward National Historic Site
Ft. Seaward Dr.
Mud Bay Rd.
**4**
**5**
To Portage Cove Park/ Battery Point
F.A.A. Rd.

0   1/10 mi
0   100 m

### Haines Area

0   3 mi
0   3 km

Mt. Ripinski
Mt. Ripinski Trail
Lutak Hwy.
Chilkoot Inlet
To Chilkat Bald Eagle Preserve & Canada
**HAINES**
Portage Cove State Wayside
Battery Point Trail
F.A.A. Rd.
Chilkat River Tide Flats
Chilkat Inlet

ALASKA
Anchorage   Haines
Juneau

**8**

THE PORTS & GLACIERS | Haines

the beach space to the facilities. Both docks are within walking distance of many of the town's main attractions.

**INFORMATION**   Pick up some walking-tour information on Haines at the **Haines Convention & Visitors Bureau visitor center,** on 2nd Avenue (© **800/458-3579** or 907/766-2234; http://haines.ak.us/visitor-information-center; open summer Mon–Fri 8am–5pm, Sat and Sun 9am–4pm). It's easy to explore the town on foot, or you can rent a bike at Sockeye Cycle, on Portage Street, right up the street from the cruise-ship dock (© **907/766-2869;** www.cyclealaska.com); it's $15 for a 2-hour rental, $25 for 4 hours, and $35 for the entire day. The shop also offers escorted tours.

# Best Cruise-Line Shore Excursions

**Chilkat Cultural Tour & Meal** (4 hr.; $159 adults, $99 children): Travel by bus for 22 miles on the Haines Highway, a national scenic byway, through the Chilkat Bald Eagle Preserve on your way to Klukwan, a small Alaska Native village. Here you'll visit a recently built replica of a Long House, see a performance by the local Jilkaat Kwaan Heritage Dancers, watch carvers, learn about smokehouse techniques, and have time to chat with Chilkat Tlingit people. Also included is a meal of salmon or chicken.

**Eagle Preserve Wildlife River Adventure** (3¼ hr.; $159 adults, $105 kids): A bus takes you to the world-famous Chilkat Bald Eagle Preserve, where you board small boats specially designed to traverse the narrows of the Chilkat River. Eagle spotting is the thing on this excursion, where you may also spy bears, moose, and beavers.

**Kroschel Wildlife Park** (3½ hr.; $139, $99 children): Steve Kroschel worked with wild animals for movies including *Never Cry Wolf* and the PBS "Wild America" series. At his private and interactive wildlife center, he now provides a home for orphaned and rescued critters including a Kodiak bear, moose, wolves (and wolverines), mink, reindeer, and more. Kids will love the fact many of the animals can be touched (also a great photo op). The drive to Kroschel's property is through the Chilkat Bald Eagle Preserve.

**A Taste of Haines** (1½ hr.; $79 adults and children): Sample some of the fresh products of Haines on this intimate tour, headed by a local guide. You'll visit Dalton City, a gold-rush town created for the 1989 Disney film *White Fang,* and tour Haines Brewing Company (with an annual production of only 350 barrels), sampling ales and stouts with the brewmaster. The tour also includes a visit to the Dejon Delights seafood shop in Haines to learn how the experts make smoked halibut and salmon. Samples are provided, and there's time for shopping.

**Wilderness Kayak Experience** (4 hr.; $119 adults, $59 children 7–12): Located as it is at the top of the Inside Passage, Haines is an ideal place for kayaking. A short bus trip will take you to the launch site, and the goal as you glide in your kayak is to see wildlife—depending on your luck, this might include humpback whales, porpoises, seals, sea lions, sea otters, moose, brown bears, and, of course, Haines' famous bald eagles.

## Excursions Offered by Local Operators

**Chilkat Guides,** on Portage Street (℗ **907/766-2491;** www.raftalaska.com), takes a rafting trip twice a day in summer down the Chilkat River to watch eagles. The rapids are pretty easy—there's a chance you may be asked to get out and push—and you'll see lots of eagles. The 4-hour trip includes a snack and costs $94 for adults, $65 for children. **Alaska Nature Tours** (℗ **907/766-2876;** www.alaskanaturetours.net) has a variety of escorted tours, including a 4-hour walking tour of the Chilkat Bald Eagle Preserve ($88 adults, $73 children 12 and under; lunch is included).

## On Your Own: Within Walking Distance

**Alaska Indian Arts** ★   Located in the old fort hospital on the south side of the parade grounds, the center has a small gallery and a carvers' workshop where you may be able to see totem-pole carving in progress.

On the south side of the parade grounds. ℗ **907/766-2160.** Daily 9am–5pm.

**American Bald Eagle Foundation Natural History Museum** ★★  Haines is proud of its position in prime eagle territory, and this natural-history museum celebrates the raptors. You can view live eagles (three bald eagles as of summer 2013) along with owls, hawks, and ravens in an enclosed aviary, and up close during live bird presentations by staff. In the main building is an impressively large diorama of the Chilkat Bald Eagle Preserve—all 48,000 acres.

113 Haines Hwy. (at 2nd Ave.), 2 blocks from the town center. ℂ **907/766-3094.** www.baldeagles. org. Admission $10 adults, $8 seniors, $5 children 8–12, free for children 7 and under. Mon–Fri 9am–5pm.

**Fort William Seward** ★★★  The central feature of the town, rising right above the docks, Fort Seward was retired after World War II and redone by a group of returning veterans. It's not the kind of place you think of when envisioning a fort. It has no parapets, no walls, no nothing—just an open parade ground surrounded by large wood-frame former barracks and officers' quarters that today have been converted into private homes, the Hotel Hälsingland, a gallery and studio, and the Alaska Indian Arts (see above). In the center of the sloping parade ground, you'll find a replica of a Tlingit tribal house. Also added—thanks to a local collector—is a harpoon gun on the parade grounds. It looks like a cannon and is fired on special town occasions.

The area is just inland from the cruise-ship dock. Open all day.

**Hammer Museum** ★★  You'll learn more uses for hammers than you ever imagined at this quirky museum. The collection was started by Dave Pahl, a longshoreman and hammer nut (he even constructed the giant hammer in front of the building). On display are more than 1,500 hammers from around the world, designed to do everything from bang nails to test the quality of cheese. Prized pieces in the collection include an 800-year-old Tlingit war hammer and an ancient Egyptian tool used around 2500 B.C. (donated to the museum by an archaeologist in 2008).

108 Main St. ℂ **907/766-2374.** www.hammermuseum.org. Admission $3, free for children 12 and under. Mon–Fri 10am–5pm.

**Sheldon Museum & Cultural Center** ★★  Named for a man who moved to Haines in 1911 (and not affiliated with the better-known Sheldon Jackson Museum in Sitka; see p. 211), this small museum has a collection that includes Tlingit artifacts, gold-rush items, and assorted Haines memorabilia. Those interested in traditional crafts will want to see the Chilkat blankets and baskets; those interested in local history, the historical photos. A guided tour of the displays is available on request. A rotating exhibit (that changes every 6 weeks) showcases the work of contemporary artists, giving insight into the local arts scene. A gift shop is on the first floor.

Corner of Main and Front sts. ℂ **907/766-2366.** www.sheldonmuseum.org. Admission $5, free for children 12 and under. Mid-May–mid-Sept Mon–Fri 10am–5pm, Sat–Sun 1–4pm; Mid-Sept–mid-May Mon–Sat 1–4pm.

# On Your Own: Beyond the Port Area

**Chilkat Bald Eagle Preserve** ★★★  Haines may be the best place in the world to see bald eagles. And this 48,000-acre park along the Chilkat River is ground zero for the species. From around mid-October to December, some 3,000 eagles reside here. But even during cruise season, you're likely to glimpse a few—a couple hundred live here year-round. The best viewing is on the Haines Highway, between miles 18 and 21. The preserve is managed by the Alaska State Parks.

ℂ **907/766-2292.** www.alaskastateparks.org.

# SKAGWAY

No port in Alaska is more historically significant than this small town at the northern end of the picturesque Lynn Canal. In the late 19th century, a steady stream of prospectors began the long trek into Canada's Yukon Territory, seeking the vast quantities of Klondike gold that had been reported in Rabbit Creek (later renamed Bonanza Creek). Not many of them realized the unspeakable hardships they'd have to endure before they could get close to the stuff. They first had to negotiate either the **White Pass** or the **Chilkoot Pass** through the coastal mountain range to the Canadian border. To do so, they had to hike 20 miles, climbing nearly 3,000 feet in the process, and, by order of Canada's North-West Mounted Police, had to have at least a year's supply of provisions before they could enter the country. Numbed by temperatures that fell at times into the −50s Fahrenheit (−40s Celsius) and often blinded by driving snow or stinging hail (they were, after all, hiking through mountain passes that gave Skagway its name—in Tlingit, *Skagua* means "home of the North Wind"), they plodded upward. They ferried some of their supplies partway up, stashed them, and then returned to Skagway before repeating the process with another load, always inching their way closer to the summit. The process took as many as 20 trips for some, and often enough, their stashes were stolen by unscrupulous rivals or opportunistic locals. Prospectors who thought themselves lucky enough to be able to afford horses or mules found their pack animals to be less than sound of limb. One stretch of the trail through the White Pass (the more popular of the two routes through the mountains) is called **Dead Horse Gulch.**

Arduous as it was, that first leg was just the beginning. From the Canadian border, their golden goal lay a long and dangerous water journey away, part of the way by lake (and, thus, relatively easy), but most of it down the mighty Yukon River and decidedly perilous.

The gold rush brought to Skagway a way of life as violent and lawless as any to be found in the frontier West. The Mounties (the law in Canada) had no jurisdiction in Skagway. In fact, there was no law whatsoever in Skagway. Peace depended entirely on the consciences of the inhabitants—saloonkeepers, gamblers, prostitutes, and desperadoes of every stripe.

The most notorious of the Skagway bad men was Jefferson Randolph "Soapy" Smith, an accomplished con man. He earned his nickname in Denver, Colorado, by persuading large numbers of gullible people to buy bars of cheap soap for $1 in the belief that some of the bars were wrapped in larger denomination bills. They weren't, of course, but the scam made Smith a lot of money. In Skagway he and his gang engaged in all kinds of nastiness, charging local businesses large fees for "protection," exacting exorbitant sums to "store" prospectors' gear (and then selling the equipment to others), and setting up a telegraph station and charging prospectors to send messages home (though the telegraph wire went no farther than the next room).

The gold-rush days of Skagway had their heroes as well. One of them, city surveyor Frank Reid, put an end to Soapy's reign; he shot Smith dead and was himself mortally wounded in the gunfight. In his honor, the local citizenry erected an impressive granite monument over his grave in the Gold Rush Cemetery; Smith's marker, on the other hand, is very simple, and his remains aren't even underneath it (they're 3 ft. to the left, outside consecrated ground). Perversely, though, it is the villain Smith whose life is

# Skagway

**ATTRACTIONS ●**

1898 Red Onion Saloon **10**
Case-Mulvihill House &
  Nye House **3**
Eagles Hall and
  Days of '98 Show **9**
Gault House **4**
Gold Rush Cemetery **2**
Historic Moore Homestead **8**
Jefferson Smith's Parlor **11**
Klondike Gold Dredge **1**
Skagway City Hall **7**
Skagway Museum & Archives **6**
Skagway Visitor
  Information Center **10**
White Pass and Yukon Route
  Railway **12**

⬛ Cruise Ship Dock
ⓘ Information
✉ Post Office

**DINING ◆**

Red Onion Saloon **10**
Skagway Brewing
  Company **5**

8

THE PORTS & GLACIERS | Skagway

commemorated annually on July 8, with songs and entertainment. The women of the gold-rush days are also given tribute—at least, those of ill repute—in a shore excursion called the "Ghosts & Goodtime Girls Walking Tour" (see below).

Unlike many other Alaska frontier towns, Skagway has been spared the ravages of major fires and earthquakes. Some of the original buildings still stand, protected by the National Park Service. The **Klondike Gold Rush National Historic District** contains some striking examples of these buildings. Other little touches of history are preserved around town, such as the huge watch painted on the mountainside above town—an early billboard for the long-gone Herman Kirmse's watch-repair shop. Also remaining from the old days is the White Pass and Yukon Route narrow-gauge railroad, opened in 1900 to carry late stampeders in and gold out. A ride on the train is a must for visitors. The round-trip to the summit of the pass, following a route carved out of the side of the mountain by an American/Canadian engineering team backed by British money, takes 3 hours from a departure site conveniently located a short walk (or an even shorter shuttle-bus ride) from the cruise-ship piers.

229

Having a sweet little historic town is nice for Skagway's 960 or so year-round residents, of course, but by itself, history doesn't pay the bills. So although Skagway is trying to hang on to its gold-rush heritage, it's also trying to make money off it. Businesses, including restaurants and jewelry stores (one shop even serves Starbucks coffee products!), have taken over much of the downtown, many of which have gold-rush connotations only in the sense that they've opened to cash in on visitors' "gold." We were rather shocked to see even a Harley-Davidson merchandise shop on a recent visit. (What's next? A Hard Rock Cafe?)

Clerks standing outside fancy jewelry stores that have followed cruise passengers here from the Caribbean stand in doorways urging passengers to come in, luring customers with offers of free charms and raffles. Step inside and you may be in for a hard sell—to make the sale, they may offer discounts, including a refund of sales tax.

For a respite from shopping, check out the beer and lunch specials at the **Red Onion Saloon,** which has been the town's honky-tonk since 1898 (look for the impressive façade made of thousands of pieces of driftwood at Broadway and 2nd Ave.), or, down Broadway at 7th, test the product at the **Skagway Brewing Company** (www.skagway brewing.com), one of the few places in town where you can check your e-mail; the signature Spruce Tip Blonde is brewed with spruce tree tips.

The shops in Skagway are mostly touristy, with many items made outside of Alaska (and most outside the country). But you can find high-end crafts, including Tlingit masks and silver jewelry, at **Inside Passage Arts,** at 340 7th Ave. (© **907/983-2585;** www.insidepassagearts.com). **Inspired Artworks,** 555 Broadway (© **907/983-3443;** www.inspiredartworks.com), also sells regionally made art, jewelry, and crafts.

**COMING ASHORE** Most ships dock at the cruise pier, at the foot of Broadway. But if a number of ships are in town, two other docks are available—the walk from those is no longer than 10 minutes, with shuttles provided. From the closest point, it's about a 5-minute walk from the pier across the train tracks to downtown, but shuttle buses are also provided. The only street you really need to know about is Broadway, which runs through the center of town and off of which everything branches.

After you've docked, take a few minutes to study the paintings of ships' and captains' names and dates, which cover the 400-foot-high cliffs alongside the pier. It's not graffiti; it is a genuine history of the development of the cruise industry in Skagway over the past 4 decades or more. All the paintings, mostly of shipline logos, were done by crew members from visiting ships. Some of the pictures are placed hundreds of feet up the cliffs. Local authorities have put a stop to it. For several years, it's been a case of "paint a rock, go to jail," and the rock face, which used to be so colorful, is beginning to fade without new creations. Occasionally, some enterprising crew members attempt to revive the tradition, but they are quickly shepherded away from the cliff.

**INFORMATION** Maps with routes for walking are available at the **Skagway Visitor Information Center** (© **907/983-2854**), at the Arctic Brotherhood Hall, 245 Broadway, between 2nd and 3rd avenues. Located in the restored railroad depot, the **National Park Service Visitor Center,** 2nd Avenue and Broadway; © **907/983-2921;** www.nps.gov/klgo), is the focal point for activities in Skagway. Rangers answer questions, give lectures, and show films; five times a day, they lead an excellent walking tour. The building houses a small museum that lays the groundwork for the rest of what you'll see. The park service's programs are free. The visitor center is open May through September daily 8am to 6pm, and during the rest of the year Monday through Friday 8am to 5pm.

# Best Cruise-Line Shore Excursions

**Eagle Preserve Float Adventure** (6½ hr.; $207 adults, $115 children 7–12): This outing combines a fjord cruise (45 min. to Haines) with a leisurely raft float (no whitewater rapids here) through the Chilkat Bald Eagle Preserve.

**Ghosts & Goodtime Girls Walking Tour** (2 hr.; $40; minimum age 16): Take a walking tour of Skagway's streets and back alleys, led by a costumed Red Onion madam, and end with a champagne toast at the infamous Red Onion Saloon. Be on the lookout for the brothel's resident ghost.

**Golden Glass-Blowing Experience** (3 hr.; $207 adult; $125 children; minimum age 7): Visit a working glass-blowing studio to learn how to blow or mold molten glass. You'll get to create your own ornament, complete with 24-karat gold.

**Gold Panning & Sled Dogs** (3 hr.; $89 adults, $69 children): Gold mining never actually happened in Skagway—it was only a transit point—but the town now gets more gold-rush tourists than any other place. This kid-friendly excursion combines the popular activity of gold panning with a lesson in how dogs played a part in the Klondike Gold Rush—with a dog-sledding demonstration and an opportunity to interact with Iditarod sled dogs and their puppies. You also suit up in a parka and snow boots to step into a cold chamber to experience what 40 degrees below zero feels like, at least for a few minutes. At the gold fields, costumed characters join the fun.

**Horseback Riding Adventure** (3½ hr.; $179; minimum age 12): Giddy-up on horseback to see the remnants of Dyea, once a booming gold-rush town, and explore the scenic Dyea Valley. Participants, of course, must be able to mount a horse and maintain balance in a saddle.

**Skagway Street Car** (2 hr.; $44 adults, $24 children): This is as much performance art as it is a historical tour. Guides in period costume relate tales of the boomtown days as you tour the sights both in and outside of town aboard vintage 1930s sightseeing limousines. Though theatrical, it's all done in a homey style, as if you're getting a tour from your cousin Martha.

**White Pass Scenic Railway** (3 hr.; $122 adults, $61 children 3–12): The train makes two round-trips a day, three on Thursday. The sturdy engines and vintage parlor cars of this famous narrow-gauge railway take you from the dock past waterfalls and parts of the famous Trail of '98, including Dead Horse Gulch to the White Pass Summit, the boundary between Canada and the United States. Don't take this trip on an overcast day—you won't see anything. If you have a clear day, though, you can see all the way to the harbor; you might even spot a marmot fleeing the train's racket. Or take the train to Fraser, BC (in Canada), and ride mountain bikes on the way back (4 hr.; $199). All the trains are wheelchair-accessible.

**Yukon Jeep Adventure** (5 hr.; $169 adults, $105 children): Retrace the steps of the gold miners along the Trail of '98 from the comfort of a four-wheel-drive Jeep Wrangler. Interactive headphones permit drivers in the convoy to keep in touch with guides as they describe the events of '98. The convoy passes all the historic gold-rush sights.

## Excursions Offered by Local Agencies

Independent tours, representing a number of operators, are sold at a tour center at 7th Avenue and Broadway. Tours are priced in the $45 to $55 range for a 2½-hour city and White Pass Summit tour by van. **Chilkat Cruises** (© **888/766-2103;** www. hainesskagwayfastferry.com) has a fast ferry that takes you to Haines in about 45 minutes. It runs several trips a day, costing $68 adults, $34 children 3 to 12. Introduced last year, the **Ultimate Zipline Adventure,** operated by Alaska Excursions (© **907/ 983-4444;** www.alaskaexcursions.com), picks passengers up at the pier and travels 9 miles to Dyea, where a course with 12 ziplines (up to 750 ft. long) and four suspension bridges offers thrills plus views of waterfalls and forest. For 4 hours, it's $169 for adults, $149 for children.

## On Your Own: Within Walking Distance

### The Case-Mulvihill House, the Gault House & the Nye House ★★★

All within a block of one another, these three buildings are striking examples of gold-rush-era Skagway architecture. You can view these three, from the street only, as part of a guided walking tour conducted by officers of the National Park Service.

The Case-Mulvihill House and the Nye House are on Alaska St., btw. 7th and 8th aves. The Gault House is on Alaska St., btw. 5th and 6th aves.

### Eagles Hall and Days of '98 Show ★★

This is the venue for Skagway's long-running (since 1927) *Days of '98* show, a live melodrama of the Gay '90s featuring dancing girls and ragtime music. Follow the events leading up to the historic shootout that led to the end of Smith's crime reign. Daytime performances are at 10:30am, 12:30pm, and 2:30pm, timed so cruise passengers can attend.

Southeast corner of 6th Ave. and Broadway. © **907/983-2545.** Daytime performances $20 adults, $10 children 12 and under.

### Historic Moore Homestead ★★

The Moore Cabin was built in 1887 as the home of Capt. William Moore, the founder of Skagway. The cabin was restored recently by the National Park Service.

5th Ave. and Spring St. Free tours early May–mid-Sept daily 10am–5pm.

### Jefferson Smith's Parlor ★★

Also known as Soapy's Parlor, Jefferson Smith's Parlor was a saloon and gambling joint opened by the notorious bandit in 1897. The building has been relocated twice, but it looks pretty much as it did at the time of Smith's death in a gunfight in 1898.

2nd Ave., just off Broadway.

### Skagway City Hall ★

This is not, strictly speaking, a tourist site, but as the town's only stone building, it's worth a peek.

Spring St. and 7th Ave.

### Skagway Museum & Archives ★

This small, city-run museum collects things significant to Skagway history. The eclectic displays include everything from a Tlingit canoe to a carving of a Moorish Queen (which used to sit in front of a cigar shop) to a 1931 Ford AA truck. It has items from the Klondike Gold Rush and some Native artifacts (including baskets and carvings), as well as historic photographs. The building dates to 1900.

7th and Spring sts. ✆ **907/983-2420.** Admission $2 adults, $1 students, free for children 12 and under. May–Sept Mon–Fri 9am–5pm, Sat 10am–5pm, Sun 10am–4pm.

## On Your Own: Beyond the Port Area

**The Gold Rush Cemetery ★★**   This is the permanent resting place of Messrs. Smith and Reid. The cemetery is small and is a short walk from scenic Reid Falls, named for the heroic one-time surveyor. Aside from Reid's impressive monument, most of the headstones at the cemetery are whitewashed wood and are replaced by the park service when they get too worn. You can get a good look at it from the White Pass & Yukon Rail carriages.

About 1½ miles from the center of downtown, up State St. (walkable if you have the time and inclination).

# HUBBARD GLACIER

Alaska's longest glacier accessible by cruise ships—it's about 76 miles long and 7 miles across—Hubbard lies at the northern end of **Yakutat Bay.** It also has a rather odd claim to fame: It is one of the fastest advancing glaciers in Alaska. So fast and far did it move about a dozen years ago that it quickly created a wall across the mouth of **Russell Fjord,** one of the inlets lining Yakutat Bay. That turned the fjord into a lake and trapped hundreds of migratory marine creatures inside. Scientists still can't tell us why Hubbard chose to act the way it did or why it receded to its original position several months later, reopening Russell Fjord.

Cruise ships in Yakutat Bay get spectacular views of the glacier, which, because of the riptides and currents, is always in motion, its visible 350-foot face (another 250 feet are below the waterline) calving into the ocean and producing lots of white thunder. It should be noted, however, that only one ship can get close to the glacier at a time, and if another ship is hogging the space, your ship may have to wait or may not get close at all.

# COLLEGE FJORD

College Fjord is in the northern sector of Prince William Sound, roughly midway between Whittier and Valdez. It's not one of the more spectacular Alaska glacier areas, being very much overshadowed by Glacier Bay, Yakutat Bay (for Hubbard Glacier), and others, but it's scenic enough to merit a place on a lot of cruise itineraries, mostly for **Harvard Glacier,** which sits at its head. On one visit, coauthor Fran got within 1,000 feet of the glacier on a Carnival ship, and it was calving every few minutes. What this means in terms of global warming aside, it was an unforgettable sight to behold.

The fjord was named in 1898 by an expedition team that opted to give the glaciers lining College Fjord and their neighbor, Harriman Glacier, the names of Ivy League and other prominent Eastern universities—hence, Harvard, Vassar, Williams, Williams, Yale, and so on.

# CRUISETOUR DESTINATIONS

No matter how powerful your binoculars, you can't see all of Alaska from a ship, and that's why the cruise lines invented the **cruisetour** (or what Holland America Line now calls Land + Sea Journeys): vacations that include a week on a ship and several days touring on land. In this chapter, we give you information on the most popular cruisetour destinations. See "Cruisetours: The Best of Land & Sea," in chapter 2, for a discussion of the various cruisetour packages offered.

## 9

# DENALI NATIONAL PARK & PRESERVE

This is Alaska's most visited—environmentalists say overvisited—national park area, with roughly 400,000 people a year coming by bus and train to soak up the park's scenic splendor. It used to be difficult to stay overnight anywhere in or near the park, but it's become easier in recent years with the opening of the Talkeetna Alaskan Lodge and the Princess McKinley Lodge—both with spectacular views of the Alaska Range and Mount McKinley (just be warned that both lodges are more than an hour's drive from the park's entrance). An addition to the McKinley Chalet Resort, located just north of the park, has brought the room count to 345 in the area. There also are rooms in nearby Healy, Alaska, and the Denali Princess just outside the park has increased its capacity. There are, however, times when demand for rooms in the area outstrips supply, so book early.

**Wildlife** is the thing in Denali: Somewhere in the realm of 169 bird species, 39 mammal species, and 758 vascular plant species are found there.

The **Alaska Railroad** operates a service daily between Anchorage and Fairbanks that passes just within the eastern boundary of the park, towing the private railcars of Holland America Line and Princess, as well as those of Royal Celebrity Tours (Royal Caribbean and Celebrity Cruises' joint tour product). You can do the tour in either direction. Eight years ago, the Alaska Railroad added its own domed viewing cars in addition to its more basic (but less expensive and perfectly adequate) carriages. The train stops at a station inside the park near the Denali Visitor Center.

Besides the wildlife, the focal point of the park is North America's highest peak, **Mount McKinley** (also known by its original Native name, *Denali,* which means "the high one"). You could argue that McKinley

# A mountain BY ANY OTHER NAME . . .

We've long been taught that the Athabascans of Interior Alaska called the mountain *Denali,* meaning "the high one." But at least one historian contends that the word *Denal'iy* actually referred to a mountain near Anchorage, now known as Pioneer Peak, and means "one that watches," and that the Native word for McKinley, "the high one," is actually *Doleika.* In any event, Alaska Natives only used the area for seasonal hunting, as in, no permanent settlements, and white men came only in search of gold. In 1896, a prospector named the mountain after William McKinley of Ohio, who was elected president of the United States that year.

All well and good, except that most Alaskans prefer the name Denali and since 1975 have petitioned to officially change it back. Ohio won't allow it. Although congressmen from Alaska and Ohio compromised on the issue in 1980, changing the name of the national park to Denali and leaving the mountain named McKinley, Alaskans have kept pushing for Denali. However, the U.S. Board on Geographical Names cannot consider an issue that is also before Congress, and the Ohio Congressional delegation repeatedly introduces a one-paragraph bill stating that the name should stay the same. This bill never goes anywhere, but just introducing it has been enough to thwart any name change. There is currently a bill that has passed the Senate to name it Mt. Denali.

comprises the two highest peaks in North America: Its south peak towers over the Alaska Range at 20,320 feet, while its north peak rises to 19,470 feet. Permanently snow-covered mountains dominate the surrounding expanse: Mount Foraker, which stands a mere 17,400 feet; Mount Silverthrone, at 13,320 feet; Mount Crosson, at 12,800 feet; and many, many more giant heaps. It's an awesome sight, even from a distance. You just have to hope you can see it.

As with all enormous mountains, the High One creates its own weather system, and hidden-from-clouds seems to be its favorite flavor. Sadly, it's possible to be in the area for days and never catch a glimpse of the Alaska Range. Trust us, though: When you finally see it in all its splendor, you'll realize that it's worth the wait. It is one of Gene's favorite Alaska views.

Most visitors experience the park by bus. Private vehicles are tightly restricted, for environmental reasons, and are allowed only to about mile 15 on the park road. That cuts down on your wildlife viewing chances. However, you can get a ticket on a park shuttle bus or sign up for a **Tundra Wilderness Tour,** both operated by the park concessionaire, which is allowed to operate much more deeply in the park. The tour buses have been upgraded in recent years to include drop-down video screens on which the driver shows live video of the animals you see along the road, allowing everyone a better view. The drivers of these buses are knowledgeable about the flora and fauna of the area. They always seem to be able to spot Dall sheep on the mountainside or caribou in the vegetation—even bears. When the wildlife is close enough, the driver/guide will ask for quiet so as not to startle the animals. And you'd better be quiet! The tour or shuttle ride demands a long day—about 8 hours in not particularly luxurious

# FIRST TO THE top

It's the biggest. That's why climbers risk their lives on Mount McKinley. You can see the mountain from Anchorage, more than 100 miles away. On a flight across Alaska, McKinley stands out grandly over waves of other mountains. It's more than a mile higher than the highest peak in the other 49 states. It's a great white triangle, always covered in snow, tall but also massive and strong.

The first group to try to climb Mount McKinley came in 1903, led by Judge James Wickersham, who also helped explore Washington's Olympic Peninsula before it became a national park. His group made it less than halfway up, but on the trip they found gold in the Kantishna Hills, setting off a small gold rush that led to the first permanent human settlement in the park area. Wickersham later became the Alaska Territory's nonvoting delegate to Congress and introduced the bill that created the national park, but the government was never able to get back land in the Kantishna area from the gold miners. Today that land is the site of wilderness lodges, right in the middle of the park.

On Sept. 27, 1906, renowned world explorer Dr. Frederick Cook announced to the world by telegraph that he had reached the summit of Mount McKinley after a lightning-fast climb, covering more than 85 miles and 19,000 vertical feet in 13 days with one other man, a blacksmith, at his side. On his return to New York, Cook was lionized as a conquering explorer and published a popular book of his summit diary and photographs.

In 1909, Cook again made history, announcing that he had beaten Robert Peary to the North Pole. Both returned to civilization from their competing treks at about the same time. Again, Cook was the toast of the town. His story began to fall apart, however, when his Eskimo companions mentioned that he'd never been out of sight of land. After being paid by Peary to come forward, Cook's McKinley companion also recanted. A year later, Cook's famous summit photograph was re-created—on a peak 19 miles away and 15,000 feet lower than the real summit.

In 1910, disgusted with Cook, four prospectors from Fairbanks took a more Alaskan approach to the task. Without fanfare or special supplies—they carried doughnuts and hot chocolate on their incredible final ascent—they marched up the mountain carrying a large wooden

vehicles—but if the weather holds and the viewing is good, it'll be the best $125.50 you ever spent ($57.75 for children 14 and under). The cost for the shuttle bus varies by the destination—from $26.25 to Tolkat (6 hr. round-trip) to $50 to the end of the road at Kantishna (12 hr. round-trip).

# FAIRBANKS

Alaska's second-largest city (after Anchorage) is friendly, unpretentious, and easygoing in the Alaska tradition, although its downtown area is drab and a little depressing. Fairbanks' major attraction is the ***Riverboat Discovery,*** 1975 Discovery Dr. (© **866/479-6673** or 907/479-6673; www.riverboatdiscovery.com), a three-deck stern-wheeler that operates 4-hour cruises twice a day throughout the summer on the Chena (*Chee*-nah) and Tanana (*Ta*-na-naw) rivers. The boat visits a re-created flagpole they could plant on top to prove they'd made it. But on arriving at the summit, they realized that they'd climbed the slightly shorter north peak. Weather closed in, so they set up the pole there and descended without attempting the south peak. Then, when they got back to Fairbanks, no one could see the pole, and they were accused of trying to pull off another hoax.

In 1913, Episcopal archdeacon Hudson Stuck organized the first successful climb to reach the real summit—and reported he saw the pole on the other peak. Harry Karstens led the climb (he would become the park's first superintendent in 1917), and the first person to stand on the summit was an Alaska Native, Walter Harper.

Although McKinley remains one of the world's most difficult climbs, about 10,000 people have made it to the top since Hudson Stuck's party. Since 1980 the number of climbers has boomed. Garbage and human waste disposal are a major problem. In 1970, only 124 made the attempt all year; now more than 1,200 try to climb the peak every year, with about half making it to the summit. The cold, fast-changing weather is what usually stops people. From late April into early July, climbers fly from the town of Talkeetna to a base camp at 7,200 feet on the Kahiltna Glacier. From there, it takes an average of about 18 days to get to the top, through temperatures as cold as –40°F (–40°C).

Climbers lose fingers, toes, and other parts to frostbite, or suffer other, more severe injuries. More than 90 climbers have died on the mountain, not counting plane crashes. During the season, the park service has a station for rescue rangers and an emergency medical clinic at the 14,200-foot level of the mountain, and a high-altitude helicopter is kept ready to go after climbers in trouble. In 2002, under pressure from Congress, the park service started charging climbers a $150-a-head fee, defraying a portion of the rescue costs. The park and the military spend about a half-million dollars a year rescuing climbers, and sometimes much more. The cost in lives is high as well. Volunteer rangers and rescuers die as well as climbers. Plane crashes, falls, cold, and altitude all take a toll. Monuments to those who never returned are in the cemetery near the airstrip in Talkeetna.—*Charles Wohlforth*

Indian village, a sled-dog training school, and an Athabascan Indian fish camp (with narration), and a flyby is performed by a bush pilot. The cruise costs $59.95 adults, $39.95 children 3 to 12, and free for children 2 and under. Sailings are mid-May to mid-September.

The Binkleys, the family that owns the stern-wheeler, also own **El Dorado Gold Mine,** off the Elliott Highway, 9 miles north of town (© **866/479-6673** or 907/479-6673; www.eldoradogoldmine.com). Here visitors can pan for gold and, while riding on the open-sided Tanana Valley Railroad, study the workings of the mine just as it was a century ago. It's hokey, for sure, but good fun, especially for youngsters. Tours, which run daily (call for times), are $39.95 adults, $24.95 children 3 to 12, and free for children 2 and under. If you buy the Gold Mine tickets at the same time as you do the riverboat cruise, you can save $2 a head off the combined price.

# denali CHANGES

Been to Denali before? If it's been a few years, you may be surprised by the changes to the park's visitor facilities, which have undergone a major upgrade over the past decade. Among the additions:

○ A complete rebuilding of the **Eielson Visitor Center**—the more remote of the two visitor centers in the park. Long a small and limited facility, the center was completely demolished in 2005 and rebuilt bigger (but more environmentally friendly) over several years, finally reopening in 2008. Located 66 miles inside Denali's borders and reached by shuttle bus only (cars are not allowed), it has new exhibits and viewing areas. The shuttle bus from the park entrance to the center costs $33.50 for adults and is free for children 15 and under.

○ The **Murie Science and Learning Center,** located near the entrance to the park, which doubles as a visitor center in the winter months (when the regular visitor centers are closed).

○ The **Denali Visitor Center,** near the entrance to the park, which includes exhibits and a theater housing an award-winning film, *Heartbeats of Denali*. The building has won kudos for its environmentally friendly design, including the use of integrated photovoltaic solar panels on its south-facing side and renewable and recycled materials for walls, ceilings, and carpeting. The center is open from mid-May to late September.

○ A revamped **transit center** near the entrance to the park (formerly the Visitor Access Center), where travelers board buses and get permits for campgrounds and backcountry tours.

**Pioneer Park** (formerly **Alaskaland**), at the intersection of Airport Way and Peger Road (*©* **907/459-1087**), is a low-key Native culture theme park with a couple of small museums, a playground, and a little tour train. It will never be confused with Disneyland. The park is open year-round, but the attractions operate only from Memorial Day weekend to Labor Day, daily from noon to 8pm. And the best part of all? Admission is free (for general admission; several of the museums charge a small fee).

Your cruisetour may include a tour of the gold mine or a visit to **Gold Dredge No. 8,** a huge monster of a machine that dug gold out of the hills until 1959 and is now on display for visitors. Shore excursions and cruisetours almost always include the *Riverboat Discovery* and the El Dorado Gold Mine.

# PRUDHOE BAY

Prudhoe Bay is at the very end of the Dalton Highway, also known locally as the Haul Road, a 414-mile stretch built to service the Trans-Alaska Pipeline. The road connects the Arctic coast with Interior Alaska and passes through wilderness areas that include all sorts of scenic terrain—forested rounded hills, the rugged peaks of the Brooks Range, and the treeless plains of the North Slope. The route provides lots of wildlife-spotting opportunities, with strong chances of seeing caribou, Dall sheep, moose, and bear.

But the real reason to come way up here is to view the **Prudhoe Bay Oilfield.** (Indeed, Prudhoe Bay is, essentially, a company town run by oil giant BP, with a population of just 50 people or so, give or take.) Although touring an oil field may not be high on your vacation must-do list, the bay complex is no ordinary oil field. It's a historic and strategic site of great importance and a great technological achievement. (And chances are, you'll be the only one on your block who's actually been there!) The industry coexists here with migrating caribou and waterfowl on wet, fragile tundra that permanently shows any mark made by vehicles.

One of the few ways to catch a glimpse of the oil field is via the **Arctic Ocean Shuttle tour,** which operates between late May and early September from nearby Deadhorse Camp to the Arctic Ocean and passes through the oil field. It is operated by Deadhorse Camp, which works with the oil-field security company to allow access. Reservations for the shuttle are made online through a **reservation system** (www. arcticoceanshuttle.com) and must be made in advance. The tour emphasis is on the Arctic Ocean and not the oil fields, and it would not be considered an industrial tour in that guests are not going into any buildings and are only on a very small portion of the oil fields. Shuttle trips are 1½ hours round-trip and depart from Deadhorse Camp at 9am and 3pm. Tickets are $49.

To get to the starting point, you usually drive the Dalton Highway one-way in buses and then fly back, with either **Fairbanks** or **Anchorage** being the other connecting point.

Two companies offer multi-night tours to Prudhoe Bay from Fairbanks. The **Northern Alaska Tour Company** offers a 3-day/2-night Arctic Ocean Adventure (fly/drive tour) from the city. Participants stay at Deadhorse Camp and take the Arctic Ocean Shuttle to the Arctic Ocean (www.northernalaska.com/arctic-ocean.htm). The **1st Alaska Outdoor School** also offers a 3-day/2-night Arctic Ocean/Prudhoe Bay trip from Fairbanks (driving both ways), also with a stop at the Arctic Ocean to let guests dip their toes into the (frigid) water (www.1stalaskaoutdoorschool.com).

Those wishing to drive to Prudhoe Bay/Deadhorse independently have two options for accommodations. The **Prudhoe Bay Hotel** (www.prudhoebayhotel.com) located in Deadhorse, only makes reservations for independent travelers 7 to 10 days out. The Prudhoe Bay Hotel has 180 rooms, but most are occupied by employees of the oil companies. Guests staying at the Prudhoe Bay Hotel who want to take the Arctic Ocean Shuttle would have to make shuttle reservations in advance and drive 2.5 miles south on the Dalton Highway to the Deadhorse Camp and depart on the tour there. The Prudhoe Bay Hotel does not offer any tours for guests.

**Deadhorse Camp** (www.deadhorsecamp.com) is located at mile 412.8 of the Dalton Highway—just before you arrive into Deadhorse. It has 12 rooms available for independent travelers, which usually fill up a few weeks in advance. Rooms accommodate two people. This is the starting point for the Arctic Ocean Shuttle.

*Be aware:* The drive to Prudhoe Bay is a long one over not particularly good roads, and it's not always terribly comfortable.

# NOME & KOTZEBUE

There's no place like Nome. Well, we had to say it. But, really, this Arctic frontier town is a special place, combining a sense of history, a hospitable and silly attitude (we're talking about a place that holds an annual Labor Day bathtub race), and an exceptional location on the water before a tundra wilderness.

What it does not have is anything that remotely resembles a tourist destination. Anthropological, yes; touristy, no. It's little more than a collection of beat-up residences and low-rise commercial buildings. It looks like the popular conception of a century-old gold-rush town—which isn't really surprising, because that's what it is. But if it seems to be in need of a face-lift, the inhabitants make up for all that with the warmth of their welcome. They're probably glad to see a strange face in the summer because they know they'll see precious few in the winter, when the weather turns ugly and the sun disappears for 3 or 4 months. There are local roads, but no highway link with the rest of the state.

The name Nome is believed to have been an error by a British naval officer in 1850, who wrote "? Name" on a diagram. The scrawl was misinterpreted by a mapmaker as "Nome." The population boom here in 1899 also happened by chance, when a prospector from the 1898 gold rush was left behind because of an injury. He panned the sand outside his tent and found that it was full of gold dust.

Undoubtedly, on your visit, you'll find time to try gold panning. The city also has a still sloppy, gold-rush-era saloon scene, as well as bargains on **Iñupiat Eskimo** arts and crafts.

Your tour will also visit **Kotzebue** (pronounced *Kot*-say-bue) to the north, one of Alaska's largest and oldest Iñupiat Eskimo villages. Here you'll tour the **NANA Museum of the Arctic,** run by a regional Native corporation representing the 7,000 Iñupiat who live in the northwest Arctic region.

To get here, you fly from Anchorage to Nome, then to Kotzebue, and then fly back to Anchorage, as part of itineraries that typically include an overnight in Anchorage and a visit to Denali and Fairbanks.

# THE KENAI PENINSULA

The Kenai (*Kee*-nye) Peninsula, which divides Prince William Sound and Cook Inlet, has glaciers, whales, legendary sportfishing, spectacular hiking trails, bears, moose, and high mountains. And it's easy to get to, to boot. At least it's not a long way from Alaska's tourist hub, Anchorage, and there's a good road to help you get there. The trouble is that there's an awful lot of traffic on it—not just from tourists, but also from Alaskan locals who drive down from Anchorage on weekends for outdoorsy pursuits. The traffic jams on Friday evenings and Saturday mornings, especially, can make the most jaded Los Angelenos forget the crush on the I-405 at rush hour, or New Yorkers the Lincoln Tunnel. Try to get to Anchorage a day or two before your cruise begins (or stay a day or two afterward) and make the trip in midweek. The scenery alone is well worth the effort. There are two main towns on the peninsula, Kenai and Soldotna, the former slightly bigger than the latter, but neither a major metropolis by any stretch of the imagination.

People from Anchorage come here for the weekend to hike, dig clams, paddle kayaks, and, particularly, to fish. There's a special phrase for what happens when the red

# The Kenai Peninsula & Prince William Sound

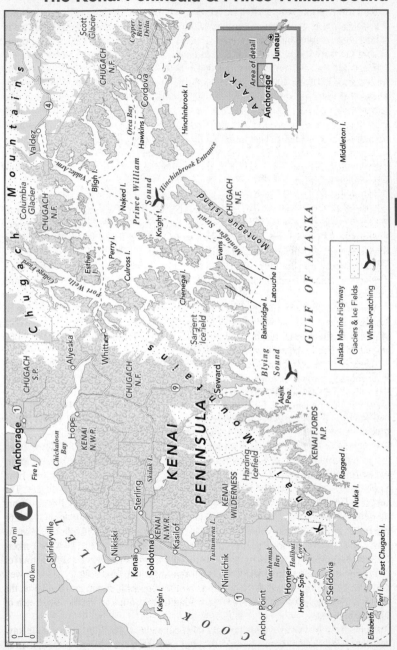

Area of detail

Juneau

ALASKA

Anchorage

Scott Glacier

Copper River Delta

CHUGACH N.F.

Cordova

Hawkins I.

Hinchinbrook I.

Middleton I.

Orca Bay

Valdez

Valdez Arm

Columbia Glacier

CHUGACH N.F.

Bligh I.

Naked I.

Prince William Sound

Hinchinbrook Entrance

Knight I.

CHUGACH N.F.

Montague Island

College Fiord

Perry I.

Esther I.

Culross I.

Chenega I.

Montague Strait

Evans I.

Bainbridge I.

Latouche I.

GULF OF ALASKA

C h u g a c h   M o u n t a i n s

Port Wells

Sargent Icefield

Alyeska

CHUGACH S.P.

Whittier

CHUGACH N.F.

Blying Sound

Anchorage

Hope

Fire I.

Chickaloon Bay

KENAI N.W.R.

KENAI N.W.R.

Seward

Aialik Pen.

Alaska Marine Highway
Glaciers & Ice Fields
Whale-watching

KENAI PENINSULA

K e n a i   M o u n t a i n s

Harding Icefield

KENAI WILDERNESS

KENAI FJORDS N.P.

Ragged I.

Sterling

Skilak L.

Shirleyville

Nikiski

Kenai

Soldotna

Kasilof

Tustumena L.

Ninilchik

Kalgin I.

Anchor Point

Kachemak Bay

Homer

Halibut Cove

Homer Spit

Seldovia

Nuka I.

East Chugach I.

Elizabeth I.

Perl I.

C O O K   I N L E T

40 mi

40 km

salmon are running in July on the Kenai and Russian rivers: **combat fishing.** Anglers stand elbow-to-elbow on a bank, each casting into his or her yard-wide slice of river, and they still catch plenty of fish (as well as, occasionally, each other!).

Cruisetours to the Kenai Peninsula include options for fishing, **river rafting,** and other soft-adventure activities.

You typically travel here by bus or rail from Seward or Whittier. Princess includes an overnight stay at its own Kenai Princess Lodge, a wilderness resort with a gorgeous setting on a bluff overlooking the river; other cruise lines provide overnight stays at other properties. Some tours combine a visit to Kenai Peninsula with an overnight in Anchorage.

# THE YUKON TERRITORY

You'll pass plenty of beautiful scenery along the way, but today the real reason to cross the Canadian border into this region is the same as it was 100 years ago: **gold** (or, rather, gold-rush history).

Gold was discovered in the Canadian Klondike's Rabbit Creek (later renamed Bonanza Creek—for fairly obvious reasons) in 1896. In a matter of months, tens of thousands of people descended into the Yukon for the greatest gold rush in history, giving birth to Dawson City, Whitehorse, and a dozen other tent communities. By the turn of the century, the gold rush was on in earnest, and in 1900 the White Pass & Yukon rail route opened from Skagway to the Canadian border to carry prospectors and their goods.

Once part of the Northwest Territories, the Yukon is now a separate Canadian territory bordered by British Columbia and Alaska. The entire territory has a population of just over 33,000, two-thirds of them living in **Whitehorse,** the capital of the region since 1953. Located on the banks of the Yukon River, Whitehorse was established in 1900, 2 full years after the stampeders began swarming into Dawson City. Today the city serves as a frontier outpost, its tourism influx also giving it a cosmopolitan tinge complete with nightlife, good shopping opportunities (with some smart boutiques and great outdoor shops), fine restaurants, and comfortable hotels. The up-to-the-minute nature of the town—with the **Canada Games Centre,** a sports/convention center; its modern **Visitor Information Center;** a **Waterfront Trolley** rail service ($2 one-way) that runs from the Games Centre all the way to the other end of town, allowing passengers to disembark at any of several stations along the way—contrasts it with most of the Yukon.

**Dawson City** was once the biggest Canadian city west of Winnipeg, with a population of 30,000, but it withered to practically a ghost town after the gold-rush stampeders stopped stampeding. Dawson today is the nearest thing in the world to an authentic gold-rush town, with old buildings, vintage watering holes, dirt streets flanked with raised boardwalks, shops (naturally), and some particularly good restaurants. On a visit to Dawson a few years ago, we were much impressed by the excellent **La Table,** in the Aurora Inn at the corner of 5th Avenue and Harper Street, an eatery that compares to the dining spots in the nation's largest cities. There is always, of course, the Dawson staple—**Diamond Tooth Gertie's Gambling Hall** (full-service bar, poker, blackjack, roulette, and slots), where you can eat a casual meal in truly fun surroundings. There's a $6 admission charge for adults—and don't bring the kids! The place is operated by the Klondike Visitors Association, and it's all good fun. The proceeds go to maintain the gold-rush-style architecture and ambience of the town. Another establishment worth a visit is **Bombay Peggy's Inn & Pub,** at 2nd Avenue and Princess Street. The pub features—along with a selection of locally brewed libations—artworks by Dawson-area artists. (And no, there is no plan to change the name to Mumbai Betty's!) Take a look also at the **city museum,** in the Old Territorial Building on 5th Avenue, with one of the most comprehensive narrations found anywhere of the tumultuous years of the gold rush.

If you're on a Holland America cruisetour—highly likely, as that company operates more Yukon cruisetours than any other—you'll take a 1-hour flight between Fairbanks and Dawson City, a new option this year that eliminates the need for up to 2 days on a motorcoach and a hotel night. You'll also travel between Dawson City and the tiny Alaskan town of Eagle via the MV *Yukon Queen II,* a high-speed, 115-passenger catamaran. It makes the trip along the Yukon River in 5 hours, passing through incredibly beautiful wilderness scenery, where the only sign of civilization is the occasional fisherman.

Holland America also has two more Yukon strings to its bow—exclusive rights to enter the UNESCO World Heritage Site known as **Kluane National Park,** a protected Canadian wilderness area that was hitherto all but inaccessible (a few backpackers, campers, and cyclists made up almost the only traffic into the park), and **Tombstone Territorial Park,** about a 90-minute drive from Dawson City.

# THE CANADIAN ROCKIES

Canadian Rockies cruisetours typically include travel by bus and/or train between Vancouver and either Seattle or Calgary.

Highlights of the tour include a visit to the parks at **Jasper** and **Banff,** which together comprise 17,518 square kilometers (6,832 sq. miles). The parks are teeming with wildlife, with some animals—such as bighorn sheep, mountain goats, deer, and moose—meandering along and across highways and hiking trails. There are also coyotes, lynx, and occasional wolves (though they tend to give humans a wide berth), as well as grizzlies and black bears, both of which are unpredictable and best photographed with a telephoto lens.

The two "capitals," Banff and Jasper, are 287km (178 miles) apart and connected by scenic Highway 93 (a destination unto itself). Banff is in a stunningly beautiful setting, with the mighty Bow River, murky with glacial till, coursing through town.

The stylish **Fairmont Banff Springs** (© 866/540-4406 or 403/762-2211; www.fairmont.com/banff-springs) was originally built in 1888 as a destination resort by the Canadian Pacific Railroad. Ever since then, tourists have been visiting this area for its scenery and hot springs, plus nearby fishing, hiking, and other outdoor activities. Today the streets of Banff are also an attraction, lined with trendy cafes and exclusive boutiques with international fashions.

**Lake Louise** is located 56km (35 miles) north of Banff and is a famed spot, deep green from the minerals it contains (ground by the glaciers above the lake) and surrounded by forest-clad, snowcapped mountains. The village near the lake is a resort destination in its own right. Nearly as spectacular as the lake is the **Fairmont Château Lake Louise,** 111 Lake Louise Dr., Lake Louise (© 866/540-4413 or 403/522-3511; www.fairmont.com/lake-louise), built by the Canadian Pacific Railroad and one of the most celebrated hotels in Canada.

Between Lake Louise and Jasper is the **Icefields Parkway,** a spectacular mountain road that climbs through three deep-river valleys, beneath soaring, glacier-notched mountains, and past dozens of hornlike peaks. Capping the route is the **Columbia Icefields,** a massive dome of glacial ice and snow that is the largest nonpolar ice cap in the world.

Jasper isn't Banff. It was born as a railroad division point, and the town does not have the glitz of its southern neighbor. **Jasper National Park** is Canada's largest mountain park and provides an outdoor-oriented experience with opportunities to hike, ride horseback, fish, or even climb mountains.

# ALASKA IN CONTEXT

Alaska is the largest state in the U.S. Just how big is it? If you put together Texas, California, and Montana—the next biggest states—Alaska would still be bigger. If Alaska were a country, it would be ranked at number 33, right before Venezuela—Alaska is twice as big as Sweden. We're talking 570,665 square miles. Yet in 2012, Alaska had a population of just 731,449, according to the U.S. Census Bureau, making it the fourth least populous state in the Union. Theoretically, every resident could have nearly a mile to him or herself if they wanted it. There are remote parts of the 49th State that haven't even been visited by humans—but don't think temperatures that can reach minus 40 degrees are a deterrent. Alaskans are as hearty as they come.

## A SHORT GOLD-RUSH HISTORY

The big Alaska historic event that cruise passengers will hear a lot about is the 1898 **Klondike gold rush.**

The first prospectors actually came in search of gold even before Russia sold Alaska to the United States in 1867, and the American flag went up over Sitka. A few of them even struck it rich. In 1880 there was a major find on the Gastineau Channel that led to the creation of the city of Juneau.

Other finds got some minor press attention, including one on the **Kenai Peninsula** in 1895. More people started to seek their fortune in Alaska.

In 1896, prosecutor George Washington Carmack and his Native partners, Dawson Charlie and Skookum Jim Mason, found gold in a tributary to the Klondike River in Canada's Yukon Territory. Word of the find traveled downriver fast. The three men set off one of the biggest gold rushes in history.

Prospectors flocked to the Klondike to stake claims and dig gravel from the water. Big chunks of gold were found and some prospectors became instant millionaires.

"GOLD!" read newspaper headlines in 1897, as the men returned to Seattle with their riches.

At the time, the country was in the midst of a deep economic depression—unemployment at 18percent.

**Fun Fact**

Before 1983, Alaska had four time zones, but now there are two.

Alaska was a place largely ruled and inhabited by indigenous people—and little changed for thousands of years. There were only 500 white residents in the 1880 census.

But an instant population was on its way. By 1898, some 100,000 gold-seekers had headed north, arriving in **Skagway** and **Dyea,** with plans to head on to the Canadian interior. Even the mayor of Seattle left for Alaska in hopes of striking it rich.

What the stampeders learned when they arrived was that most of the good claims had already been staked and getting to available gold fields would require a 600-mile wilderness trek. Most were unprepared for the arduous trek.

The **White Pass** above Skagway and the **Chilkoot Pass** above Dyea were the routes. To prevent famine, Canadian authorities required each miner to carry a year's worth of supplies—but this made for an exceptionally miserable journey. The White Pass was so difficult some 3,000 horses died on the route—their bones still at the bottom of Dead Horse Gulch. The Chilkoot was so steep you couldn't even use animals to carry your supplies and instead had to carry them on your back.

The journey also required the miners to cross Lake Bennett to get down the Yukon through dangerous rapids. Many did not survive. Stampeders also died from everything from murder and suicide to malnutrition and hyperthermia. But 30,000 gold-seekers did make it to Dawson City in the Yukon Territory.

While only a few of the Klondike gold-rush miners struck it rich, entrepreneurs saw opportunity and became prosperous building the towns and businesses that catered to the miners, saloons, and brothels included.

The gold rush is credited with marking the beginning of contemporary Alaska. Within a few years Alaska had cities—albeit lawless ones. There were even telegraph lines, riverboats, and mail routes (via dog sled).

Some prospectors took their search for gold farther afield in Alaska and in the process founded dozens of towns.

While some of the gold-inspired communities eventually became ghost towns, many survived. Created in the gold rush, for instance, were Nome (1899) and Fairbanks (1902).

The arrival of the railroad through White Pass in 1901 meant **Dyea** and the **Chilkoot Pass** were abandoned. The gold-rush town of **Skagway** has in modern times found riches from tourists as a popular cruise port (see chapter 8).

**Fun Fact**

The state bird of Alaska is not the bald eagle, but the Willow ptarmigan (*Lagopus lagopus*).

There are actually still people looking for gold in Alaska, and occasionally there is a strike of significance. In 1987, for instance, north of Fairbanks, one find produced as much as 1,000 ounces of gold per day for years.

# INTRODUCTION TO SOUTHEAST ALASKA'S NATIVE CULTURES

A memorable part of your cruise to Alaska will be the opportunity to experience Alaska Native culture. The presence of Alaska Native people can be traced back hundreds of thousands of years—to when the first descendants came across the Bering Land Bridge from Asia to North America.

Today, Alaska Native people make up about 16 percent of the state's population. The majority are **Eskimo, American Indian,** and **Aleut** and live in villages along the coastline and rivers of Alaska.

Many still practice traditional crafts and customs and lead traditional hunting and fishing lifestyles, though in cities including Anchorage, Fairbanks, and Juneau, Alaska Natives have very much embraced Western lifestyles, including tourism—blending language and social customs with modern life.

Alaska's Native people are divided into 11 distinct cultures with 11 languages and 22 dialects, from the **Inupiat** of the cold Arctic to the **Tlingit** (pronounced Klink-get) of the warmed Inside Passage. No other state holds such a range of Native cultures.

Cultural heritage is passed down from generation to generation, and while language and customs vary from region to region, many values and spiritual beliefs are shared.

Cruise passengers are most likely to encounter members of the Tlingit group. No one knows for sure when the Tlingit first settled on the Alaska coastline and islands. The language is similar to the Athabascan of Interior Alaska and Canada, but also similar to the Navajo of the American Southwest.

It is known that in the 1700s, Tlingit paddlers steered cargo canoes as far as the Channel Islands off the coast of Los Angeles. In the 18th and 19th centuries, the Tlingit people were trade partners with the Russians, British, Americans, and interior tribes of Canada—they demanded tolls for use of the waterways of Southeast Alaska. In the 1800s, the Tlingits allowed gold miners to travel over the rugged Chilkoot Pass, between Skagway and the Klondike gold fields—for a fee.

Relative newcomers to Southeast Alaska include the **Haida** and **Tsimshian,** both entering Tlingit territory from British Columbia.

Today, many Alaska Natives live in small villages such as Hoonah (home to Icy Strait Point) on Chichagof Island and Metlakatla on Annette Island as well as in major port cities including Juneau, Ketchikan, and Sitka.

In villages, you may see such traditional practices as the drying of seaweed or salmon on wooden planks. You may have a child ask, as we once did, if we'd ever seen a bear before peppering us with questions about what big cities like Anchorage were like. Just don't expect things to look as they did in the 1800s. While some traditions are upheld, you'll likely see more cars than canoes, people hauling bags from the Costco in Juneau, and satellite-TV dishes on many homes.

Although commercial fishing and logging are the primary income streams for some Natives, tribes have also heavily invested in the tourism infrastructure.

In 1971, Natives gained economic clout when the Alaska Native Claims Settlement Act answered the 100-year-old question of aboriginal land rights. Congress deeded title to 44 million acres to Alaska Natives and approved payment of close to $1 billion to compensate for the loss of an additional 331 million acres.

The act created 13 regional corporations and more than 230 village corporations to receive federal money and manage land on behalf of Native shareholders. In Southeast Alaska, Native corporations have considerable clout when it comes to tourism. For instance, Goldbelt operates the Mount Roberts Tramway, the Goldbelt Juneau Hotel and Auk Nu Tours. Huna Totem developed the tourist destination known as Icy Strait Point—home to one of the world's longest ziplines. Native corporations have invested in first-class hotels, sightseeing ships, and more.

The cultural influence is obvious when you tour Southeast Alaska. Towering totem poles, intricate works of art—some reaching 90 feet tall—can be found in places including Ketchikan, Sitka, and Chief Shakes Island in Wrangall. You can compare the distinctive styles of the Tlingit, Haida, and Tsimshian craftspeople. In Ketchikan alone there are more than 70 standing totem poles, plus a museum dedicated entirely to the oldest poles collected from abandoned Tlingit villages.

Alaska Native cultural centers and museums across the state are a good place to get an overview of Native culture.

You can, for instance, observe Native carvers working on commissioned masks, canoes, and totem poles at places such as Saxman Native Village, 3 miles south of Ketchikan, and in private studios. Many Native artists, including carvers and blanket weavers, have their work in private and museum collections throughout the world.

Most towns in Southeast Alaska have museums filled with artifacts and traditional art. Those with the largest collections are the Alaska State Museum in Juneau and the Sheldon Jackson Museum in Sitka, but smaller museums shouldn't be missed. The Sheldon Museum & Cultural Center in Haines has Tlingit exhibits on basketry and carvings, as well as exhibits on fishing and dance. If your itinerary includes Anchorage, a must-do stop is the Alaska State Museum, with its exhibit of Native artifacts that are part of the Smithsonian collection.

The 26-acre Alaska Native Heritage Center in Anchorages showcases the 11 major groups with interactive displays, live dance performances, and six authentic housing sites.

Raven and Eagle clan symbols, representing two of the major clan divisions, adorn everything from beach blankets and T-shirts to greeting cards. These clan symbols, plus other totem figures, such as salmon, killer whales, frogs, and bears, represent the strong family ties that reach back far into the past. Learn firsthand the stories associated with the symbol from Native tour guides and artisans.

There is also opportunity to experience the drums and dance at a Native Alaska gathering, including those in Sitka at the Sheet'ka Kwaan Naa Kahidi Community House, a gorgeous hall modeled after the old clan houses.

# ALASKA WILDLIFE

t's all but guaranteed that you will see plentiful wildlife on your cruise, on land, sea, and in the air, from majestic bald eagles to some of the 16 different species of whales that spend time in Alaska waters. Keep your binoculars at the ready. Listen for announcements from the bridge—cruise crews are well versed in spotting critters in places such as Glacier Bay National Park, Tracy Arm Fjord, and the waters near Sitka. Be on the lookout from your ship's open decks for Dall sheep hanging out on cliffs and sea lions sunning on rocks. Keep your eyes peeled, too, during shore excursions, whether on land or in small boats. You may even spot a bear perched at a forest stream hoping to munch on some salmon. Here is a brief directory of some of the wildlife you may encounter.

## ON SEA

**Beluga Whale**  These small white whales with a cute rounded beak prefer the cold and don't head south for winter. They grow to only about 16 feet and might be confused for dolphins—though dolphins are smaller and have the addition of a dorsal fin. Baby belugas are gray. They tend to swim in large groups, feeding on salmon, including at the mouths of rivers.

**Where to spot them:** Cook Inlet, Kenai Peninsula. A favorite viewing spot is the beach near the mouth of the Kenai River in Kenai.

**Gray Whale**  These mottled gray whales are nearly the size of humpbacks (40–50 ft. in length), though without the humps or dorsal fins. They are also among the friendlier whales, even swimming up to small boats to get their pointy-heads patted.

**Where to spot them:** In late May and late September they migrate past Southeast Alaska on their way to and from the waters of Northern Alaska. If you see one, you're lucky, but Sitka Sound is a prime spot.

**Humpback Whale**  These migratory whales spend summers feeding in the cool waters of Alaska before heading to the warmer waters of Mexico and Hawaii in winter. You can recognize a humpback by the hump on its back—which you can spot as they cruise along the surface of the water—and the flukes on their huge tails as they dive. They grow to a length of about 53 feet.

**Where to spot them:** Icy Straight, Frederick Sound (near Petersburg) and Sitka Sound. Also, Kenai Fjords National Park (near Seward).

**Minke Whale**   Minkes are less than 26 feet in length, the smallest of the baleen whales. They have a blackish-gray body and a white stomach, a triangular head, and distinctive white bands on their flippers. When they breach, they gracefully reenter the water headfirst. They are often confused for dolphins, but the dark color is your first clue.

**Where to spot them:** Glacier Bay and Prince William Sound, as well as the Cook Inlet.

**Orca (Killer Whale)**   It's easy to spot these whales, the ocean's top predator, by their impressive black-and-white color and impressive dorsal fins. With a maximum length of about 30 feet, these whales tend to move around in pods, as they hunt for salmon, seals, sea lions, porpoises, and even small whales.

**Where to spot them:** Resurrection Bay and Prince William Sound (on cruises from Vancouver, also keep a lookout as you pass Robson Bight in Johnstone Strait).

**Steller Sea Lion**   Listen for a honking and sniff for a yucky smell. When you get close to sea lions you'll know it. They like to hang out in large groups, sunning on rock outcroppings and plopping in and out of the cold water. They are super-fun to watch, though you don't want to get too close. Males weigh as much as 1,500 pounds, while females average 600 pounds.

**Where to spot them:** Throughout Southeast Alaska, in the cool coastal waters and gathering on secluded rocky islands.

# IN THE AIR

**Bald Eagle**   America's majestic symbol, the bald eagle is very common in Alaska—the population is estimated to exceed 30,000. Chances are you will spot one or more of the adult birds, with their familiar white head and tail (juveniles are brown). In Ketchikan and other fishing towns in Southeast Alaska, they swarm around the docks looking for freebies. Look for them too in Anchorage and Juneau, perching on power lines, in tall trees and flying around office buildings. Over waterways, you may be treated to the sight of an eagle plopping from the air to make a catch. In Sitka and Ketchikan there are rescue centers for injured birds, where you can get up close and personal with the raptors.

**Where to spot them:** Practically anywhere in Southeast Alaska. The birds congregate in particularly big numbers around Haines in the fall.

**Raven**   Ravens are the largest species of songbird, noted for their heavy bill and distinctive "kaw." The all-black, scavenger birds are prolific in Southeast Alaska forests and important in Alaska Native stories—where they have magical powers.

**Where to spot them:** Like the bald eagle, ravens are very common in Southeast Alaska.

# ON LAND

**Alaskan Moose**   Alaskan Moose can be somewhat elusive in summer, but in winter they lumber on roadways, eat shrubs, and are considered a bit of a nuisance by locals. The largest member of the deer family, they number in Alaska between 144,000 and 166,000 and can grow as large as 1,600 pounds—as big as a horse but with a long bulbous nose. The ones with the antlers are male.

**Where to spot them:** Look for them standing around freshwater ponds or near streams—especially if you do a pre- or post-cruise land tour on the Anchorage-Denali-Fairbanks route.

**Black Bear** Black bears are common in Alaska. While they live on fish, berries, bugs, and vegetation, they also show a fondness for human garbage. Because of this they are considered pests by the human populace. In Southeast Alaska, communities have strict rules on garbage handling to discourage the bears from coming into town. They bears stand up to 6 feet, nose to tail, but are not typically dangerous—though you wouldn't want to approach one. Black bears are not always black—they may also be brown, blond, or even blueish. Unlike the brown bear, their back is straight (brown bears have a large hump at the shoulder).

**Where to spot them:** Black bears live in forests all over Alaska, but your best bet for sighting one in Southeast Alaska in summer is on a riverbank or salmon stream.

**Brown Bear** There are an estimated 32,000 to 43,000 of these big and ferocious bears, also known as grizzlies, in the 49th State. In coastal areas of Southeast Alaska, they feed on salmon and can grow to well over 1,000 pounds. In Denali National Park and other inland locales, the bears eat rodents, berries, and insects and the largest are just 500 pounds. You can recognize the bears by their shoulder humps and long faces—though size will be your first clue. Their color actually ranges from almost black to blond.

**Where to spot them:** Admiralty Island near Juneau and Kodiak are prime places. Brown bears are large enough that you can see them from floatplanes.

**Caribou** Alaska's caribou and Europe's reindeer are genetically identical. The animals were never domesticated in Alaska but are hunted as a food and hide source for the Iñupiaq and Athabascan people (killing a caribou for sport or recreation is illegal in Alaska). The caribou travel in small groups in Denali. Both male and female caribou have antlers, which they shed annually.

**Where to spot them:** If you see a creature that looks a lot like a reindeer in Denali National Park, you're not hallucinating.

**Dall Sheep** You probably won't spot these curly-horned sheep—similar to bighorn sheep but smaller—unless you are scanning a cliff with good binoculars. Look for white spots in high, rocky places, then zoom in. Males can grow to 300 pounds, females to 150.

**Where to spot them:** Denali National Park is your best bet for a sighting.

**Mountain Goat** If it's not a Dall sheep you spot on the cliffside, it will likely be a goat. They are shaggy creatures with black horns and a Billy goat beard.

**Where to spot them:** Look for them on the Kenai Peninsula, including the Turn-again Arm (Cook Inlet) and at higher elevations around the icy fjords in Southeast Alaska.

**Sitka Black-Tailed Deer** These relatively small deer (males weigh around 120 pounds) can be spotted in coastal rainforest regions including in Southeast Alaska. They can have a reddish-brown coat in summertime.

**Where to spot them:** Prince William Sound, Chichagof Island, and Baranof Island, among other places.

# Before, During, or After your use of an EasyGuide... you'll want to consult

# FROMMERS.COM

## FROMMERS.COM IS KEPT UP-TO-DATE, WITH:

### NEWS
The latest events (and deals) to affect your next vacation

### BLOGS
Opinionated comments by our outspoken staff

### FORUMS
Post your travel questions, get answers from other readers

### SLIDESHOWS
On weekly-changing, practical but inspiring topics of travel

### CONTESTS
Enabling you to win free trips

### PODCASTS
Of our weekly, nationwide radio show

### DESTINATIONS
Hundreds of cities, their hotels, restaurants and sights

### TRIP IDEAS
Valuable, offbeat suggestions for your next vacation

### *AND MUCH MORE!

*Smart travelers consult Frommers.com*